AN HISTORICAL ATLAS OF NORFOLK

AN HISTORICAL ATLAS OF NORFOLK

edited by

Peter Wade-Martins

assistant editor

Jane Everett

Maps drawn by Phillip Judge

Second Edition
Published by Norfolk Museums Service
in association with the Federation of Norfolk Historical
and Archaeological Organisations

Editorial Committee: John Ayton, Christopher Barringer, Jane Everett, Judy Sims, Peter Wade-Martins and Tom Williamson

First published 1993 by Norfolk Museums Service, Castle Museum, Norwich NR1 3JU in association with the Federation of Norfolk Historical and Archaeological Organisations

Second Edition 1994

ISBN   0 903101 60 2

Text typed by Joan Daniells

Index of place-names appearing in the text compiled by Jane Everett

Cover design by Phillip Judge

Printed by Witley Press Ltd., Hunstanton, Norfolk

Front cover: Cley Next the Sea, from the West. *Photo by Derek A. Edwards.* Ref DFJ 6
Back cover: Middleton Towers, from the South. *Photo by Derek A. Edwards.* Ref DDRI5

Contents

Folding plans in back cover pocket: Maps of Norfolk parishes *c.* 1923 and modern

Foreword

Norfolk is a large county with a rich variety of landscape. The light soils of Breckland, the heavy clays, the Broads, the Wash and the fens combine to produce a diverse tapestry which has evolved over thousands of years as a result of the county's geology and the impact of man. Variety in every aspect of life is the result, from patterns of settlement to building materials, from windmills to monasteries, from ports to markets. The *Norfolk Historical Atlas* is a most ambitious project which charts the county's fascinating progress from prehistoric past to ever-changing present. This *Atlas* fills a gap in the literature on local history and archaeology. I congratulate those who have produced it, and I wish it every success.

Timothy Colman D.C.L.
H.M. Lord Lieutenant of Norfolk

List of Contributors

Alderton, D.L., B.A. — Fellow of the School of Education, University of East Anglia

Ayers, Brian S., B.A., F.S.A., M.I.F.A. — Principal Field Archaeologist, Norfolk Archaeological Unit

Ayton, John, B.A., Dip. T.P., M.R.T.P.I. — Head of Planning, Norfolk County Council

Barnes, Pam, Ph.D. — Chairman of Anglia Lead Ltd

Barringer, Christopher, M.A. — Director of Extra-Mural Studies, Centre of Continuing Education, University of East Anglia

Batcock, Neil, B.A. — Teacher, Shipdham School

Blackwood, Gordon, B.A., B. Litt., D. Phil., F.R. Hist.S. — Early-retired Head of History, Felixstowe College

Campbell, Bruce M.S., B.A., Ph.D. — Lecturer, Department of Economic and Social History, The Queen's University of Belfast

Corbett, W.M., B.Sc., M.Sc. — Senior Demonstrator, University of East Anglia

Cornford, Barbara, B.A.

Davison, Alan, M.A., F.S.A.Scot. — Landscape Archaeologist

Davison, Andrew P., M.A., Dip. Post Ex. — Inspector of Ancient Monuments, English Heritage

Davison, Caroline, B.A. Hons., Grad. Dipl. Cons (A.A.) — Conservation Officer, Norfolk County Council

Dent, D.L., B.Sc., M.Sc., Ph.D. — Senior Lecturer, University of East Anglia

Digby, Anne, M.A., Ph.D. — Reader in Humanities, Oxford Polytechnic

Douet, Alec., Ph.D. — Oral History Project Coordinator, Centre of East Anglia Studies, University of East Anglia

Dymond, David, M.A., F.S.A., F.R.Hist.S. — Board of Continuing Education, University of Cambridge

Earl, Stephen, Dip. T.P., M.R.T.P.I. — Conservation Officer, Great Yarmouth Borough Council

Ede, Janet, B.A. — Norfolk Nonconformist Chapel Survey

Evans, Nesta, M.A., M.Phil. — Historian and local history lecturer

Fawcett, Richard, B.A., Ph.D, F.S.A. — Principal Inspector of Ancient Monuments, Historic Scotland

Fewster, Mary Innes, B.Ed.(Hons) M.Phil. — Head of History, Hewett School, Norwich

Funnell, Brian M., M.A., Ph.D., C.Geol., F.G.S. — Professorial Fellow, University of East Anglia

George, Martin, O.B.E., Ph.D.

Green, Barbara, B.Sc., F.S.A., F.M.A. — Keeper of Archaeology, Norfolk Museums Service (retired)

Gurney, David, B.A., M.I.F.A. — Principal Landscape Archaeologist, Norfolk Museums Service

Harris, S.P., B.Sc. — Senior Countryside Officer, Norfolk County Council

Heywood, Stephen, Lic. ès Lettres, M.A., F.S.A. — Conservation Officer, Norfolk County Council

Holderness, J., B.A., M.A., Ph.D., F.R.H.S. — Reader in Economics and Social History University of East Anglia

Joby, Richard, M.Sc. (Econ)., Ph.D. — Author and lecturer

Jones, John

Kent, Peter, M.A.

Lawson, Andrew J., M.Sc., F.S.A. M.I.F.A. — Unit Director, Trust for Wessex Archaeology

Lewis, Charles, M.A., A.M.A. — Curator, Great Yarmouth Museums

Lucas, Robin, B.A., M.A.,Ph.D. — Librarian for Art History and Archaeology, University of East Anglia

Mackley, Alan, B.A. B.Sc.

Manning, Mary — Industrial Archaeologist

Murphy, Peter, B.Sc., M.Phil. — Environmental Archaeologist, Centre of East Anglian Studies, University of East Anglia

Palgrave-Moore, Patrick, B.A., F.S.A., F.S.G. — Professional Genealogist

Penn, Kenneth, B.Ed., M.I.F.A. Unit — Project Manager, Norfolk Archaeological Unit

Pound, J.F., M.A., Ph.D. — Lecturer in Education, University of East Anglia

Reid, Andy, M.A., M.Ed.

Rickett, Robert J., B.A., P.G.C.E. — Teacher, Mattishall Middle School

Rogerson, Andrew, B.A., F.S.A., M.I.F.A. — Senior Landscape Archaeologist, Norfolk Museums Service

Rose, Edwin J. Diploma in Archaeology — Sites and Monuments Records Officer, Norfolk Museums Service

Rowe, Joy, B.A. — Former Archivist, West Suffolk Record Office

Rutledge, Elizabeth, LL.B. — Archivist and Local Historian

Rutledge, Paul, M.A. — Senior Assistant Archivist, Norfolk Record Office

Scott, Martin A.C., B.A., M.Sc., M.R.T.P.I. — Assistant Director, Environment, Norfolk County Council

Silvester, R.J., B.A., M.I.F.A. — Deputy Director, Clwyd-Powys Archaeological Trust

Skipper, K.R., M.A. — Research Assistant, University of East Anglia

Tolhurst, Peter, M.A., Dipl. T.P., M.R.T.P.I. — Conservation Officer, Breckland District Council

Turner, Michael, B.Sc., Ph.D. — Professor of Economic and Social History, University of Hull

Virgoe, Norma, B.A. — Norfolk Nonconformist Chapel Survey

Wade Martins, Susanna , Ph.D. — Research Associate, Centre of East Anglian Studies, University of East Anglia

Warren, Martin R., B.Sc., A.M.A. — Curator, Cromer and Walsingham Museums

Warren, Pamela, B.A., M.A. — Historian and Lecturer

Williamson, Tom, M.A., Ph.D. — Lecturer in Landscape History, University of East Anglia

Wright, John, B.A., Dip. T.P., M.R.T.P.I. — Principal Planner, Department of Planning and Property, Norfolk County Council

Wymer, J.J., M.A., F.S.A., M.I.F.A. — Self-employed Archaeologist

Yaxley, David, B.A. — Writer, Artist and Lecturer

Note: The views expressed in this Atlas are those of the authors and not their employers

Introduction

The publication of the first edition of the *Norfolk Historical Atlas* has proved extremely popular. In response to this demand, a second edition has been published which incorporates a number of corrections. The preparation of the *Atlas* has involved 61 contributors preparing maps for 93 different topics concerned with the history of Norfolk. In a sense this is a county history presented in a rather unusual form. The inspiration for the *Norfolk Historical Atlas* was the successful *Suffolk Historical Atlas* published in 1988 with 62 topics on similar lines. Indeed, the Editorial Committee of the Norfolk *Atlas* has unashamedly modelled this volume on its Suffolk counterpart. The theme which holds each volume together is the use of distribution maps based on parish boundaries. The maps used were either the parish boundary pattern in 1923 or the modern parish system. Both maps are reproduced as folders inside the back cover. Where the same subjects are carried in both volumes, it will be possible to obtain a regional overview, and obvious examples of this are moated sites and markets (Maps 28 and 33) . While for a subject like moats, a distribution map represents a fairly accurate and genuine distribution pattern, for other periods and for other features much of our knowledge still depends on chance discoveries. In these cases, the maps should be seen primarily as a progress report on our current state of knowledge and not a definitive distribution.

The problem with presenting a county history in this way is that knowledge is broken up into a rather segmented form, with divisions which inhibit flow between subjects and between time periods. The apparent interaction between themes is also minimised. However, despite these obvious problems, the lavish use of distribution maps, often so meaningful yet often under used, has considerable advantages; the patterns of Roman roads, medieval deer-parks and methodist chapels have a tremendous fascination all of their own. And, indeed, to have such a wide range of specialists all contributing to one volume has seldom been possible in any previous study of the county.

Each contributor was limited to 900 words for a full topic, which has in many cases led to considerable condensation of the writers' favourite themes. The texts can not therefore be regarded as a full exposition of particular subjects, but rather as amplification and explanation of the maps. The contributors have provided an introduction to subjects which can, in most cases, be followed further by reference to the *Further Reading* section at the back of the *Atlas*. The reader is encouraged to make full use of these lists to explore subjects in more detail.

The Norfolk Museums Service was delighted to co-operate with the Federation of Norfolk Historical and Archaeological Organisations which made a major contribution to the project by sponsoring the production of the maps for publication.

Special thanks are due to Phillip Judge, who has drawn the maps to a very high standard, to Jane Everett, who carried the burden of seeing the text through all its stages, and to the many authors who have undertaken a considerable amount of research to make this publication possible.

Peter Wade-Martins B.A., Ph.D., M.I.F.A., F.S.A.
County Field Archaeologist

1. SOLID GEOLOGY

Brian Funnell

Norfolk is underlain by a platform of ancient rocks which inclines from about 200 m below sea-level in the south west to more than 1,000 m below sea-level at the coast in the north east. These ancient (Precambrian and Palaeozoic) rocks are similar to those found at the surface today in Wales, the Pennines and Charnwood Forest, but in Norfolk they never reach the surface.

Overlying this ancient platform are Mesozoic and Cenozoic sediments, arranged in a series of superimposed sheets, which incline eastwards towards the southern North Sea. The oldest occur at the surface in western Norfolk, the youngest near the coast in eastern Norfolk. These sediments are of variable composition and hardness.

The oldest Mesozoic sediments are the West Walton Beds and the Kimmeridge Clay formation, which are relatively soft. Ice Ace glaciers excavated the Wash and the Fenland Basin in these deposits and transported vast quantities,of Kimmeridge Clay in particular, southwards and eastwards to form the chalky boulder clays (tills) of southern and central Norfolk (Map 2).

Overlying the Kimmeridge Clay are a complex series of sands, (and some clays), that constitute the Lower Cretaceous geology of west Norfolk. Some of the sands (Sandringham Sands) are completely uncemented and have been extensively worked for glass manufacture. Others (Carstone) are cemented by iron oxides to form sandstone, which occurs at the base of the colourful cliffs at Hunstanton and has often been used as a picturesque building stone in west Norfolk

Following a thin seam of latest Lower Cretaceous Red Chalk, (also seen in the Hunstanton cliffs, and also used as a building stone), the Upper Cretaceous consists of white Chalk, which underlies glacial deposits across most of Norfolk. The Lower Chalk, (again seen in the Hunstanton cliffs, and again used as a building stone), is harder and often greyer than higher levels in the Chalk,

but it does not contain the characteristic flint nodules found in the Upper Chalk. The Lower Chalk forms the lower part of the Chalk escarpment, which faces westward over the Fenland and the Wash. The escarpment rises relatively gently to the east, (it was substantially eroded by the passage of Ice Age glaciers across it), and at its crest forms subdued downland. Along this crestal area, from south-south-east to north-north-west, strikes Peddars Way.

The main outcrop (dip-slope) of the Chalk inclines very gently eastwards across all of central and eastern Norfolk. Usually concealed on higher ground by variable but often thick deposits of clay and gravel laid down by glaciers, it is mainly seen at or near the surface on the sides of river valleys. It is important as a source of groundwater, emerging from springs and accessible from wells. It is also a widespread source of flint from its contained nodules, including good quality flint for flint knapping, as at Grimes Graves, as well as rough flint for building. The chalk itself, after calcining, provides a ready source of lime and lime mortar.

From Norwich eastwards the Chalk is overlain by marine, and sometimes shelly, sands and gravels (Norwich Crag formation) laid down, not long before the advent of Ice Age glaciers, by a North Sea that extended rather further inland then than it does today. These sands and gravels are almost entirely uncemented and occupy a similar postion in the landscape to the overlying glacial deposits.

Note on the Solid Geology Map

The British Geological Survey publishes two main types of geological map at the 1 to 50,000 scale; (a) 'Solid' or 'Pre-Quaternary' maps, representing rocks deposited or created before the Quaternary Ice Age (i.e. prior to 1,770,000 years ago), and (b) 'Drift' or Quaternary maps showing deposits laid down during the Ice Age and the present Post-Glacial Epoch. Occasionally Pre-Quaternary and Quaternary information is combined on the same

map. Usually it is not. (Details of all currently available maps are obtainable from the British Geological Survey, Keyworth, Nottingham NG12 5GG.)

'Solid' geology maps represent Pre-Quaternary rocks as if the Quaternary sediments had been removed. If there is a cover of Quaternary (Pleistocene or Holocene) sediments at any point the 'Solid' geology will not actually appear at the ground surface, but will be a variable distance beneath it. This needs to be clearly kept in mind when studying 'Solid' geological maps, particularly in Norfolk where Quaternary sequences may be more than 100 m thick.

A further characteristic feature of 'Solid' geology maps is that they are intrinsically 3-dimensional. The intersection of the 'Solid' rocks with the ground surface or sub-Quaternary topography, serves to define the geometry of the rock bodies in such a way that their underground extensions can be projected below the surface. On the other hand, 'Drift' or Quaternary maps simply represent deposits as they occur at the land surface.

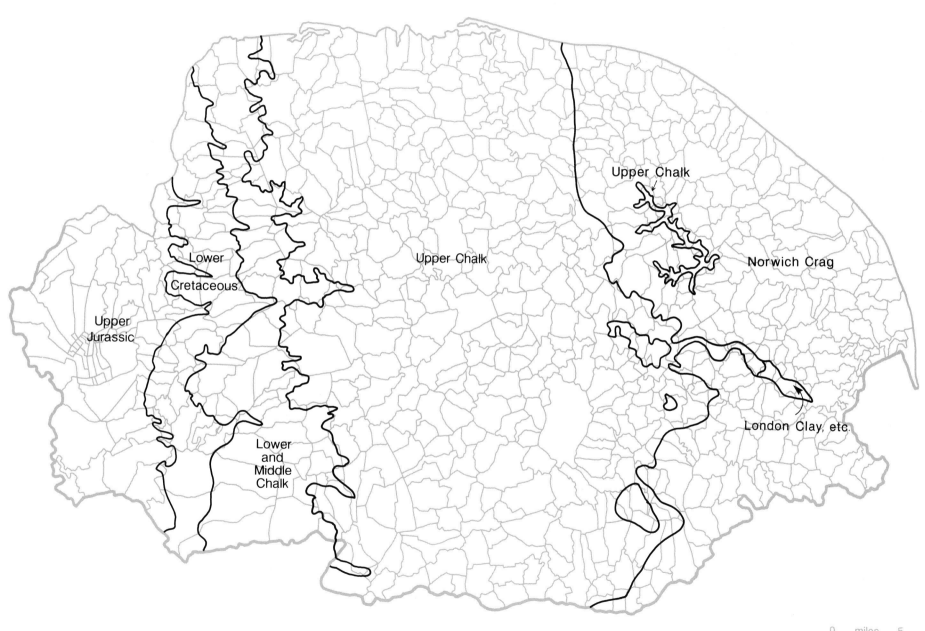

1. SOLID GEOLOGY

Upper Chalk

Upper Chalk

Lower
Cretaceous

Norwich Crag

Upper
Jurassic

London Clay, etc.

Lower
and
Middle
Chalk

0   miles   5

0   km   10

2. GLACIERS CHANGE THE LANDSCAPE

Brian Funnell

Much of the contemporary landscape of Norfolk has been shaped, not by the processes which are observed operating today, but by the activities associated with the repeated growth and decay of continental ice sheets during the late Cenozoic (Quaternary) Ice Age. More than once these continental glaciers spread as far south as Norfolk, either crossing the county altogether or just reaching as far as the north Norfolk coast. The precise number of occasions on which this has happened, and the exact extent of individual glaciers, is still disputed. (Later glaciers have ploughed up, disturbed or even destroyed the deposits of earlier episodes, and deposits datable by fossil remains or radiometric methods are not always present.) However, a general sequence of events, which satisfactorily explains the overall distribution of glacial deposits and landforms in Norfolk can be formulated.

Following shortly after the marine episode of the Norwich Crag formation a proto-Thames river was flowing northwards across eastern Norfolk, and the Cromer Forest Bed formation, rich in large and small mammal and plant remains, was deposited in the vicinity of the present north east coast. At some periods the river waters were supplemented by glacial meltwaters originating in the Midlands, and gravels containing substantial quantities of quartz and quartzite pebbles were laid down on top of the Norwich Crag. However, there is no evidence that the glaciers themselves actually reached Norfolk at that time.

Sometime later, during the Anglian Glaciation, the glaciers reached Norfolk in strength. First they arrived at the north east coast, containing some erratics from as far away as Oslo, and deposited the dark grey clayey Cromer Till of the coast, and the brown sandy Norwich Brickearth inland. Another glacier lobe arrived from central England loaded with Jurassic (including Kimmeridge) clay and Chalk, now called the Lowestoft Till. In places the deposits of these two glacier lobes are superimposed on one another, usually with an intervening layer of outwash sands and gravels. Generally the Cromer Till lobe is confined to the area north east of Norwich and becomes more clayey towards the coast, whereas the Lowestoft Till lobe crossed the entire county from west to east depositing very chalky (marly) till or boulder clay towards the north coast and increasingly clayey (Kimmeridgic) till towards the border with Suffolk. Where the two lobes met in the vicinity of Cromer huge contortions were induced, not only in the glacial deposits themselves, but also in the underlying geological deposits, and a great ridge (Cromer Ridge) was thrown up, which equals in height the elevation of the Chalk escarpment of western Norfolk.

The glacial deposits left by the Anglian Glaciation are very variable both in thickness and composition. Since they make up most of the surface of Norfolk they exert a strong influence on the soils of Norfolk (Map 4) and have significantly influenced both the early colonisation of the county and subsequent agricultural development. In the north these deposits are more sandy and heathy, whereas to the south they support heavier soils that were originally heavily forested. After the decay of the glaciers of the Anglian Glaciation a temperate (interglacial) period ensued, called the Hoxnian Interglacial, after a site on the Suffolk border, where there is good evidence for human occupation. Interglacial conditions probably persisted for no more than 10,000 years, before glacial conditions returned again.

It is not certain whether glaciers reached Norfolk during the glaciation following the Hoxnian temperate period. If they did they only reached the north Norfolk coast and the entrance to the Wash. Otherwise the only effect of that glaciation in Norfolk was the widespread introduction of frozen ground (periglacial) conditions, leading to superficial disturbance and water- and ice-logging of the soil and sub-soil.

There followed another interglacial period, called the Ipswichian after a site in Ipswich. The climate was sufficiently warm at that time (around 126,000 years ago) for hippopotamuses and the European pond tortoise to live in Norfolk, and human beings returned too.

The final glaciation started gradually, but eventually reached a maximum 18,000 years ago. This Last Glaciation, (referred to as the Devensian), may well have brought a glacier front as far as north Norfolk. There is a glacial till, the Hunstanton Till, along much of the north Norfolk coast, up to elevations of 30m above sea level, from Hunstanton to Stiffkey. There are large fans of outwash gravels forming Salthouse and Kelling Heaths. There are eskers (formed by sub- or en-glacial meltwater streams) in Old Hunstanton Park and near Blakeney, and other outwash features in the Glaven valley. For none of these is it quite certain whether they were created during the Last Glaciation or the one before. At the present time they still form such fresh features in the landscape that it is certainly possible to believe they were produced during the Last Glaciation. Periglacial (frozen ground) conditions were also widespread in Norfolk during the Last Glaciation, forming patterned ground and soil disturbance in many places, but particularly in Breckland and adjacent areas on thin Chalk soils.

The end of the Last Glaciation was quite rapid, although it took some 10,000 years finally to melt the glaciers back to essentially their present limits. During that time, lakes outside the glacier limits, including several in Norfolk, were accumulating Late Glacial deposits, which include evidence of the presence of Mesolithic man (Map 7).

Norwich Brickearth, "Contorted Drift", etc.

Boulder clay (mainly Lowestoft Till, and other Anglian tills)

Glacial sands and gravels (of Anglian and later ages)

0   miles   5

0   km   10

3. RECENT GEOLOGY

Brian Funnell

As we have seen (in Map 2) the last major expansion of continental ice sheets in the northern hemisphere peaked about 18,000 years ago. Sea-level around the world was lowered by 120 or more metres, such was the volume of water from the oceans that was trapped as glacier ice on the continents at that time. At the end of the glacial period the continental glaciers melted, and water was returned to the oceans causing sea-level to rise.

At first the coast was situated far beyond the present coastline in the vicinity of the Dogger Bank. However, the sea moved rapidly landward as post-glacial conditions established themselves, and by 8,000 years ago it was approaching close to the present-day Norfolk coast. The drainage of freshwater from the lower river valleys and from springlines, particularly along the north Norfolk coast, was impeded, and substantial deposits of freshwater peat began to form. As time went on the incoming sea flooded these freshwater marshes, covering the peat with silty, marine or estuarine clay. We find general evidence of this marine incursion (transgression) in the Fenland, along the whole of the north Norfolk coast, and in the Yare and Waveney valleys around 6,500 years ago, (although details of the timing vary from place to place).

At about 4,500 years ago, (possibly associated with the initiation of spits across the mouths of estuaries, as at Great Yarmouth, or of barrier islands such as Scolt Head Island seaward of salt marsh), marine waters were excluded from estuaries and stretches of coastal marsh for a time, and freshwater, peat-forming conditions resumed. Along the course of the Yare, the Waveney and their tributaries, these peats largely formed the resource exploited by medieval peat diggers in creating what we now call the Broads.

However, long before the medieval period, from about 3,000 to 1,600 years ago, the sea reasserted its power over these alluvial and coastal tracts, and during Romano-British times the estuaries and coastal marshes were again extensively inundated by the sea, laying down another layer of silty clay. In places this clay covered or eroded the underlying 'Middle Peat', reducing its availability or accessibility to later exploitation.

In post-Roman times it appears that water-levels were lower and marine incursion less extensive in the Broadland estuaries, particularly during the time of most intensive peat-digging. By the 13th century, however, flooding events were again becoming more frequent.

From Roman times onwards it is sometimes difficult to distinguish clearly between natural and human influences on conditions in the estuarine and coastal zones. Drainage schemes and embankments, to reclaim land and prevent flooding from the sea, have continued to be built, (and destroyed), up to the present day. Indeed, if it were not for these constructions the sea and its salt water would certainly reign over much wider tracts of lowlying country at the present day than it actually does.

The recent geological processes which we have been describing are historically important in two ways. Firstly, they have been responsible for depositing sediments that form the basis of some of the richest and most valuable soils in the county (Map 4). Secondly, because of the value of these soils, and their proximity to water transport, successive generations have inevitably been drawn into actions designed to exert some human control on the natural processes which affect them.

Outside the coastal and estuarine zones geological changes since the last glaciation have been much less dramatic. In fact relatively little change has taken place. Except in the vicinity of rivers and meres, where fluctuating river flows and ground-water levels have produced some local changes, the physical landscape over most of Norfolk owes much more to its inheritance from the last glaciation than it does to subsequent events.

Note on the Glacial and Recent Geology Maps

Maps of Quaternary (Glacial and Post-Glacial) deposits only depict the latest and uppermost layer of deposit immediately underlying the soil. There may well be other Quaternary deposits present, even at shallow depth, which do not appear on the map. Many of these hidden Quaternary deposits are, and always have been, relatively easily accessible to human activity.

Post-Glacial (i.e. Recent) deposits, in particular, may arbitrarily overlie both 'Solid' and earlier Quaternary rocks and deposits. In Norfolk they generally comprise a veneer on the top and sides of the Glacial blanket. They merge imperceptibly into the currently accumulating river, estuary, tidal-flat and beach sediments.

In this Atlas, to achieve greater clarity, we have separated onto two maps the Quaternary deposits mainly laid down by Glacial action from those laid down in the Post-Glacial. The actual types of sediment: gravels, sands, clays and peats, are often very similar.

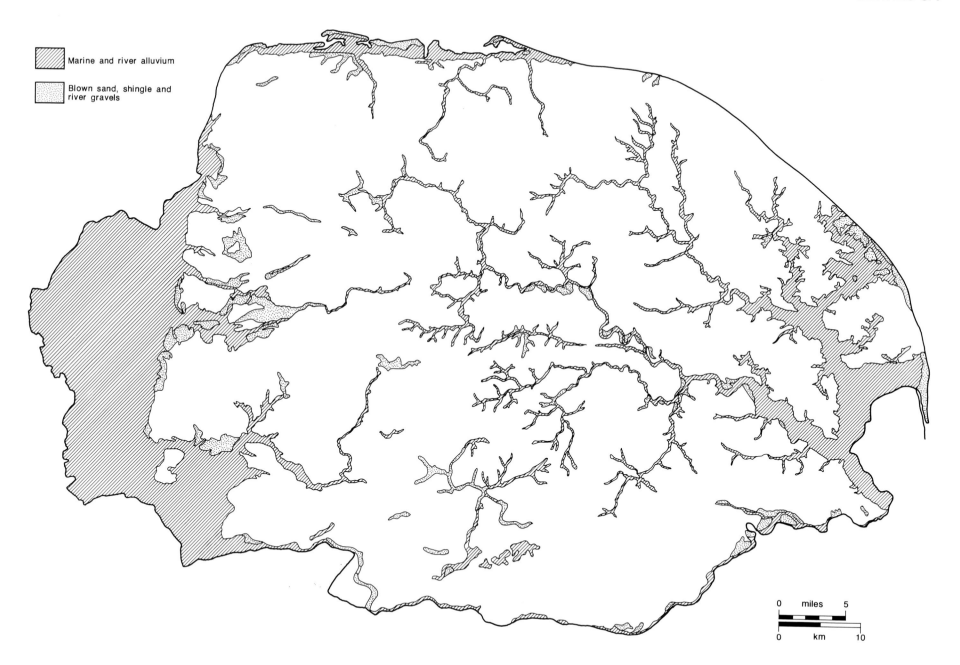

Marine and river alluvium

Blown sand, shingle and river gravels

0 miles 5

0 km 10

4. THE SOIL LANDSCAPES

William Corbett and David Dent

Surprisingly for a county long famed for its farming, most soils in Norfolk are inherently poor or difficult to work. The broad pattern was recognised by Young in 1804 and more detail has been supplied by modern surveys.

The Boulderclay Plateau is a broad upland spanning the north-to-south watershed. Boulderclay is a stiff, grey, clayey glacial till rich in chalk stones. It overlies coarse-textured outwash and is itself thinly covered by wind-blown sand. Topsoil texture is related to the thickness of the coversand. The clay subsoil is impermeable and supports a perched watertable. The most common soil is a gley with dark, rather flinty, sandy clay loam topsoil over mottled brown and grey clay. The present dominance of arable farms on this heavy and often wet land has been made possible by extensive tile drainage and the use of powerful machinery.

The Rich Loams. North-east Norfolk has a cover of loamy loess over glacial till or coarse outwash. The most widespread upland soil is a well drained brown earth with about 0.5 m of almost stone-free brown loam over sand and gravel. Downslope, the loam thickens to 1 m or more. These thick loams are amongst the most productive soils in the country. Their water storage capacity sustains crops through droughty spells and they are responsive to fertilizers.

The Good Sands. The upland of north-west Norfolk has coversand over a red, strongly-weathered clayey subsoil, over chalky till. Contrasting soils occur on spreads of coarse outwash and, again, on slopes where shallow loams lie directly on chalky drift. The most common soil is a brown earth with a dark loamy topsoil over a reddish clay loam. These versatile soils are used for arable, fruit and vegetable farming, and for grassland.

The Cromer Ridge is the high ground, parallel to the coast, inland of Sheringham. The crest, at about 100 m, falls steeply to the north but to the south more gradually.

Except on the steepest slopes, a thin coverloam overlies outwash gravels. Podzols on the gravels of the ridge crest carry pine plantations and heath. Southwards, well drained brown sands alternate with loamy brown earths on footslopes and valley floors. This intricate pattern of droughty sands and rich loams present management problems, especially of soil erosion and timeliness of cultivations.

The Chalk Scarp delineates the northern and western boundary of High Norfolk. The shallowest and most extensive soil is a rendzina with a dark loamy plough layer over chalk rubble. The gentler slopes carry a deeper loamy topsoil. On crests, some patches of well drained brown sands are on remnants of outwash. Land use is almost entirely arable and soil erosion is a problem on the steeper slopes.

Breckland is the most distinctive landscape in East Anglia. It is a low plateau with long, gentle slopes leading to flat bottomlands. Soils are developed in coversand over chalk-sand drift. On the plateau, the coversand is about 1m thick and the dominant soil is a brown sand with a thin red line of clay enrichment at the boundary with the underlying chalky drift. Periglacial action has produced striped soil patterns of rendzinas and brown sands on the slopes and polygonal patterns on the plateau. In the bottomlands, sandy colluvium sometimes develops a striking podzol. Without irrigation, farming is marginal because of the droughty soils and liability to wind erosion. Present land use includes extensive pine plantations, military training areas and some very large arable farms.

The West Norfolk Lowland, between the chalk scarp and Fenland, is mostly sandy with well drained swells and wet hollows. Brown sands and podzols occur on the swells. This very mixed landscape also includes distinctive orange brown sands on the Carstone and heavy soils on Boulderclay.

The Wensum Sands, lying immediately west and north of Norwich, are on outwash. Rolling land around Ringland has well drained brown sands but, elsewhere, subdued relief and high watertables give gleys and gley podzols. Land use is a mixture of arable, pine plantations, heath and scrubby deciduous woodland.

The Black Fens. Since drainage in the early 17th century, 2-3 m of peat have been lost by shrinkage, oxidation, and erosion by the wind. The land is now below sea level and wastage has produced complex patterns of residual peat in hollows between exhumed sandy, clayey or marly substrata. Deep peats remain only in Feltwell and Methwold Fens. Intensive vegetable farming, especially of potatoes, developed on the peat, must now adjust to the complex soil pattern of droughty sands and some severely acid peat and clay.

Marshland is calcareous, estuarine silt and clay, mostly reclaimed from the Wash since the 17th century. The soils have a large water storage capacity and support the most extensive, intensively-farmed, arable land in the country.

Broadland and the North Coast. The lower reaches of the Broadland rivers drain calcareous silty to clayey marine alluvium, fingering inland to deep peat. Similar soils occur along the north coast with, in addition, extensive saltings, dunes and shingle bars. Gleys on alluvium under old grassland have developed a humose topsoil, a mottled, columnar subsoil, with unripe clay below the watertable. Some of the traditional grassland has been ploughed over the last 20 years. Inland, the deep peats have sulphidic subsoils that become severely acid when drained. These are mostly under reed marsh and alder carr.

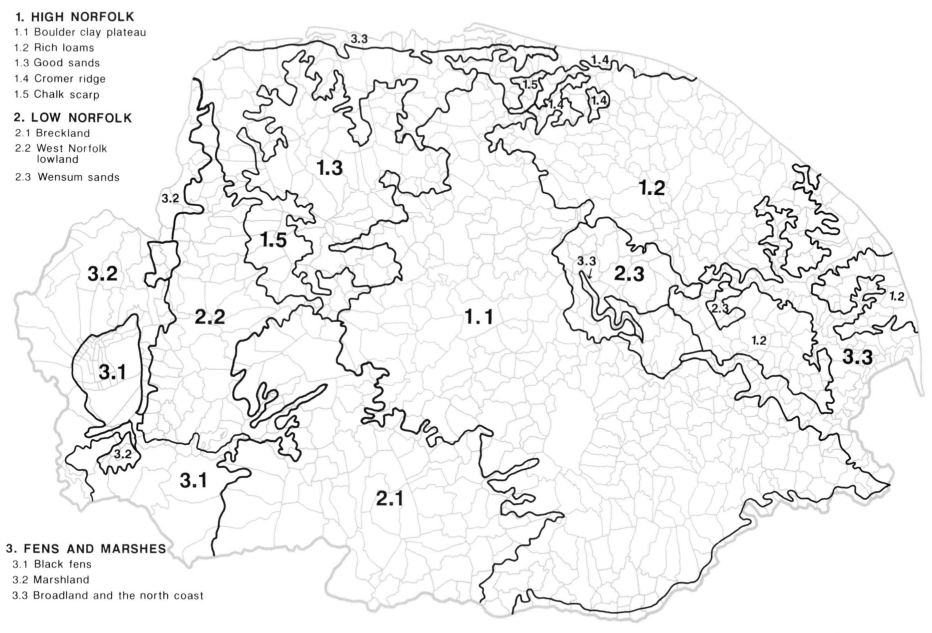

4. THE SOIL LANDSCAPES

1. HIGH NORFOLK
1.1 Boulder clay plateau
1.2 Rich loams
1.3 Good sands
1.4 Cromer ridge
1.5 Chalk scarp

2. LOW NORFOLK
2.1 Breckland
2.2 West Norfolk lowland
2.3 Wensum sands

3. FENS AND MARSHES
3.1 Black fens
3.2 Marshland
3.3 Broadland and the north coast

0 miles 5

0 km 10

5. PRE-NORMAN VEGETATIONAL CHANGES AND WOODLAND CLEARANCE   Peter Murphy

Information on the post-glacial vegetational history of Norfolk comes from several sources. Pollen analysis of sediments from meres (particularly Hockham, Old Buckenham, Diss and Seamere), from coastal peat sections (eg at Titchwell) from the Fenland and from the Broadland river valleys has provided a picture of habitat change from the end of the latest (Devensian) glaciation. Analysis of pollen and macrofossils (seeds, insects etc) has also been undertaken at archaeological sites in valley locations. Sites in dry situations, too, have yielded useful data from pollen and macrofossils in buried soils and other features. The list of Further Reading provides a starting point for exploring the literature.

During the early post-glacial period, as temperatures rose, trees spread northwards from southerly refuges. Birch, with *Populus* (probably aspen) and *Salix* (probably sallows) colonised the landscape, replacing the late glacial vegetation of grasses, sedges, and herbs. Later, pine and hazel spread into the area. There would have been local variations in vegetation, depending on soil-types, but results from Fishergate, Norwich give an impression of a typical Norfolk river valley during this period. The Wensum was then a slow-flowing river, in which waterlilies and pondweeds grew, fringed by a fen swamp. The surrounding landscape - the site of Norwich - was covered with woodland, at first mainly of birch, later mainly of pine. There is no sign of a human presence. Evidence for Mesolithic activity from pollen analysis is slight and often controversial, but at Spong Hill dense deposits of pine charcoal, associated with Mesolithic flints, have been found in natural hollows originally formed by processes of freezing and thawing in the latest glaciation. It seems that pine woods, growing on the sandy soils of this site, may have been intentionally burnt by a Mesolithic group, possibly to improve grazing and encourage game. In the later Mesolithic, between about 6500-4500 BC, further climatic amelioration permitted the spread of trees requiring higher temperatures, to produce a densely wooded landscape showing local characteristics of species composition, but including a high proportion of lime, hazel, oak and elm.

Around 4,000 BC, in Norfolk as elsewhere, there was a dramatic decline in the production of elm pollen. The significance of this has been much disputed, but it was associated with the spread of farming, for there is evidence for a contemporary rise in pollen of weedy herbs and, sometimes, cereals (though it is now thought that there was some cereal growing before this Elm Decline). The balance of opinion is that woodland clearance by Neolithic farmers encouraged the spread of an elm disease. The true extent of Neolithic clearances for farming is still uncertain, though there are grounds for thinking that earlier investigators may have over-estimated them. The heaths of the Breckland, for example, were formerly thought to have been produced by very large-scale, permanent deforestation in the Neolithic, but the most recent pollen studies at Hockham Mere indicate that really substantial woodland clearance did not begin until the Late Bronze Age/Early Iron Age, whilst the spread of heath vegetation occurred still later in the Iron Age. Late Neolithic pits cut into the chalk at Redgate Hill, Hunstanton contained subfossil snail shells with a high proportion of species characteristic of woodland. Neolithic communities do not seem to have exploited landscapes to their full agricultural potential, but nevertheless they did initiate a process of clearance which accelerated through later prehistory.

This opening-up of the landscape is marked by declines in pollen percentages of lime and other trees and by increases in pollen of grasses, weeds, cereals and heathland plants. Analysis of pollen from buried soils gives a more detailed local picture. For example, pollen from the soil sealed beneath a Bronze Age barrow at Mintlyn Wood, Bawsey shows that before the mound was raised there was open woodland of lime and hazel at the site, with alder in nearby valley floors. Open heath vegetation (which covered the site before modern conifer plantations) became dominant after the mound was constructed, as a result of deterioration in soil structure and nutrient status following the loss of tree cover. A similar process of clearance and heath development took place at many localities on sandy soils in west Norfolk and in the Breckland. Elsewhere, on the Chalky Boulder Clay soils, for example, intensively farmed landscapes - pastoral and arable - covered increasingly large areas by the time of the Roman conquest. Patterns of land-use established in the Iron Age seem to have continued in many respects unchanged through the Roman period.

The disturbed political and economic conditions during the collapse of the Roman administration were at one time thought to have resulted in widespread abandonment of farmland and extensive regeneration of woodland. There is, indeed, some evidence - from Diss Mere and Staunch Meadow, Brandon, for example - for a small-scale and transient increase in pollen of trees such as hazel, birch and ash at about this time, but this does not amount to large-scale development of secondary woodland. The expansion of arable farming in Anglo-Saxon times, involving the cultivation of cereals, hemp, flax and other crops - for which there is pollen evidence from several sites - does not seem to have taken place in an untamed woodland landscape but in a varied and diverse landscape which was the product of millennia of human activity.

5. PRE-NORMAN VEGETATIONAL CHANGES AND WOODLAND CLEARANCE

TITCHWELL

REDGATE HILL
HUNSTANTON

SPONG HILL

BROADLAND CORES

MINTLYN WOOD
BAWSEY

WIGGENHALL
ST GERMANS

NAR VALLEY

FISHERGATE
NORWICH

SAHAM TONEY
MERE

OXBOROUGH
WOOD

SEAMERE

NORDELPH

THOMPSON COMMON

THE MERE
STOW BEDON

BROOME HEATH

FELTWELL COMMON

HOCKHAM MERE

OLD BUCKENHAM
MERE

STAUNCH MEADOW
BRANDON

LOPHAM
LITTLE FEN

DISS MERE

0   miles   5

0   km   10

6. THE PALAEOLITHIC PERIOD

John Wymer

Human populations were spreading into the temperate latitudes of Europe about half a million years ago, probably from Africa where fossil human bones and associated stone tools can be dated back at least two million years. When these people reached Europe they would have looked much more like ourselves than the earliest known human beings, but distinctive enough to warrant the name of *Homo erectus*. None of their skeletal remains have been found in Britain, let alone Norfolk, but there is mounting evidence of their presence in the country from flint tools and debitage found in sediments thought to date to this time. This was in the period before the advent of the major glaciation of the British Isles, estimated as occurring between 472,000 and 440,000 years ago, when Norfolk and most of East Anglia was covered by a thick ice sheet. One possible trace of their presence in Norfolk is a very worn stone tool known as a hand-axe, actually found in glacial boulder clay at Stibbard. However, as it is made of quartzite it may have been transported by the ice from the Midlands. Hand-axes in gravel at South Acre may also be of this age, but caution is necessary until geologists can be more certain of its date. There is more definite evidence in nearby Suffolk, so *Homo erectus* was seemingly around.

When this great ice sheet had receded, Norfolk had assumed most of its present topography, although the rivers flowed at higher levels along their valleys and the coastline was much further away. The English Channel had been broached during the glaciation but a land connection with the continent would have existed except perhaps at times of very high sea levels during the numerous oscillations of climate that occurred from then until now. The find spots of hand-axes shown on the distribution map relate almost entirely to tools which were discarded at various times during this enormous span of time between the recession of the major glaciation, known to geologists as the Anglian Stage, and the last cold period known as the Devensian Stage. Small groups of people must have intermittently occupied the area that is now Norfolk, for their stone tools have been found in the gravels of former channels of most of the present valley systems. Clearly, they have been washed into the ancient river deposits from nearby beaches or land surfaces and nowhere in Norfolk have any sites been found where chance has gently covered material lying in its original position with fine sediments. The most prolific sites are in the valleys of the Little Ouse, Yare and Nar, particularly at Keswick and Whitlingham near Norwich, Thetford and Weeting and at South Acre. Most of these gravels, if not all of them, were deposited during cool conditions and, to judge from many other similar sites in southern Britain, it would seem that these palaeolithic groups preferred the periods when the landscape was relatively open, i.e. at the beginnings and ends of interglacial periods. This may have been because the heavily forested environments of mid-interglacials restricted movement and hunting. Thus, these people had to contend with cooler climates and, although no evidence has survived, they could only have done this by making clothes and erecting simple shelters. Foraging for vegetable food was probably as important, if not more so, than obtaining meat. Doubts have been expressed as to whether the much-quoted role of 'Man the Hunter' should really be 'Man the Scavenger'. The most likely reality is that both roles were true.

By the end of the interglacial that followed the major Anglian glaciation, known as the Hoxnian Stage, more modern types of humans were in Europe, but not necessarily our ancestors, for it seems they belonged to a branch of *Homo sapiens* that was evolving towards the Neanderthalers, who became extinct about 40,000 years ago. These latter people made very distinctive flake tools and hand-axes. Some of the hand-axes are of a thin and flat-butted form and several have been found in Norfolk, especially at Lynford and Little Cressingham, so Neanderthalers may have been present. Otherwise, there is little to show for any so-called progress through about 400,000 years! However, things did alter towards the latter part of the last glaciation (the Devensian Stage), from about 35,000 years ago, with the arrival in Europe of modern humans, physically the same as ourselves. This period is known as the Upper Palaeolithic and human society, although still dependent entirely upon a hunting and foraging economy, was much more advanced and sophisticated. The earlier part of this period, before the last ice advance reached as far as the north Norfolk coast about 20,000 - 16,000 BC, is not definitely represented in the county. Flint leaf points have been reported from Heacham and Feltwell and may belong to this period, but it cannot be certain that they are not products of later, Neolithic industries which also include leaf points. But this was a time of very low sea level and much of the North Sea was land. Rivers had to cut deep channels in their lower reaches and sites may exist along them, now buried by sediments below present sea level. It was not until the ice receded and the climate warmed that bands of these resourceful hunters came into Norfolk and left evidence of their presence.

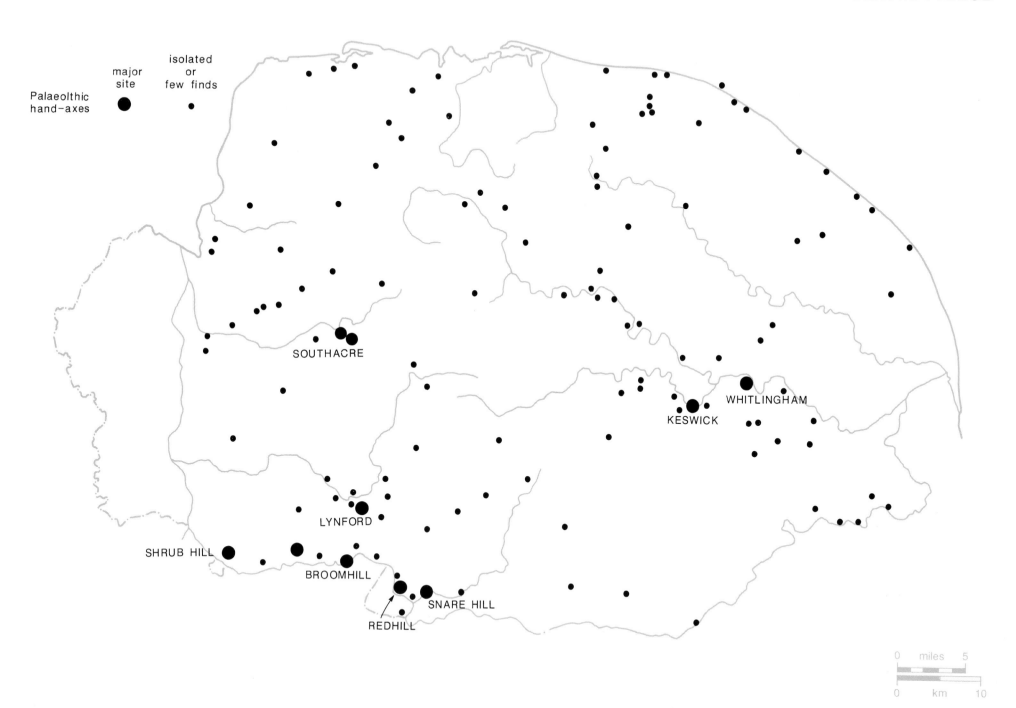

Palaeolithic
hand-axes

major
site

isolated
or
few finds

SOUTHACRE

WHITLINGHAM

KESWICK

LYNFORD

SHRUB HILL

BROOMHILL

REDHILL

SNARE HILL

miles 5

km 10

7. LATE GLACIAL AND MESOLITHIC HUNTERS

John Wymer

The Mesolithic period is defined in Britain as the time between the final retreat of glacial ice, about 8,300 BC, and the advent of societies which based their livelihood on farming. Norfolk, like most of Britain, was occupied by small groups of hunters and gatherers, descendants of the elaborate hunting communities which had peopled Europe from about 35,000 years ago. Some of these people were already in Britain during the Late Glacial period before the very last, small ice sheet in Scotland had disappeared. They seem to have survived with little change up to if not into the early Mesolithic period. Their distinctive flintwork including long blades has been found at several places in Norfolk, particularly along the valleys of the Little Ouse, Lark and Wissey, and under the peat of the Fens.

There was a rich site on the coast at Titchwell during the Late Glacial and Early Mesolithic period, beside a small stream with the coastline 60-70 kilometres away. The sea level was at least 60 m below its present level, so much of what is now the North Sea was dry land. Norfolk was merely the western extremity of the great European plain. This is emphasised by the remarkable find made by a trawler off the Leman and Ower Banks, 40 km off Norfolk, in 1931: a barbed antler point radiocarbon dated to about 9800 BC, dredged off the sea bed. Many Early Mesolithic sites must exist under the North Sea but newcomers made their way into the valleys and the then relatively open landscape of Norfolk. Kelling Heath is one of the richest known sites of this time, in terms of scattered flintwork found over a large area. Unfortunately, nothing but the flintwork has survived on the intensely acid soil of this part of the Cromer Ridge, but it can be assumed that the magnificent view across the wide plain that is now sea allowed the hunters to spot browsing or migrating herds of animals, such as deer and aurochs (the extinct giant ox). This must have been the reason for visitations, probably seasonal, from generation to generation over many centuries. Hundreds of the tiny flint points known as microliths have been found there, testifying to the production and repair of arrows and spears for the hunt, although not all microliths were necessarily used as barbs for such weapons.

Gradually, as the climate ameliorated and coniferous forest spread, the wide, open landscape was lost. Hunting and food-gathering methods had to be modified to cope with the changes, and the Mesolithic people seem to have done this very successfully. Their major contribution to progress was the use, if not the invention, of the hafted flint axe. With these axes, clearings were made in the forest and, to judge by other areas where conditions have been more favourable for the preservation of organic material, they worked the timber into a variety of equipment such as boats. Settlements were often along river banks, such as at Two Mile Bottom, Thetford. The distinctive axes, skilfully resharpened by striking a transverse blow across a worn cutting edge (thus called tranchet axes) are found over much of Norfolk, as can be seen from the accompanying map, together with the flint blades, scrapers, burins and debitage of their traditional style of flintwork. Some concentrations of material away from the river valleys in what must have been forest, as at Great Melton near Norwich, appear to have been temporary hunting camps.

As much of the polar ice sheet melted, so the sea level rose. Continental connections became difficult, hazardous and eventually impossible without suitable sea-going craft. By about 6,500 BC Britain was an island and the coastline of Norfolk was little different from that of today. The coniferous forest had given way to even denser deciduous forest and the climate was becoming warmer, but wetter. The Fens were becoming inundated and Mesolithic people had to adapt accordingly. Little is know of the life of these people. There is nothing to identify their presence, in the absence of good, sealed datable archaeological sites: only scatters of flintwork on the surface, distinguished by the presence of different forms of micoliths. These are often of neat, geometrical shape, such as crescentic or triangular, and rod-like forms sometimes absurdly minute. It has been suggested that different Later Mesolithic groups had these particular shapes so that each group could be recognised by the variations of them. This could imply a concept of territory, thus preventing one group straying into the hunting grounds of another. The lighter soils, particularly in Breckland, were much favoured during this Later Mesolithic period, but there is a very prolific site on the heavier boulder clay of the Norfolk till plain at Banham. This site has produced more flint tranchet axes than any other in East Anglia, together with rich spreads of other flintwork. The people were presumably clearing the forest for some reason. Across the North Sea and the English Channel many people were adopting the farming economies that were spreading across Europe, either partly or completely abandoning the traditional, nomadic life of the hunter and food-gatherer. How the Mesolithic people of Britain came to follow suit, if they did so at all, is still unclear, but it can be no coincidence that their distinctive flintwork disappears at about the same time as the evidence for prehistoric farming appears.

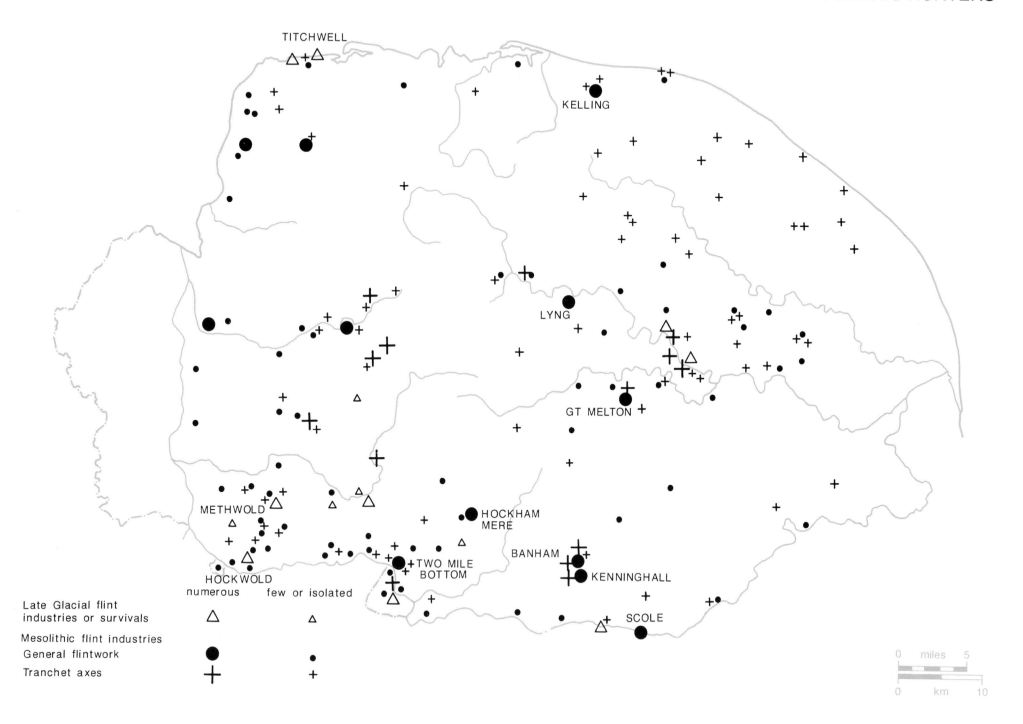

TITCHWELL

KELLING

LYNG

GT MELTON

METHWOLD

HOCKHAM
MERE

BANHAM

TWO MILE
BOTTOM

HOCKWOLD

KENNINGHALL

SCOLE

numerous   few or isolated

Late Glacial flint
industries or survivals

Mesolithic flint industries
General flintwork

Tranchet axes

0   miles   5

0   km   10

8. THE NEOLITHIC PERIOD

John Wymer

From about 4,500 BC more settled communities gradually arose in Britain, partly or fully dependent on arable farming or stock-raising. Whether these farmers were mainly the descendents of the indigenous Mesolithic population who had changed their way of life, or were immigrants, is unknown. The former is more likely but both may have been true. Some connection with the established Neolithic communities there must have been, in order to acquire seed grain and domesticated strains of animals, especially cattle. As far as Norfolk is concerned, this need not imply direct contact with the continent, for the stock and grain could have been obtained from adjacent territories where farming economies seem to have developed earlier.

The new life style is reflected in the type of tools and equipment that has been found over most of Norfolk. Flint axes have their cutting edges sharpened by grinding, arrowheads bear no resemblence to the microlithic barbs of Mesolithic people, sickles can be identified, there are querns for grinding grain and axes made of fine-grained rocks imported from the Highland zones of Britain. One of the most important changes in the archaeological record is the appearance of pottery; round-based plain vessels in the earlier phase and more elaborate, decorated forms in the later one. The distribution of Neolithic axes, as shown on the adjacent map, records the presence of these early farmers throughout the whole of Norfolk during the Neolithic period with the exception, as noted above, of the very earliest phase. Unfortunately, little else has survived apart from this nearly imperishable material. Settlement sites can only be recognised by scatters of domestic rubbish, pits and a few postholes. There is no excavated site in Norfolk that gives enough evidence to allow any reconstruction to be made of contemporary dwellings or out-buildings, but a C-shaped enclosure of bank and ditch on Broome Heath encloses over a hectare of scattered potsherds and flints. Other large spreads at Eaton Heath and Spong Hill suggest quite large communities may have been present, apart from small, isolated farmsteads.

The characteristic monumental earthworks that arose in response to the larger, more socially-organised population, so dramatically represented in Wessex and other parts of Britain, exist rather sparsely in Norfolk. To some extent this may reflect destruction of them through the intensive agriculture of later periods, for aerial photography has revealed several marks which may indicate their former existence. There are only four known, visible long barrows in Norfolk, at West Rudham, Harpley, Broome Heath and Felthorpe. Crop-marks at Roughton and Marlingford look suspiciously like ploughed-out examples of this type of Neolithic burial mound. There are no visible causewayed enclosures which may have been communal meeting places, but there are possible crop-marks of them at Roughton and Hainford. Neither is there any example of the long, parallel banks and ditches known as cursus earthworks save for a crop-mark at Beachamwell which may qualify. However, there is the fine henge monument at Arminghall, near Norwich. Its circular ditches are still visible and the timbers which made the great feature in the centre gave a radiocarbon date of about 2,500 BC. Several crop-marks may record the existence of other, smaller but similar ceremonial monuments.

Perhaps the most impressive of Neolithic monuments in the county is the flint-mining site at Weeting, known as 'Grimes Graves'. More than 360 closely-spaced hollows mark the partly-filled vertical shafts dug to the fine quality flint that was brought to the surface and worked into knives, axes and other tools. This flint-mining industry does not seem to have started until fairly late in the Neolithic period and continued well into the Bronze Age. It is thought that the prodigious effort expended in obtaining the flint may have been more connected with producing prestigious objects for ritual exchange more than functional, everyday tools. Smaller industrial sites where flint could be found outcropping on the surface of the Chalk, such as in the river valleys of east Norfolk, would have supplied some of the domestic requirements. Movement and trade can be traced to some extent from the distribution of axes of exotic stone and demonstrate transport along the general line of the Icknield Way.

The latter part of the Neolithic period in Norfolk, as elsewhere, was a time of complex change in both the economy and society. Distinctive styles of pottery, including beakers with their origins in the Low Countries and Germany, point to continental influences, if not migrations; metal knives, of copper and later bronze, appear as imports; inundations of the Fens removed large areas of valuable pasture. There is an impression of a major economic collapse in the mid third millenium BC followed by a slow but gradual revival. Flint daggers, as opposed to domestic knives became fashionable, being skilfully-made copies of their metal counterparts. It does not seem tenable to regard the Neolithic population any more as peaceful, hard-working families, living in simple plenty, independent and free. There is ample evidence for flint arrowheads being used by people against each other in a few other parts of Britain. Nothing has been found in Norfolk to support this, but the large numbers of Late Neolithic arrowheads found in certain parts of the Breckland may indicate some form of warfare rather than the sport of the hunt.

8. THE NEOLITHIC PERIOD

▲   Settlement

C   Enclosure

⊙   Henge monument

—   Long barrow

\\\\   Cursus earthwork

◇   Flint mine

○   < 5 Flint axe

◯   > 5 Flint axe

●   Stone axe

0   miles   5

0   km   10

9. EARLY FARMING IN NORFOLK
Peter Murphy

The earliest farming in Britain is conventionally supposed to have arrived as part of a cultural package including permanent settlements, pottery, polished axes and leaf-shaped arrowheads. Things may not, however, have been so simple. Recently, cereal pollen grains have been reported from peats pre-dating the Elm Decline and it seems quite possible that indigenous Mesolithic communities may have incorporated some cereal-growing into their gatherer-hunter economies. In Norfolk there is at present no direct evidence for such early cultivation; the earliest results we have relate to well-established Neolithic farming.

At Spong Hill, North Elmham and Broome Heath, Ditchingham impressions of plant material on pottery and carbonised plant remains point to an earlier Neolithic economy involving the growing of einkorn and emmer wheats and barley and the collection of hazelnuts and crab-apples. Later Neolithic plant remains have come from Redgate Hill, Hunstanton (emmer, bread-type wheat, naked barley and hazelnuts) and Grimes Graves (acorns, barberry, hawthorn etc.). The consistent presence of wild plant foods here, as elsewhere in Britain, is thought to indicate that wild plant food gathering remained very important throughout the Neolithic. Bones from pits at Redgate Hill were (in order of abundance) of domestic pigs, cattle, goat, possibly sheep, roe- and red-deer, wild-cat and dolphin, and were associated with shells of mussels, oysters and cockles, whilst at Grime's Graves Later Neolithic deposits produced bones of cattle, sheep/goat, pig, deer and horse.

Information from the Bronze Age in the county is, again, sparse though results from pollen analysis show that at this time woodland was being more extensively cleared for agriculture (Map 10). At some sites, for example a barrow at Little Cressingham, land snails indicate open grassland habitats, which could only have been maintained by continued grazing. Early Bronze Age bones from Redgate Hill are mainly of sheep/goat and at Grime's Graves the predominance of cattle, and the age-

and sex-structure of the herds represented suggest an economy based on dairying in the Middle Bronze Age. Carbonised seeds from this site indicate cultivation of barley, emmer and peas. Unfortunately there is no information in Norfolk from the Late Bronze Age/Early Iron Age, a critical period for agricultural change when the pace of clearance increased and new crops were introduced.

By the Late Iron Age there are grounds for thinking that intensively-farmed landscapes had been established in many areas (Map 11). At Fison Way, Thetford carbonised remains of spelt wheat, six-row hulled barley and emmer were recovered and there is evidence from the site for grain storage in large pits. Roman rural sites typically produce large cereal deposits, mainly of spelt and barley, including both grain and waste chaff. These are often associated, as at Fengate Farm, Weeting, with ovens used for grain drying and probably malting. Large amounts of cereal processing waste were available for tempering clay used in the salt industry around Denver. At present the available evidence seems to suggest a continuation and intensification of the Iron Age arable system, based on spelt and barley. More affluent Roman Britons were able to enjoy introduced crops, such as grape and walnut, which were identified in the fills of wells at Scole. This site also produced one of the few collections of bones as yet published from a Roman site in Norfolk. Cattle, followed by sheep, supplied most of the meat consumed, together with pigs, domestic fowl, duck and deer, and it appears that Scole may have been a market for surplus stock from surrounding farms (Map 12).

Results from sites in Suffolk and Essex show that spelt-growing continued into Early Saxon times, though sunken-featured buildings at Spong Hill, Witton and Redcastle Furze, Thetford (Map 13) have produced only free-threshing cereals (bread wheat, rye and barley) with horse-beans and probably flax. Most evidence for Late Saxon and medieval crops and herds comes from urban sites, some of which, as at Whitefriars Street and St.

Martin-at-Palace Plain, Norwich, included waterlogged organic deposits. In the Norwich area there is reason to think that some rye was grown on impoverished sandy soils, and barley on more productive land in the Early Middle Ages. Barley was widely used for malting, and medieval kilns associated with charred malt have been found at Alms Lane, Norwich and Redcastle Furze, Thetford. Urban deposits commonly produce a wide range of other crops, including peas, beans, flax, hemp, opium poppy, celery, fennel, coriander, hop, plums, cherries, apples, medlars, mulberries, fig, grape, hazel and walnut. Few rural sites have been studied, though at Barton Bendish 14th-16th century features contained carbonised cereals and pulses with walnut shell. As yet remains of rivet, a wheat crop introduced about the 11th century and known from sites in Suffolk and Essex, has not been reported from Norfolk.

The urban sites have also yielded large bone assemblages. Cattle, sheep/goat and pig bones usually predominate, though hare, deer and wildfowl also contributed to the diet. Rabbits, originally reared in managed warrens, are also represented and their bones occur in deposits of 11th century and later date. However, fish bones - mainly herring, cod and eel - are often extremely abundant and fish may well have supplied much of the animal protein in the medieval urban diet. Eggshell of domestic fowl is not uncommon, and fowl and goose bones occur frequently. The earliest record of the turkey - later a Norfolk speciality - comes from 17th-century deposits at Alms Lane.

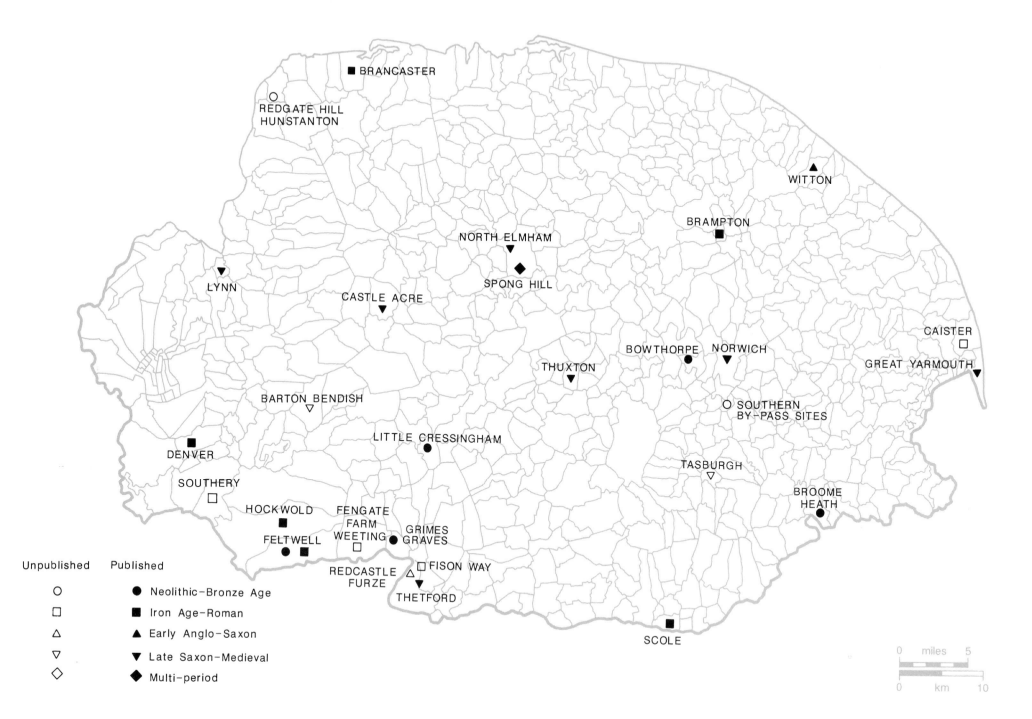

■ BRANCASTER

○ REDGATE HILL
HUNSTANTON

▲ WITTON

BRAMPTON
■

NORTH ELMHAM
▼

◆
SPONG HILL

▼ LYNN

CASTLE ACRE
▼

CAISTER
□

BOWTHORPE NORWICH
●   ▼

GREAT YARMOUTH
▼

THUXTON
▼

○ SOUTHERN
BY-PASS SITES

BARTON BENDISH
▽

LITTLE CRESSINGHAM
●

TASBURGH
▽

■
DENVER

BROOME
HEATH
●

SOUTHERY
□

HOCKWOLD
■

FENGATE
FARM
WEETING
□

GRIMES
GRAVES
●

FELTWELL
● ■

REDCASTLE
FURZE

□ FISON WAY

△
▼
THETFORD

■
SCOLE

Unpublished   Published

○   ● Neolithic–Bronze Age

□   ■ Iron Age–Roman

△   ▲ Early Anglo-Saxon

▽   ▼ Late Saxon–Medieval

◇   ◆ Multi-period

0   miles   5

0   km   10

10. THE BRONZE AGE

Andrew Lawson and John Wymer

Objects of copper, or bronze (an alloy of copper and tin) were first introduced into Norfolk about 2,500 BC. The casting of even simple objects represented a very significant technological advance over the production of earlier stone implements because it required a knowledge of the sources of ores (outside Norfolk), of smelting, and casting in a pre-shaped mould. The skill of the smiths who perfected bronze casting is demonstrated in the many finds, more than six hundred in number, from the county. Until its replacement by iron in about 800 BC, bronze was the principal material used for tools, weapons and ornaments. The quality and quantity of metal objects from Norfolk is surpassed in few other areas of England and indicates the presence of a sizeable population of some wealth.

Early Bronze Age metalwork which included daggers, axes, pins and awls, required relatively simple casting techniques. However, in the Middle and Late Bronze Age (1,500-800 BC) the ready supply of metal from western Britain and the continent together with recycled scrap enabled smiths to produce prolific quantities of intricately cast bronze tools, weapons, ornaments, harness and dress fittings. In this later period hoards of objects were occasionally buried or lost. At least 60 hoards, each containing a number of objects, have been reported, although another 35 are suspected but poorly recorded. The Foulsham hoard, with 141 objects, is the largest from the county. At this time gold was also used for necklaces and bracelets (torcs) or dress fasteners. The concentration of metal finds dating from before 1,000 BC on the eastern edge of the Fens suggests a centre of metalworking in that area, but later production appears to be more dispersed throughout the county and concentrations of Late Bronze Age hoards in the Norwich and Snettisham areas as well as in the Fen Edge may indicate important social centres.

Evidence for the lifestyle, burial customs and environment of the Bronze Age population has been derived from nearly 200 archaeological excavations within the county. However, three quarters of the excavations have been on burial sites. There has not been a corresponding number of excavations on settlements because these are more difficult to identify. The majority of metalwork finds are isolated discoveries which provide little information on contemporary daily life.

The introduction of metal technology is associated with the widespread use of Beaker pottery, a fine earthenware of continental origins, frequently highly decorated with geometric designs. Concentrations of Beaker sherds in the modern ploughsoil, particularly on the Fen edge, have indicated the sites of farming settlements, although few traces of buildings have been revealed. It is probable that most people lived in small circular timber huts with conical thatched roofs: ground plans of earthfast posts have been found at Hockwold and Hunstanton.

The best evidence for daily life during the later Bronze Age comes from the uppermost filling of the earlier flint-mine shafts at Grimes Graves. Here large quantities of pottery, flint tools and animal bones, also charred seeds and metalworking debris, characterise the lifestyle of the local dairy farmers of the 14th century BC. Sheep bones and loom weights suggest that they were comfortably clad in sheepskin, leather and fabrics woven from wool. At West Harling, one of the few buildings of the Bronze Age, dating to its latest phase in the 10th century BC, has been excavated.

By contrast, round barrows, the circular burial mounds favoured by early Bronze Age people are ubiquitous. Approximately 1,200 barrows or their plough-flattened remnants (ring-ditches) are currently known in Norfolk, and more are discovered by aerial photography each year. Their distribution suggests that the heavier clay soils of central Norfolk were largely avoided, and information in Fenland is obscured by later peat or silt deposits. Few barrows remain in good condition but it is possible to recognise cemeteries which incorporate different barrow designs: the best are at Little Cressingham, Salthouse and Weasenham All Saints. The dead people beneath them were buried with a variety of different pots, jewellery (in jet, amber or gold, as at Little Cressingham), or weapons.

Environmental evidence derived from meres, fens and barrow ditches together with the distribution of Bronze Age sites indicate that the people of the time swept aside considerable areas of the ancient wildwood, a process which had already started in the Neolithic, but which accelerated in the later Bronze Age as arable farming and pasture were established for the controlled production of food for an expanding population. Barrows would have been visible landmarks in an open landscape. Although the climate may have deteriorated slightly towards the end of the Bronze Age, it is unlikely that this seriously affected the Norfolk farmers except in Fenland.

If the living places have been difficult to find, so also have the cemeteries, because in the later Bronze Age elaborate barrows were no longer built. Instead the cremated remains of the dead were placed in coarse, bucket-like pots in cemeteries now unmarked on the surface. Many thousands of Bronze Age people must have used, discarded or lost the many bronze tools which have been found, but only five small cremation cemeteries are known.

The evidence of the Bronze Age population in Norfolk may be imperfect and unbalanced, but it points nonetheless to an extensive and industrious farming community.

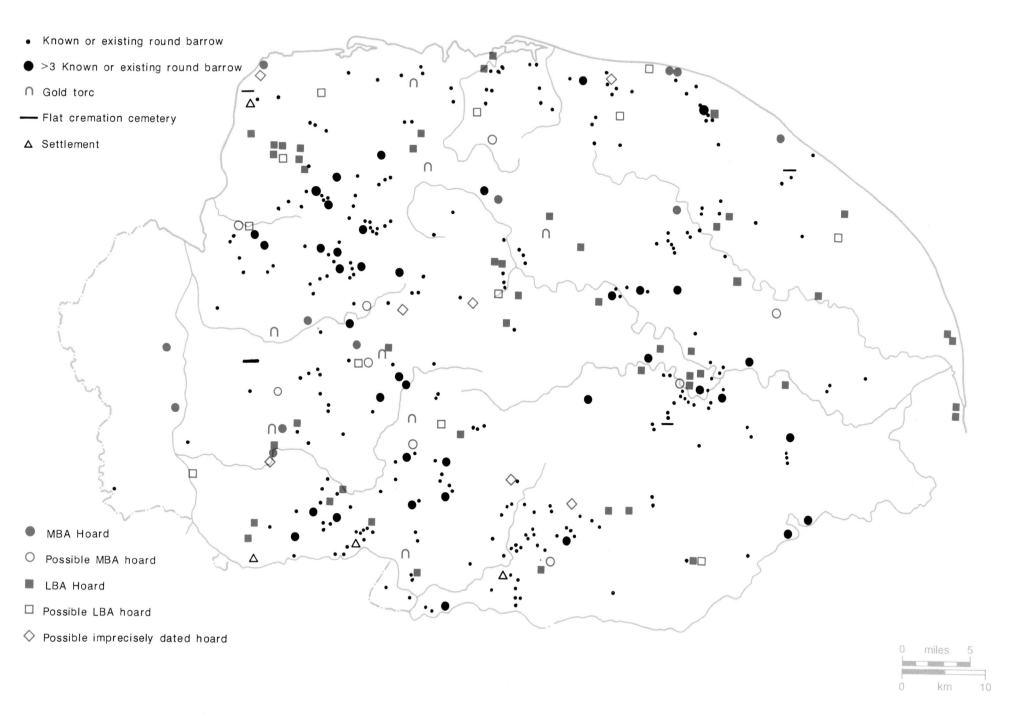

Known or existing round barrow

>3 Known or existing round barrow

∩ Gold torc

— Flat cremation cemetery

△ Settlement

● MBA Hoard

○ Possible MBA hoard

■ LBA Hoard

□ Possible LBA hoard

◇ Possible imprecisely dated hoard

11. THE IRON AGE

Barbara Green

Tools and weapons made of iron were sharper than those of bronze and soon replaced them. The earliest iron objects came from the continent, but at about 650 BC British smiths learnt how to work iron. Because of rust, few iron objects survive. Bronze continued to be used for a wide range of objects, while gold and silver were used for jewellery and coins, especially late in the Iron Age.

Iron Age people lived in a tribal society, but until the 1st century BC there is no evidence for either the name or the extent of the tribal area. Julius Caesar lists the Cenimagni as one of the tribes which submitted to him during his raid on Britain in 54 BC. The name Cenimagni is perhaps more correctly Iceni or Eceni Magni - the Great Iceni. The name Iceni was recorded by Tacitus in the 1st century AD. The distribution of their coins indicates that in the 1st century AD the tribal area covered Norfolk, north Suffolk and part of Cambridgeshire.

Our knowledge of Iron Age Norfolk is limited, as few sites have been excavated to modern standards and pottery is difficult to date. However, we know most people lived in round houses in scattered, undefended farmsteads. They kept cattle, sheep, pigs and horses and grew cereals, particularly spelt (a wheat) and barley. The area under cultivation expanded during the period, leading to the permanent clearance of woodland and the development of heaths in Breckland. Carefully laid-out field systems have been recognised near Scole and may have been widespread. There is evidence, too, for woodland management. This is likely to have included coppicing to provide, for instance, more than 60,000 timbers needed for a recently excavated artificial 'oak grove' at the 1st century AD ceremonial site at Thetford. By the 1st century AD much of upland Norfolk was settled. In Fenland, however, by the 2nd/1st century BC settlement was restricted to the Fen islands and the Fen edge, because of flooding from the Wash. The distribution of sites here suggests farmers exploited the adjacent Fenland as well as cultivating the upland. Detailed fieldwork in Broadland might produce a similar pattern there.

Two types of defended site have been recognised, but little is known of their date or function. Five belong to a large type of fort with massive earthworks. Those at Holkham, Warham, South Creake and Narborough form an arc around north-west Norfolk; the fifth is at Thetford. They may mark a boundary or be an indication of the status of the persons who controlled them. The second type of defended enclosure, known mainly from air photographs, is square and much smaller, enclosing about 1/4 ha. Most lie near artefact concentrations in north Norfolk and possibly relate to settlement boundaries. The slender dating evidence suggests 1st century AD construction.

North-west Norfolk within the arc of larger forts may have been the tribal centre in the 1st century BC. This area has produced a unique concentration of gold and silver alloy torcs (neckrings); the largest group of about 180 from Snettisham was probably buried about 70 BC. This find has been interpreted as a treasury buried in response to some threat. The many bronze horse-harness and vehicle fittings recorded from Norfolk show the widespread use of chariots drawn by pairs of ponies whose use in war is described by Julius Caesar. These, together with the large number of torcs and the absence of imported wine-vessels and certain types of pottery, show that the Icenian nobility expressed their wealth and rank in a quite different way from neighbouring tribes of south-eastern England.

A few continental gold coins of the late 2nd/early 1st century BC date are recorded from Norfolk, mainly from hoards such as were found at Snettisham and Weybourne. There is some evidence that these were melted down and their gold re-used. The main series of Icenian gold and silver coins began late in the 1st century BC and continued until about AD 60. In the 1st century AD the names of the rulers and, uniquely, the tribal name ECE(NI) appear on the coins. The coin types suggest the Iceni were divided into three sub-tribes. It is difficult to know how far coins were used commercially within the tribal area. The presence of Iron Age pottery and coins at places such as Saham Toney suggest that some of the Roman towns began as native market centres perhaps after the Roman Conquest. Coins may have been used for trading between tribes, because those struck by the Trinovantian and Catuvellaunian tribes of south Suffolk, Essex and Hertfordshire have been found in south Norfolk, while Icenian coins were recorded from south Suffolk sites. The distribution of Icenian coins suggests that by the mid 1st century AD the tribal centre was in Breckland, perhaps at Thetford where the major ceremonial centre was constructed, reconstructed and demolished probably between the 40s and 60s AD.

In AD 43 the Romans invaded Britain. In AD 49 the Iceni were given the status of client-kingdom with their own ruler, probably Prasutagus. His death in AD 60 was followed by a revolt led by his widow Boudica (Boadicea). After its failure, the Icenian kingdom ceased to exist and the area came under direct Roman control from the new centre at Caistor St. Edmund (Map 12).

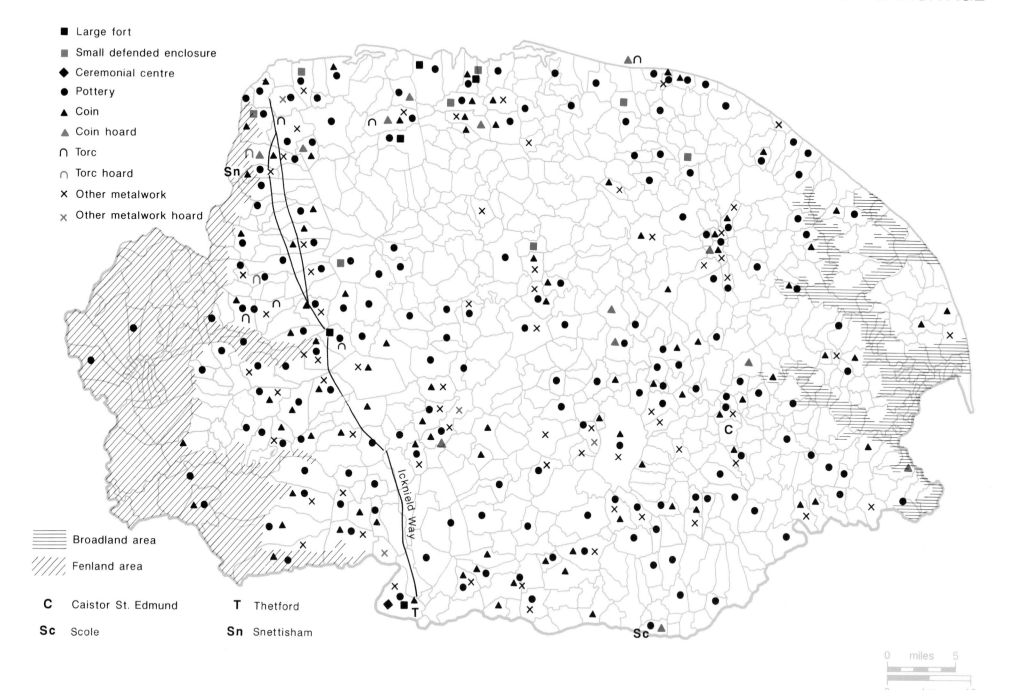

Large fort

Small defended enclosure

Ceremonial centre

Pottery

Coin

Coin hoard

Torc

Torc hoard

Other metalwork

Other metalwork hoard

Broadland area

Fenland area

Icknield Way

C   Caistor St. Edmund

T   Thetford

Sc   Scole

Sn   Snettisham

0   miles   5

0   km   10

12. THE ROMAN PERIOD

David Gurney

The conquest of Britain in AD 43 saw the absorption of south-east England into the Roman Empire, as the Roman army established and consolidated its control by the construction of forts and effective means of communication. In Norfolk, early forts are known at Threxton, Ashill, Swanton Morley and Horstead, while the principal Roman roads - the Pye Road (the modern A140), the Peddars Way and the Fen Causeway - are probably of military origin. These main routes formed the infrastructure for the development of a more comprehensive road network, linking the major towns and larger villages.

The Roman advance westwards into Wales led to troop withdrawals from the south-east, and to safeguard the rear, the Iceni were disarmed. This led to a rebellion in AD 47 by at least one faction of the tribe, but this appears to have been easily quashed.

After this, the tribe under the rule of Prasutagus became a client kingdom enjoying considerable independence, but this came to a dramatic end in AD 60 on his death. The emperor Nero enforced the return of the territory to Roman rule, and this resulted in a major rebellion led by the widowed queen, Boudicca. After successfully sacking the new Roman towns of Colchester, London and St. Albans, the rebels were eventually defeated in battle, probably at Mancetter (Warks).

Thereafter, Norfolk was firmly established as part of the Roman province, and there followed three centuries of a new order, with peace, prosperity and culture. During the Roman period, large areas cleared of forest in earlier times continued in occupation, and inroads were made into the less-easily farmed afforested boulder clay region of central Norfolk. In the east of the county, there was a great estuary between the islands of Flegg and Lothingland, while in the west, the Fenland was becoming dry land allowing settlement for the first time. The climate appears to have been somewhat warmer but wetter than at present.

With the new order came a new administration, and the centre for this, called *Venta Icenorum* (meaning 'market place of the Iceni'), was established at Caistor St. Edmund. It was a large planned town, founded around AD 70, with a regular street grid, forum and basilica, baths, temples, town houses, shops and evidence of glassmaking, metalworking and pottery manufacture. This bustling 'county town' and centre for commerce and industry, probably had a population of several thousand.

At Brampton, a second smaller town enclosed by a defensive ditch was built, with a bath-house and metalworking areas inside. To the west of this was an extensive pottery with at least 141 kilns, which mainly produced kitchen wares for local markets.

Smaller towns or large villages developed at a dozen or more sites, usually where there were major crossroads (Threxton, Toftrees) or river crossings (Scole, Billingford). Each of these probably fulfilled various needs, acting as local markets, centres of manufacturing industries (Kempstone) and religious centres (Crownthorpe, Hockwold).

Most of the population of Roman Norfolk (probably several hundred thousand) lived in the countryside, either in villages or in native-style farmsteads, with an economy based on agriculture or animal husbandry following patterns of land-use and settlement of Iron Age (or earlier) origin. Dotted among these smaller sites were Roman-style villas, which were the residences of officials, prosperous landowners or farmers. Sixteen certain villas are known, while surface finds suggest that many more existed. The densest area of these comfortable and well-appointed farmhouses, which show aspirations to a Roman life-style, with mosaics, wall-plaster and hypocausts, is in north-west Norfolk, where there is a string of evenly-spaced villas along the Icknield Way, a prehistoric track reused as a road in the Roman period. Surrounding these houses were largely self-sufficient working farms or estates with a mixed economy.

In the west of the county, a fall in sea level in the first century AD meant that vast tracts of hitherto uninhabitable Fenland became dry. This new and highly fertile land, previously lacking an owner, automatically became the property of the emperor, and it was run as a massive Imperial Estate, administered from a headquarters at Stonea (Cambs). The main activities of the estate were sheep-rearing (for milk, wool and hides) and salt-production from the evaporation of saline water from tidal creeks. The considerable profits of this estate are not reflected in the character of most Fenland sites, so these probably went into the Imperial coffers while the estate workers led a very humble lifestyle.

Other industrial activities in Norfolk were the manufacture of pottery, with large potteries at Brampton and in the Nar Valley, and smaller kiln sites or individual kilns known or suspected at some 30 other locations. Metalworking took place on the Greensand deposits in west Norfolk, and in several of the towns and villages.

In the 3rd century, the threat of Saxon raiders led to the construction of coastal defences, with forts at Brancaster, a possible fort (now lost through erosion) in the Cromer area, and Caister-on-Sea. Inland, the core of the town of Venta Icenorum was defended by a wall and ditch, giving some inhabitants at least a place of refuge. In AD 410, the emperor Honorius withdrew the last army units, leaving the occupants of late Roman Norfolk to fend for themselves. A gradual decay set in, and the visible evidence that Norfolk had ever been part of the great Roman Empire crumbled slowly away.

12. THE ROMAN PERIOD

Legend:

- ● Defended town
- ○ Large village
- — Road
- --- Probable road
- ■ Early fort
- □ Late fort
- ⋯ Coastline
- ▲ Settlement with substantial building
- • Settlement

- ◇ Pottery kiln
- M Metalworking
- S Salt production
- T Temple
- ▽ Hoard

Labelled places:

Brancaster
Toftrees
Billingford
Brampton
Narford
Kempstone
Caister on sea
Fincham
Crownthorpe
Caistor St Edmund
Burgh Castle
Fen Causeway
Denver
Threxton
Hockwold
Long Stratton
Ditchingham
Scole

Peddars Way
Icknield Way
Pye Road

0 miles 5
0 km 10

13. EARLY SAXON SETTLEMENT

Kenneth Penn

Roman rule in Britain came to a formal end in AD 410 when the province was told to defend itself against the barbarians. The next two centuries saw a migration of Angles, Saxons and other small tribes from the coastal lands of north-west Europe to eastern England, including many from Scandinavia, until the old Roman province became thoroughly Anglo-Saxon in character. However, these newcomers did not come to an empty country, but encountered many Romano-Britons, their farms and fields, small towns (by then deserted) and their roads (some still in use today) (Map 12). We know little about the relationships between these peoples, although historians believe that many Romano-Britons continued in their farms and villages; however, their culture seems to have been rapidly replaced by the customs and language of the Anglo-Saxons and they became indistinguishable from these new people. In the cemeteries, which are the main evidence of the Anglo-Saxons, there is almost no hint of Romano-British objects amongst the gravegoods, which are resolutely Germanic. This is true even at Caistor St. Edmund, where the Anglo-Saxons established a cemetery within sight of the walls of the old Roman town. Some hint of British survival may be seen in a few of the place-names which survived until Domesday Book. The Roman fort at *Branodunum* became Bran-caster, the Anglo-Saxons borrowing the word *castra* (fort) from the Britons, as they did for Caister (-on-Sea) and Caistor (St. Edmund), both Roman walled places; the Roman name of Caister, *Gariannonum*, survives in the river-name, Yare. The survival into Anglo-Saxon times of a British church *ecles*, is suggested by the name Eccles, at two places in Norfolk; near Eccles on the coast is Walcott, perhaps from the Anglo-Saxon word for serf or foreigner (meaning Briton) *wala*.

The first record of almost all Norfolk place-names is Domesday Book, but some are thought to belong to a very early period, especially some of the names ending in -ham, such as Reepham, Gresham and Fransham, and their distribution (with cemeteries) may indicate the general area of early settlement. Some names are thought to point to the existence of local 'tribes' or groups, for example, the Framingas (Framing-ham), Happingas (Happisburgh) and Morningas (Morningthorpe), whilst Swaffham seems to be the "ham of the Swabians". Some of these places are close to an early cemetery, for example, Swaffham, Elmham, Bridgham and Brettenham.

The early Saxon settlement pattern was probably much like the prehistoric and Roman one, with thin settlement in central Norfolk and towards the north-east coast, possibly reflecting woodland or boulder-clay (which at Domesday coincided closely). However, on the boulder-clay in parts of south Norfolk (and north Suffolk) were extensive areas of ancient field systems, at least of early Roman date, which seem to have been taken over and maintained by the early Saxons, and cemeteries and -hams along the rivers. Breckland in south-west Norfolk is an area of dry sandy heaths, with little woodland at Domesday, but here too, along the river Thet and its tributaries, there was probably settlement, indicated by the -ham names (Shropham and Bridgham, both with nearby cemeteries, Hockham and Wretham, on the heath close to a mere). Excavations have revealed a small village of at least 12 huts on the west bank of the Little Ouse at Thetford (Map 18); a contemporary cemetery stood on the opposite bank, on a slope overlooking the river, and perhaps contained the people of this village.

This pattern of -ham names near rivers, often on patches of light gravelly soils, and burial-places on high ground nearby is repeated along many of Norfolk's river systems, leaving the interfluves thinly settled, especially in regions of poor soils, such as the high sandy areas of north-west Norfolk, and Breckland, and probably the northern part of the belt of boulder-clay. However, it is in this area, in (North) Elmham parish, that one of the most interesting discoveries has been made, of both a settlement and a large cemetery next to each other on a hill, Spong Hill, overlooking a stream. The cemetery contained over 2000 cremation pots, and 58 inhumation graves, and was in use for most of the 5th and 6th centuries. The settlement has not been fully excavated, but so far, six 'sunken' huts and several post-built houses have been found. It was probably just one of the settlements served by this cemetery. Only a handful of early Saxon settlements have been discovered in Norfolk, but the existence of the early -ham names, which may refer to fairly important 'central places' and not mere hamlets, suggests that many more await discovery.

Some hint of their existence comes from Scole, Hemsby, Loddon, Postwick and Congham, where scatters of potsherds must indicate early Saxon occupation. At Witton, in north-east Norfolk, on a hillside overlooking a small stream, two groups of sunken huts have been found, nine huts altogether, possibly part of a larger settlement.

By the time that we have the first written evidence for the Anglo-Saxons in East Anglia, around AD 600, it is clear that society was not composed of independent peasant communities, indeed, never had been, but was complex and sophisticated, with a royal dynasty and many kinds and conditions of people, from nobles to slaves. The land they occupied was organised around quite large territories, containing important places, small villages and perhaps seasonal sites for the fishermen and herdsmen of Early Saxon Norfolk.

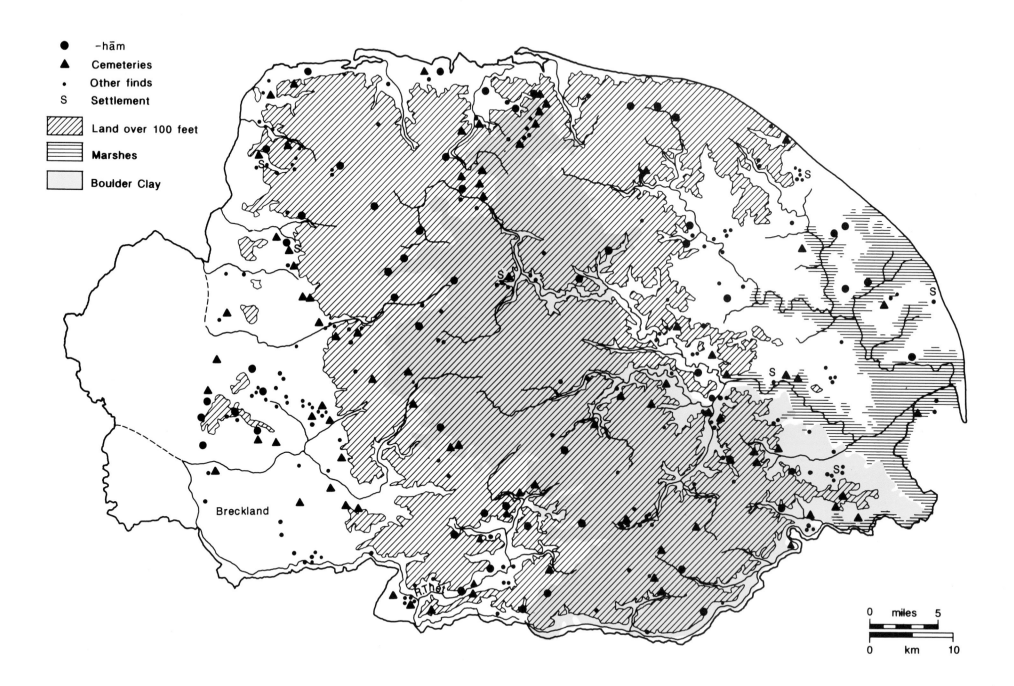

-hām
Cemeteries
Other finds
S   Settlement
Land over 100 feet
Marshes
Boulder Clay

Breckland

R.Thet

0   miles   5

0   km   10

14. THE MIDDLE SAXON PERIOD

Andrew Rogerson

From the earlier 7th century the nature of the archaeological evidence for Anglo-Saxon activity begins to change, a transformation completed by shortly after AD 700. Whereas in the pagan period of the 5th and 6th centuries cemeteries replete with grave-goods form the mainstay of Anglo-Saxon studies, the 7th century sees the introduction of Christianity and the eventual disappearance of accompanied burials. Only five sites are known to contain Middle Saxon cemeteries, Caister-on-Sea, Caistor St Edmund, Burgh Castle, Thornham, and possibly Sedgeford.

The disappearance of datable cemeteries in the early 8th century is balanced by the introduction throughout East Anglia, in c.650, of a distinctive type of pottery, Ipswich ware, which permits easier identification of settlement sites, with 420 sites and findspots so far recorded in the county. The introduction of silver coins, 'sceattas', into East Anglia in c.680 adds a class of evidence largely absent since the beginning of the 5th century.

Without doubt the Middle Saxon period saw the completion of settlement over the whole of the upland and much of the silt fen of Norfolk. Middle Saxon settlements were usually situated on different sites to their Early Saxon predecessors, and continued to be occupied after the Danish invasion of the late 9th century. Probably every modern parish within upland Norfolk contained a settlement of some type, although large tracts of land were left unexploited. Most place-names, apart from those with a Danish element, had been introduced by the mid-9th century. Contemporary written evidence, however, is sparse. Only two Norfolk places are named in documents: Dereham (probably West) and *Cnobheresburgh.* Recent fieldwork has shown not only the widespread nature of Middle Saxon use of the landscape but also that settlement size, status, wealth and type were greatly variable.

Although there were no Middle Saxon towns, recent discoveries point to settlements of some importance at Norwich and Thetford. That at Norwich lay on the north bank of the river (Map 32), and was perhaps the North wic or trading settlement, while the precursor of Anglo-Scandinavian Thetford spread along the southern bank of the Little Ouse outside the defences of the later town (Map 18). Neither site has been excavated on any scale, and the degree of urbanisation at both remains uncertain.

In the pre-Danish period there were surely many monasteries in Norfolk, but the names of only two, Dereham and *Cnobheresburgh,* are known. The latter, founded by the Irishman, Saint Fursey, in c.630, can be identified with either Caister-on-Sea or Burgh Castle. Both have been partly excavated. At the former a huge cemetery was located outside the walls of the Roman fort. Burials ranged in date from the 7th to 11th century, and included a group of extraordinary pseudo-ship burials. Limited work was carried out at Burgh Castle within the Roman fort. A cemetery of the 8th to 10th centuries lay adjacent to the flimsy remains of a timber building, perhaps a church. In the opposite corner of the fort seven curious oval timber structures were probably of similar date. At North Elmham excavations revealed parallel ditches defining roadways, with a few timber buildings. The site lay near the edge of an area which in the 10th century contained a cathedral, and which in the Middle Saxon period was, if not monastic, certainly associated with the Bishopric of East Anglia.

Near the Roman town at Caistor St. Edmund an exceptional site has produced, as surface finds, over thirty coins of the mid-7th to later 8th centuries, but very little contemporary metalwork and no pottery. Perhaps this assemblage represents a seasonal market or fair on an open site, exchange rather than settlement. A similarly prolific site at Bawsey has a coin series extending into the 9th century as well as pottery and abundant metalwork. The latter includes six styli, surely indicative of literacy, in other words monasticism. This site probably had two functions, as permanent religious centre and periodic market. A scattered hoard of proto-pennies of King Beonna of East Anglia (c.750) was found at Middle Harling. Excavations showed that the hoard had been deposited towards the edge of a Middle Saxon settlement, which metalwork finds suggest was of high status. The coins and other finds, however, were far less prolific than those from Bawsey. On Wormegay island a dense surface concentration of Ipswich ware containing an area of scattered human bone also produced one stylus after a very brief metal-detector survey. This site may have monastic origins.

An arc of large and ceramically prolific Middle Saxon sites span Norfolk Marshland from east to west set back behind the later Sea Bank. One, at Hey Green, Terrington St Clement, was huge, stretching for c.1.5 km along a roddon or extinct watercourse. These sites represent an intense and organised pastoral exploitation of rich silt-land grasses.

Fieldwalking and metal detecting continue to augment our stock of knowledge of Middle Saxon sites and finds, and it will soon be possible to establish a settlement hierarchy based on predominantly surface evidence from rural areas and excavations in the towns. This will indicate the range of settlements, from rural sites, small and large, poor and rich, to monastic sites, cemeteries, markets and fairs, and trading centres.

Excavation and survey will also trace the origins of each site-type as well as their fates during and after the Danish invasion which marks the start of the Late Saxon period.

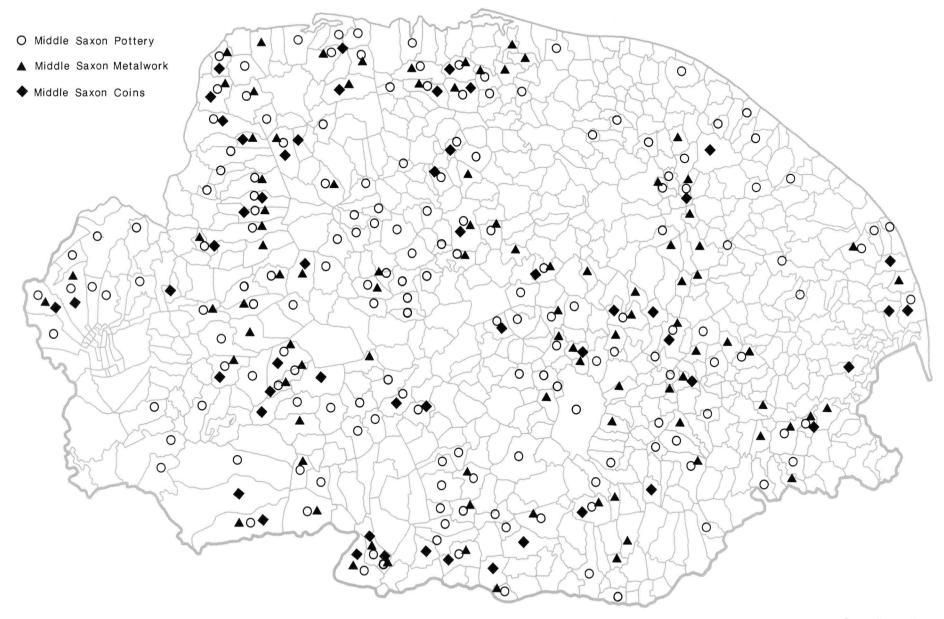

○ Middle Saxon Pottery

▲ Middle Saxon Metalwork

◆ Middle Saxon Coins

15. LATE SAXON SOCIAL STRUCTURE

Kate Skipper and Tom Williamson

Norfolk had a highly complex system of tenurial organisation at the time of the Norman Conquest. Domesday shows that vills on the familiar text-book pattern, containing a single manor and a population of villeins, bordars, and cottars, were rare. Instead, most contained several estates, and, in particular, many had large numbers of individuals described as free men (*liberi homines*) or sokemen (*sochemanni*). There has been much discussion about the origin of these social groups, which were also a characteristic of neighbouring counties. Some historians have seen them as the direct result of Danish settlement - as descendants of the demobbed Danish army. Others have suggested that the upheavals of Danish incursions interrupted, and retarded, an inexorable decline in the status of the English peasantry, which continued unabated in areas further to the west. The three maps opposite do not solve the problem of the East Anglian free peasants, but they may help to refocus the questions which historians should be asking about them.

Sokemen and free men have been mapped by historians before, but usually in combination. Indeed, they had much in common: unlike villeins and bordars, they were not listed by Domesday among the chattels of a manor. Nevertheless, it is clear that the two groups were, in theory if not in practice, distinct. Sokemen varied greatly in the amount of land they held; a few possessed substantial estates, but many existed on only a few acres. What they had in common was their semi-dependent status. *Soc*, in origin, was an Old English (*not* a Scandinavian) term for customary rights to control, and to profit from, a person. These rights had originally been royal, but during the Middle and Later Saxon periods they had often been usurped or alienated. They included the right to justice over an individual, and to the profits which might accrue from this. But it is also likely that many, perhaps most, East Anglian sokemen owed other obligations, including services, and may have been distinct from villeins principally in that they were able to alienate their land. The extent of this freedom could, however, be limited, as at Blofield, where there were 43 sokemen 'who could not sell or grant their lands'.

Domesday makes it clear that a sokeman's taxes were usually paid through the manor or estate to which he was attached. As far as the government was concerned, therefore, the pre-eminent rights in their land presumably lay with the local lord. It is hardly surprising that in the following centuries sokemen disappear from the county, depressed to villein status, or surviving as a class of dependent cultivators, often described as 'molmen', distinguished from the villeins only by the less onerous terms of their tenure.

Those described by Domesday as *liberi homines*, in contrast, seem to have had a more direct relationship with public authority. Domesday implies that they were generally responsible for paying their own taxes, and they presumably attended the hundred court. They were indeed free men, although their land might sometimes be the property of another individual, to whom they might also be bound by personal ties of fealty and obligation. Some had substantial estates with dependent cultivators, others minute holdings. In part, this was because free land was subject to partible inheritance, leading to the rapid fragmentation of estates. Domesday occasionally shows us the early stages of this process, as at Buxton, where 'five free men, brothers' held seven carucates of land.

Poverty could lead to an inability to meet public obligations, and might thus bring a free man down to the level of a sokeman. So too, perhaps, could ties of commendation, particularly when these had been made to an individual from who the person in question also held land. Many must have been hovering on the borderline between these two groups, and the Domesday commissioners must often have been uncertain about how an individual should be classified. In theory, however, the two groups *were* still distinct. But they probably had similar origins. Most were the descendants, not of Danish soldiers, but of the general mass of the early Anglian population, of free lineages which had originally owed obligations to no lords but the *Wuffingas*.

Whereas, by 1066, sokemen were widely spread throughout the county, *liberi homines* had a more limited distribution. They clustered in the south and east of the county and, to a lesser extent, in the south west. Although they were numerous in Flegg, where there was probably a major influx of Danish settlers in the 9th century, in general their distribution was much wider than, and correlates poorly with, that of Scandinavian place names. They seem to have been most common in areas of particularly fertile soils; and in peripheral areas, especially on the clayland interfluves, or on the edges of the fens. This pattern is open to a number of possible interpretations. It probably reflects the greater opportunities for economic expansion in these areas, and the fact that they were more distant from the residences of great landowners. The descendants of free lineages residing in such areas had managed to maintain, or enhance, their ancestral status. Where the power of great lords was more pervasive, in contrast, and where population pressed on limited resources, sokemen predominated.

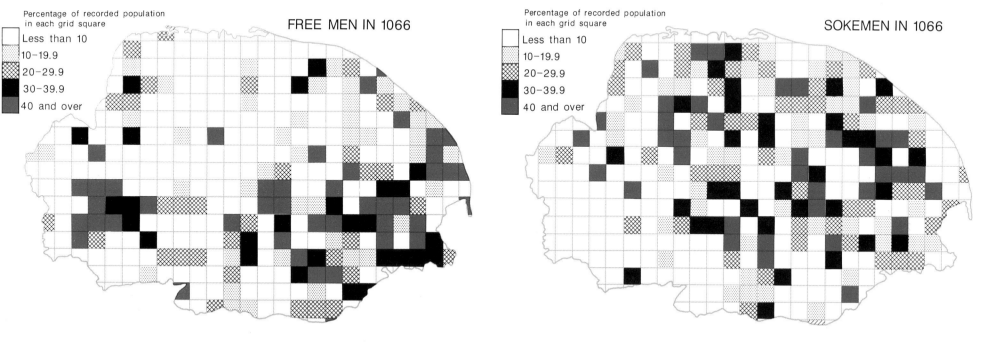

Percentage of recorded population
in each grid square

Less than 10
10–19.9
20–29.9
30–39.9
40 and over

FREE MEN IN 1066

Percentage of recorded population
in each grid square

Less than 10
10–19.9
20–29.9
30–39.9
40 and over

SOKEMEN IN 1066

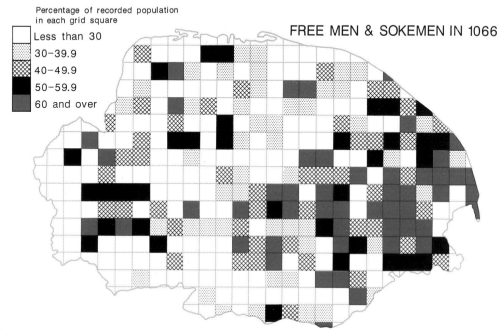

Percentage of recorded population
in each grid square

Less than 30
30–39.9
40–49.9
50–59.9
60 and over

FREE MEN & SOKEMEN IN 1066

16. LATE SAXON POPULATION DENSITIES

Tom Williamson and Kate Skipper

The Domesday Inquest did not, unfortunately, aim to provide any record of population. Its creators were only interested in collecting information about those holding land, and owing tax and other obligations. As a result, it has provided later historians with ample scope for debate and disagreement about the correct 'multiplier' necessary to convert its statistics into real population figures, a choice which depends on untestable assumptions about average family size, and structure. Rather than enter into these difficult debates, the map simply shows the density of the tenant population as recorded, retrospectively, for 1066.

Domesday population densities in Norfolk have been mapped before, by H.C. Darby, but on the basis of hundreds. This map attempts to provide a more detailed break-down. To do this, it would have been most satisfactory to calculate the population density of each vill, but for a number of reasons this is not feasible. We do not really know the area of the vills mentioned in the survey. In particular, it is not safe to assume that they were the same as the parishes which, in most cases, later bore their names. Parish boundaries only seem to have become finally fixed during the century or so after the completion of the survey. Moreover, some medieval parishes do not appear as Domesday vills, while some Domesday vills never became parishes.

The map therefore takes another approach, although one which, we freely admit, is open to a number of objections. It rests on a simple, although possibly flawed assumption. Because fieldwalking surveys suggest that Late Saxon settlement usually took the form of small nucleations, near or adjacent to the sites of parish churches, we have assumed that the latter make the sites of all those vills recorded by Domesday which later developed into parishes, and the residences therefore of those listed within them. In the case of those vills that did not so develop, we have identified the main focus of settlement as the hamlet, farmstead, or manorial site which bears, or bore, its name (only a handful of such

places mentioned in Domesday cannot be identified in this way, and most of these had negligible populations). Having identified the likely residences of the listed population, we have mapped the overall densities on the basis of a grid of squares, each measuring 4 by 4 km, based on the framework of the National Grid.

The problems inherent in such an approach will be obvious. It does not allow for the possibility that there was more than one focus of settlement within a vill. More importantly, there must be doubts about whether the free men or sokemen which the Survey often listed as 'lying in' a particular vill necessarily dwelt within it. Nevertheless, for all its problems, the exercise is worth doing, for it produces a map which serves, in a number of ways, to modify the picture of population densities represented by a hundred-based mapping technique.

Like Darby's map, ours shows that the highest population densities were in the south and east of the county, the lowest in the north and west. But, in part, the overall densities in the latter region were lowered by the absolute absence of settlement from certain areas, most notably the high, dry interfluves away from the principal river valleys. Where major valleys occurred, in the Burnhams or the Creakes, for example, the population density was comparable to that in the south and east. Moreover, mapping by hundreds tends to obscure the fact that in the south east, population densities were not uniformly high. On the heaviest soils, lying on the poorly-draining watersheds between the major valleys, the densities were lower than in the valleys themselves. It was the latter, and especially those of the Chet, the Tiffey, the Tas, and the Yare, that were really densely settled. Indeed, they were among the most densely-settled areas in the whole of England. In both the south east, therefore, and in the north west, we see a contrast between the river valleys and the watersheds. This was a contrast vital in the development of early settlement in the county, one which was as important as the overall distribution of soil-types, and one which is also reflected

in the distribution of certain kinds of place-names (Map 17).

The population densities in Late Saxon Norfolk were, therefore, related in some measure to aspects of topography. But variations are difficult to explain solely in environmental terms. There are some puzzling anomalies. Thus, for example, it is not immediately apparent why population densities in the clayland valleys were so much higher than those in the fertile soils of Tunstead or South Erpingham hundreds, areas which were densely populated in subsequent centuries. To some extent, areas of high population correlate with those in which free tenures were also thick on the ground (Map 15), and it is possible that the custom of partible inheritance (equal division between male heirs) associated with such tenures may have encouraged rapid population growth. But the coincidence is not a close one. The distribution of Late Saxon population in Norfolk, like that within the country as a whole, was presumably the consequence of the complex interplay of many factors, operating over a long period of time: social and economic, as well as environmental.

Recorded individuals
per square kilometre

Less than 4

4–5.9

6–7.9

8–9.9

10 and over

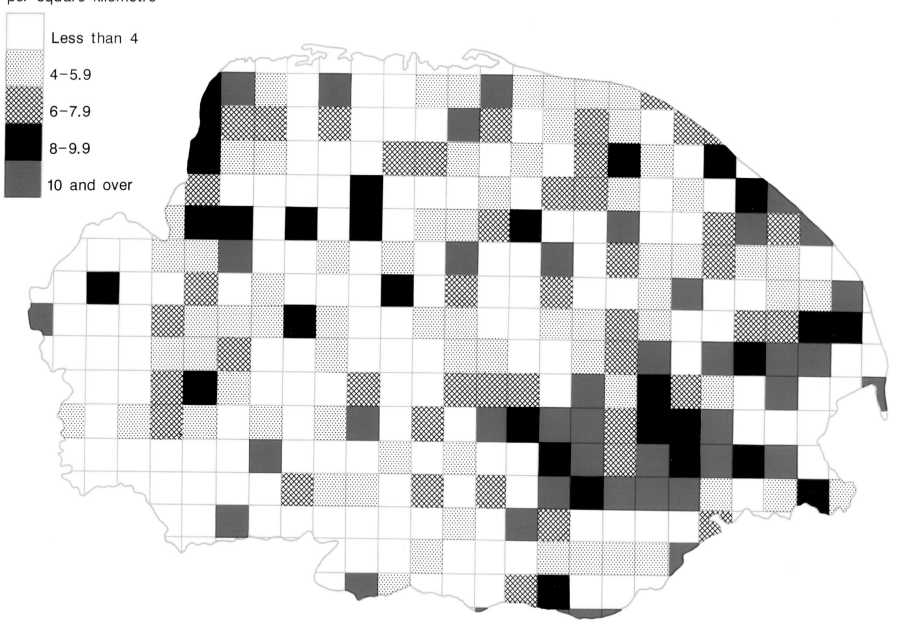

Different kinds of place name are not randomly scattered across Norfolk. Most have a highly structured distribution, forming patterns which are sometimes informative, more often obscure and challenging. The maps opposite illustrate some of the problems and possibilities.

The first two maps show the contrasting distributions of the two most common suffixes in the county: -ham ('village, estate') and -tun ('farm, settlement'). The former are largely restricted to the better-drained soils and the main river valleys. The latter, in contrast, are more widely distributed, occurring in large numbers in more marginal and peripheral locations, especially on interfluves away from the major valleys.

Most large and administratively important vills recorded in Domesday were hams, and many, like Aylsham or Wymondham, later became important market towns. In contrast, most tons were comparatively small: many of those mentioned in Domesday disappeared altogether in the late medieval period. Names ending in ham are often shared by several neighbouring parishes, distinguished from each other by the addition of the name of the saint to whom the parish church is dedicated (e.g., Weasenham St. Peter, Weasenham All Saints) or by some directional qualifier (South, East and West Raynham). This is rarely the case with names containing tun. Lastly, the prefixes used to qualify the two kinds of element are different. Hams tend to be associated with very early personal names, or with topographic terms (Burnham, the 'river estate'). Tuns, in contrast, are more likely to be associated with later personal names; to have a first element suggesting some specialised economic function (such as growing apples (Appleton) barley (Barton) or rye (Roughton); or to lie north, south east or west of some other, presumably more important, place (Norton, Sutton, Easton, Weston).

These aspects suggest that the locational differences exhibited by the two kinds of name are not simply a reflection of settlement chronology. That is, tuns are not necessarily places established later in the Anglo-Saxon period than hams, but rather places which were once subsidiary settlements attached to them, and which became separate estates comparatively late in the Anglo-Saxon period. Place-names ending in wick, stead, and worth exhibit similar tendencies.

Many names ending in ham thus represent the foci of large, early estates or territories. Some early territories are represented by other kinds of name: Creake, for example, bears a pre-Anglian, Celtic name. Other early territorial names survived into the later Anglo-Saxon periods as those of hundreds. Loddon hundred is derived from Lodningas, a name containing the element ingas, usually translated as 'people of'. The name thus meant something like 'people of the Lodne', the earlier name for the river Chet. Happing hundred, which preserves the name of 'the people of Haep', is another example. But it is noteworthy how most examples of -ingas names, and also of those containing the related element -ingaham, do not occur in the kinds of primary, river-valley sites favoured by hams. They occur in more marginal locations. Perhaps some lie at what was once the boundary of an early territory, the tribal name having been dislodged from the estate centre by social changes - the decline in the importance of tribal groups, and the development of a more hierarchical society - occurring early in the Anglo-Saxon period.

The third map shows the principal place names asscociated with woodland. Names in the first category, containing the elements thveit and leah, are given the most prominence, on the basis that they probably indicate clearance, and therefore more extensive areas of woodland, than names in the second category, which might indicate no more than a small grove. Other elements, most notably feld, are also mapped, but with even less prominence. Feld, meaning 'open country', merely implies that adjacent areas were densely treed.

Together, these names suggest that in Early and Middle Saxon times the distribution of woodland was not determined in any simple or direct way by soils. The heavy clays in the south of the county are noticeably deficient in woodland names. Instead, many cluster on the watersheds between the principal valleys, or around the upper reaches of streams and rivers. Thus, there is a noticeable concentration along the great watershed which runs in an arc through the middle of the county - between the rivers draining east, and those draining north and west. This region was also that in which most of the largest areas of woodland recorded by Domesday were located. More perplexing is the marked concentration on the edge of the Yare/Bure marshes. This is not clearly mirrored in Domesday, and has no obvious explanation.

The last map shows place names containing Scandinavian elements, or showing Scandinavian influence. It omits those with the element thorp, which are widely distributed: this term for a small hamlet seems to have been generally adopted by English speakers. Otherwise, Scandinavian names tend to cluster, most obviously on the island of Flegg: a cluster so distinct that it must surely represent Danish peasant settlement in the ninth century. A less marked concentration occurs around the lower reaches of the Yare and the Waveney; and others, somewhat surprisingly, in the upper reaches of the tributaries of the Bure, and around the headwaters of the Thet and the Wissey. Whether these similarly represent Danish settlement, or have a chronological explanation - as areas settled, or (more probably) hived off from large estates, at a particularly late date - remains obscure.

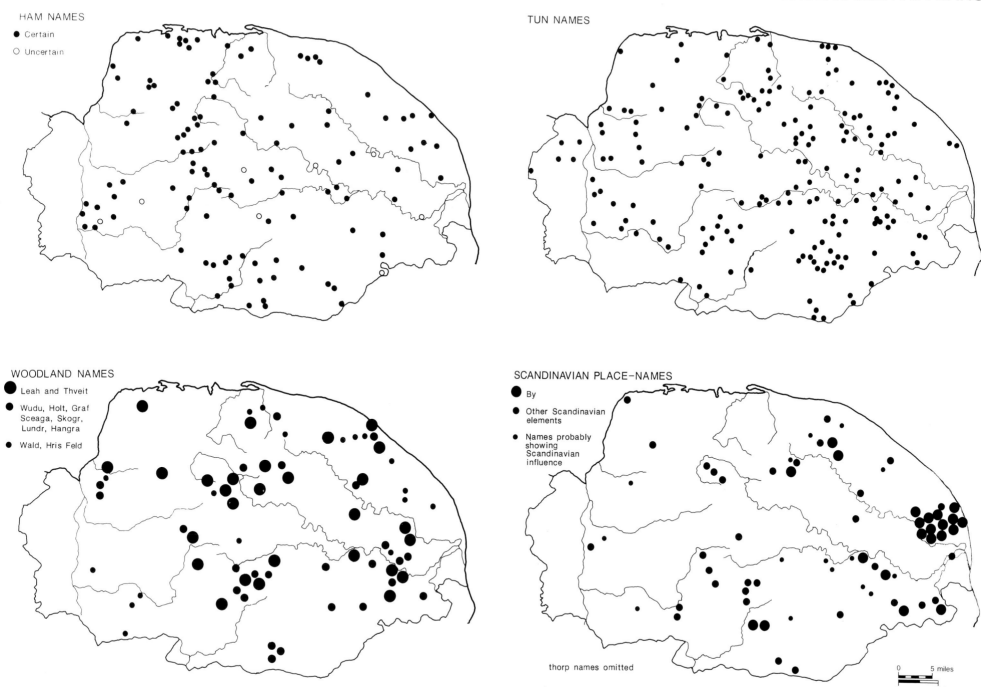

17. PLACE-NAME PATTERNS

HAM NAMES
- ● Certain
- ○ Uncertain

TUN NAMES

WOODLAND NAMES
- ● Leah and Thveit
- ● Wudu, Holt, Graf Sceaga, Skogr, Lundr, Hangra
- ● Wald, Hris Feld

SCANDINAVIAN PLACE-NAMES
- ● By
- ● Other Scandinavian elements
- ● Names probably showing Scandinavian influence

thorp names omitted

0   5 miles
0   10 km

18. SAXON THETFORD

Kenneth Penn

The town of Thetford (Thetford means something like 'chief' or 'people's' ford) probably had its beginnings around 870 when 'the raiding army [of Vikings] rode...into East Anglia and took up winter quarters at Thetford'. However, there had been at least one important river crossing in the area for over a thousand years.

The Iron Age fort at Thetford Castle was probably sited to guard the point where the Icknield Way crossed the river at Nuns' Bridges (Map 11). Only a short distance to the north lay the major Iceni religious or ceremonial centre at Gallows Hill. Several small Roman sites have been found, one near the central ford and another near the Red Castle ford, to the west. It was around the three fords that Thetford developed.

The Early Saxon settlement started near the Red Castle ford, and at least a dozen 6th century huts have now been excavated here, probably part of a small village. Middle Saxon objects and features have been found in the same area, attesting to extensive activity along the river bank around AD 700. Finds from north of the central ford may indicate its continued use, while pottery and coins from the Iron Age fort may come from its use as a meeting-place, possibly for markets and fairs.

Difficulties in precise dating of pottery make it impossible to say if there was a break in occupation between the end of the Middle Saxon settlement and the start of the Late Saxon town towards the end of the 9th century, on a site some way along the river bank to the east.

The long looping line of the Late Saxon defences on the south bank has long been known from excavation. This has also shown that in one place the ditch had silted up and been built over by the late 10th century, suggesting that these defences were built early in the life of the town, and that they initially enclosed a large but scattered settlement, only here and there densely packed. Elsewhere, there were areas of open ground and paddocks.

Excavations in the 1940's by Guy Knocker and in the 1960's by Brian Davison at various places within the defences on the south bank have shown us much else about the town's character in the Late Saxon and Norman period. At its peak, Thetford was a town of loosely-arranged timber buildings, often set back from gravelled streets, in their own yards with associated cesspits, wells and rubbish pits. Many seemingly casual burials have been found, singly or in larger groups, not associated with any known churchyard.

These excavations also revealed a group of kilns which made 'Thetford-type' pottery, and the traces of a timber church in its churchyard (perhaps one of those mentioned in Domesday Book). Thetford was an industrial town, with a mint, and also had trade-links with other areas of eastern England, perhaps based on its pottery and textile production.

It was once thought that the southern ditch must be the original and only defensive circuit, but in 1963 a circuit on the north bank was suggested, a theory untested by excavation until 1989 when a small excavation in Guildhall Street found a ditch of Late Saxon date, either part of the suggested circuit, or an addition. The origins and dates of the two sets of defences are unclear; it is likely that the West Saxons, when they took East Anglia from the Danes in 917, built a new 'burh' here and perhaps this is represented by the defences on the north bank. Recent excavations on the north bank show that, apart from a few Middle Saxon finds, occupation here in the Late Saxon period began sometime in the 11th century.

Thetford reached its greatest importance and extent in the Late Saxon and Early Norman period (it was briefly the site of the bishopric 1071-1094). Domesday Book reveals that Thetford was one of the largest towns in Late Saxon England with 934 burgesses, occupying land on both the Norfolk and Suffolk sides of the river Little Ouse. Twelve churches were recorded, including St. Mary and its dependants, St. Peter, St. John, St. Martin and St. Margaret. By 1086 there were 724 burgesses and 224 empty houses, possibly a sign of the slow decline that afflicted Thetford from the late 11th century. This eventually left the area south of the river with little more than scattered farms.

Between the possible town defences and the Iron Age fort, in which a Norman motte was built, a small grid of streets may represent a 'planned suburb', whilst the streets within the Iron Age castle defences may be evidence of another medieval market-place. St. Nicholas Street was perhaps built to replace Minstergate whose route out to the west was blocked by the Cluniac priory, built in 1114. Red Castle, on the edge of the town, is a 12th-century earthwork, and was probably hastily thrown up in the civil war of Stephen's reign (and may hint at one of the steps in Thetford's decline and abandonment on the south bank). Even in medieval decline, Thetford remained an important local centre with several religious houses, but all these disappeared at the Reformation.

46

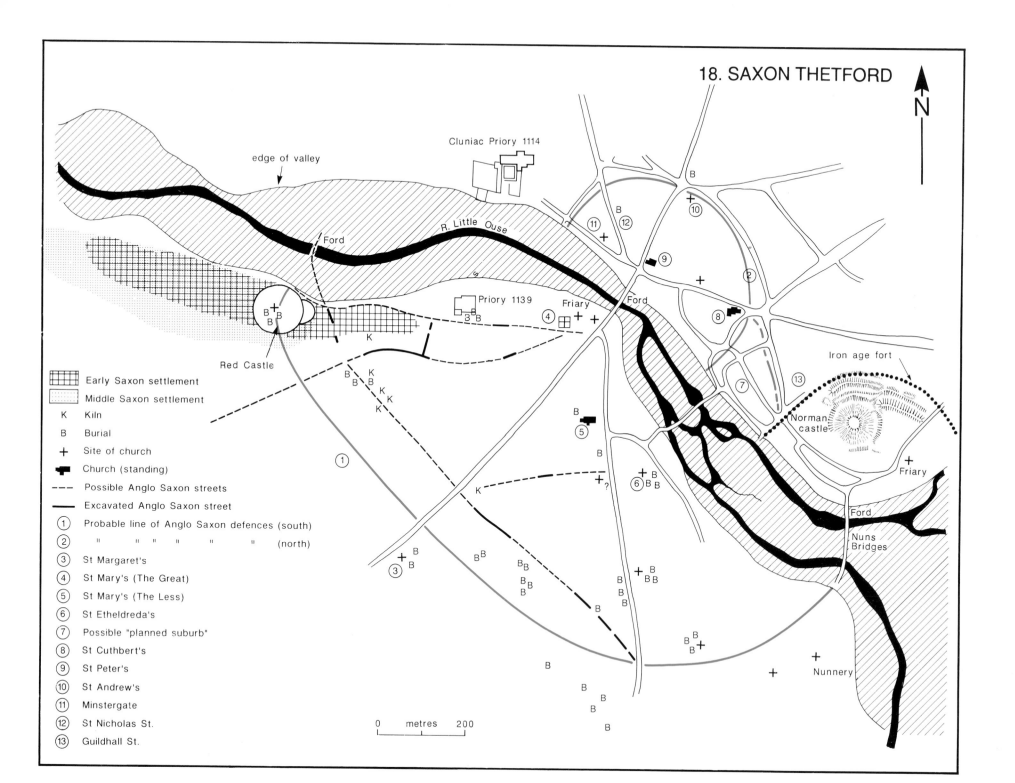

18. SAXON THETFORD

N

edge of valley

Cluniac Priory 1114

R. Little Ouse

Ford

Ford

Priory 1139

Friary

Ford

Iron age fort

Red Castle

Norman castle

Friary

Ford

Nuns Bridges

Nunnery

Early Saxon settlement

Middle Saxon settlement

K   Kiln

B   Burial

+   Site of church

Church (standing)

- - -   Possible Anglo Saxon streets

⎯⎯   Excavated Anglo Saxon street

①   Probable line of Anglo Saxon defences (south)

②   "   "   "   "   "   (north)

③   St Margaret's

④   St Mary's (The Great)

⑤   St Mary's (The Less)

⑥   St Etheldreda's

⑦   Possible "planned suburb"

⑧   St Cuthbert's

⑨   St Peter's

⑩   St Andrew's

⑪   Minstergate

⑫   St Nicholas St.

⑬   Guildhall St.

0   metres   200

19. MEDIEVAL LAND USE AND LAND VALUES

Bruce M. S. Campbell

The years around 1300 mark the culmination of two centuries of demographic and economic expansion, during which the national population rose to a new and unprecedented maximum. The premium which this placed upon agricultural land in general, and arable land in particular, was considerable, and nowhere more so than in the closely settled and intensively exploited countryside of Norfolk. Unfortunately, there is no one comprehensive and consistent source, such as the Domesday Survey of 1086, by which the balance of land use within the county at this early climax of development may be gauged. Instead, reliance has to be placed upon the many hundreds of separate surveys or 'extents' compiled for individual manors at a variety of different dates. By far the largest and most consistent collection of these survives in conjunction with the *Inquisitiones Post Mortem* (IPMs) preserved at the Public Record Office, London. Information from these extents relates exclusively to the holdings of those lay lords who held directly from the Crown. Common pastures, which in parts of Norfolk formed a prominent and crucial component of land use, are omitted and there are grounds for supposing that the true extent and value of other resources are sometimes understated. IPMs are therefore of value as a relative rather than absolute guide to the amounts and values of resources.

The IPMs confirm Norfolk's early 14th-century status as one of the country's most pre-eminently arable counties. On average landlords' holdings of arable were worth almost four times the combined value of their meadow and pasture (the 'grassland ratio'). This implies a much more decided arable bias than prevailed at the time of Domesday. As will be seen from the first map, more favourable ratios of grassland to arable only persisted where the advance of the plough was halted by specific environmental circumstances: in Broadland, on the Fen edge, on the fringes of Breckland, and on the heavy soils of south Norfolk. By contrast, in much of central, north-eastern, and, especially, north-western Norfolk there were below-average quantities of privately-owned grassland. Here significant numbers of landlords, like their tenants, were largely dependent upon common pastures and grazings, fallows, and fodder crops for the support of their livestock.

Woodland as well as grassland had been sacrificed to the imperialism of the plough. The Domesday Survey portrays a countryside already largely cleared of woodland, with the most important surviving stands mostly confined to the heavy soils of central Norfolk. Some vestiges of these woodlands survived to c.1300 and are recorded by the IPMs, but it was in south Norfolk that the greatest concentration of woodland was now to be found, much of it small in scale and carefully managed on a coppicing system. By contrast, much of western, northern, and eastern Norfolk wore a relatively treeless aspect. Indeed, in Broadland and on the Fen edge, peat had long displaced wood as the principal fuel.

If early 14th-century Norfolk was largely given over to arable cultivation, the per-acre valuations given in the IMPs indicate that the returns thereby obtained were far from uniform. These values represent the anticipated annual 'rent' which the land was expected to yield rather than its full capital value. As such they are a function of many things, not least the physical productivity of the land itself and the relative costs of production - especially ploughing - on different soils and under different husbandry systems. Light soils were relatively cheap to cultivate but often yielded poorly. Heavy soils were potentially more productive but more difficult and expensive to till, and medieval cultivators rarely experienced much success with them. Instead, their best results were obtained on moderate soils where output could be maximised without incurring excessive costs.

Norfolk possessed all three types of land, their contrasting potentials reflected in their per-acre values. On the good sands of northern and north-eastern Norfolk, moderate values of 4-7d an acre generally prevailed, and similar or higher values were returned for some of the heavier soils of central and southern Norfolk. Values were, however, conspicuously lower on the most sterile sands (Breckland and the greensand belt of west Norfolk) and intractable clays (parts of south-eastern Norfolk). This contrasts with the situation prevailing on the loam soils of central and eastern Norfolk, the best of which constituted some of the finest and most intensively cultivated arable land in the country and commanded per-acre values which were correspondingly impressive. Values of 12d are common and on the rich, deep and productive loams of Flegg they attained a national maximum of 36d.

If Norfolk contained some of the most highly valued arable in the country the same cannot be said of its meadow. The environmental conditions which made much of its arable so productive were less conducive to the production of lush crops of grass. Thus, notwithstanding the acute scarcity of meadowland on the free-draining soils of the north-west its indifferent quality ensured that it rarely commanded a value of more than 18d an acre. As in later centuries, it was in the south of the county, in the vicinity of the Waveney Valley, that grass grew best to judge from the concentration of meadow values of 24d or higher. There was also some comparably highly-valued meadow in north-central and north-eastern Norfolk, where it formed an integral part of an intensive mixed-farming system geared, on the pastoral side, towards cattle-based dairying.

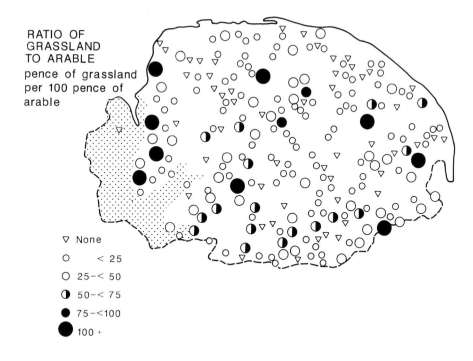

RATIO OF
GRASSLAND
TO ARABLE
pence of grassland
per 100 pence of
arable

▽ None
○ < 25
○ 25-< 50
◑ 50-< 75
● 75-<100
● 100 +

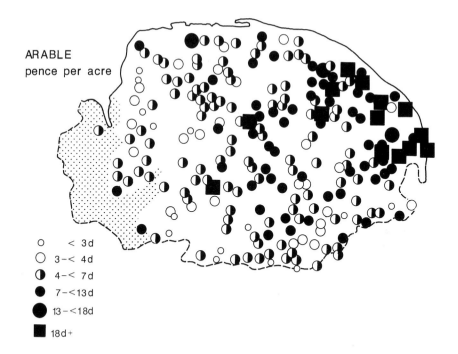

ARABLE
pence per acre

○ < 3d
○ 3-< 4d
◑ 4-< 7d
● 7-<13d
● 13-<18d
■ 18d+

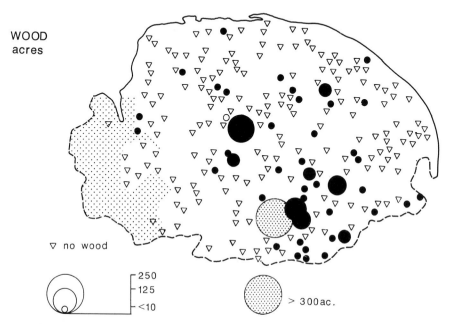

WOOD
acres

▽ no wood

250
125
<10

> 300ac.

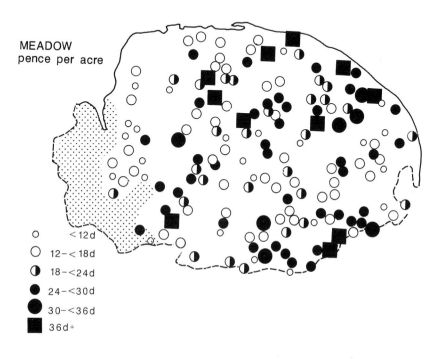

MEADOW
pence per acre

○ <12d
○ 12-< 18d
◑ 18-<24d
● 24-<30d
● 30-<36d
■ 36d+

20. MEDIEVAL ARABLE AND PASTORAL HUSBANDRY, 1250-1349   Bruce M. S. Campbell

By the late 13th century Norfolk was already one of the most distinctive farming counties of England. For one thing, Norfolk farmers favoured quite distinctive combinations of crops and animals. Barley was grown on a larger scale than anywhere else in the country. Rye - very much a light-land alternative to wheat - and legumes - principally peas and vetches - were also grown on a larger scale than was usual elsewhere. Moreover, for all that Norfolk was pre-eminently an arable county, it was better stocked with livestock than many supposedly more 'pastoral' parts of the country. Part of the explanation lies in the replacement of oxen by horses for draught power. Horses were costlier but worked harder and faster than oxen and operated to particular advantage on medium to light soils. Their adoption helped to liberate the pastoral sector from a narrow subservience to the arable, with the result that non-working animals accounted for an exceptional two-thirds of all farm livestock. Although sheep were undoubtedly present in significant numbers, cattle were actually of greater importance and few demesnes were without a well-developed dairy herd.

These particular combinations of crops and livestock went hand-in-hand with relatively intensive methods of production. On the better managed farms the ground was thoroughly prepared for cultivation, crops were systematically weeded, livestock were stall-fed with hay and fodder crops, and crop yields were pushed to levels unsurpassed until the 18th century. None of this would have been possible had Norfolk farmers not been active in the adoption of many of the technological innovations of the age. They were among the first to cultivate legumes for their nitrifying properties, to develop a form of convertible husbandry and devise rotations which minimised fallowing, to employ horses for farm work, and, above all, to reconcile the competing demands of arable and pastoral husbandry through the development of integrated mixed-farming systems.

Nevertheless, for all that Norfolk farmers stood in the van of medieval agricultural progress, the pattern of husbandry within the county was itself far from uniform. The variations which existed may be investigated using manorial accounts. These survive in large numbers - almost 130 demesnes are documented by over 1,300 individual accounts during the period 1238-1349 - and record in graphic detail the agricultural activities of a wide range of landlords: but not, alas, their tenants.

On the evidence of the principal crops cultivated and animals stocked, seven basic cropping and seven basic pastoral types may be identified in the tables and maps. The pattern, in the case of both crops and livestock, is kaleidoscopic, and admits of no simple subdivision into a tidy set of self-contained agricultural regions. Certain general trends and associations do, however, stand out.

On the arable side a clear contrast is apparent between cropping systems adapted to moderate-light soils (types 1-4), those adapted to heavy (types 5-6), and those adapted to the lightest and most infertile soils of all (type 7). The first accorded greatest prominence to barley, the second sowed wheat and oats or dredge (a barley/oats mixture) in greatest quantities, whilst on the third rye and oats - both poor-soil crops - were particularly conspicuous. But soil conditions were by no means the only determinant of cropping practice. The lure of the Norwich market was no doubt one reason why so many of the demesnes in its immediate vicinity devoted such an exceptionally large share of their sown acreage to the production of malting barley (type 4). Similarly, a plentiful supply of labour and relative freedom from communal controls helped to underpin the intensive and productive cropping systems associated with the Flegg district of east Norfolk (type 1). Indeed, farmers in this locality enjoyed the triple benefits of naturally fertile and easily cultivated loam soils, excellent access to major urban markets, and a cheap, abundant, and enterprising workforce.

On the pastoral side the pattern was somewhat different,

since the influence of soils was less direct, wool and cheese were better able to bear the costs of overland transport, and animals were themselves capable of walking to market. Nor was a cheap and abundant labour force of quite such crucial importance. Hence, the most advanced and intensive pastoral systems (types 1 and 2) - with their strong reliance upon horses rather than oxen, substantial non-working sector, and well-developed dairy herds - were widely distributed throughout the county. Insofar as this pastoral type was associated with any particular locality it was with north-central and north-eastern Norfolk, where dairy producers found a ready market for their products both in Norwich and the local textile-producing villages. In contrast, on the Breck edge, in the north-west, and in the vicinity of Norwich many demesnes practised a dual cattle/sheep economy (type 3). In most cases this represents a specific response to the opportunities presented by access to extensive common grazings. Nevertheless, a more-or-less exclusive emphasis upon sheep was unusual. 'Sheep-corn' demesnes (type 4) were few in number and relatively scattered in distribution. Of the remaining three pastoral types, types 5 and 6 were distinguished by the retention of oxen as their principal work animal. They were closely associated with areas of heavy soil and abundant pasturage, notably central and south-eastern Norfolk and the Fens and Fen edge. Finally, types 6 and 7 were demesnes which for a variety of reasons stocked working animals only.

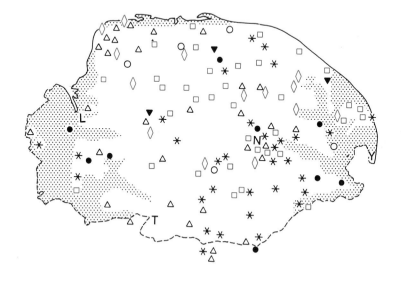

L=Lynn　　　　　N=Norwich　　　　　T=Thetford　　　　　Y=Yarmouth

CROP COMBINATIONS 1250-1349

PERCENTAGE OF TOTAL CROPPED ACREAGE

		WHEAT	RYE	BARLEY	OATS	MIXED GRAIN	LEGUMES
□	Cluster 1	15.74	2.10	51.48	8.11	0.28	22.33
◇	Cluster 2	19.07	7.32	44.36	13.42	1.25	14.62
△	Cluster 3	6.37	11.46	48.22	20.53	0.10	13.31
○	Cluster 4	6.01	21.45	55.46	9.10	0.02	7.98
✳	Cluster 5	20.57	13.01	26.05	16.36	12.35	11.69
▼	Cluster 6	30.76	4.63	21.80	26.11	1.10	15.63
●	Cluster 7	5.33	39.88	28.93	23.81	0.65	1.45
	NORFOLK	15.73	11.86	41.37	16.06	1.52	13.48

LIVESTOCK COMBINATIONS 1250-1349

PERCENTAGE OF TOTAL LIVESTOCK UNITS
(horses x 1.0)+(oxen x 1.2)+(adult cattle x 1.2)+
(young cattle x 0.8)+(sheep x 0.1)+(swine x 0.1)

		HORSES	OXEN	ADULT CATTLE	YOUNG CATTLE	SHEEP	SWINE
□	Cluster 1	17.21	9.59	50.76	16.70	3.65	2.09
◇	Cluster 2	20.45	5.62	31.57	16.62	13.79	11.95
△	Cluster 3	14.48	7.00	29.97	10.14	36.74	1.68
○	Cluster 4	26.43	3.39	0.39	0.34	63.85	5.59
✳	Cluster 5	19.44	23.55	25.88	19.44	9.49	2.21
▼	Cluster 6	87.36	12.64	0.00	0.00	0.00	0.00
●	Cluster 7	33.63	58.23	2.00	0.83	2.96	2.35
	NORFOLK	20.59	15.22	30.98	13.67	16.35	3.20

SOURCE: MANORIAL ACCOUNTS

The manorial system lay at the core of medieval agrarian life: it was fundamental to all aspects of land tenure, to law and local administration, and to the organisation and conduct of agriculture. Yet it was superimposed upon the country with anything but uniformity. Manors varied greatly in their size and composition and in their relationship to the village community, with the result that lordship did not weigh equally everywhere. Quite why this was so is intimately bound up with the history of English regional differences in ways which are as yet imperfectly understood.

East Anglia, for whatever reason, was an area of generally complex lordship and this was undoubtedly one source of the region's socio-economic distinctiveness and the dynamism of specific localities within it. A high proportion of tenants within the region were of free or semi-free status and there was little coincidence between manor and township. D. C. Douglas, commenting on the situation depicted by Domesday Book in 1086, observed that the rights involved in lordship were here more miscellaneous and loosely organised than in any other part of the country. During the next two centuries arrangements became more complex still, as free tenants proliferated in numbers, great lords made land grants to their followers, and individual manors were fragmented by inheritance. In Norfolk the dense and, in places, tangled web of manorial tenancies which had been brought into being by the beginning of the 14th century is captured in outline by the *Nomina Villarum* of 1316. This comprises a list of the townships in each hundred and the names of their lords. A carefully checked version of these lists was published by W. J. Blake in 1952. On its evidence only 163 of the 695 enumerated townships - 23 per cent - were held by a single head lord; the rest were divided among several lords. Moreover, significant geographical variations existed in the extent to which individual townships were divided between lords and the corresponding size and value of their lordships.

The first map endeavours to illustrate this variation by classifying each hundred according to the relative number, size, and taxable value (from the 1334 Lay Subsidy) of the lordships contained within it. As will be seen, an area of heavily divided lordship is clearly identifiable in the Hundreds of Wayland, Forehoe, Humbleyard, Blofield, Walsham, and Tunstead, in south-central and north-eastern Norfolk. This contrasts with the south-eastern Hundreds of Earsham and Clavering and the north-western Hundreds of Freebridge and Smithdon, where lordships were altogether more substantial and there was a greater measure of coincidence between manor and township.

The *Nomina Villarum* can also be used to illustrate another aspect of manorial structure, namely the relative importance of lay and ecclesiastical lordship, as in the second map. The distinction is an important one, for ecclesiastical lordships are disproportionately represented by surviving manorial records and the manors concerned were characterised by greater continuity of ownership and management and a tendency towards the exaction of higher levels of feudal rent. Ecclesiastical lordships accounted for approximately a sixth of all manors and were present in roughly a third of all townships. In distribution they were particularly well represented in the Fens and on the Fen edge and in central and north-eastern Norfolk. Nevertheless, for all that ecclesiastical manors were widespread, only one in twelve of all townships was under exclusive ecclesiastical control.

On the larger ecclesiastically owned manors substantial arable demesnes were maintained, usually worked in part by servile labour. The size of demesnes shown in the third map therefore provides a further guide to variations in manorial structure. This map is compiled from the recorded arable acreages in *Inquisitiones Post Mortem* and manorial accounts. The former may, or may not, include land lying fallow; the latter relate exclusively to land that was sown. Demesnes of less than 150 acres and even of less than 75 acres were to be found in all parts of the county, but it was in precisely those areas where lordships were smallest and most numerous that they formed the predominant type. Demesnes with a sown acreage in excess of 225 acres were a rarity in central and north-eastern Norfolk, and demesnes with a sown acreage of more than 300 acres were virtually unknown. All the largest demesnes were to be found in either the south or the north-west of the county.

Intriguing and suggestive as these distribution patterns are, none of them does justice to the full complexity of manorial arrangements within the county. This is exemplified by the diagram which reconstructs the manorial structure of the township of Hevingham in the Hundred of South Erpingham (a locality of generally complex lordship). The evidence for this reconstruction is a probable draft Hundred-Roll return of 1279. It demonstrates how manors were often inter-twined and merged in such a way as to blur any clear distinction as to the fiefs and baronies from which the lord of the manor actually held its various components. Here, as elsewhere, large holdings of complicated structure occurred among the free holdings of a manor, with a demesne and dependent holdings of their own, which fully merit the title of manor. Sometimes on such a sub-manor a further sub-manor appeared in its turn, and so on. A complex tier of tenures and obligations thus separated those who actually occupied the soil from those who ultimately owned it.

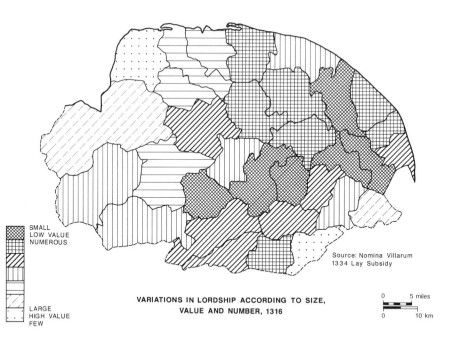

SMALL
LOW VALUE
NUMEROUS

LARGE
HIGH VALUE
FEW

VARIATIONS IN LORDSHIP ACCORDING TO SIZE, VALUE AND NUMBER, 1316

Source: Nomina Villarum
1334 Lay Subsidy

0   5 miles

0   10 km

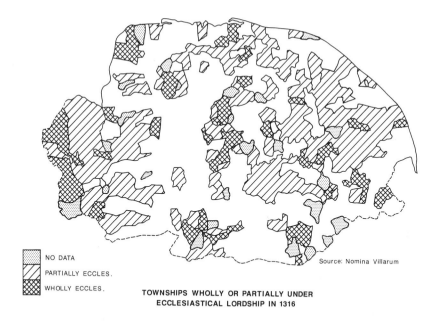

NO DATA

PARTIALLY ECCLES.

WHOLLY ECCLES.

Source: Nomina Villarum

TOWNSHIPS WHOLLY OR PARTIALLY UNDER ECCLESIASTICAL LORDSHIP IN 1316

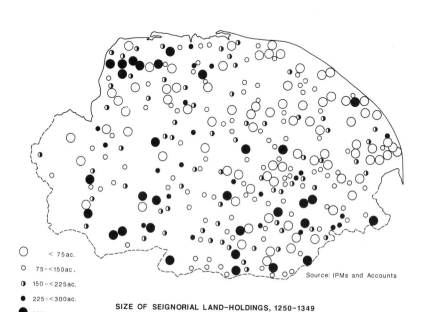

○ < 75 ac.

○ 75 - <150 ac.

◑ 150 - <225 ac.

● 225 - <300 ac.

● 300 ac.+

Source: IPMs and Accounts

**SIZE OF SEIGNORIAL LAND-HOLDINGS, 1250-1349
(ACRES OF ARABLE)**

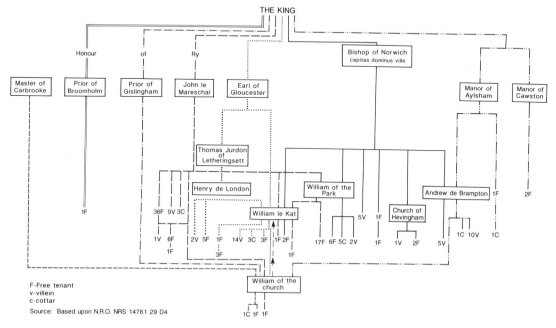

THE KING

Honour   of   Ry

Bishop of Norwich
capitas dominus ville

Master of
Carbrooke

Prior of
Broomholm

Prior of
Gislingham

John le
Mareschal

Earl of
Gloucester

Manor of
Aylsham

Manor of
Cawston

Thomas Jurdon
of
Letheringsett

Henry de London

William of the
Park

Andrew de Brampton

1F

2F

William le Kat

Church of
Hevingham

1F

36F 9V 3C

5V   1F

1V

2F

5V

1C 10V

1C

1V   6F
1F

2V 5F 1F   14V 3C 3F   1F 2F

17F 6F 5C 2V

1F

3F

1F

F-Free tenant
v-villein
c-cottar

Source: Based upon N.R.O. NRS 14761 29 D4

William of the
church

1C 1F 1F

HEVINGHAM, NORFOLK: SIMPLIFIED DIAGRAM OF MANORIAL STRUCTURE, c.1279

22. MEDIEVAL DEER-PARKS

David Yaxley

Although the red deer may have been present in medieval Norfolk, it seems likely that the fallow deer, introduced into England in early Norman times, was by far the more numerous. Venison was an important part of medieval upper class diet, and the pursuit of deer was an aristocratic and regal sport. There was no royal forest in medieval Norfolk, although there were at least five chases, open areas devoted to hunting deer and smaller animals; the most important was Rising Chase, which came into the hands of the Crown in the early 14th century. However, the easiest way to keep an accessible stock of deer was to create a deer-park by enclosing an area with an impenetrable boundary, usually a ditch with a bank outside it topped with a hedge or, more commonly, a fence of oak pales with sharpened tops. Most parks were roughly circular or polygonal: surviving or traceable ditch-and-bank park boundaries, e.g. at Wymondham, Thornage, Mileham, and Old Buckenham, run in a broad curve across the landscape. Elmham park was seven-sided and contained 300-348 acres in the late Middle Ages. The dimensions of many parks are not known, but they varied considerably. Medieval estimates of large areas are not altogether reliable, but for what they are worth some known figures are: 60 acres (Pulham 1277), 80 acres (Winfarthing 1389), 100 acres (Horsford 1310), 260 acres (Hempnall 1327), 310 acres (Shelfanger 1412), and 500 acres (Whinburgh 1253). Parks might expand or contract over the centuries. Of 19 parks whose rough circumference was given in 1581, seven, including Winfarthing, averaged 45 acres, nine, including Whinburgh, averaged between 100 and 200 acres, and the remaining three were larger: Kenninghall (about 280 acres, though stated to be 700 acres in 1610), Attleborough (about 410 acres), and Lopham (about 560 acres, though recorded as 423 acres in 1612).

Much of the deer-park was mature woodland, interspersed with rides and open grazing spaces, often called 'Le laund'; but as 'Laund' sometimes meant a meadow in a wood, or simply a grazing meadow, it has not been used as a sure indicator of a park unless corroborative evidence has been found. At Elmham 'Le Laund' had a ditch round it. The park might also have other divisions or enclosures in it for the management of the deer and woodland or the pasturing of cattle; 'herbage' or grazing for cattle could bring in a welcome income to the lord, and timber and underwood could also be sold. There were also smaller enclosures: the Norman deer-park at Denton had a rectangular ditched enclosure measuring 85 by 45 yards within it, and in 1708 the Elmham park included a 'deer penn'. Some parks may also have contained wild boar; in December 1593 a wild boar was sent to Sir Nathaniel Bacon from Thornage park, where a tributary of the Glaven provided good wallowing conditions.

Entry to the park was by tall wooden gates, the inner ditch being crossed by a 'grate' or cattle-grid. Some parks had deer-leaps, which allowed deer to enter the park but not to leave it. There was usually a lodge, attached to or within the park and used by the parker or warrener; it would serve as a temporary residence for the lord if the park were any distance from the manor house. A surviving example of a medieval warrener's lodge can be seen in Thetford Chase.

Although most parks must have been established with royal approval, few actual grants for emparking survive for Norfolk. Many must have been established before 1200, and most can only be dated by their earliest occurrence in such documents as inquisitions, records of complaints, or prosecutions for unlawfully entering the park and taking game there. Of the 92 sites on the map, 24 occur in documents before 1300 and another 19 before 1350, while 31 are included on documentary evidence from the 16th and 17th centuries, although some of these latter were undoubtedly established well back in the middle ages.

Most deer-parks occur on the boulder clays of south and central Norfolk, the sandy heathlands north of Norwich, and the loams of north Norfolk. Half a dozen are in the greensand belt of west Norfolk, but there are very few on the chalk downlands, the sandy breckland area, and the rich soils and sandy gravels of the extreme east of the county. However, this pattern is not necessarily dictated by geology alone; the possession of a deer-park was a mark of social status in all periods, and the power and will to enclose a park must always have been of at least equal importance as any question of terrain. By the 16th century, although the economic value of the deer-park had declined, it was just as much a status symbol as in the middle ages; but it was more desirable to have it adjacent to the owner's house, and this, together with the natural changes in ownership, led to the decay of detached parks. The 17th century was a transitional period when a medieval-type deer-park might be created around a large house, but by the middle of the 18th century the landscape park, which seldom provided for the keeping of deer, had taken over. Fewer than a score of deer-parks were incorporated into landscape parks.

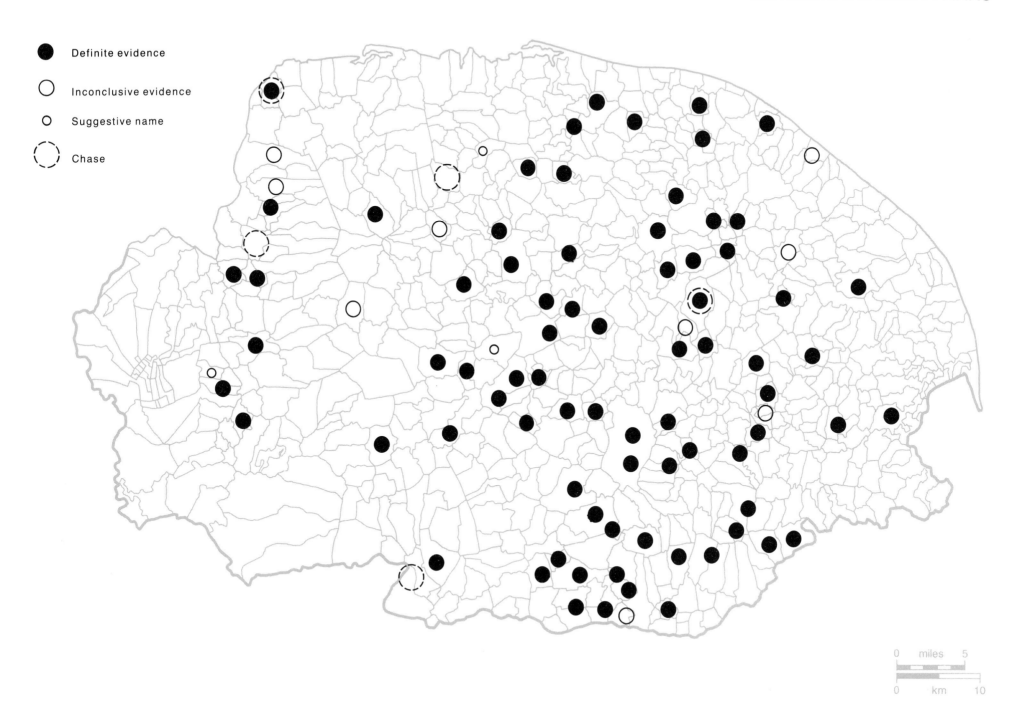

Definite evidence

Inconclusive evidence

Suggestive name

Chase

0 miles 5

0 km 10

23. ROUND-TOWERED CHURCHES

Stephen Heywood

The circular western tower is a characteristic of East Anglian medieval ecclesiastical architecture. The largest numbers are in Norfolk. The statistics are as follows:

	Standing	Ruinous	Disappeared
Norfolk	123 (after 1974)	11	10
Suffolk	38 (after 1974)	3	2
Essex	6	-	2
Cambridgeshire	2	-	-
Sussex	3	-	-
Berkshire	2	-	-
Kent	-	-	1
Surrey	-	-	1
Egilsay (Orkney)	-	1	-

It is clear that the greatest concentration of round-towered churches is in south-east Norfolk and the majority of the Suffolk round towers are in the north-east quarter of that county. This convergence towards the valleys of the rivers Yare and Waveney simply reflects a greater population of the area during the early Middle Ages (Map 16).

The number of round-towered churches in Norfolk built during the Romanesque period of the 11th and 12th centuries far outnumbers the parish churches with conventional square western towers or axial towers (i.e. tower with or without transepts, standing between the nave and the chancel). There are 15 with axial towers and only six with square western towers. This shows that the round tower was not only a characteristic of Norfolk parish churches, but was almost obligatory during the Romanesque period.

In function the round tower is no different from other western towers. This is, principally, to house bells. There are several architectural features, however, which are particular to round-towered churches. The quadrant pilaster, a fillet of masonry in the acute re-entrant angle

between the round tower and the west wall of the nave, appears to be unique to East Anglia and occurs on about 30 round-towered churches. It is purely decorative and has no function apart from being a convenient way of filling the awkward acute angle between the tower and the nave. The best example is at Haddiscoe Thorpe.

Another decorative device which deserves mention is shallow undressed recessed blind arcading on three towers at Haddiscoe Thorpe, Tasburgh and Thorington (Suffolk). The stumps of masonry at ground level at Kirby Cane may represent the remains of arcading of a similar type.

Round towers are often described as 'Saxon' towers and local antiquarians have claimed great antiquity for a number of them. The reasons for these claims are probably due to the lack of parallels in Norman or French architecture together with the high incidence of techniques of construction considered to be of Anglo-Saxon date, namely: rubble dressings, double-splayed windows, triangular-headed openings, stripwork (thin strips of masonry surrounding openings as decoration) and tall, narrow openings. Whilst some of these techniques are undoubtedly indicative of Anglo-Saxon workmanship they cannot be used as evidence for pre-Conquest origin because they commonly occur in buildings of post-Conquest date. For example, the west range of the cloister at Norwich Cathedral (begun in 1096 or possibly 1094) was lit by a row of round double-splayed windows. The bell openings at Haddiscoe are triangular headed and surrounded with stripwork yet they have scalloped capitals and the strips are decorated with Norman billett moulding. The doorways at Haddiscoe show that the building could not have been built before c.1130. Thus, Bessingham has a round-towered church with similar bell openings to Haddiscoe but without Norman decoration and without capitals or bases to the mid-wall shafts. Nothing in the tower is specifically Norman in character, yet it is impossible to substantiate a date more precise than the second half of the

11th century because these techniques survive up to eighty years after the Conquest.

It remains to attempt an explanation for the high concentration of round towers in Norfolk. The almost universally accepted view is the functionalist explanation that towers were built round because of the lack of a local source of freestone to form quoins. This does not stand up to the mildest scrutiny, if only in the light of the square towers built virtually without freestone such as Heigham (Norwich), Weybourne and Hethel. Similarly there are many round structures built of materials more suited to right angled buildings. For example the round tower at West Dereham is faced with large blocks of ironbound conglomerate, the round radiating chapels at Norwich Cathedral are faced entirely with cut limestone and countless other circular structures are faced with ashlar. It is inescapable that in all these examples the circular form is chosen for cultural not functional reasons. The effort required to lay out, construct shuttering and build a round tower and to incorporate it with a straight nave gable wall far outweighs the difficulty of constructing a square western tower whatever material is used.

There is only one other region in Europe where single round western towers are used. This is in north Germany in Schleswig-Holstein and the area around Bremen and the Lüneburg Heath with a few examples in southern Sweden. Round towers as stair turrets *cum* bell towers on major buildings were current practice in the Empire since the Carolingian period (9th century). The use of single round western towers on minor churches is probably due to imitation within the economic constraints of a small community. The round-towered churches in Norfolk must be seen in this context and they are a reflection of the strong cultural links which existed during the early Middle Ages with countries bordering the Baltic and North Seas.

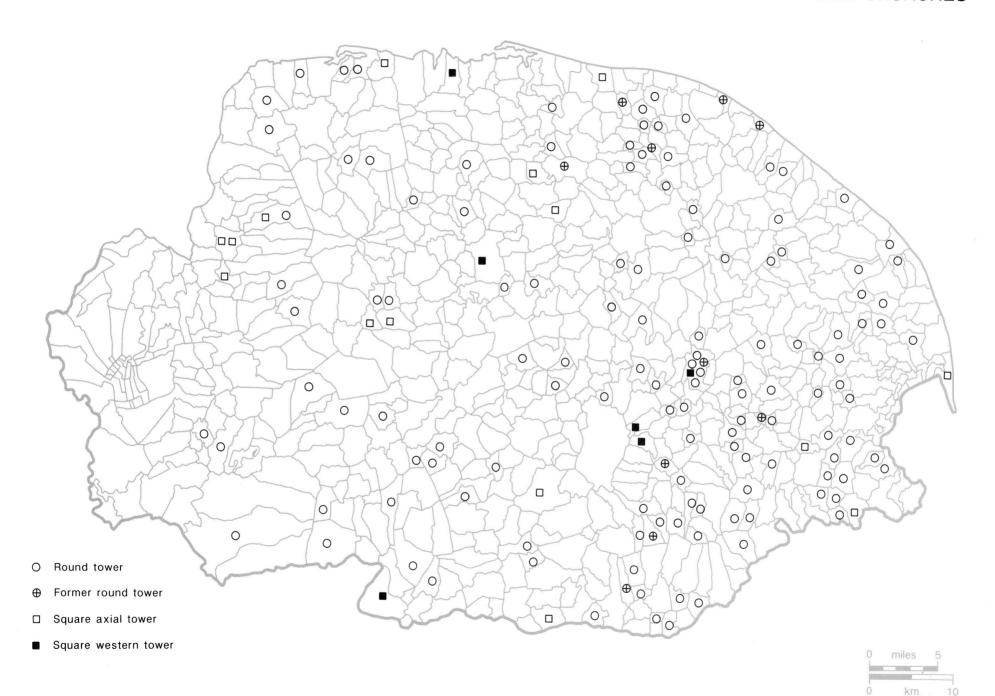

Round tower

Former round tower

Square axial tower

Square western tower

0 miles 5

0 km 10

For the great majority of medieval masons, whose names have not come down to us, the only evidence for their careers as designers is to be found in the buildings they constructed. One possible way of identifying masons is to study masons' marks which can be found in a number of related churches in western and central Norfolk. English masons' marks were probably mainly used as a method for the master mason to assess the quantity and quality of output of his workmen. Because of this it would perhaps be dangerous to think that the presence of similar marks in related buildings meant any more than that a master mason had employed some of the same men at different building operations.

Research in Norfolk has suggested that, for the parish churches of the later Middle Ages, the most convincing way of identifying many of the designing masons is likely to be through careful analysis and comparison of the details of the buildings. The ten masons whose work is plotted on the attached map are among those who seem to be identifiable in this way, although it is possible that more buildings would be found to be by the same masons if further research could be carried out and, of course, many more masons still wait to be discovered.

The principle on which these masons have been identified is that personal design preferences will be most clearly seen in the details in which no-one other than the mason was likely to have an interest. Taking these as a starting point, a fuller picture can be built up by considering the way in which they are related to the building as a whole, bearing in mind, though, that contracts show us that patrons might expect to have their say in the design of some of the more prominent features.

On this basis, it can be assumed that the mind of a mason is best seen in minutiae such as the decorative mouldings which were cut into the stonework of piers, arches, doorways and windows. Although the successful design of these mouldings required great technical expertise and judgement, contracts suggest it was their overall impression - and cost of production - rather than their detailed design which interested the patron. As a result it seems that, in the later Middle Ages at least, masons relied on mouldings they had already tried and found successful. Sometimes very complex moulding formations could be repeated on several occasions in a way which shows that the same template must have been re-used, as in the work of the master mason of Wiveton. In other cases, although new templates must have been cut for each job, the repeated combinations of details reliably reveals the mind of the designer, as in the work of the mason of Martham.

Nevertheless, the information provided by mouldings must be supported by other evidence to be acceptable. Otherwise we could not be sure that the stone was not being supplied with the mouldings ready-cut from the quarry, or that templates for them were not being shared between masons - we certainly know that templates could be bequeathed by one mason to another. After mouldings, the detail which can often be most useful as a pointer to personality is the tracery of the windows. Even when patrons gave orders about the size of a window and insisted on the examples which were to be taken as models, the design of a window involves so many technical decisions that there is still scope for the mason's personal preferences to show through. This is seen most strikingly in the angular forms of the King's Lynn St. Nicholas mason. Beyond this, in building up a picture of a mason's personal style we must also take into account factors such as the way the windows and doorways relate to the wall, the design of the buttresses and wall heads, and the general approach to the grouping and proportion of all the parts.

But in all efforts to identify masons from their own work it is particularly important to look for evidence of dating, such as building counts, or heraldry and inscriptions on the fabric. In addition to these, the most invaluable source of dating information is now Paul Cattermole and Simon Cotton's list of references to Norfolk churches in wills. There must be, of course, as much care in the use of documentary as of architectural evidence, since building operations might be unduly extended or might be interrupted, and a false impression of dating could be given by references surviving to only one part of the operation. With this word of caution, however, it may be said that late medieval Norfolk offers many cases in which a combination of architectural and documentary evidence convincingly points to the presence of the same designing mason in parts of two or more buildings.

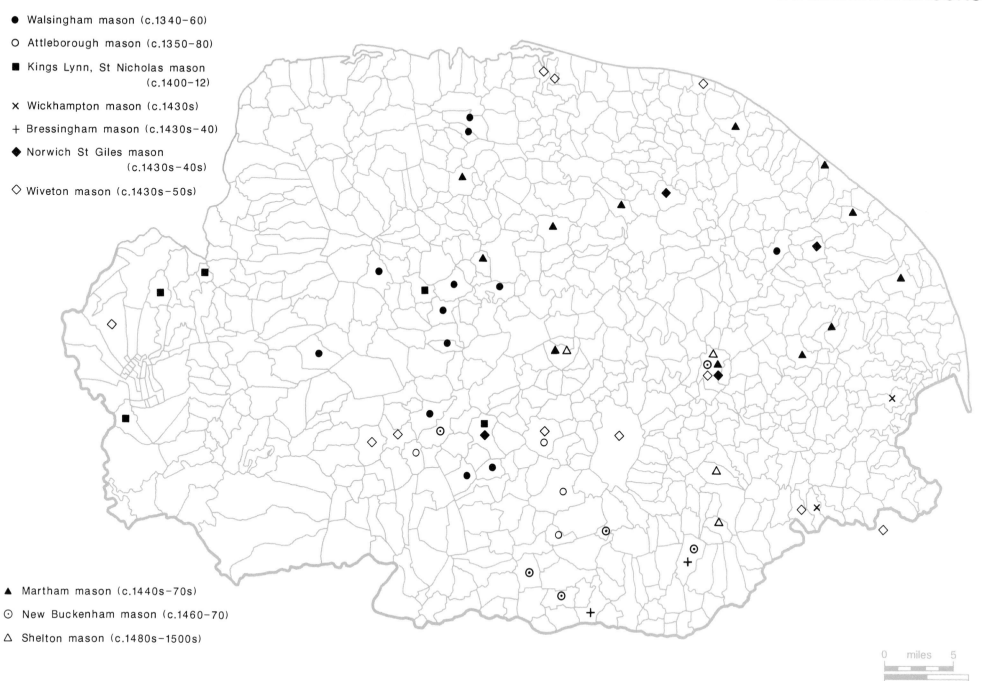

24. MEDIEVAL MASONS

- ● Walsingham mason (c.1340-60)
- ○ Attleborough mason (c.1350-80)
- ■ Kings Lynn, St Nicholas mason (c.1400-12)
- × Wickhampton mason (c.1430s)
- + Bressingham mason (c.1430s-40)
- ◆ Norwich St Giles mason (c.1430s-40s)
- ◇ Wiveton mason (c.1430s-50s)

- ▲ Martham mason (c.1440s-70s)
- ☉ New Buckenham mason (c.1460-70)
- △ Shelton mason (c.1480s-1500s)

0 miles 5

0 km 10

25. MEDIEVAL CHURCHES IN USE OR IN RUINS

Neil Batcock

Norfolk possesses an astonishing number of medieval parish churches. At least 921 were built between the 11th and 16th centuries (excluding Lothingland), and some 610 are still used today. These figures exceed, by quite a large margin, those of any other county: the nearest to approach Norfolk are the neighbouring counties of Lincolnshire and Suffolk, the former with around 600 medieval churches built and 445 still in use, the latter with about 580 churches built and 460 still in use.

Many of the Norfolk churches, probably the vast majority, were already in existence by the time of the Domesday Survey. Some 330 churches were recorded in 1086 (including a small number of churches mentioned in the contemporary *Liber Eliensis*), but this is clearly an incomplete list. For example, in the south Norfolk hundred of Clavering, 13 out of 17 medieval churches were recorded in 1086, while in neighbouring Earsham only three out of 14 merited attention. The towns of Thetford and Norwich comprised a multiplicity of parishes, with ten and 62 churches respectively. Likewise, some 26 rural parishes contained more than one church at Domesday. Excavations of churches at Norwich, Thetford and Barton Bendish suggest that during the late 10th and 11th centuries there was a remarkable expansion of new parishes being founded, with their churches built on a virgin site. Few new parishes were created after 1086, save in areas of population expansion such as the Marshlands.

The 'Norwich Valuation' of 1254 gives a more complete picture. A total of 818 parish churches are recorded for the county, which must come close to the correct total for this period. There are some notable omissions, including Great Yarmouth (although this is picked up in the 'Pope Nicholas' Taxation of 1291), Attlebridge, Emneth, Needham, Plumstead and Worthing. But relatively few escaped the efficient eyes of those who prepared the 1254 Valuation, as the map demonstrates. Most of the churches mentioned in 1086 were also recorded in 1254, but some had probably already ceased to function, such as

Thurketeliart and the second churches at Carleton Rode and Stoke Holy Cross; although it needs to be noted that of the many parishes with two churches, only one is usually mentioned in the 1254 Valuation, suggesting that the two churches were valued together.

By the end of the 13th century, the number of parish churches had remained fairly constant for some 200 years. Thereafter, the numbers declined, although by no means at a steady rate. The 14th century saw 30 churches abandoned, although the 15th witnessed a reduction of only 19 churches. Neither compared with the 16th century, which saw the closure of a massive total of 98 churches throughout the county. From the 17th to the end of the 19th century the pace of abandonment slowed down considerably, averaging about ten churches per century. This century has seen a return to a rate of abandonment comparable with the 16th century, with a total (thus far) of 71 churches falling into disuse.

The causes of the abandonment of churches are varied. Depopulation of the village in which the church stands is one reason. Many of the abandoned churches, around 100, stand (or stood) within the site of a deserted (or greatly shrunken) village. Four of the villages were deserted as recently as 1942, when they were cleared to make way for the Stanford Training Area. The causes of village desertion are too complex to go into here (Map 37): suffice it to say that hardly any were wiped out by the Black Death. Some churches stood within villages that flourish to this day, but were abandoned because of ecclesiastical reorganization or rationalization: in villages with more than one church, the smaller or less valuable church was usually closed down, especially in the 16th century. Some 76 rural churches met their fate in this way. A similar process occurred in the towns, with a further 70 churches being abandoned after the unification of small parishes, a large number of these closures taking place over the last 30 years. Other churches were lost for a variety of reasons, including being washed away to sea, catching fire or being bombed; one

was even destroyed by a riotous mob in the 13th century! In the 19th century there developed the strange fashion of 'church moving': if the centre of population of the village was some distance from the church, the church was dismantled and re-erected some distance nearer the centre, thus transporting the church to the people, rather than the people to the church.

It is possible to become gloomy when considering the numbers of medieval churches which have been destroyed or lost to use for whatever reason. However, it is much more cheering to reflect on the enormous number of medieval churches still in use in the county (some 610) and to marvel at the care and dedication which has resulted in the survival of so many. The breakdown of figures for the county (excluding Lothingland) is as follows: 610 still in regular use; 59 redundant and fully standing, but no longer used; 100 in ruins; and 152 with no above-ground remains. Although Norfolk remains unique in the number of churches it has lost, it is also unique in the number of medieval churches it has kept in use for regular worship.

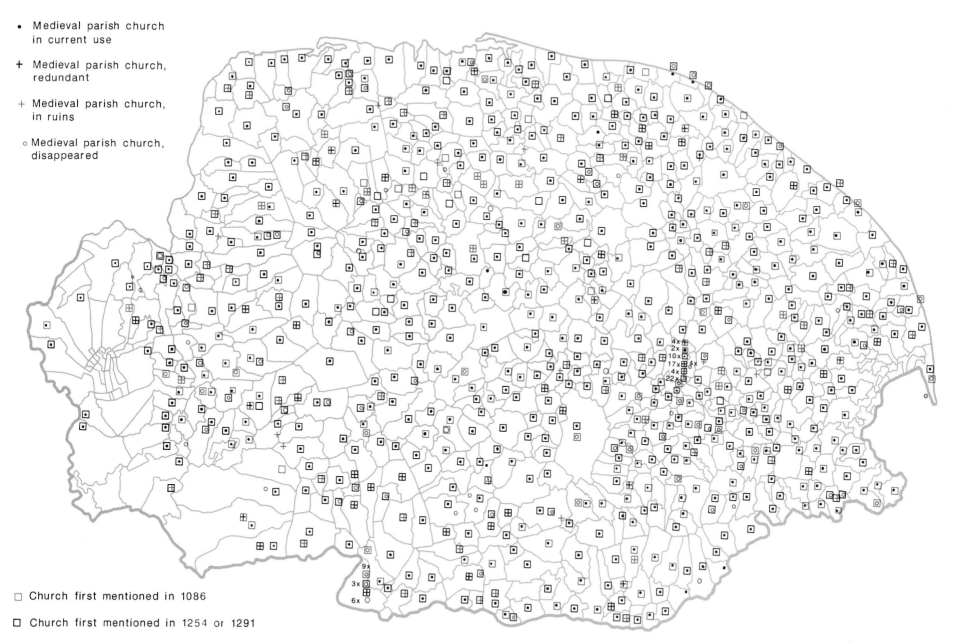

• Medieval parish church
in current use

+ Medieval parish church,
redundant

+ Medieval parish church,
in ruins

○ Medieval parish church,
disappeared

□ Church first mentioned in 1086

▢ Church first mentioned in 1254 or 1291

9x
3x
6x

4x
2x
10x
17x 4x
4x
22x

0 miles 5
0 km 10

Parishes vary greatly in shape and size, and their origins are shrouded in some mystery. We do however have relatively unexploited information about the medieval livings (benefices) which in each parish went to the support of a resident priest. Incumbents were usually provided with a house (parsonage), land (glebe), offerings and tithes, but the total value of individual livings varied markedly - even in the same deanery. Furthermore, monastic and other religious institutions, mostly founded from the 12th century onwards and often short of money, were allowed to take endowments formerly intended for the parochial clergy. Large numbers of pensions and 'portions' were paid, but parishes lost most by the seemingly piratical practice known as 'appropriation' or 'impropriation'.

When a living was appropriated, the religious house legally became 'rector'. Commonly it took over most of the parochial endowments and left what remained (often no more than a third or a quarter) to support a resident priest known as 'vicar' (Latin *vicarius* meaning 'a substitute'). This involved an elaborate division of responsibilities and assets. Thus in 1202 the bishop of Norwich approved the appropriation of Gayton by St. Stephen's Abbey at Caen: the vicar was to receive a suitable house, offerings and the lesser tithes of the parish; the abbey retained the valuable 'great tithes' and still expected a pension of two marks a year from the vicar. When in 1349 the Benedictine nuns of Bungay appropriated Redenhall, a wall had to be built across the double-moated parsonage to divide the vicar's part from the rector's (i.e. the nunnery's).

Not all such take-overs resulted in the establishment of formal vicarages. In many cases the appropriating institution chose to pay a stipendiary priest or to send one of its own members to serve 'the cure of souls'. This gave rise to large numbers of 'perpetual curacies' which were relatively poorly paid, while the religious house gratefully swallowed all the endowments of the parish or farmed them out for a rent.

The map opposite plots those parishes known to have been appropriated in the Middle Ages. The main sources were the *Ecclesiastical Taxation* of 1291 and the *Valor Ecclesiasticus* of 1535. Total accuracy cannot be claimed because the sources contain omissions, some early appropriations were short-lived, and some vicarages were purely personal and temporary arrangements. However, the map shows that about 37% of Norfolk's parishes, in all parts of the county, were taken over. Some 33 of the appropriating institutions were in Norfolk itself, but as many as 20 others were elsewhere in England or abroad.

Many religious houses acquired, or were given, livings in their own vicinities which were therefore quite easy to control. For example, the block of appropriated parishes south-east of King's Lynn marks 'Norfolk's Holy Land' with its string of religious houses in and around the Nar Valley; a similar concentration can be seen in Broadland. However, much more distant parishes could be appropriated. For example, Norfolk livings were acquired by monastic houses at Battle in Sussex, Lilleshall in Shropshire and Longueville in Normandy. The livings of towns also tended to be appropriated; Norfolk has examples varying in size from Yarmouth and King's Lynn to New Buckenham and Watton. Five parishes in Thetford were taken over and 23 in Norwich. It needs stressing that some parishes were coveted by outside institutions because they were valuable. In 1291 valuations were given for 34 Norfolk vicarages: before being carved up the average *total* value of these benefices had been £26, whereas the average values of all livings in the county was under £13. After appropriation the vicars of those 34 parishes were left with an average income of only £7.

After the Reformation, appropriated livings and vicarages survived as private property, frequently known as 'lay rectories'. Thus in 1835 a Parliamentary report shows that Norfolk still had 175 vicarages, 84 perpetual curacies, 13 mere curacies and five donatives (livings under the total control of their patrons). However, these numbers fluctuated over time because some livings recovered their lost endowments and were once again regarded as full rectories, and during the 19th century many perpetual curacies were upgraded to vicarages. Of particular interest in Norfolk is the influence of Sir Henry Spelman (1564?-1641) who himself restored the living at Middleton, persuaded his uncle to give up the appropriate rectory of Congham and put pressure on other neighbouring gentry to do likewise. He argued that to retain lay rectories not only 'tended to the defrauding of the Church' but also invited personal 'misfortunes and grievous accidents'.

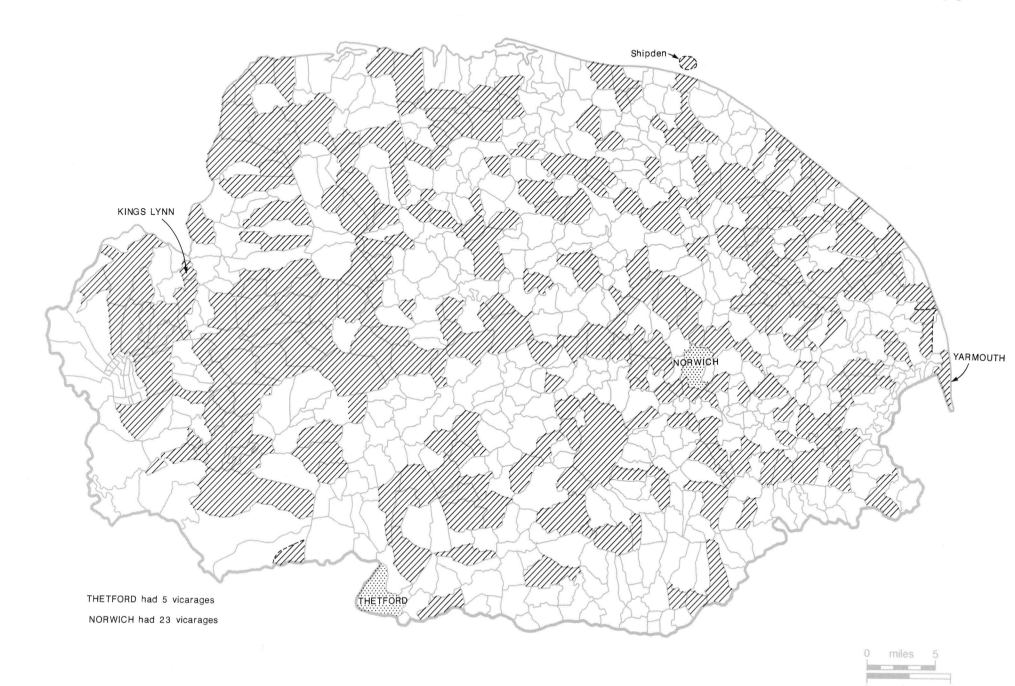

Shipden

KINGS LYNN

NORWICH

YARMOUTH

THETFORD had 5 vicarages

NORWICH had 23 vicarages

THETFORD

0   miles   5

0   km   10

27. MONASTIC HOUSES

Robert Rickett and Edwin Rose

Monastic communities were founded to enable groups of monks or nuns to live in isolation from the outside world, in the worship of God. The earliest sites were therefore in remote places, such as Fursa's monastery at *Cnobheresburg*. This was either the old Roman fort at Burgh Castle, or possibly Caister-on-Sea. Sigheburt, King of the East Angles, gave the land to the Irish saint about 630, and King Anna and his nobles endowed it with 'still finer buildings and gifts'.

The Late Saxon period witnessed a decline in the monastic ideal, and the Viking raids disrupted many communities. However, in the late 10th century, a revitalisation of monasticism occurred, and new reformed orders originated on the continent. These eventually came to this country, the earliest being the early 11th century foundation of St Benet at Hulme, following the Rule of St Benedict.

The new Norman order fostered the growth of monasticism, and several lords founded religious houses, such as Earl Warenne's Cluniac Priory at Castle Acre. Religious life blossomed, and along with it many crafts such as metalworking, carving and sculpting, and schools of illumination.

These religious houses were built to a fairly standard plan, differing only to suit the local site conditions. In the centre was the cloister walk around a garden; on the north side the church; on the west side the cellarer's or stores range, with guest accommodation and lodgings for the head of the community; on the south side the refectory and kitchens; and on the east side the chapter house, dormitories and living room. Detached buildings included the rere-dorters or toilets, small hospitals, bakeries, breweries and barns. There was often a farm in the precinct, which also enclosed gardens, vineyards, cemeteries and fish ponds. The gatehouse frequently survives today when other buildings have gone. Well preserved monasteries can be seen at Castle Acre, Binham, Thetford and North Creake.

Extensive remains of the cathedral monastery in Norwich survive, although many of the claustral buildings are inaccessible due to modern use. The later communities of Friars were founded in towns, and although the provision was similar to earlier religious houses, lack of space resulted in constricted accommodation and upper storeys projecting over the cloister walks. Good examples of Friaries can be found at Little Walsingham, and the Blackfriars in Norwich.

All the major religious orders had foundations in the county; in the 11th and 12th centuries there were many Benedictine foundations, such as Norwich, Binham and Blackborough Nunnery. Many were also parish churches and thus partly survived the dissolution.

During the 11th and 12th centuries the Cluniac order founded several houses, some of which were dependencies of mother houses abroad. This gave rise to problems during the French wars, until they were naturalised. This order was very aristocratic, feudal, and hierarchical and in returning to the Rule of St Benedict, placed high emphasis on the liturgy. With many endowments, it became very wealthy and lost its popularity. The best examples are Thetford, Castle Acre and Bromholm.

In the 12th and 13th centuries there occurred many foundations by the Augustinian order. This included the Canons Regular in the monasteries, and the Canons Secular who were priests in the local churches outside their community. There was no rigorous monastic discipline, and the order was very popular. The best examples are at North Creake, The Canons of the Holy Sepulchre in Thetford, and Little Walsingham, which contained the Shrine of the Virgin Mary. This was the biggest centre of pilgrimage in Norfolk, where the pilgrim routes converged, labelled on old maps as 'Palmer's Way', 'Walsingham Way' and 'Pilgrim's Way'. In 1511 Erasmus described the shrine as 'the seat of the Gods, so bright and shining it is all over with jewels, gold and silver'.

The reforming order of Premonstratensian Canons, strict vegetarians, heavily involved in parochial and missionary work, established three foundations, all in rural locations. An extensive plan of West Dereham Abbey has been compiled from aerial photographs showing reasonably clear cropmarks.

The Trinitarian Canons, a semi-military order concerned with the fate of captives, had one house in the county at Ingham.The Cistercian order established houses in remote places, leading a life of hardship, with strict ideals, contemptuous of declining standards in the other orders. They established two houses at Marham Nunnery and Field Dalling.

The purely English order of Gilbertines had one house at Shouldham. The two military orders, the Knights Templar, who enlisted people for pilgrimages, and the Knights Hospitaller established houses at Haddiscoe, Horsham St Faith and Great Carbrooke.

In this country, in the early 13th century, as a reaction to the wealth of the religious houses, the Friars were formed, renouncing property ownership and living off charity. They were active, and preached in towns and anywhere else that provided a suitable congregation, such as in the pilgrimage town of Little Walsingham. All the four main orders, the Dominicans (Black Friars), Franciscans (Grey Friars), Carmelites (White Friars), and the Augustinians (Austin Friars) established houses in the towns. Remains of these houses can be found in Norwich, Great Yarmouth, King's Lynn, Thetford and Blakeney. At Little Walsingham the Grey Friars, established in 1347, is one of the best preserved Friaries in the country.

After the Dissolution of the religious houses by Henry VIII in the 1530s, many buildings were sold and disappeared without trace. Fortunately some still survive to testify to the architectural wealth and splendour of the medieval period.

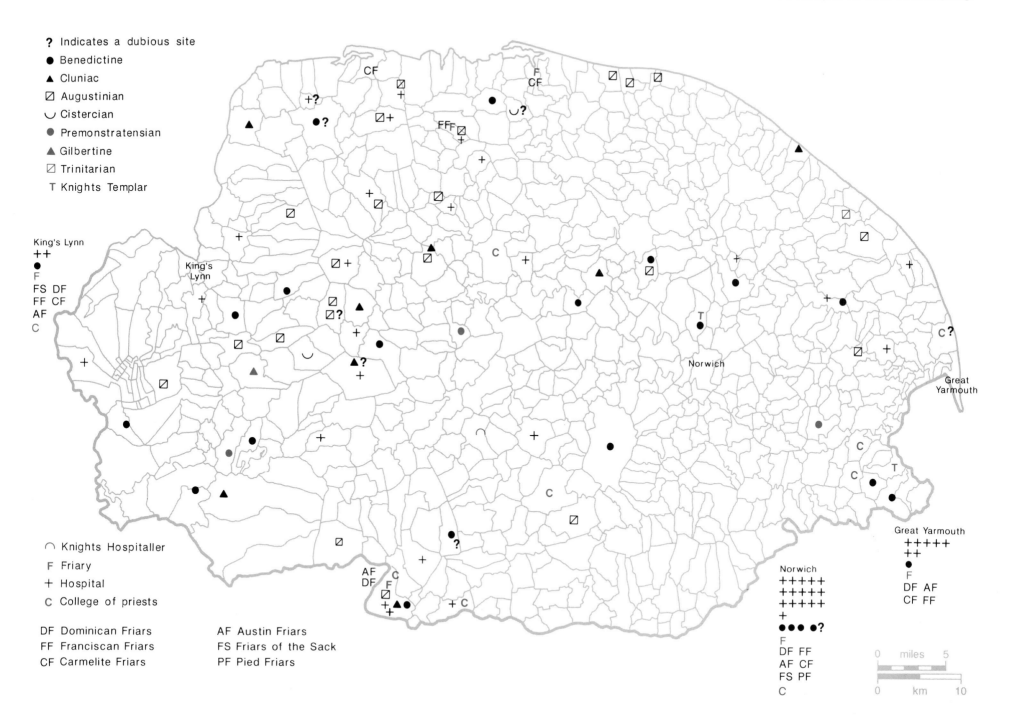

? Indicates a dubious site
● Benedictine
▲ Cluniac
◨ Augustinian
∪ Cistercian
● Premonstratensian
▲ Gilbertine
◫ Trinitarian
T Knights Templar

∩ Knights Hospitaller
F Friary
+ Hospital
C College of priests

DF Dominican Friars
FF Franciscan Friars
CF Carmelite Friars

AF Austin Friars
FS Friars of the Sack
PF Pied Friars

King's Lynn
++
●
F
FS DF
FF CF
AF
C

Great Yarmouth
+++++
++ ++
●
F
DF AF
CF FF

Norwich
+++++
+++++
+++++
+
●●● ●?
F
DF FF
AF CF
FS PF
C

0   miles   5

0   km   10

28. MOATED SITES
Andrew Rogerson

Over 400 medieval moated sites exist or are known to have existed in Norfolk. They were constructed between the mid-12th and 16th centuries, with the majority dating to the 13th and earlier 14th centuries.

Approximately 70% of moats lie in the Boulder Clay region, where the retention of water was not normally a problem. In areas of freely draining subsoil almost all moated sites are situated in valley bottoms. On the Boulder Clay, moats are found in a variety of topographical locations, on plateaux, on valley bottoms and/or edges. A few sites may be considered to be moated although their ditches no longer contain water. Some may always have been dry, such as the remarkable round moat at Horningtoft. Where the water-table is low and the subsoil pervious, considerable trouble was expended in the collection and retention of water, with the diversion of streams, the cutting of feeder ditches, the construction of leats, and the lining of moats with clay. The present appearance of an earthwork may give few clues as to the ingenuity of the hydro-engineering that once kept its ditches full of water.

The locations of moats in relation to contemporary settlements are variable. They can lie in the centre of nucleated villages often but not always adjacent to parish churches, on common edges, isolated close to parish boundaries, in or adjacent to woodland, and within deer parks. Their present condition can range from those that are ploughed over and only visible as soilmarks or cropmarks, such as one at Grimston, to those under woodland, such as in Moat Plantation, Honing, through finely preserved earthworks under grass as at Hall Carr, Besthorpe, to moats enclosing houses both humble and grand. The latter, which merge in the categories of late medieval castles and 'maisons fortes', include such impressive houses as Middleton Towers and Mannington Hall, while the former include many fine early post-medieval houses on the south Norfolk clays.

The majority of moats surrounded manor houses, and only in the southern part of the clay region, where the subsoil is heavier, are some moats associated with non-manorial free tenements. Even there many examples of non-moated manor houses occur. Some parishes are particularly well endowed with moated sites; Bradenham for example has ten, not all of which were manorial. In some parishes an excess of moats over manors may be the result of the migration of manors. Documentary evidence sometimes shows that a manor was enclosed not by moats but walls of cob or clay which have since vanished.

Moats normally surrounded a dwelling house, but other buildings, barns, granaries, dovecots etc. could also be enclosed. Other ancillary buildings, with yards, orchards and gardens were often situated within outer ditched or walled enclosures. Most such enclosures have been swept away by later changes, particularly arable farming. The moated island that survives today is the least easily destroyable element in a complex that contained manor house, demesne farm and their attributes. Fish ponds of varying sizes and forms are frequently associated; that at Park Farm, Shipdham is an impressive example.

Moated islands are usually rectangular and sometimes approximately square. Double rectangles occasionally occur, as do irregular and incomplete rectilinear forms. The latter, often moated on three sides only, may be the result of infilling. Sometimes only one arm is now visible, as at the site of Gelham Hall, Dersingham. Circular moats, often assumed to be early, i.e. 12th century, are rare, with only eight examples known. That at Shotesham is a fine example.

Although moat construction began at a time of great insecurity, it is unlikely that defence was a major consideration. It is generally agreed that fashion, influenced by the defensive moats that surrounded the castles of the seignurial class, was the main stimulus behind moat digging carried out first by the manorial classes and later by the yeomanry; in other words even in the medieval period the English were preoccupied with emulating their social betters, a case of keeping up with the Warennes! Clay extraction for building is unlikely to have been an important aim of moat digging. A water supply for fire-fighting and the provision of fish are feasible additional aims. The width of the water-filled moat would certainly have afforded some security against wild animals, although not against determinedly hostile humans.

Most Norfolk moats surround an island of between 0.5 and 1 acre. There are a few exceptionally large moated complexes, for example the double moat at the Candle Yards, Kenninghall, which enclosed the seat of the Howards until the early 16th century, surrounding an area of over 7.5 acres.

Excavation in Norfolk has added few details on the physical lay-out of moated sites. Fieldwork has been restricted almost entirely to the recording of earthworks, with a few small-scale excavations. At Hempstead a 14th-century manor house had rubble walls and a floor of relief-decorated tiles, but the rest of the island was not examined. At Kelling a complicated sequence of masonry buildings stretched from the 13th to the 18th century covering most of the island, on a site occupied since the Middle Saxon period. The period of occupation on ploughed sites can be gauged from surface pottery. Few moats seem to have been dug around pre-Conquest sites. However, most ploughed examples are isolated and those with early origins may lie inaccessible in village centres.

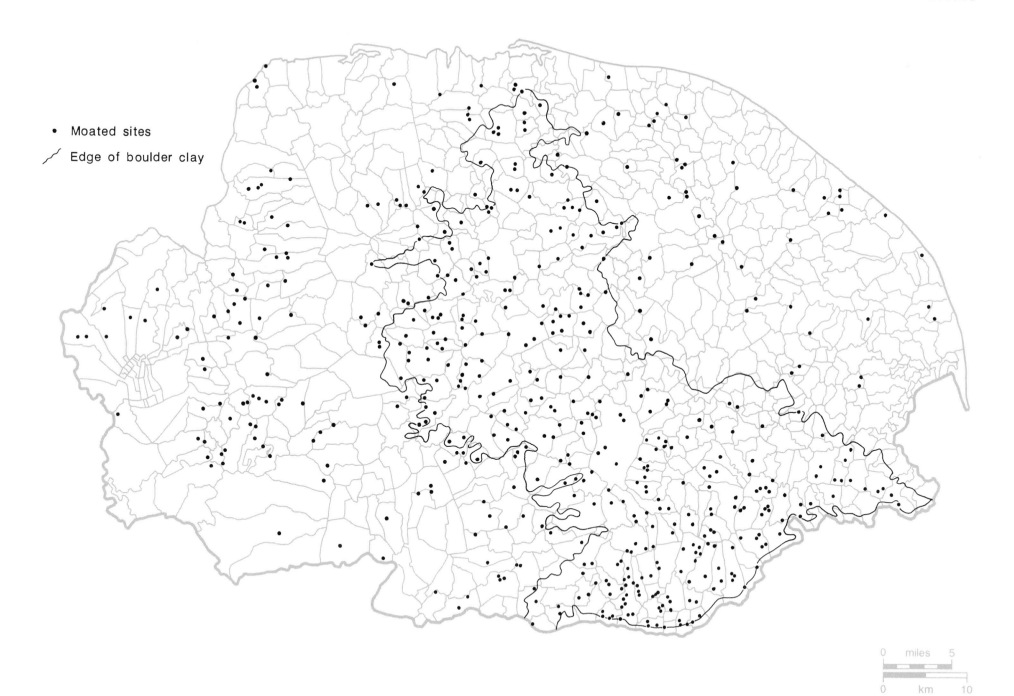

- • Moated sites
- ⌇ Edge of boulder clay

0   miles   5

0   km   10

Norfolk '...was never part of a credible invasion shore. Moreover, it formed a strategic blind alley, lying off any route from one part of the country to another...no-one would ever fight in Norfolk unless he had gone there to fight, or to be ready to fight others there. This is not a situation conducive to the building of castles' (King 1983, 305). Relatively few castles were constructed in Norfolk; only one per 231 sq.km. are known to have existed.

There were no castles in Norfolk before 1066, and few elsewhere in England. The castle was an alien form of military architecture introduced with the Norman Conquest. Between the aftermath of Hastings and the end of the Anarchy (1136-54) castles were built across the country, guarding the borders of Norman rule, reflecting centres of seignurial power and controlling communication lines.

William I's only East Anglian castle was in Norwich. It was constructed in the years immediately following the Conquest, so quickly that by 1075 it was in a position to withstand a siege during the rebellion of Earl Ralph Gauder. The motte must first have carried timber structures, but by the second quarter of the 12th century was crowned by a magnificent square keep. The keep's construction may well have necessitated a considerable increase in the size of the motte, and it was probably at this period that the complex of massively defended outer baileys, recently excavated, was laid out. Despite being refaced in the 1830's, the keep, with its fine external ornament of string-courses, blind arcading and pilasters, remains a potent symbol of Norman royal power.

The superbly conical motte at Thetford set within the refurbished defences of an Iron Age fort and placed so as to guard the crossing of the Icknield Way over the Rivers Thet and Little Ouse, may have been thrown up by the Earl of East Anglia soon after 1066. This castle went out of use before the widespread use of masonry, perhaps after the rebellion of Earl Ralph in 1075. In any event it was destroyed in 1172/3.

Both Great Yarmouth and Lynn, towns and ports which grew up after 1066, had castles. At Yarmouth a stone keep-like tower has vanished, while a probable motte and bailey at Lynn survives incorporated within later town defences and surmounted by the Red Mount Chapel built in the late 15th century.

Small motte and bailey castles, such as those at Wormegay, Denton and Horsford, may have been constructed in the later 11th century, but are more likely to have sprung up in the Anarchy of 1136-54, during which, according to the Anglo-Saxon Chronicle, the warring parties 'filled the whole land with castles...and filled them with devils and wicked men'. These were earthwork castles with buildings and defences of timber. Mileham, on the other hand, had a square stone keep set within a motte flanked by two baileys. Other sites, such as Middleton, Raveningham, and Quidenham simply consist of a motte, without visible evidence of baileys. Excavations at Middleton have shown that there was once a small bailey, now long since levelled. It is very likely that some lesser earthwork castles have entirely vanished without record. The motte set within the late Roman fort of Burgh Castle, for example, was levelled in 1839, with only traces of the encircling ditch now remaining.

As an alternative to the motte and bailey the Normans frequently constructed ringworks, which consisted of a roughly circular rampart and surrounding ditch. Examples occur at the Redcastle, Thetford, and probably at Castle Hill, Hunworth and Moot Hill, Wymondham. Excavations at the Redcastle, Thetford have indicated that it was constructed in the earlier 12th century, and was edged on one side by a small bailey.

The elaborate external decoration at Norwich was the inspiration for the treatment of the elevations of the keep at Castle Rising, a much smaller affair built by William de Albini on the eastern side of the Wash in c.1160, and set within approximately contemporary earthworks of

impressive proportions. Castle Acre castle, a stronghold of the Warennes which sits astride the Peddars Way, has been shown by excavation to have begun life in the later 11th century as a lightly defended but large stone-built country residence. Before long, probably during the Anarchy, the house was converted into a keep and the defences massively strengthened. These included a bailey which continued in use after the keep was abandoned in the later 12th century.

The circular keep at New Buckenham is the earliest in England, having been constructed by William de Albini in c.1150. It is set within a ringwork, which is accompanied by an outer bailey (Map 31). Subsequent heightening of the bank has partly buried the keep and engulfed the adjacent gatehouse. New Buckenham was built to replace a castle at Old Buckenham, of which nothing visible remains apart from a rectangular island surrounded by a moat. Similar earthworks at Weeting enclosed 12th century and later stone buildings, as well as the remains of a small motte containing a post-medieval icehouse.

There is no firm dividing line between later medieval 'castles' such as Caister or Baconsthorpe and fortified moated manor houses, 'maisons fortes', such as Oxburgh. In the 13th to 15th centuries licences to crenellate were issued for buildings known as castles at such places as Gresham, Great Hautbois, Oxburgh, and Marham.

29. CASTLES

- ● Castles
- ○ Probable castles
- △ Late medieval castles & maisons fortes

Baconsthorpe △ △ Gresham

○ Hunworth

△ Wood Norton

Castle Rising ●○

North Elmham ●

△ Great Hautbois

○ Kings Lynn

Mileham ●

Horsford ●

● Middleton

Castle Acre ●

Caister △

● Wormegay

Norwich ●

Great Yarmouth ○

△ Marham

Claxton △

Burgh Castle ●

△ Oxburgh

Wymondham ○

Raveningham ○

Old Buckenham ●

● New Buckenham

Weeting ●

Denton ●

Quidenham ○

Thetford
●●

miles 0 — 5

km 0 — 10

30. EARLY UNPLANNED TOWNS

Kenneth Penn

Most medieval towns were actually very small, never achieving real borough status but remaining firmly in the hands of their manorial lord, only distinguished from villages by their markets, for towns were, above all, places of trade. Probably, some small towns had beginnings in Saxon times as markets set up next to the lord's hall, or outside the gates of an abbey, but good evidence for this is missing. For most small towns, their origins and plans belong to the 12th and 13th centuries, when so many planned towns were laid out. Sometimes a market-grant for a manor merely regularized an existing market, perhaps held near the church, or even in the churchyard. As late as 1285, the Statute of Winchester ordered that 'neither Fairs nor Markets be kept in churchyards'. The association of church and weekly market - often held on a Sunday originally - is an old one which allowed trade to be supervised and would benefit both. At first a weekly event on fixed days, the market and its site gradually became permanent, and market stalls and booths were then replaced by solid buildings which colonised the market place. Sometimes a row of *shoppa* would be built at one side of the market-place, leaving a narrow back-street for access. Often the first colonists were butchers' shops, known as 'shambles' (Latin *scamellus* = little bench) but later, other traders became permanent.

Some hint of control is evident in the laying-out of streets and siting of the market-place, sometimes a wide street, a meeting of roads or an open square, perhaps next to the church. Most market-places had narrow entrances, sometimes barred, perhaps to control animals or to enforce market tolls, and around the market, houses were more tightly packed, to make best use of their frontages. Although the 12th and 13th centuries were the height of town foundation, these were followed by times of famines, plagues and social unrest; cloth-manufacture revived the fortunes of some small towns but however they fared, their patterns of streets and markets remained, rarely altering after they were first laid out.

Aylsham: A market existed here before 1296, possibly held in the existing market-place, next to the church, now much reduced by colonisation.

The several manors of *Burnham*, each with its own church, became divided at an early date but remained linked by the establishment of *Burnham Market*, around a long green with a church at each end, both of at least 12th century date.

A market existed at *Dereham* by the late 13th century, possibly originally in the wide Church Street; the large rectangular market-place, partly colonised, may be a later addition, possibly even laid out as late as 1581, after a 'great fire'.

Diss: The triangular market-place at Diss is nearly completely colonised, with the church and Guildhall at one end, 'shambles' and 15th century chapel in the centre, possibly built to supervise trade and tolls.

Harleston was a deliberate creation (possibly 13th century), set up on a few acres of land in the parish of Redenhall, as a long triangular market-place, now entirely colonised. Its ancient church (probably 15th century), set up in the market-place, had no burial ground and was merely a chapel-of-ease to Redenhall. Harleston also had a fair on Midsummer Day, ie. the Nativity of St. John the Baptist to whom the chapel was dedicated.

Hingham and *Worstead* are two of many places (Foulsham, Harling, Shipdham etc.) with a market-place but which remained little more than villages; another examples is *Pulham Market*, an Ely manor which was granted a market in the 12th century, perhaps the time when the village and market-place (The Green) was laid out, but which declined rapidly after 1600.

The large market-place at *Holt*, possibly the centre of a large Anglo-Saxon estate, was probably deliberately laid out a little distance from the church, and has become completely colonised by rows, so that the original shape is almost lost.

A market and two fairs existed at *Swaffham* by the mid 13th century, probably held in the enormous triangular market-place, at an important crossroads. Colonisation has added the Shambles, a scatter of buildings and probably the whole row on the east side, in front of the churchyard.

Reepham was probably the centre of a large Anglo-Saxon estate, but its market-place may be much later and belong to the 13th century, when a market-grant was given. The churchyard held three churches, each belonging to a separate manor in Reepham.

Little Walsingham became an important place of pilgrimage in the mid-12th century, when a shrine and then a Priory were built here. To serve the pilgrims, a busy town grew up outside the walls of the Priory, with two market-places, hostels, a lazar-house and in the mid-14th century a Friary, placed next to a market, and blocking the old road south.

Wymondham, the centre of a large Anglo-Saxon estate, had an important church which became an abbey in 1107, and probably had a market long before Henry I granted a market and three fairs.

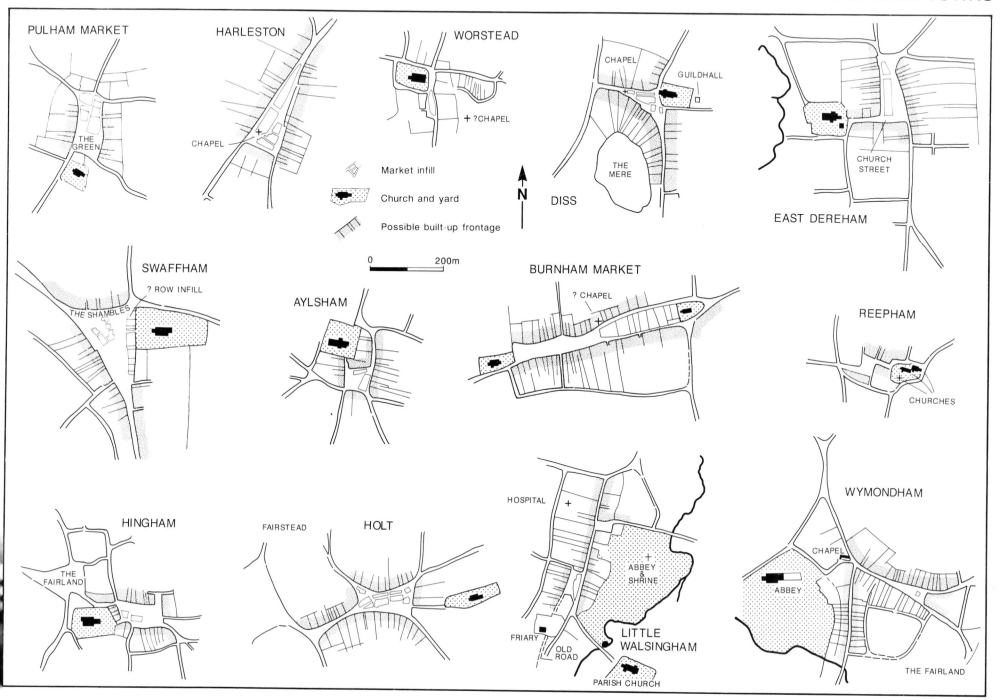

30. EARLY UNPLANNED TOWNS

PULHAM MARKET

THE GREEN

HARLESTON

CHAPEL

WORSTEAD

+ ?CHAPEL

DISS

CHAPEL

GUILDHALL

THE MERE

EAST DEREHAM

CHURCH STREET

Market infill

Church and yard

Possible built-up frontage

N

0   200m

SWAFFHAM

? ROW INFILL

THE SHAMBLES

AYLSHAM

BURNHAM MARKET

? CHAPEL

REEPHAM

CHURCHES

HINGHAM

THE FAIRLAND

FAIRSTEAD

HOLT

HOSPITAL

LITTLE WALSINGHAM

ABBEY & SHRINE

FRIARY

OLD ROAD

PARISH CHURCH

WYMONDHAM

CHAPEL

ABBEY

THE FAIRLAND

31. PLANNED TOWNS

Brian Ayers

Norfolk in 1086 had very few boroughs compared with other counties of lowland England. Only three places are recorded in Domesday as having 'burgesses' - Norwich, Thetford and Yarmouth. Of these, Yarmouth seems to have been little more than a fishing village, but Norwich and Thetford (the latter partly in Suffolk) were very large towns, perhaps the fourth and sixth largest respectively in the kingdom. The urban pattern, particularly in relation to the countryside, was thus very atypical; a densely-populated county was served by a very small number of towns which dominated the region.

The balance began to be redressed in the centuries after the Conquest. The growing importance of *Yarmouth* was consolidated by Herbert de Losinga, first Bishop of Norwich, who founded the church and priory of St. Nicholas and perhaps the market as well. Yarmouth is here included in a section of planned towns as it had (prior to the Second World War and post-war clearance) a unique plan, the origins of which remain obscure but which, in the transverse 'Rows', probably contained a planned element supplementing the north-to-south streets. These latter appear to reflect successive alignments of the river.

De Losinga also consolidated development at *Lynn* in about 1095 by founding the church of St. Margaret. He may have founded a market as well although it seems likely that such was already in existence. The market became the Saturday Market, next to Losinga's foundation of St. Margaret's church and priory. The town lay between the Purfleet and the Millfleet, with the sinuous streets emphasising its riparian origin.

By the middle of the 12th century further expansion was necessary. This was undertaken north of the Purfleet (in the area of 'Newelond' or 'Newland') as a planned development, streets and burgage plots being laid out around a splendid new market place, the Tuesday Market, close to the new church (technically a subordinate chapel) of St. Nicholas.

The ports of Yarmouth and Lynn were to grow rapidly as major trading centres of medieval England. Neither was a true plantation, both being developed out of earlier settlements. The same was probably true of another borough which did not emulate their success. This was *Castle Rising*, refounded after the construction of the great castle by William d'Aubigny forced relocation of the existing church and settlement in the 1130's. The general layout of the present village implies that it may be a rectilinear plantation but other evidence is lacking.

A more obvious attempt to create a town occurred at *Castle Acre*. Here, the earthwork fortress of the Warennes lies to the east of a small, rectilinear planned town which is itself defended by a ditch and bank. The town, almost certainly a 12th-century addition, had gates to the north and south (the north gate survives) with the parish church standing just outside the defensive line. The castle dominates the Peddar's Way which, at Acre, is thus forced to divert through the plantation. Even so, the town was not successful; to the present day development within the bank is limited while the centre of the village has grown up on the green to the north.

A documented plantation, also associated with a castle, is that of *New Buckenham*. William d'Aubigny acquired land in the parishes of Banham and Carleton Rode in the 1140's to build a castle to replace his existing castle at Old Buckenham. The new castle stood next to the Norwich-to-Thetford road and d'Aubigny planted a borough east of the fortress. The road diverts through the town which is set within a small ditch and bank in a square with a rectilinear pattern of streets. The plantation was endowed with a market but originally it did not have a church, being served by the chapel (which chapel survives near the castle as a barn). Commercially the borough never thrived and, even today, the modern town stands entirely within the bank and ditch laid out in the 12th century.

Two further plantations should be mentioned here in passing, both at *Norwich* (Map 32). The first of these was created by Ralph de Guader, Earl of East Anglia, who established a borough for the 'Franci de Norwic' to the west of the royal castle before 1075. This area of 'Newport' ('new town') was built on the open fields of the Anglo-Saxon settlement, the name 'Mancroft', now attached to the principal church of St. Peter, probably meaning '(ge)maene' croft ('common land'). The borough is centred on the market place with east-to-west streets ('Lower' and 'Upper' Newport) running off westward.

Between *c*.1138 and *c*.1154 Eborard, Bishop of Norwich, planted a small suburb on the north bank of the River Wensum in an area of land that probably belonged to his manor of Thorpe. This suburb was created around the church and hospital of St. Paul. There is, however, considerable evidence to suggest that the streets of Cowgate, Rotten Row or Peacock Street (Blackfriars Street) and probably Whitefriars predate the Conquest and the area may, therefore, be a 'planted' but not a 'planned' part of the borough.

Finally it has been asserted that *Wymondham* might have been a planted town, associated with the priory. There is little evidence to support this assertion and the town could as easily be the result of organic growth given the importance of the priory and the existence of its fair.

Castle Rising

Kings Lynn

Castle Acre

Great Yarmouth

Norwich

Wymondham

New Buckenham

0　miles　5

0　km　10

32. NORWICH

Brian Ayers

Norwich came into existence as a series of small settlements on either bank of the River Wensum, probably in the 8th century. These settlements were generally established on gravel terraces next to the river and were associated with roads, one or two of which were probably Roman in origin (along Bishopsgate, through the Cathedral Close and along St. Benedict Street; and the line of Ber Street). There is increasing evidence to suggest the birth of an urban economy, particularly on the north bank of the river, in the 8th and 9th centuries but nothing comparable with contemporary Ipswich.

Danish incursions and settlement may have stimulated urban growth. The town was defended by a bank and ditch on the north side of the river, perhaps before 917 AD, a pattern which has parallels in other Anglo-Scandinavian towns. Following the reconquest in 917 AD Norwich became an administrative centre of the English kings. Coins were being minted here by the 930s. The town probably continued to grow in the 10th century but archaeological work has yet to confirm this. The borough was sacked in 1004 but underwent spectacular growth thereafter.

It seems that the central importance of the town was concentrated on the south bank by the beginning of the 11th century. Excavations in the last twenty years have uncovered evidence of commercial and industrial activity as well as ecclesiastic and domestic occupation. The river foreshore at St. Martin-at-Palace Plain was consolidated from the 11th century with brushwood and wickerwork fencing while the eastern end of Pottergate (now Bedford Street and Lobster Lane) developed as a centre of pottery production. Known pre-Conquest church sites, such as that of SS Simon and Jude, have been supplemented by the discovery of previously unrecorded churches and cemeteries at the Anglia Television site and at Castle Mall. Also at Castle Mall, excavations have recently recorded complete groundplans of 11th-century buildings for the first time. Domesday Book entries imply a settlement which was perhaps the fourth largest in the country by 1066.

The town was augmented in size and importance by the Norman Conquest. A great castle was constructed and a new borough for the 'Franci de Norwic' laid out, both by 1075. The seat of the Bishopric was established in Norwich after 1094 and construction of the cathedral and its close started in 1096. Development south of Mountergate on King Street was undertaken after about 1100 while further expansion took place in the north-east about 1140.

The various settlements of the Middle Saxon, Anglo-Scandinavian, Late Saxon and Norman periods coalesced to occupy an extensive area on both banks of the river. Defences were constructed from the 1280s onwards (although there is a suggestion that some form of communal defence in the western part of the city may date from the 12th century) and it was finally fortified with a wall containing twelve gates and 40 towers.

By the late 13th and 14th centuries Norwich was an extremely important market, industrial town and administrative centre. Its population was probably well in excess of 20,000 and it had between 60 and 70 churches as well as about 30 monastic institutions and dependencies. Its river was crossed by no less than five bridges.

At the turn of the 15th century the city authorities spent considerable sums on public works. The Cow Tower was rebuilt in 1398/99 as an early artillery fortification with gunloops and probable provision for cannon on the roof. The Guildhall was started about 1410 and the New Mills were working by about 1430. The city's wealth is still exemplified by the surviving churches, many of which were rebuilt in the 15th century. In the 16th century the city was still largely confined within its walled boundaries. Economic problems were alleviated by a revitalisation of the cloth trade, stimulated by many refugees fleeing the Spanish Netherlands. At least 6,000 of these seem to have arrived by 1579 (archaeological deposits containing evidence for immigrant communities have been uncovered on a number of sites, notably on the north bank of the river). By the 17th century the cloth trade was easily the single most important element in the city's economy.

Immigrants brought other industrial techniques to Norwich and introduced the earliest recorded production of tin-glazed pottery in England in 1567. A kilnyard was established on Ber Street and, although the precise location remains unknown, waster sherds have been found.

Suburban development began on Bracondale in the late 16th or early 17th century and had probably started even earlier on Barrack Street. The Civil War made little impact on the fabric of the city, other than artillery earthworks improving the defences in certain areas. The walls continued to be maintained as late as the 1720s with most occupation remaining within them until the 19th century.

Large scale development outside the walls only began in the last quarter of the 19th century with the construction of characteristic terraces in the years preceding the First World War. Between the wars the growth of the city accelerated, an acceleration developed since 1945 with the boundary of the city now encompassing Bowthorpe to the west. The population is currently about 130,000 and is set to grow considerably in the next decade.

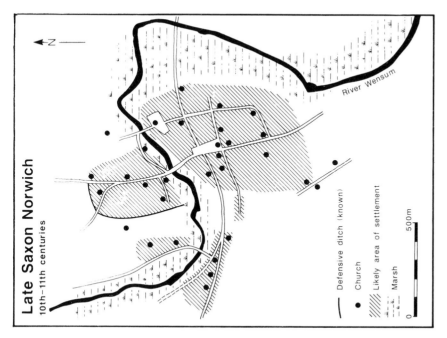

Late Saxon Norwich
10th–11th centuries

Defensive ditch (known)
● Church
Likely area of settlement
Marsh

0   500m

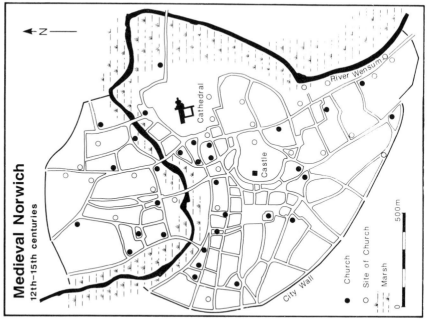

Medieval Norwich
12th–15th centuries

Cathedral
Castle
City Wall
River Wensum

● Church
○ Site of Church
Marsh

0   500m

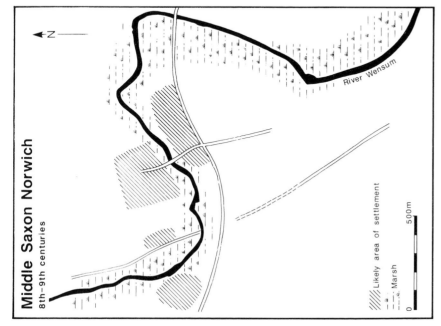

Middle Saxon Norwich
8th–9th centuries

River Wensum

Likely area of settlement
Marsh

0   500m

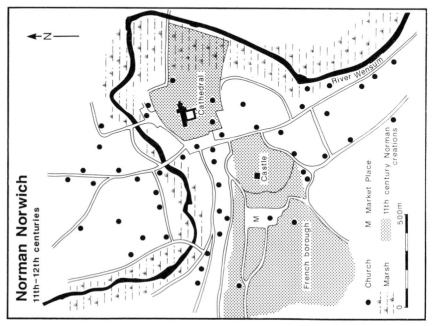

Norman Norwich
11th–12th centuries

Cathedral
Castle
M Market Place
French borough
River Wensum

● Church
M Market Place
11th century Norman creations
Marsh

0   500m

33. MEDIEVAL AND LATER MARKETS

David Dymond

Norfolk has a wealth of historic towns, large and small, and its urban life has had a long history (Maps 30-32). Towns already existed in Roman times, both planned and informal, and there was a major revival of urban life in the later Anglo-Saxon period. By 1066 Norwich and Thetford were already major towns, the two ports of Yarmouth and Lynn were taking shape, and minor marketing centres must have existed widely (though only three are specifically mentioned in Domesday Book at Holt, Dunham and Litcham). But all these developments are overshadowed by a major 'Commercial Revolution' in the 11th to 14th centuries which led to a rapid proliferation of towns and markets all over the county.

Strong Norman government was a great encouragement to commerce and urban development. The existing towns of Norwich and Lynn were extended by planned developments known respectively as the New or French Borough and the New Land, while three grid-like towns were laid out beside Norman castles at Castle Acre, Castle Rising and New Buckenham. However, the great majority of medieval markets were created after 1150 as the result of charters granted and sold by the Crown. These gave a manorial lord the right to hold a weekly market on a specified day, often with an annual fair centring on a particular saint's day.

The map opposite shows the distribution of all known medieval markets, whether held by charter or by custom. The total number is about 140, giving a higher density than anywhere else in England. This means that one in every five or six parishes had a market sometime in the Middle Ages, or that there was a market for every 10,000 acres. Yet the true number is probably greater because of undoubted gaps and inaccuracies in the printed evidence which is the basis of this survey.

Medieval markets were peppered fairly evenly across the county, but were thickest in the centre, east and south where contemporary populations were highest. However, there are areas with few or no examples. Thus the Peat Fen of south-western Norfolk which carried a low population appears quite empty. By contrast, the apparent hole around Norwich must represent not a lack of inhabitants, but the way in which the city was able to discourage potential rivals. The precise sites of markets were largely determined by the wishes of individual lords of manors. Some landowners probably hoped for the best but others were more calculating: they knew that their chances were better in places on or near major roads (like Attleborough), or where rivers were crossed by bridge or boat (as at Acle and Stoke Ferry).

Many markets were grafted onto older agricultural villages, and the historian therefore has to distinguish the original nucleus from later commercial developments. For example, the old village of Watton was probably near the church and manor-house, while the new 13th-century town was laid out to the west - with a market-place into which a north-south road was diverted. Occasionally however, a market was laid out on a completely new site as at New Buckenham where advantage was taken of a major road from Norwich to Bury St. Edmunds. Any place of worship provided for such a new town was usually a chapel-of-ease, subordinate to an older mother church in a rural parish. Thus for centuries Harleston remained a chapelry within the parish of Redenhall, and Pulham Market a chapelry of Pulham St. Mary.

The granting of a charter does not necessarily represent the true origin of a market. We know for example that Heacham and Reepham were holding markets well before the dates of their charters. It therefore seems likely that many lords ran an experimental market before facing the expense of buying royal authorisation. Nor must we assume that all markets shown on the map were necessarily in existence at the same time. They were created at different dates over a period of more than two hundred years, and some failed abjectly or were relatively short-lived.

Where markets close to each other operated on the same day, adjustments could be made. For instance, in 1349 Worsted changed its market from Tuesdays to Fridays because it was competing with nearby Sutton. Although rivalries could be minimised in this way, it is remarkable that so many markets co-existed in the early Middle Ages, often much closer together than the 6.7 miles recommended by the 13th-century lawyer Henry Bracton. The map is therefore good testimony to the vigorous agriculture and commerce of the period, and to the distances which people could travel on contemporary roads in a single day.

Few new charters were granted after the Black Death of 1349. Indeed, over the next 150 years some 75% of medieval markets declined and died. In the 17th century only 31 places in Norfolk were rated as market towns, which means that those communities which previously contained markets had sunk back to the status of ordinary agricultural villages. This process of weeding-out, which continued into the 18th century, is interesting in its own right and deserves much greater study. Although the primary cause after 1349 was a catastrophic decline of population, the death of many markets and the survival of a few also reflects factors like increasing commercial specialisation and improvements in transport.

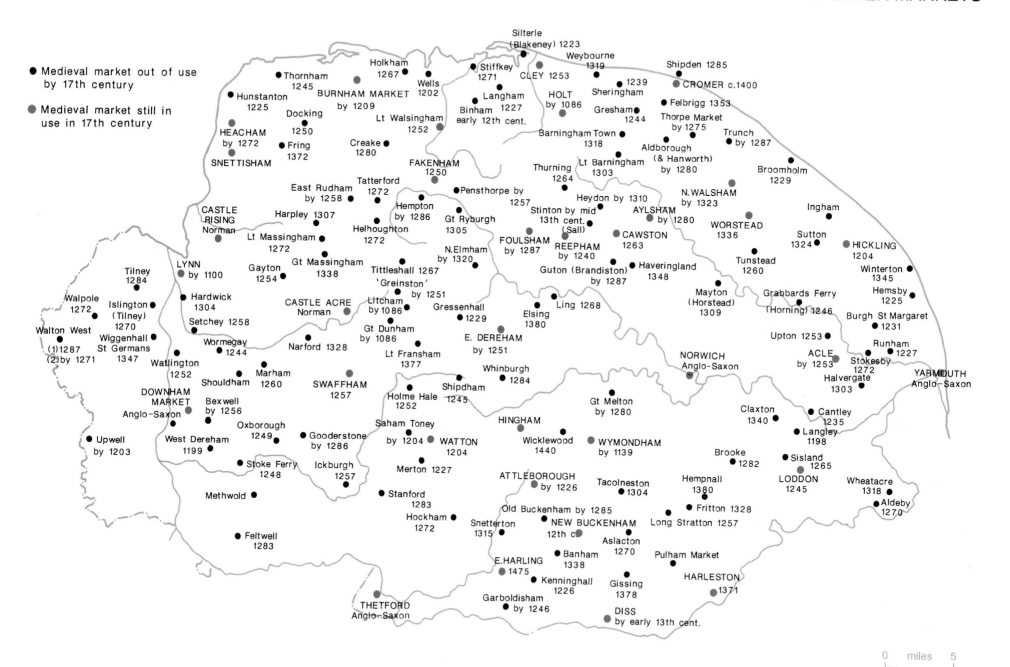

Medieval market out of use by 17th century

Medieval market still in use in 17th century

Silterle (Blakeney) 1223
Weybourne 1319
Shipden 1285
Holkham 1267
Stiffkey 1271
CLEY 1253
1239
CROMER c.1400
Thornham 1245
Wells 1202
Sheringham
Felbrigg 1353
Hunstanton 1225
BURNHAM MARKET by 1209
Langham 1227
HOLT by 1086
Gresham 1244
Thorpe Market by 1275
Trunch by 1287
Docking 1250
Lt Walsingham 1252
Binham early 12th cent.
Barningham Town 1318
Aldborough (& Hanworth) by 1280
Broomholm 1229
HEACHAM by 1272
Fring 1372
Creake 1280
FAKENHAM 1250
Lt Barningham 1303
SNETTISHAM
Tatterford 1272
Pensthorpe by 1257
Thurning 1264
Heydon by 1310
N. WALSHAM by 1323
Ingham
East Rudham by 1258
Hempton by 1286
Stinton by mid 13th cent. (Sall)
AYLSHAM by 1280
WORSTEAD 1336
CASTLE RISING Norman
Harpley 1307
Gt Ryburgh 1305
Sutton 1324
HICKLING 1204
Lt Massingham 1272
Helhoughton 1272
FOULSHAM by 1287
CAWSTON 1263
LYNN by 1100
Gayton 1254
Gt Massingham 1338
N.Elmham by 1320
REEPHAM by 1240
Tunstead 1260
Winterton 1345
Tittleshall 1267
Guton (Brandiston) by 1287
Haveringland 1348
Hemsby 1225
Hardwick 1304
'Greinston' by 1251
Mayton (Horstead) 1309
Grabbards Ferry (Horning) 1246
Walpole 1272
Islington (Tilney) 1270
CASTLE ACRE Norman
Litcham by 1086
Gressenhall 1229
Ling 1268
Burgh St Margaret 1231
Tilney 1284
Setchey 1258
Elsing 1380
Walton West (1)1287 (2)by 1271
Wiggenhall St Germans 1347
Wormegay 1244
Narford 1328
Gt Dunham by 1086
E. DEREHAM by 1251
Upton 1253
Runham 1227
Watlington 1252
Lt Fransham 1377
ACLE by 1253
Stokesby 1272
NORWICH Anglo-Saxon
Halvergate 1303
YARMOUTH Anglo-Saxon
DOWNHAM MARKET Anglo-Saxon
Marham 1260
SWAFFHAM 1257
Whinburgh 1284
Shouldham
Bexwell by 1256
Holme Hale 1252
Shipdham 1245
Gt Melton by 1280
Claxton 1340
Cantley 1235
Upwell by 1203
West Dereham 1199
Oxborough 1249
Gooderstone by 1286
Saham Toney by 1204
WATTON 1204
HINGHAM
Wicklewood 1440
WYMONDHAM by 1139
Langley 1198
Brooke 1282
Sisland 1265
Stoke Ferry 1248
Ickburgh 1257
Merton 1227
ATTLEBOROUGH by 1226
Tacolneston 1304
Hempnall 1380
LODDON 1245
Wheatacre 1318
Methwold
Stanford 1283
Old Buckenham by 1285
Long Stratton 1257
Aldeby 1270
Feltwell 1283
Hockham 1272
Snetterton 1315
NEW BUCKENHAM 12th c.
Aslacton 1270
Pulham Market
E.HARLING 1475
Banham 1338
Gissing 1378
HARLESTON 1371
Kenninghall 1226
Garboldisham by 1246
THETFORD Anglo-Saxon
DISS by early 13th cent.

0 — miles — 5
0 — km — 10

The history of shipping and sea-borne trade in medieval Norfolk is dominated by the ports of Great Yarmouth and King's Lynn. Both were among east-coast towns that flourished after the Conquest and eventually supplanted river ports such as Norwich. When King John imposed a duty of a fifteenth on sea-borne exports and imports, Norwich still merited its own customs officials. However, the relatively small amount of duty collected at Norwich in 1203-1204, namely £6 19s 0d, as against £54 15s 6d at Yarmouth and £651 11s 11d in Lynn, marks its evident decline as a port. No officials were stationed there when the customs system was reorganised in the early 14th century.

Yarmouth and Lynn both lay at the mouths of extensive river systems. As well as serving Norwich, Yarmouth was the outlet for east and south Norfolk and north Suffolk, through the Bure, the Waveney and the Yare. Lynn served not only west Norfolk and Suffolk via the Little Ouse but, through its connections with the Great Ouse, the Nene and the Welland it had access to Bedfordshire, Cambridgeshire, Huntingdonshire and Northamptonshire. The map can show but few of the goods that were handled by Lynn and Yarmouth and little is known about the coastal trade before the 16th century. Corn from its wide hinterland provided the basis for Lynn's foreign trade, already so extensive by 1203-1204 that the total duty collected was the fourth highest of any south- or east-coast port, London included. Corn was supplemented by wool and then by cloth. From at least the 12th century Yarmouth's fortunes were founded on its autumn herring fishery, and herring comprised its principal export.

Little wool left from Yarmouth but the port handled three quarters of English worsted exports in the 14th century, with 12,000 worsteds passing through in 1400/1. Its merchant fleet in 1300-1350 possibly contained 60 to 100 vessels of 100 tons and many more smaller ships, and the port was of national importance as a supplier of shipping to royal campaigns; in 1301 Yarmouth was ordered to send six ships to Berwick against the Scots. Lynn sent three but was principally established as the port from which northern armies or garrisons were provisioned.

The Hundred Years War with France interrupted trade, and by the 15th century both ports were in decline. Lynn's attempts to establish trading links with Iceland in the early 15th century were frustrated by Hansa Merchants, though fishing for cod continued in spite of Norway's opposition. Yarmouth experienced further difficulties with the Low Countries dominating the herring fishery and silting at the harbour mouth. The latter remained a problem until the 1560s. When markets revived, command of the sale of worsteds, like the wine trade, had passed to London. Nevertheless, of the two ports Yarmouth, with the demands of Norwich to satisfy, remained the more active. Most overseas trade in the late 15th and early 16th centuries was with the Low Countries, exporting grain for salt and timber, but the changing political situation later in the century encouraged Yarmouth to resume its former trading contacts and initiate new routes to Norway, Spain and Italy. Though a busy port with more ships in 1580 (122) than the other Norfolk harbours combined, Yarmouth never regained its earlier national status. Lynn's 16th-century revival was based not on overseas trade but on a growing coastal traffic in coal from Newcastle.

Because of few and intermittent sources much less is known about the minor Norfolk ports. By far the most important of these was the Blakeney haven complex which comprised the harbours of Blakeney alias Snitterley, Cley and Wiveton. In 1301 Blakeney was to send two ships to Berwick while the other lesser ports contributed just half a ship each, and from the 14th to the 16th century it was the only Norfolk harbour apart from Yarmouth and Lynn with customs officials. Up to the 17th century the Blakeney channels could take most merchant shipping and the complex boasted more vessels than Lynn in the Elizabethan shipping surveys, with 36 to Lynn's 32 ships in 1580. By the late 16th century Blakeney was facing some competition from Wells. Wells harbour had 19 ships in 1580 and local merchants petitioned for a custom house there in the 1590s.

There is even less information for the other Norfolk ports. None could muster more than three ships of over 16 tons in 1580, though the Ringstead entry (two) should probably be included with Heacham (three) which was credited with six ships in 1582. The 1580 shipping survey names more ports than those of 1565 or 1582 and is the only list to include any shipping on the east coast between Cromer and Yarmouth, namely a fishing boat apiece from Caister and Eccles. Though the lesser harbours on the Wash may have suffered through coastal accretion and embankment, Dersingham still appears in the more selective survey of 1565 with one ship of 30 tons. Many of the boats from the smaller harbours would have been primarily occupied in fishing. This need not have been local. A Cromer man was credited with the discovery of Iceland at the beginning of the 15th century and boats from several Norfolk ports engaged in the fishery trade. Such craft could also be used for the coastal trade or trips across the North Sea and the absence of custom houses save at Blakeney, Lynn and Yarmouth encouraged widespread smuggling.

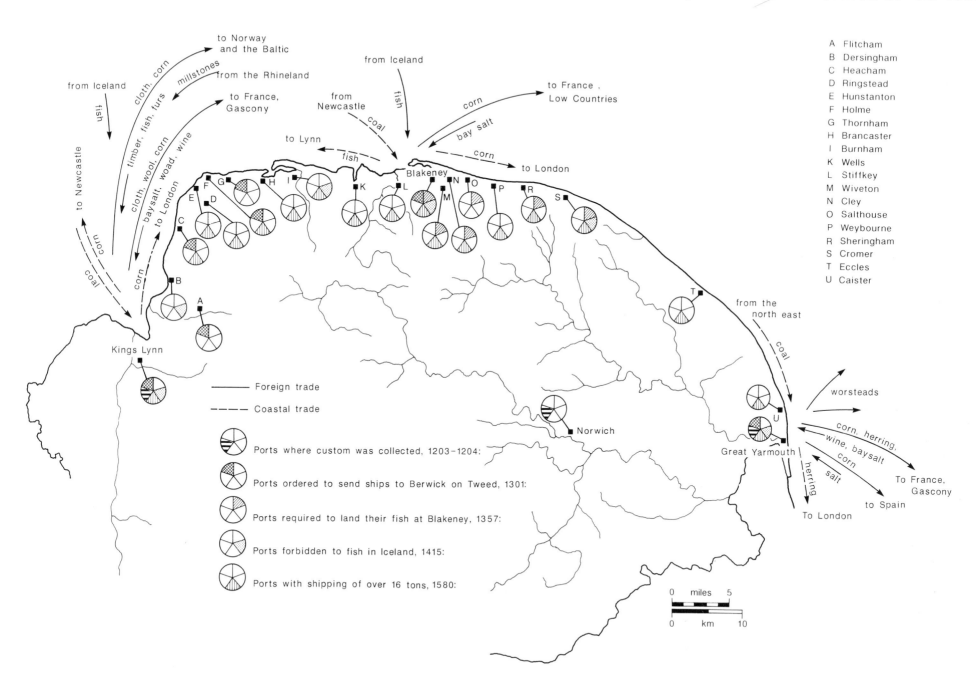

to Norway
and the Baltic

cloth, corn

millstones

from the Rhineland

from Iceland

to France,
Gascony

from Iceland

from
Newcastle

to France,
Low Countries

corn

fish

coal

to Newcastle

fish

bay salt

to Lynn

corn

to London

fish

timber, fish, furs

cloth, wool, corn

baysalt, woad, wine

to London

Blakeney

corn

coal

corn

B

A

Kings Lynn

C
D
E
F
G
H
I
K
L
M
N
O
P
R
S

T

from the
north east

coal

worsteads

corn, herring,

wine, baysalt

corn

To France,
Gascony

to Spain

salt

herring

To London

Great Yarmouth

U

Norwich

A Flitcham
B Dersingham
C Heacham
D Ringstead
E Hunstanton
F Holme
G Thornham
H Brancaster
I Burnham
K Wells
L Stiffkey
M Wiveton
N Cley
O Salthouse
P Weybourne
R Sheringham
S Cromer
T Eccles
U Caister

—— Foreign trade

‑ ‑ ‑ Coastal trade

Ports where custom was collected, 1203–1204:

Ports ordered to send ships to Berwick on Tweed, 1301:

Ports required to land their fish at Blakeney, 1357:

Ports forbidden to fish in Iceland, 1415:

Ports with shipping of over 16 tons, 1580:

0   miles   5

0   km   10

Christopher Barringer

The total area of Norfolk is 1,307,333 acres and of this some 200,000 acres were recorded by Nathaniel Kent in 1796 as being unimproved commons, marshland, warrens or sheepwalk.

The rate of enclosure of common waste slowed down markedly after Tudor concern about illegal enclosure and it can be assumed that many 16th century commons still had very similar boundaries in the late 18th century. Recent archaeological field work in Norfolk suggests that as at Hales Green the edges of at least some commons have changed very little since the early 14th century.

In 1797 William Faden produced his map of Norfolk which has been used as the major source for the map opposite. His map records many commons, heaths and marshland that were not yet enclosed. It is important to note that some enclosures had already taken place; Fincham for example was enclosed in 1772 but no area of former common is named by Faden.

Common 'waste' was of course not waste. There were several terms, at times overlapping, used to describe the 'waste'. Common was the most frequent; green, marsh, fen, heath, moor and bog were also used. The unique balance between the various types of common that occurred in a particular parish depended on its relief and surface geology. Glacial sands and gravels supported a heathy vegetation on acid soils. In the lime-rich waters of the fens and broadland river marshes a wealth of plants flourished, species suitable for animal grazing. Finally, on the dominant soil type - that of the boulder clays - the climax vegetation was either oak or lime woodland which if gradually grazed out produced wood/pasture which varied from wet meadow to drier plateau conditions depending on the particular nature of the glacial deposits.

Many parishes had sandy soils, loams and heavy clays within their boundaries and it was not unusual as for example at Mattishall to have greens (Clipping Green and South Green), a moor and a heath in one parish. In many places the local names gave clear hints as to the nature of the land - in Attleborough for example there were Ling Common, Swangey (Swan Island) Fen, Burgh Green, West Carr Common, Oak Common and Cow Common. Names of commons such as Goose Green (Little Ellingham), Neat Fen in Watton or Cows Green, Sheeps Green and Styrks Green in Martham are all functionally descriptive. It is likely that many commons have evolved from primary woodland and that commons such as Attleborough's Oak Common and Long Stratton's Wood Green evolved this way.

Common land provided a great variety of products and fulfilled many uses. Fuel was cut as wood or furze or turf; clay sand and gravel and local stone were all used in building and road making and some spaces were used for recreation - fairs, campinglands etc. The foldcourse system of managing sheep flocks needed common grazing especially on the heaths, and the greens, and wetter commons were used for milch cattle, the younger stock and for horses. The fen and valley marsh provided sedge and reed for building and for animal bedding as well as vast quantities of fish, eels and wild birds.

Rather different patterns of common occur in the major physical regions of the county (Map 46). In the Northern Fens 6,132 acres of unenclosed common existed as the 'Smeeth', a vast inter-common. In this area of marshland the layout of a group of parishes consisted of a settlement in the siltlands, salt marsh grazing on the tidal marshes and fen and smeeth rights in the south and an umbilical droveway or street green linking these settlements. Settlements grew from the 14th century southwards along these common droveways.

In the sandy Breckland many parishes had their settlement on the boundary between the valley sides and the marshy valley floor. The bulk of the parish, away from the river was heathland (once primary woodland) over which lords of manors had their foldcourses for sheep and sometimes also their warrens. One of the largest heaths, Mousehold, with an area of about 6,000 acres, was not in the Breck but lay between Norwich and the Broads on the sandy low plateau between the Yare and the Bure. In all probability this was originally woodland but by 1086 it was largely heath.

In the Broads marshland provided stretches of grazing on fen marsh above the tidal limits and salt marsh below them. The presence of peat led to the cutting of large amounts for fuel, especially for Yarmouth and Norwich and to the resultant formation of the broads after the flooding in the 14th century (Map 36). The exact ratio of common to upland in any parish was unique, but parishes such as Horsey, Hickling and Martham had a great deal of common marshland.

The north coast of Norfolk is fringed by salt marsh and these formerly wider common marshes supported summer flocks of sheep.

The bulk of the county is boulder clay upland. The valley-side parish with its low (wet) common by the river and its plateau common on its upland boundary was a very frequent type. The map makes it clear that more commons survived until 1797 in the south and south-east of the county in what is often termed the 'wood pasture' area. Whether this indicates that there had always been more common land in this area is arguable: it may be that a greater proportion of ancient commons had already been enclosed by 1797 in the other, more arable, parts of the county.

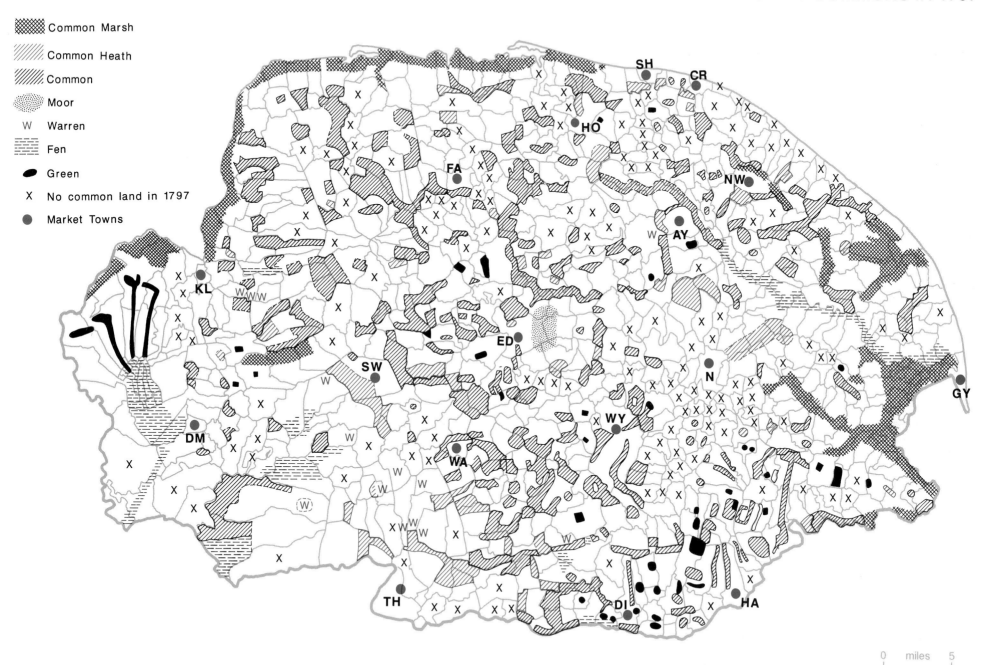

Common Marsh

Common Heath

Common

Moor

W Warren

Fen

Green

X No common land in 1797

● Market Towns

SH

CR

HO

FA

NW

AY

KL

ED

N

GY

SW

DM

WY

WA

TH

DI

HA

0 miles 5

0 km 10

36. THE BROADS

Martin George

The origin of the *c.*50 shallow lakes, known locally as 'broads', was the subject of much speculation until the late 1950s, when a multi-disciplinary team comprising an ecologist (J.M. Lambert), physiographer (J.N. Jennings), historical geographer (C.T. Smith), archaeologist (C. Green) and engineer (J.N. Hutchinson) demonstrated that the great majority of them are peat workings which became flooded in medieval times. Some of the deepest and largest broads, the Ormesby - Rollesby - Filby group - are located in Flegg, a district heavily settled by the Danes from the mid-9th century onwards, and it is suspected that they introduced the practice of exploiting the local fens for fuel, as peatlands in Denmark have been used for this purpose since about 500 BC.

Stratigraphical research showed that many of the peat pits now occupied by broads were dug to a depth of three metres or more below the present fen surface, despite the increased difficulties which would have been experienced in keeping such workings free of water, and the large expanses of surface peat nearby which could have been exploited with much less effort. Lambert and Jennings have persuasively argued that those responsible would have wished to dig as deeply as possible in order to gain access to the brushwood peat laid down during the 'Middle Peat' era (*c.* 5000 - *c.* 2250 BP). This has a much higher calorific value than the predominantly herbaceous peats which occur nearer the surface.

Whilst the pits were in use, water would have found its way into them in the form of precipitation, and also as a result of lateral seepage from the adjoining rivers and undrained fenland. Nothing is known about the type of pump or baling system which must have been employed to remove this incoming water, but baulks of unworked peat were left between the individual pits, and these would have made the task of de-watering them somewhat easier. Nevertheless, Lambert and her co-workers were acutely aware of the difficulties inherent in hand-digging pits 3 or 4 m deep so close to a large river, and they therefore sought to demonstrate that the sea level

relative to that of the land was some four metres or more lower in *c.* 1200 than it is today. Although archaeological evidence for this was presented, the author considers this suspect, and has argued that when the broads were being dug, the sea, and therefore the river levels, were only about a metre lower than they are today.

Plenty of documentary evidence was uncovered to show that peat was being produced in the region between the 12th and 16th centuries, though confirmation that it was being worked earlier than this was not forthcoming. All but one of the 12th-century records occur in the Register of St. Benet's Abbey, and Domesday makes no mention of peat being produced in the region. But as Smith points out, this is not surprising as few references to this activity are made in the survey.

The climate of north-west Europe underwent a change for the worse during the second half of the 13th century; in particular, the incidence of northerly and north-westerly gales - the conditions most likely to generate storm surges in the North Sea - increased, as did the annual rainfall. A catastrophic flood occurred in Broadland in 1287, and there is evidence that several similar, albeit less severe, events took place during the following century. The increased susceptibility of the peat pits to flooding, possibly combined with a decrease in the demand for peat for fuel, consequent upon the development of a trade in coal from ports in north-east England, led to many pits being abandoned. The life of those at Barton and elsewhere was temporarily prolonged when a technique of dredging peat from the flooded workings was adopted. But this roughly doubled the cost of production, and the method does not seem to have been employed for very long. In contrast, a similar dredging technique was used in various parts of Holland until the early 1930s.

Once peat working had finally ceased, the internal baulks within a flooded excavation would have been deliberately breached, as were those separating it from

the main river system. This enabled the workings to be used as fisheries, and documentary evidence suggests that these were of considerable importance in the local economy from the 15th century onwards. Marginal reedswamp communities would in due course have concealed the angular outlines of the broad, and thus its artificial origin.

Much research has been carried out on the ecological changes to which the broads have been subject since they were flooded. They originally supported a waterweed flora dominated by stoneworts and other low-growing species characteristic of calcium-rich water deficient in plant nutrients. Such sites are known as 'marl-lakes'. Later, as nitrogen and phosphorus concentrations in the water rose as a consequence, respectively, of changes in agricultural practice in the catchments of the rivers, and the increasing amounts of sewage discharged into the latter, this 'Phase I' flora was replaced by 'Phase II' communities. These were highly productive biologically, and were dominated by tall-growing waterweeds. As nutrient levels rose still further, this Phase II flora was, in turn, supplanted by Phase III, algal-dominated communities, and this is the condition that the great majority of the broads are now in.

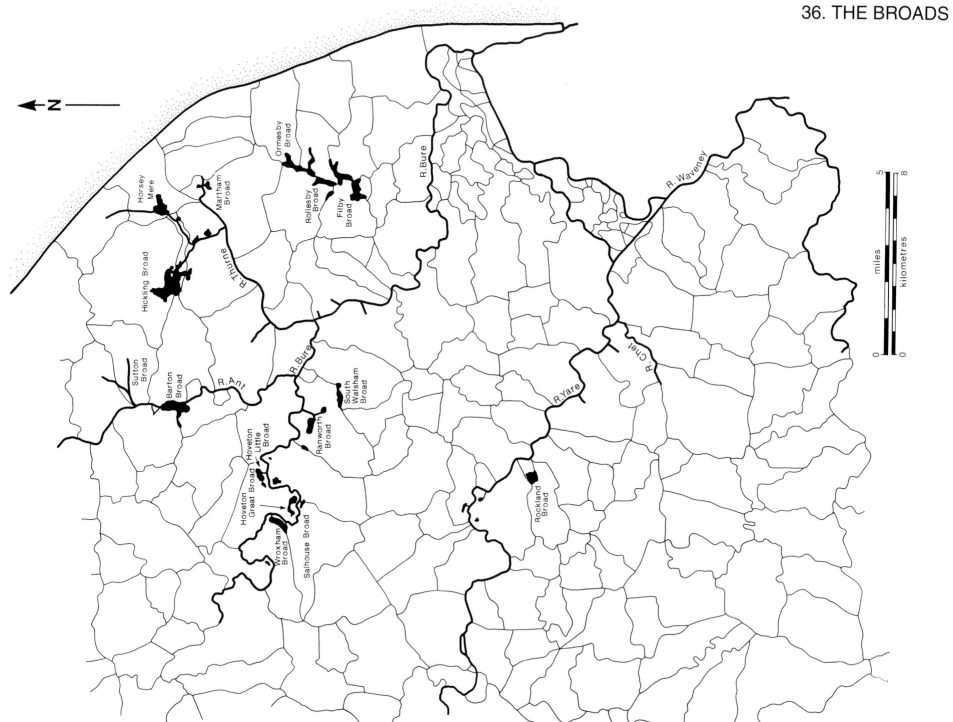

Horsey Mere

Martham Broad

Ormesby Broad

Rollesby Broad

Filby Broad

R. Bure

R. Waveney

Hickling Broad

R. Thurne

Sutton Broad

Barton Broad

R. Ant

R. Bure

South Walsham Broad

Hoveton Great Broad

Hoveton Little Broad

Ranworth Broad

R. Yare

R. Chet

Wroxham Broad

Salhouse Broad

Rockland Broad

N

miles

kilometres

5

8

0

0

37. DESERTED VILLAGES AND RURAL DEPOPULATION

Alan Davison

Defining a 'deserted' village is difficult. Although clustered earthworks, like Pudding Norton, are easy to identify, desertion can appear in ways difficult to classify. Continuing research reveals an increasingly complicated picture. Rougham, which survives, lost a large area of settlement; elsewhere scattered houses may represent a former street. West Dereham has an abandoned site near its isolated church. In Hales and Loddon medieval hamlets and farmsteads have vanished. Riddlesworth, once compact, is now no more than church, mansion and scattered buildings. Regional differences add variety. After centuries of farming many sites have been reduced to mere concentrations of pottery in the soil. With these things in mind, difficult judgements have been made in compiling the accompanying map.

Superficially, desertion appears concentrated in certain areas. Earlier research noted clusters on the Western Escarpment, in Breckland and the Good Sands and equated them with 'marginal' soils. Less easy to explain in this way are those in the south-east, Flegg and northern mid-Norfolk. Such a generalisation overlooks important local soil variations. Gaps in distribution may reflect concealment of desertion within an initially diffuse settlement pattern or absence of fieldwork.

Causes of desertion vary and more than one may be responsible. Surveys show that changes in earlier Saxon settlement had taken place by 1086. Domesday vills such as Toimere (in Stradsett), no longer named in 1316, may have been in terminal decline when recorded. Rural population, already numerous in 1086, increased until about 1300 and new greenside or common-edge settlements were established. Sometimes, as at Longham, this was at the expense of an original site, sometimes, as at Methlond in Illington, in addition. This drift was a response to increasing shortages of pasture.

Outbreaks of pestilence, beginning in 1349, brought great mortality but Little Ringstead, already weak, was probably the sole direct casualty. Nevertheless the resultant decline of population probably accounted for many minor sites, as in Loddon and Hales, and gaps appeared in surviving villages. Environmental factors may also have influenced settlement. Climatic research has shown that, for a time in the 14th and 15th centuries, Norfolk was much wetter and clayland sites less easy to drain, such as Grenstein or Godwick, may have suffered. Rising sea levels caused flooding in Broadland by 1300; in Heckingham, Loddon and Sisland some settlement moved to higher ground. Severe storms hastened coastal erosion; in 1271 West Lynn's church had to be rebuilt on higher ground and remains of Eccles church are still visible on the beach.

Economic decline after 1334 is indicated by the reduction in Lay Subsidy payments made in 1449. Places allowed reductions of 30% or more, and parishes having less than ten households in 1428 are shown. Neither index shows marked correlation with the pattern of desertion while replacement of clergy in 1349 as an indicator of plague mortality has less. Closer investigation occasionally shows such things to be misleading: Riddlesworth, weak in 1428, survived into the 17th century while Little Hockham, unmentioned after 1086, grew thereafter, surviving until the 16th century.

Human decisions based on economic opportunism were the main cause of many desertions. Although population revived after 1500, places already weakened proved easy prey for late medieval and early 16th century landlords disposed to increase their wealth by becoming flockmasters; the smaller the settlement, the less resistance offered. It seems likely that Pudding Norton suffered in this way while Sturston and Alethorpe are documented examples. Disturbances in 1381 at Rougham and Great Palgrave may have been early signs of such pressure from ambitious lords. By contrast, in a more substantial village such as Roudham, decay took longer. Purchasing of tenants' lands led to gradual enlargement of the manorial farm, bringing eventual desertion. The village ceased to be and an estate was born. This practice lingered into the 18th century in some cases. Sometimes a park might be created subsequently, as at Hargham. Whatever the fate of the village, its lands continued to be exploited.

Emparking, a fashion popular from the late 17th century onwards (Map 50), is known to have been the cause of a few desertions. At Houghton an entire village was rebuilt on a new site; at Holkham a subsidiary hamlet was enlarged to compensate for the loss of the main village. However, villages already deserted provided tempting sites for the development of extensive gardens and parks and it is not easy to separate the end of one process from the beginning of the other. Buckenham Tofts, a park by the early 18th century, had long been deserted, while a small community of 12 taxable households at Narford in 1664 would offer but a minor obstacle to such development.

Desertion is only the most extreme form of the evolution of rural settlement, a process which continues. The loss of coastal land goes on; other places may suffer the fate of the Domesday vill of Ness (in Caister) and of Eccles. In 1942, West Tofts, Tottington and Stanford were cleared to form, together with the old deserted villages of Langford, Sturston and Buckenham Tofts, a military training area. They have never been re-inhabited, the only instance of war as a depopulating agent in Norfolk. Less obvious, but more important, are the changes caused by the mechanisation of farming which has meant larger farms and fewer farmworkers. Smaller farmhouses and tied cottages have become superfluous and some of them have been demolished and their sites ploughed.

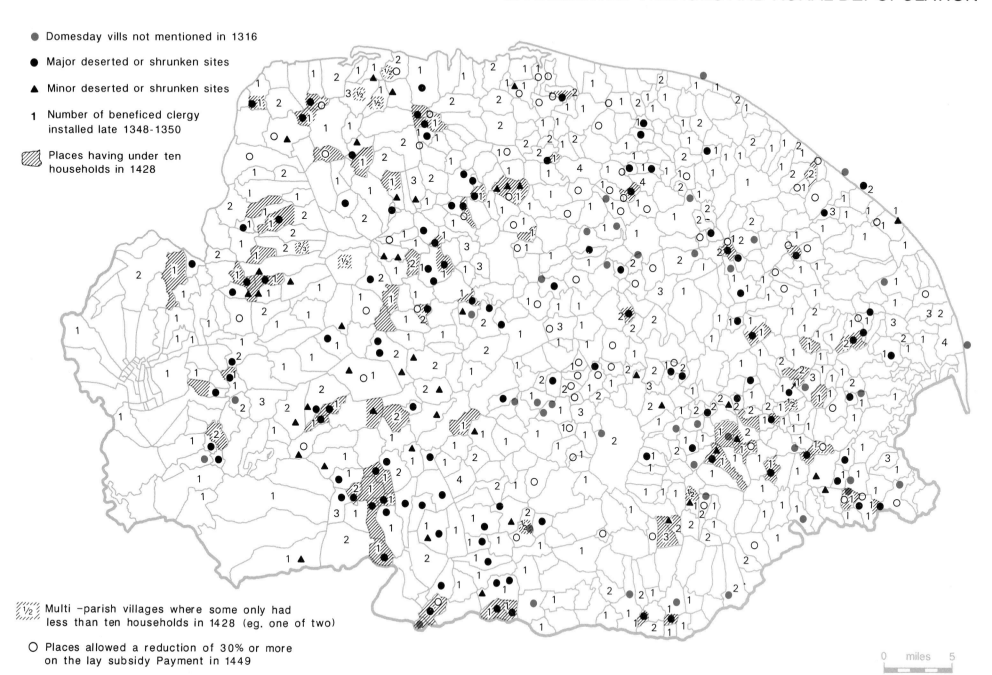

Domesday vills not mentioned in 1316

Major deserted or shrunken sites

Minor deserted or shrunken sites

1 Number of beneficed clergy installed late 1348-1350

Places having under ten households in 1428

1/2 Multi-parish villages where some only had less than ten households in 1428 (eg. one of two)

O Places allowed a reduction of 30% or more on the lay subsidy Payment in 1449

0 miles 5

0 km 10

38. THE UPRISING OF 1381

Barbara Cornford and Andy Reid

The immediate cause of the 'Peasant's Revolt' of 1381 was the imposition of an unpopular poll tax. Rebels from Kent and Essex marched to London and briefly gained concessions from Richard II, before the murder of their leader, Wat Tyler, brought the episode to an end. The rising also affected East Anglia, and Norfolk saw widespread unrest.

The map opposite contains information from the presentments made by hundred juries after the rising. These do not exist for six south eastern hundreds, and so the blankness of the map here may be misleading. Additional problems are the inconsistency of the information from different hundreds and the probable partiality of the local juries. No use has been made of other sources - manorial records, and the plea rolls of the national courts - which provide more details but raise further problems of interpretation. The rising in Norfolk occupied less than a fortnight. The first recorded incidents took place on 14 June, the date of the London insurgents' meeting with Richard II at Mile End. A group from Bury St. Edmund's arrived at Thetford and threatened to burn the town. Members of this band, together with rebels from the Brandon, Feltwell, Littleport and Diss areas, moved north across Breckland and along the Fen Edge, effectively bringing the insurrection to most of south western Norfolk. Also on 14 June in the north east of the county rebels rode from village to village urging the people to rise in the name of their leader, Geoffrey Litster. Over the next two days insurgents from areas north and east of the river Wensum gravitated towards Norwich.

On 17 June, the groups moving northwards from Breckland converged on an area north of Swaffham, joining rebels from the Wymondham district and others from the immediate locality and from places to the north. A principal target for this large congregation of insurgents was the residence of John Reed, a collector of the poll tax, at Rougham. Action was also continuing in the south western corner of the county, while in Lynn, a large body of artisans rose in revolt.

Meanwhile the insurgents from the north and east, under the leadership of Geoffrey Litster and a member of the gentry, Sir Roger Bacon, had assembled on Mousehold Heath outside Norwich. It was here that the only member of the gentry to make a firm stand against the rebels, Sir Robert de Salle, was killed. The insurgents then entered the city, where they killed a J.P., Sir Reginald Eccles, and looted the properties of their enemies.

Over the following few days, the large gatherings of rebels seem to have fragmented. Some of those in the Rougham area may have turned south again, to attack the property of a J.P. and sheep farmer, John de Pagrave. The insurrectionary craftsmen of Lynn made raids on Snettisham, East Rudham and Castle Rising.

The rebel leaders from Norwich moved on to Great Yarmouth, where they took the town's charter and plundered the houses of two influential inhabitants, Hugh Fastolf and William Elys. In the villages of north and east Norfolk the rebels now concentrated on the selective burning of manor court rolls, including those of the Abbey of St. Benet's at Holme. In the north west of the county, Edmund Gurnay, steward of the Duke of Lancaster, and John de Holkham, a king's justice, were pursued relentlessly, first by land and then by sea.

By 22 June, the rising was largely confined to the north eastern corner of the county, where Geoffrey Litster remained active. Bishop Despenser of Norwich, having rallied the gentry as he made his way across Norfolk from the west, ended the rebels' resistance near North Walsham a few days later. The chroniclers' accounts of this final confrontation differ, but they are agreed that Litster was summarily executed.

The rising in Norfolk was thus widespread but short lived. There were links with events elsewhere; some Norfolk rebels had been involved in incidents in other counties, while there is evidence from several parts of Norfolk of the influence of John Wrawe, the Suffolk leader. The targets of the Norfolk rebels included those involved in tax collection and in the administration of the county, the servants and properties of the unpopular Duke of Lancaster, and monastic and other landlords. In Lynn and Great Yarmouth, Flemish settlers were attacked. The insurgents' actions ranged from petty theft to large-scale extortion, looting, and personal threats. There were comparatively few killings. The burning of manor court rolls, which recorded the tenants' status and feudal obligations, was concentrated north east of the River Wensum; there were just three such incidents elsewhere, one at Carrow Abbey and two at manors of the Duke of Lancaster on the Fen Edge.

The loss of momentum of the rising in Norfolk after the first few days may reflect the arrival of the news of the death on 15 June of Wat Tyler. According to the chronicler Thomas of Walsingham, the Norfolk rebels sent emissaries to London to seek concessions from the king, but they were intercepted at Icklingham by Bishop Despenser. The realisation of their isolation, together with the bishop's ruthlessness and determination, probably combined to hasten the collapse of the rebels' cause.

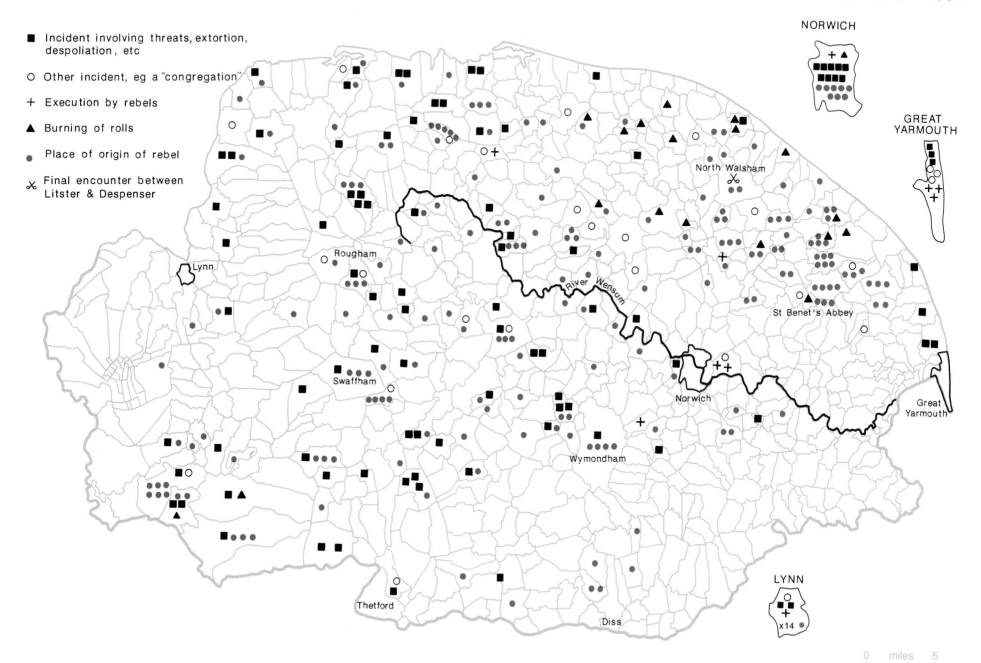

38. THE UPRISING OF 1381

NORWICH

GREAT YARMOUTH

- ■ Incident involving threats, extortion, despoliation, etc
- ○ Other incident, eg a "congregation"
- + Execution by rebels
- ▲ Burning of rolls
- ● Place of origin of rebel
- ✂ Final encounter between Litster & Despenser

North Walsham

St Benet's Abbey

Lynn

Rougham

River Wensum

Swaffham

Norwich

Wymondham

Great Yarmouth

LYNN
×14

Thetford

Diss

miles 5

km 10

Thirty three Norfolk hundreds were listed in Domesday Book in 1086, and they were clearly already well accepted units of administration and taxation by 1066. Whatever their individual beginnings, they had come by the Norman Conquest to be recognised as the sub-shire units of local government, and they remained as such until 1834. The shire was administered for the king by the sheriff; the hundreds were responsible to the sheriff and were administered by a high constable.

The origin of the Domesday hundreds of Norfolk is unclear. They probably evolved after the English reconquest of the area from the Danes in the early tenth century, but they may well have been based on earlier territorial units, units of administration in the East Anglian kingdom, ultimately perhaps ancient tribal territories. The names of Loddon hundred (Lodningas in Domesday), and of Clavering (Cnaveringas) seem to perpetuate the names of ancient folk groups. As the map makes clear, Norfolk hundreds were of very different sizes, perhaps reflecting the fact that poorer land would support fewer people and would produce lower taxable income than more fertile land.

The Domesday layout of hundreds has since undergone some slight rearrangement. Docking was later merged with Smithdon to form Smithdon Hundred. There were some minor readjustments between Brothercross and North Greenhoe, and Freebridge was split into Freebridge Lynn and Freebridge Marshland. The names of many of them survived, as in 'Mitford and Launditch' and 'Forehoe and Henstead' as local government divisions until 1974 when the tradition of a thousand years was finally discarded and the imaginative North, South and West Norfolk districts were created!

Given that hundreds may have developed out of more ancient units, it is perhaps not surprising that some were defined in part by the physical geography of the county. The two 'half hundreds' of West and East Flegg covered the 'island' of Flegg. The rivers of the county formed natural boundaries both for vills (townships) and for hundreds. Taverham for example lay between the Bure and the Wensum. In some cases the river basin seems to have been the unit rather than the river being a boundary, for example Depwade Hundred corresponded quite closely to the area of the upper Tas basin.

In a few short stretches man-made boundaries provided by Roman roads have acted as hundredal boundaries, for example the Peddars Way divided Smithdon from Freebridge. However, the major Roman road from Denver to Caister-on-Sea does not seem to have been used at all as a hundred boundary.

In several hundreds the most convenient meeting place for its men was not a major settlement but some convenient point, and many took their names from this. Tumuli form distinctive features in the otherwise relatively flat Norfolk landscape. The words 'How' or 'Hoe' imply a hill or mound, as in Carleton Forehoe. This was a distinctive clump of four tumuli which made a good meeting-place for the men of Forehoe. Fords were the key meeting-place in Mitford and Eynsford - their exact locations are, however, far from clear. Crosses as at Brothercross and Guiltcross marked places accessible to the people of their hundreds.

Already at the time of Domesday many hundreds, in Norfolk as elsewhere in England, were in the hands of particular individuals or institutions, who derived a profit from the exercise of justice at the hundred court. By 1272 there were 628 hundreds in England of which 270 were still in the King's hands and 358 in private 'control'. In Norfolk the King still held the Fleggs, but others were in private hands. Ely, for example, held Mitford and the L'Estrange family Launditch. Whether the hundred was under the King's control or that of a 'lessee' it was the unit through which royal control was exercised.

As Domesday Book shows, the men of the hundred affirmed on matters of land ownership; after 1272 this system ceased but the control of law and order through the tithing system with its view of frankpledge remained an important role of the hundred when the sheriff held *tourns* twice a year in each hundred.

The high constable was responsible for keeping the peace and if necessary for organising musters of able-bodied men for military service. Issues of dispute between manors and vills over common grazings and of straying stock were often dealt with and recorded on the hundred court rolls.

The records of the Hundred Courts only survive sporadically. As late as 1597 Forehoe Hundred's bailiff was collecting stray animals from the commons. However by this date the Justices of the Peace were more usually dealing with local disputes; for example Nathaniel Bacon was asked in 1574 to adjudicate on a dispute about Ranworth Common.

The collection of the increasing number of taxes such as subsidies, ship money and hearth and window taxes was carried out by the high constables of the hundreds. The State Papers for 1626-37 show how issues such as recruitment for military service and the cost of maintaining beacons were both dealt with through the hundredal organisation.

In 1834 the Poor Law Unions replaced the hundreds as the unit of local government.

SMITHDON

DOCKING

BROTHER CROSS

NORTH GREENHOE

HOLT

NORTH ERPINGHAM

TUNSTEAD

HAPPING

GALLOW

EYNSFORD

SOUTH ERPINGHAM

Kings Beck

FREEBRIDGE LYNN

K.L.

WEST FLEGG

LAUNDITCH

Wensum

TAVERHAM

Ant

Thurne

Bure

EAST FLEGG

FREEBRIDGE MARSHLAND

Nar

Wensum

MITFORD

N

WALSHAM

G.Y.

Great Ouse

SOUTH GREENHOE

FOREHOE

HUMBLE YARD

HENSTEAD

BLOFIELD

CLACKCLOSE

Wissey

WAYLAND

Yare

Tas

CLAVERING

LODDON

DEPWADE

GRIMSHOE

SHROPHAM

DISS

EARSHAM

Waveney

Little Ouse

GUILTCROSS

Thet

Little Ouse

0   miles   5

0   km   10

Paul Rutledge

Norfolk lies within the Archdiocese of Canterbury and until 1837 it formed with Suffolk a single bishopric. The diocese of East Anglia was established in the 630s when St Felix was sent by Archbishop Honorius to convert the East Angles. The first see was established at the unidentified *Donmoc*, undoubtedly in Suffolk and perhaps at Dunwich or Felixstowe. In the late 7th century, after 672, the diocese was split, with bishops at *Donmoc* and *Elmham*. The coincidence that North Elmham in Norfolk and South Elmham in Suffolk both have the remains of stone churches of early, though hardly pre-11th century, date has made the identification of *Elmham* also uncertain. However, it seems likely that the intention was to respect tribal divisions and give a see each to the Northfolk and the Southfolk, and that North Elmham is the site of the second cathedral.

These sees were destroyed by the Danish invasions and after the reconversion of East Anglia a single bishopric was established about 950. The bishop then had seats at Hoxne in Suffolk and at North Elmham, where excavation has shown the settlement associated with an important ecclesiastical centre. In 1071-2, however, Bishop Herfast moved the see to Thetford following Archbishop Lanfranc's injunction assigning bishoprics to major towns, and about 1095 Bishop Herbert brought it finally to Norwich and began to build the cathedral.

Under the bishop the diocese was adminstered by archdeacons and each archdeaconry was divided, perhaps from the late 11th century, into a number of rural deaneries. These jurisdictions were expressed through a hierarchy of episcopal and archdeaconry courts with oversight of such matters as church repair, will probate and moral offences. Until the move to Norwich the archdeaconry of Norfolk covered the whole county but then the premier archdeaconry of Norwich was created and given the richest parts of the county including the towns of Norwich, Thetford, Lynn and Yarmouth.

In Norfolk the twenty-six deaneries fitted into and respected the boundaries of the ancient hundreds of the county, with the exception of the deaneries of Burnham and Toftrees where there have been later hundred boundary changes. Unlike Suffolk, however, only six deaneries actually covered whole hundreds and took their names. The office of rural dean did not survive the Reformation but the deaneries continued as administrative units. The post of rural dean was revived in 1842.

Little trace of ecclesiastical areas based on great churches or minsters survived the Danish invasions in Norfolk. From the 11th century onwards the parish and the parish church are paramount. Their enormous number bears witness both to Norfolk's prosperity and to the ease with which parishes could be created before the end of the 12th century. Domesday book mentions about 50 churches and chapels in Norwich alone and by the late 13th century the number of parishes in the county approached 800. By the mid-18th century the figure had dropped to about 695. Population changes and new perceptions of spiritual need since the mid-19th century have necessitated the creation of a number of new parishes especially in and near the larger towns and within the great parishes of Marshland where the complex intermingling of boundaries, no doubt reflecting early pastoral arrangements, has also thus been rationalised; these include Little Ouse 1866, Whittington 1875, Nordelph 1909, and Marshland St. James 1922, the latter from parts of ten older parishes. A few places were deemed extra-parochial - for example Alethorpe, Choseley, Feltwell Anchor, Quarles, Redmere and Nowhere near Acle - sometimes from sheer remoteness, sometimes because of the decay of their churches, and sometimes, like the Castle Fee in Norwich, because of special status. Increasingly from the early 16th century the parish also became a unit of civil administration until the creation of parish councils in 1894, since when civil and ecclesiastical parish boundaries have tended to diverge.

There were seven peculiars (exempt from ordinary ecclesiastical jurisdiction) in the county. The two largest, scattered mainly in east Norfolk, included estates that formed the endowment of the bishopric of Norwich and the Cathedral Priory respectively. The bishop's now forgotten peculiar may have included at least North Elmham, Eccles by Thetford, Gaywood, Blickling, Langham, Thornage and Thorpe Episcopi. It lost its exempt status in 1535 when Henry VIII forced him to exchange his estate with that of the abbey of St. Benet, but Thorpe parish continued to be regarded as a bishop's peculiar. The cathedral peculiar survived the Reformation but shrank. In the medieval period it extended also into Hemsby, Hindringham, Scratby, Taverham and Winterton. The pre-Reformation Norwich parish of St. Mathew by the Palace (not shown on map) and the parish of Coston were peculiars of the Archdeacons of Norwich and Norfolk respectively. The other peculiars, in west Norfolk, comprised the five parishes within the Honour of Castle Rising, Great Cressingham where all spiritual jurisdiction was confirmed to the rector in 1297, and Emneth, belonging to the Bishop of Ely and always in Ely Diocese. The peculiars were abolished in 1857.

In 1837 Norwich Diocese lost to Ely sixteen parishes in Cambridgeshire formerly within its jurisdiction and most of Sudbury Archdeaconry in Suffolk. In 1914 on the creation of the new diocese of St. Edmundsbury and Ipswich it lost the rest of Suffolk save the deanery of Lothingland and it yielded to Ely the deaneries of Fincham and Lynn Marshland. In 1894 the new Archdeaconry of Lynn was formed and there have been reorganisations of deanery boundaries in 1918, 1931 and 1970.

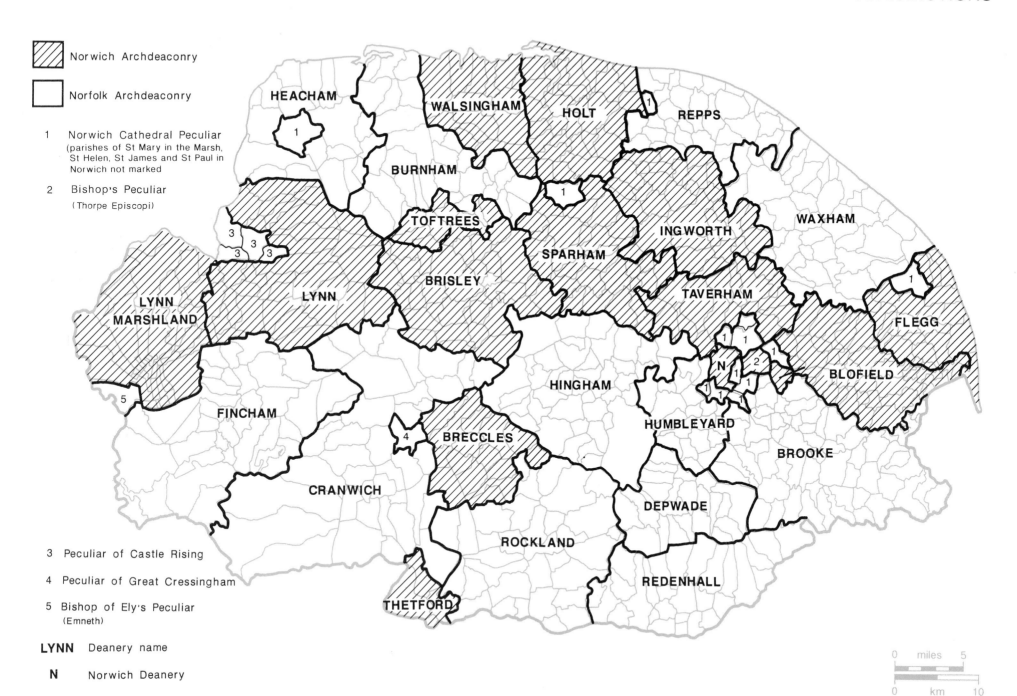

40. ECCLESIASTICAL JURISDICTIONS

Norwich Archdeanry

Norfolk Archdeanry

1 Norwich Cathedral Peculiar
(parishes of St Mary in the Marsh,
St Helen, St James and St Paul in
Norwich not marked)

2 Bishop's Peculiar
(Thorpe Episcopi)

3 Peculiar of Castle Rising

4 Peculiar of Great Cressingham

5 Bishop of Ely's Peculiar
(Emneth)

LYNN Deanery name

N Norwich Deanery

HEACHAM

WALSINGHAM

HOLT

REPPS

BURNHAM

TOFTREES

INGWORTH

WAXHAM

SPARHAM

LYNN
MARSHLAND

LYNN

BRISLEY

TAVERHAM

FLEGG

BLOFIELD

FINCHAM

HINGHAM

HUMBLEYARD

BROOKE

BRECCLES

CRANWICH

DEPWADE

ROCKLAND

REDENHALL

THETFORD

0 miles 5

0 km 10

In 1538, Thomas Cromwell, as Vicar General, ordered that registers should be kept by every parish recording weekly, all baptisms, marriages and burials. These were to be kept in the parish chest, with keys for the incumbent and two churchwardens. Several problems arose. It was often difficult to get all keyholders together to open the chest and without some form of notebook, it became impossible, particularly in the larger parishes, to remember all the ceremonies for the previous week. By 1598, when a new order from Parliament required paper registers to be copied into parchment books, maintenance of some parishes and their Catholic registers had been abandoned. It is difficult to quantify the exact number but the losses must be high. In addition, the task of copying met with little enthusiasm and comparisons of some paper and parchment registers show a degree of carelessness and lack of scholarship.

Between 1645 and 1666, ecclesiastical registration was abolished and marriages, required to be by Banns, became a civil responsibility. Few Commonwealth registers survived. Some parishes continued entries throughout this period. Some clearly attempted to copy entries into their old registers, whilst others obtained past details from those still living in the parish at the Restoration. By far the majority of registers have large gaps during this period. From March 1754, Lord Hardwick's Marriage Act, designed to prevent clandestine marriages, instituted registers independent from those for baptisms and burials and further ordered that parties should sign before witnesses or make their mark. Banns, either in separate or composite printed registers were introduced at the same time. From 1813, Rose's Act introduced standard printed registers allowing for residence and occupations to be included for baptisms and for burials, details of residence and age. In 1837, new printed registers for marriage required the names and occupations of the fathers of the two parties.

The extent of register survival is due as much to neglect as fate. Some were destroyed as they became complete; some were accidentally destroyed by fire; many suffered as a result of war bombing and in more recent times, some were stolen either through lack of supervision or burglary. Of the 710 Norfolk parishes with extant registers prior to 1837, 452 have survived from the 16th century in the form of either the original paper register or the parchment transcript. Of the remaining registers with early transcripts, 59 now commence in the 17th century, 47 in the 18th century and three in the 19th century. Of those with no known early transcripts, 88 commence in the 17th century, 58 in the 18th century and three in the 19th century.

Bishop's Transcripts

Generally, this term refers to all annual transcripts of registers sent periodically to ecclesiastical dignitaries. However, in the Norwich diocese, these are known as Bishop's and Archdeacon's transcripts both series being in the Norfolk Record Office. The former are arranged annually and the latter, with the exception of Norwich, are arranged by parish. For a few parishes in the Norfolk Archdeaconry, a long run from the 16th century survives amongst the parish papers but there are no complete runs. Annual returns with wide gaps survive from 1685. Norwich Archdeaconry Transcripts, with many gaps, survive from 1600 with the exception of Great Yarmouth (1696-1812) and Castle Rising (1736-1818). Norfolk Archdeaconry Transcripts commence only from 1725 and run to 1811. Transcripts for the Peculiar of the Dean and Chapter of Norwich run from 1706 to 1811 but there are none for the Peculiar of Great Cressingham. Indexes to Bishop's Transcripts for the years 1685-91, 1705 and 1715 have been published by the Norfolk and Norwich Genealogical Society. After 1812, all transcripts are regarded as Bishops Transcripts and are available in microform.

Copies of Parish Registers

Microforms of some registers are available in the Norwich Shirehall search room. A large number of printed, transcript and microform copies are also held by the Norfolk and Norwich Genealogical Society, whilst some transcripts are held by the Norwich Local History Library and the Norfolk and Norwich Archaeological Society. Where early registers have been lost, these copies represent the oldest record. The Norfolk and Norwich Genealogical Society has to date published 32 parish registers and an index to Norwich marriages from 1812 to 1837. Marriages for several parishes have been published by Phillimore and incorporated into Boyd's Marriage Index but the degree of inaccuracy renders both totally unreliable. A more accurate and fuller Norfolk Marriage Index from 1538 to 1812 is in the process of compilation. Invariably, commencing dates of baptisms differ from commencing dates of marriages and burials, so map dates used refer to the oldest ceremony registered but do not imply continuity from that date. Where an earlier transcript or microfilm is available, an asterisk is appended. The qualifying date for inclusion of registers is taken as 1837, the start of national registration. Where the village marked is extra-parochial, or where the parish registers have been combined as a result of parish unification and no extant registers are known, the village is marked with an 'X'.

Apart from a small number of registers still with incumbents, the majority of registers are held by the Norfolk Record Office, the Cambridgeshire Record Office and the Wisbech and Fenland Museum.

Six letters have been used where map space available does not allow the inclusion of dates; the lists for these parishes have been inserted in the *Further Reading* section.

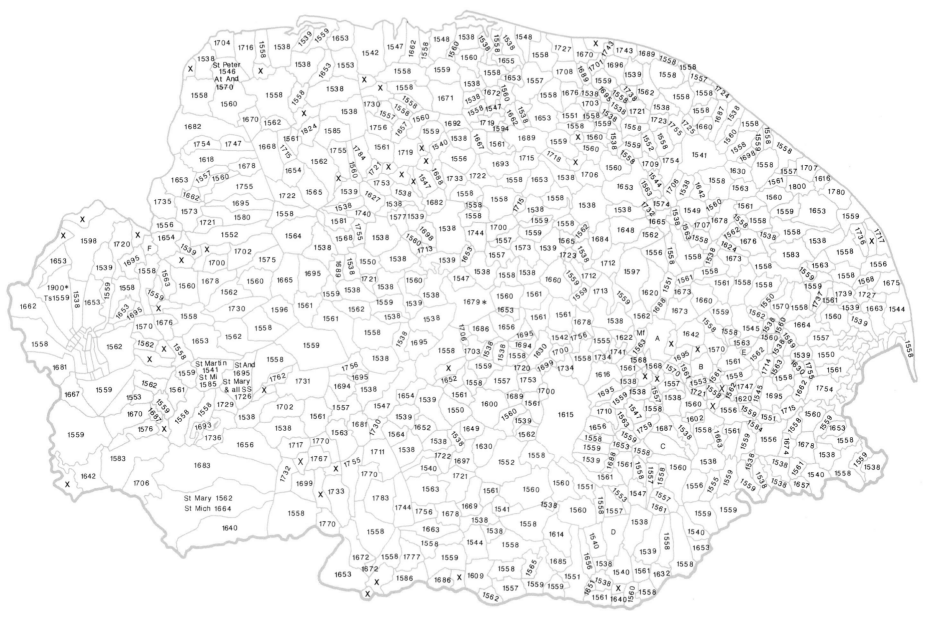

St Peter
1546
At And
1570

St Martin
1541
St Mi
1585

St And
1695
St Mary
& all SS
1726

St Mary 1562
St Mich 1664

1900*
Ts1559

1679 *

Mf

A

B

C

D

E

F

0   miles   5

0   km   10

Estimates of population in the early 16th century are based necessarily on the surviving subsidy returns of the 1520s. The wealthier members of the community were normally named in the Military Survey and in the subsidy assessments for both 1524 and 1525. The very poor were seldom or never named in their entirety, however. As the primary purpose of both the Survey and the subsidies was to extract money there was little to be gained in systematically recording everyone who had nothing to contribute, and it has been generally conceded that any listing is likely to be deficient by some 20 to 25 per cent. While the extent of omission obviously varied from place to place, it is usual to add 20 per cent or so to those actually recorded, and to use the resulting figure as the basis for calculating population.

Dr. John Patten, who originally produced the maps used in this section, after adding the usual 20 per cent to the total, plus a further 10 per cent for the very poor, assumed a similar number of females and added 40 per cent for the under fifteens.

As the map clearly indicates, there was considerable variation in the distribution of population throughout the county. The densest population was to be found in an area running north-south, mostly containing some 76 persons per 1,000 acres. To the east and west, in contrast, there were large areas of relatively low population density. As one would expect, the lower areas tended to be concentrated in those parts of the county where the soil was least productive, as in the poorly-drained fens and in the area of the poor sands in north Norfolk which was then 'a relative desert of warrens and sheep-runs'.

In complete contrast were the rich farming lands of north-east and central Norfolk, the latter including the Hundreds of Mitford and Forehoe where freeholdings of 30 acres and above predominated, and the textile-making areas to the north-east of Norwich.

Norwich contained some 8,500 people, King's Lynn and Great Yarmouth in excess of 4,000, while market towns such as Wymondham, Aylsham and East Dereham were approaching 1,000. The population of the county as a whole had reached about 112,000 in the 1520s, according to Patten's estimate, and possessed some of the highest densities of population in England.

Population figures for the next half century are derived essentially from the Communicant Returns of 1603, a source which, although defective in many ways, permits, in the opinion of Dr.Patten, 'an adequate description of the population of Norfolk and Suffolk'.

These returns suggest an overall population increase of some 27 per cent for the population of Norfolk as a whole, with the towns increasing at a slightly higher rate of 30 per cent. The increase in individual towns was higher still, reaching 37 per cent in Norwich and Great Yarmouth, although in the case of the former this was largely accounted for by a remarkable influx of alien refugees, an influx which led to the city containing some 7 per cent of the county's population by the turn of the century. By 1603 the population of Norfolk had reached some 252,000.

The information referred to above is inevitably drawn from limited data. Norwich, in contrast, provides a number of sources from which demographic data can be derived: a very full muster, taken in 1569, which listed 2,285 able-bodied males; the comprehensive census of the poor taken in the following year which recorded details of 525 men, 860 women, and almost 1,000 of their children, a total of 2,359 individuals; and, above all, the weekly listings of births and deaths which began during the severe outbreak of plague in 1579 and continued uninterruptedly until 1646.

The first of these recorded the names of most, if not all, able-bodied males in Norwich aged between 16 and 60. When allowance has been made for omissions, and an appropriate number of women and children added, the source suggests a population of some 8,190, or one little different from that of 50 years before. The situation changed dramatically during the next decade when increasing numbers of Dutch and Walloon refugees were admitted to the city. Originally limited to 30 families, their numbers had reached an astonishing 6,000 or so prior to the outbreak of plague in 1579, an influx which raised the city's population to around 15,000.

The plague of 1579-80 decimated the population, both English and alien. A positive result of the outbreak, however, was the appointment of a virtual Registrar of Births and Deaths. Initially responsible for the provision of weekly totals of deaths, differentiating between plague and ordinary deaths and between English and Dutch, the person concerned was subsequently required to record births as well as deaths. The source is especially valuable as some of the parish registers from which the figures were undoubtedly drawn have now disappeared. It is these figures which make it clear that the city's population was reduced by 5-6,000, by the plague, and although it had recovered to around 11,000 by the turn of the century, repeated outbreaks of plague ensured that it did not exceed this figure until well into the Stuart period.

Recorded Population per 1000 acres

56.8 lower quartile

75.2 median

112.2 upper quartile

0 miles 5

0 km 10

Any discussion of the distribution of wealth in the early 16th century must be based primarily on an analysis of the appropriate material in the subsidy returns of the 1520s, supplemented, if at all possible, by the surviving details of the Military Survey taken in 1522.

The Military Survey, which was the basis for a substantial loan to finance Henry VIII's French wars, was a virtual Tudor Domesday. Ostensibly inaugurated to establish details of the available arms and armour in time of war, the commissioners appointed were also required to obtain details, on oath, of the goods and freehold lands, where appropriate, of everybody above the age of 15. The information obtained was used to extract a loan of unprecedented severity and subsequently for the subsidies demanded in 1524 and 1525, when people paid on either goods or land, whichever brought in the greatest revenue.

The Military Survey, which recorded details of both goods and lands, is obviously the most useful guideline to the county's wealth, but unfortunately it has survived for only Great Yarmouth and 11 hundreds, mostly situated in the east and north of the county. The subsidy details, in contrast, largely survive in their entirety and the map provided is necessarily based on this information. Some discussion of the Military Survey is essential, however, not least because it has been examined in detail, in contrast to the subsidy material which, at the moment, has been used only to determine the tax paid by the individual hundreds.

The Survey suggests that wealth was more evenly distributed in both town and country districts in 1522 than an examination of the subsequent subsidy payments would suggest. Whereas in Great Yarmouth the traditional picture can be discerned, with an upper class of some seven per cent owning 52 per cent of the movable goods, with no more than six per cent of the property being in the possession of those worth between £1 and £2; elsewhere the bulk of the property tended to be in the hands of a middling group situated somewhere in the £5 to £39 range, with the average wealth of the taxpayers ranging from just under £5 in Happing Hundred to rather more than £10 in Great Yarmouth itself. This is especially noticeable in Blofield where the wealthy - i.e., those worth £40 and above - owned little more than 14 per cent of the hundred's wealth, in Tunstead where they owned less than one-fifth, and in Walsham where the proportion was just over one-quarter. In contrast to the larger towns assessed in 1524 and beyond where the wage-earners or those with £1 worth of goods usually comprised some 40 per cent of all the taxpayers, those in rural Norfolk seldom constituted one-third of the population and usually considerably less than that. Absolute poverty ranged from one in five in West Flegg to just over one-third in South Erpingham.

Landed wealth is a feature of the Norfolk material. Freeholders were most numerous in Gallow where they made up 68 per cent of the property-owning classes, closely followed by Great Yarmouth and Brothercross, each with around 64 per cent. More than half of those enumerated in the hundreds of North Greenhoe and Holt were similarly endowed, with the figure only falling below 30 per cent in West Flegg and Tunstead. Landholdings tended to be small, seldom reaching 30 acres, with 15 acres or less being the norm in such hundreds as Gallow, Brothercross and North Greenhoe.

While the subsidy returns are less full than this they provide a reasonably accurate picture of the nation's wealth, embracing everyone from the wealthiest peer to the humblest wage-earner. Only those with literally nothing to record escaped the net.

The major towns in the county are excluded from the map to avoid undue distortion. It should be noted, however, that Norwich, the largest and wealthiest city in England after London, paid £749 in tax, its assessment being almost five times as great as the wealthiest hundred in Norfolk, with one ward - the extremely rich Middle Wymer - itself paying more tax than the otherwise outstanding hundred of Freebridge Marshland.

All other areas are included, the map being concerned with the amount of tax actually paid and following the usual pattern of recording wealth in shillings per square mile. This suggests that the richest hundreds were to be found in the north of the county, with pockets of individual wealth in the centre and south-east, while the less prosperous areas were to the west and south, with the notable exception of Freebridge Marshland. While this method has some advantages over the 'league-table' approach which usually, although by no means invariably, places the larger hundreds at the top and the smaller ones at the bottom, it does tend to conceal the very real predominance of certain areas. Freebridge Marshland, for example, consistently paid the highest tax, the larger towns apart, from the medieval period to the late 17th century and beyond. Clackclose was similarly rich and yet in terms of wealth per square mile appears among the poorer hundreds. In contrast, the smaller hundreds of East and West Flegg who produced the least wealth in terms of tax paid feature in the middle ranks when wealth per square mile is considered.

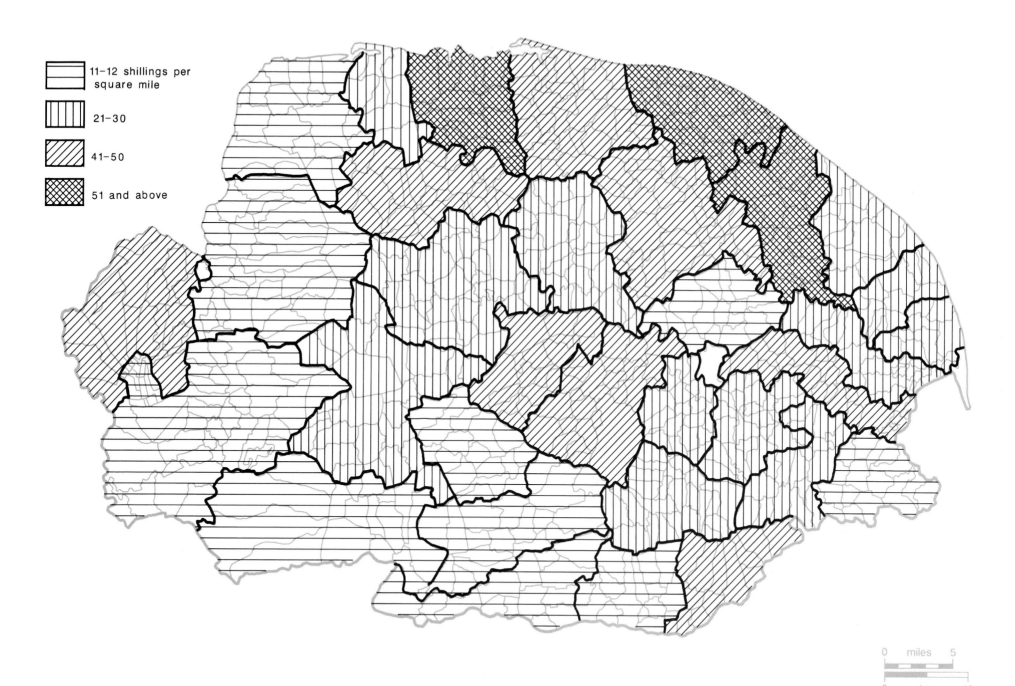

11–12 shillings per
square mile

21–30

41–50

51 and above

0   miles   5

0   km   10

The unusual nature of Kett's rebellion is summed up in the Suffolk epithet 'the campyng tyme'. Rather than attempt a march on London, the protesters gathered near administrative centres in camps that were remarkable for their order and organisation. Over 10,000 men camped for almost seven weeks in the largest, just outside Norwich, the second city in the kingdom. Here services were held daily, justice administered, warrants issued and governors chosen for 24 Norfolk hundreds (and one for Suffolk). Support came not only from individuals but also from communities. The township of Carlton Colville, Suffolk, provided money, while men from North Elmham attended with their clerk and were provisioned and paid 3d a day by the parish.

In spite of 29 articles drawn up by the Norwich camp, the causes and aims of the rising are not entirely clear. It neither opposed recent religious changes, like the Western Rebellion, nor espoused the cause of Princess Mary, later Mary I, then at Kenninghall. The uprising was sparked off by trouble over enclosures, a problem that the government was attempting to control. Several articles attacked unreasonable demands from manorial lords apart from enclosure, including the much quoted 'We pray that all bond men may be made free'. The other main target was bad local government, with the rising showing particular animosity towards administrators and lawyers. By stimulating gentry rivalries, the Duke of Norfolk's fall in 1547 may have affected adversely those rebel leaders who came from just below the governing class and local rivalry certainly precipitated Kett's initial involvement.

The rebellion grew from minor unrest in the wake of festivities at Wymondham on 6th and 7th July 1549. On 8th July a small band, engaged in destroying enclosures, was bribed by the lawyer John Flowerdew to attack Robert Kett's fences at Wymondham. Unexpectedly Kett supported their efforts and led the group against Flowerdew's Hethersett closes. So far the affair was no more serious than action already taken against enclosures in Norfolk and elsewhere, but the protesters continued towards Norwich under Kett's leadership. Refused passage through the city, they skirted it to the north and on 12th July camped on Mousehold Heath, overlooking Norwich from the east.

Although events near Norwich are the best recorded, they were accompanied by risings elsewhere in south Norfolk and north Suffolk. Within a week of the original disturbances, camps had been established at Downham Market, Bury St. Edmunds and Ipswich. The Ipswich camp later moved to Melton, Suffolk. Initially there was little violence though there were unsuccessful attempts to gain control of King's Lynn (from a camp near Castle Rising) and Great Yarmouth.

The turning point came on 21st July when the refusal of an offer of pardon branded Kett's followers as rebels and ended previous co-operation from the Norwich authorities. Military action became inevitable and Kett took the city by 23rd July. On 31st July the first relieving force, having apparently subdued the Bury camp, entered Norwich unopposed under the Marquess of Northampton. Norwich was retaken by Kett the following day, but the Melton camp accepted an offer of pardon by 3rd August. Minor camps at Watton and Hingham had already moved to Norwich and the Mousehold camp was now on its own. Two further rebel attempts to take Yarmouth on 5th and 17th August failed, and a government force under the Earl of Warwick recovered Norwich on 24th August. Two days later German mercenaries joined Warwick and Kett, perhaps to avoid being cut off from the rest of the county, decided to risk battle on open ground. Kett's army was routed at Dussindale (Thorpe St. Andrew) on 27th August. Robert Kett and his brother William survived the battle but were captured, tried and executed.

While most Norfolk incidents in the rebellion took place in south Norfolk, support was not limited to this area.

The map shows the known parishes of origin of rebels. It leaves out those whose crimes were not ostensibly part of the uprising and cannot show Suffolk supporters. There is little significance in the relative numbers of rebels, and the map reflects the chance discovery and survival of sources. Nevertheless, the distribution (except in north-east Norfolk) is supported by the largest single source used, a list of 29 prisoners at Norwich, Lynn and Yarmouth pardoned in March 1550. There is no reason why this group should show any particular topographical bias.

The resulting pattern indicates county-wide support for the rising, with the possible exceptions of north-east and south-west Norfolk. South-west Norfolk was also the area of the county not appointed governors by Kett, perhaps because it fell within the ambit of the camp at Downham Market. It has been suggested that support was greatest in the wood/pasture rather than the sheep/corn areas of Norfolk (Map 46) as enclosures could work to the tenants' advantage in the latter. However the rebels' demands indicate that the issue was enclosure of commons rather than enclosure of arable, a matter that affected manorial tenants throughout the county equally.

Kett's rebellion remains a paradox. Apparently spontaneous, its organisation and rapid spread suggest prior planning. Led by a man who was himself an encloser and minor manorial lord, it could claim with more than usual justification to uphold government policy. But such a rising had no future. In an age which treated peaceful protest as rebellion, the camps had either to disband or be destroyed.

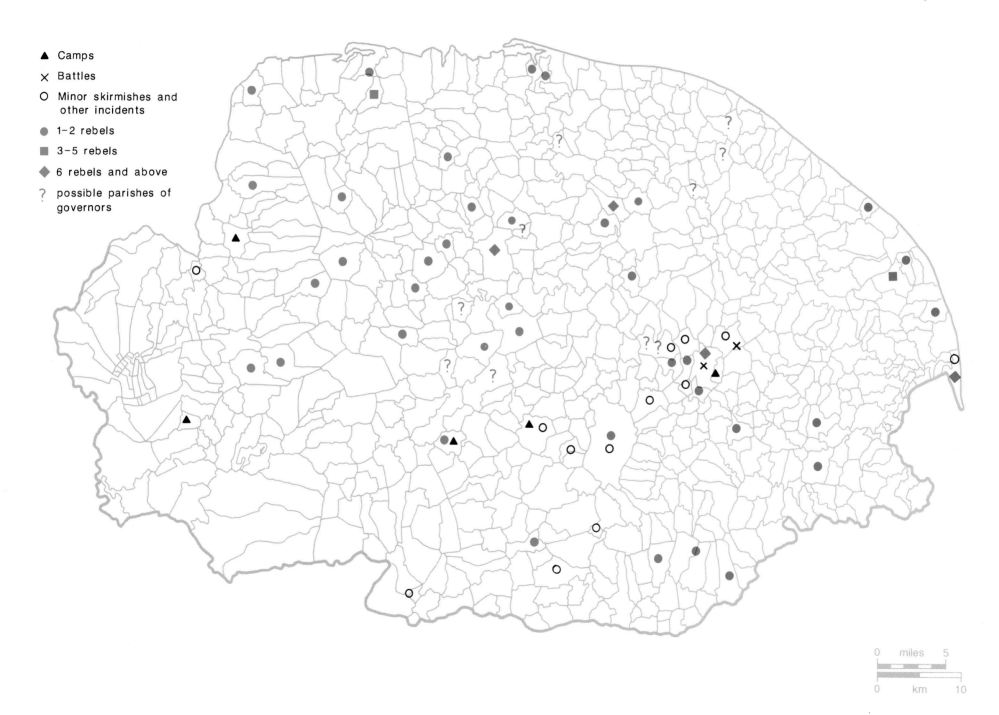

Camps ▲

Battles ✕

Minor skirmishes and
other incidents ○

1–2 rebels ●

3–5 rebels ■

6 rebels and above ◆

possible parishes of
governors ?

On 30th June 1603 Archbishop Whitgift wrote to his bishops instructing them to procure certain information about the clergy and laity of their dioceses. He needed to prepare a report for the new king, James I, on the state of the Church, and in particular on the number of recusants, i.e. those who refused to take the communion and attend the services of the Church of England. Within a fortnight Bishop John Jegon sent a copy of Whitgift's letter to all four archdeacons of his diocese, asking for answers to the questions 'att or before the 12 of August next'. The archdeacons were required to 'send for everie parson, vicar, and curat within their severall juridictions, and as secretlie and particularlie as they came to receive of them in wrightinge their severall awnswers.' This information was to be sent to the bishop, who would forward it to Whitgift. The questions to be answered were

1. 'the certaine nomber of those that doe receive the communion in everie severall parrishe'.
2. The numbers of male and female recusants within each parish.
3. The numbers of men and women who do not receive the communion.

The remaining four questions concerned the qualifications of the clergy and the value of benefices. The answers to the first three questions, and particularly question 1, form the basis of this map.

The law of the Church of England and the realm relating to attendance at church and taking the communion was complicated. The Act of Uniformity of 1559 imposed a fine of 12d. for each offence on every person not attending church on Sundays and other appointed days, and this was reinforced by later Elizabethan acts. Attendance at church, and in particular willingness to take the Holy Communion according to the Book of Common Prayer, was the touchstone of adherence to the established church and, by implication, to the Crown and its government. In the Canons of 1603/4, based on earlier codes, canon 21 ordered the clergy to provide communion regularly so that 'every parishioner may communicate at least thrice in the year', and canon 22 affirms that 'every lay person is bound to receive the holy communion thrice every year'. The rubric to the communion service in the 1559 Book of Common Prayer directs that intending communicants shall give their names to the curate (i.e. the celebrant) before the communion service; if this practice had been strictly followed it should have provided evidence in the visitations and courts of non-communication and, in 1603, for the incumbents' answers to Whitgift's questions.

In theory, the sum of the total in the answers to questions 1-3 should give the total adult population, that is, those over the age of 13-15, the usual age of confirmation - the necessary preliminary to taking the communion. The figures for recusants and those not receiving communion are little more than negligible; in Norwich archdeaconry only 116 are recorded, less than 0.37% of the total of communicants and non-communicants. In the episcopal visitation of 1597, in the same archdeaconry only 50 men and women were presented for not receiving the communion, and in some cases for not attending church, and another 48 were presented for the sole offence of not attending divine service. The impression from both visitations and the 1603 list is that there were relatively few persistent non-churchgoers or non-communicants.

The 1603 figures for communicants may be less accurate than those for non-communicants, at least in the final digit. In Norwich archdeaconry, out of 281 returns, 50 (18%) are in hundreds e.g. 100, 200, and another 168 (60%) are in intermediate round figures e.g. 60, 130. The round figures are more numerous (90%) in those parishes with over 100 communicants than in those with under 99 communicants (66%). Even allowing for those parishes where a genuine head-count produced a 'round' figure, the suspicion must remain that many parsons, especially those in larger parishes, gave an approximate figure, at best rounded up or down to the nearest unit of ten.

Even if the communicant figures are approximately correct, they represent only the adult population, i.e. those over the age of 13-15. Assuming that roughly three-fifths of the population at this time were adults, an approximate total population could be obtained by multiplying the 1603 figure by 10/6. Crude checks against baptismal figures from a few parish registers suggest that communicant-derived population figures may not be too inaccurate. However, the use of multipliers cannot be guaranteed to produce a reliable figure for total population, and the best use of the 1603 return, as most taxation and population figures before 1801, is to compare parish with parish and area with area.

The map shows that the most populous parishes were in a broad belt that ran from the coast, between Walsingham and Waxham deaneries, through central Norfolk before turning south east to Redenhall. This pattern is similar to that on other maps e.g. the boulder clay, Domesday woodland, medieval moats, and medieval deer-parks, though it bears no obvious relationship to any of these; neither is the acreage of parishes critically related, as parishes in the western third of the county are on average up to twice as large as those in the central belt.

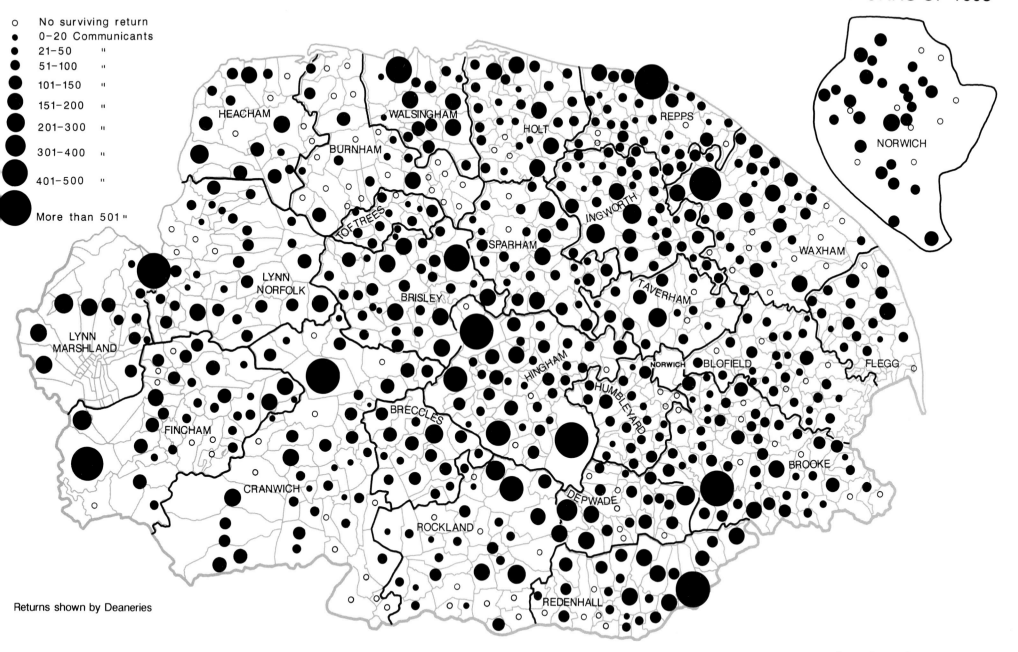

Legend:

○	No surviving return
●	0–20 Communicants
●	21–50 "
●	51–100 "
●	101–150 "
●	151–200 "
●	201–300 "
●	301–400 "
●	401–500 "
●	More than 501 "

HEACHAM
WALSINGHAM
REPPS
BURNHAM
HOLT
NORWICH
TOFTREES
INGWORTH
SPARHAM
WAXHAM
LYNN NORFOLK
BRISLEY
TAVERHAM
LYNN MARSHLAND
HINGHAM
NORWICH
BLOFIELD
FLEGG
BRECCLES
HUMBLEYARD
FINCHAM
CRANWICH
DEPWADE
BROOKE
ROCKLAND
REDENHALL

Returns shown by Deaneries

0 miles 5
0 km 10

Expressed simply, Norfolk was divided into five agricultural zones in the early modern period. These zones were characterised by differences of surface geology, especially between the sands and gravels of the heath districts and the loams and clays of east Norfolk. Soil, however, was not the only influence. Access to markets, manorial tradition, estate administration also contributed to the practice of husbandry, while the structure of rural society was variously founded upon prevailing inheritance customs, population density and the existence of manufacturing in the countryside. The distinction between woodland (by 1580 essentially deforested) and fielden (open-field) Norfolk turned more upon the social environment of their villages than upon the conventional differences between pastoral and arable regimes of production.

East Norfolk was divided into two zones; the south-eastern quadrant, including Diss, Loddon and Wymondham, made up largely of boulder clay soils, was celebrated for its rural textile industries and its dairies; the north-eastern area contained some ancient weaving townships, Aylsham, Cawston and Worsted, but it was pre-eminently agricultural, producing high quality malting barley, wheat and fat cattle. This north-eastern area was the most advanced part of the county from the 13th to the 18th centuries. Much of it enjoyed a fertile, free-draining loam, good for crops, for dairies and for out-wintering cattle. Sheep were less important than cattle throughout east Norfolk. In the 16th century farmers who kept dairies chiefly for butter also reared young cattle. Feeding bullocks attained considerable dimensions. On both clay and loam soils by 1650 this activity encouraged the purchase of leanstock, exemplified in the expansion of bullock fairs such as St. Faiths and Hempton and brought about experiments with fallow-break plants, first pulses, then clover and trefoil and turnips, to supplement the winter diet of straw. Hay was scarce in east Norfolk but the *economic* benefits of feeding cattle depended upon overwintering. By 1650 the great fairs were supplied with store beasts from the north of England, Wales and, above all, from Scotland. East Norfolk was not predominantly pastoral. Open-fields were small and irregular; arable cultivation was not confined to the fields and farmers were not restricted by manorial regulation in their choice of crops. On the clays at least half of the land was in grass; on the loams probably around one-third, including marsh and water meadows.

The Heathlands were also divided. On the good soils, sands, gravel and light loam, around Fakenham and Holt, where the later reputation of Norfolk for its agricultural excellence was established, a complex field system interspersed with common heath or sheepwalk had developed. The fields were usually irregular in size and the traditional three-shift rotation was organised around furlongs (segments of the open fields). Most tenants had begun the process of piecemeal enclosure by 1600, especially by reclaiming parts of the heath in what were called 'brecks' which were cultivated intermittently in a sequence of crops and grass. Enclosing the heath was, however, made difficult by the continued existence of the lords' fold-rights, since even in the 17th century most heathland manors retained 'fold courses', or an exclusive right to graze a number of sheep over the land of the manor. Tenants were discouraged from keeping sheep on their own account so that the characteristic sheep-corn system of the sandlands depended for its viability upon the lords' flocks.

South-west Norfolk was a county of poor, arid soils in which arable production was more precarious than on the 'good sands' north of Swaffham. Here irregular cropping in the heath was practised beside a system of 'every year' lands, in which crops were taken in each season, thanks largely to careful fertilisation and the spreading of marl. Sheep were folded on the 'every year' lands and also ranged freely on the heaths grazing on rough pasture or on sainfoin sown in the 'brecks' after corn.

The Marshland or fen land of Norfolk was a complex region in which agriculture depended on the state of draining, attended to but not very successfully in the 17th century. Much of the zone was in permanent grass, feeding large herds of bullocks and, less frequently, equally large flocks of long-wool sheep. Part was always water-logged in winter. This land could carry stock in summer or bear late-spring-sown crops, oats, hemp or tick beans. There was also a stretch of land under regular all-year cropping, which even grew winter beans and wheat, in something like a three-field system. The Norfolk Marshland was characteristically the same as the fens of Suffolk, Cambridgeshire or Lincolnshire.

These details changed through time, for agriculture was subject to market forces before 1750. In general however, the agrarian economy of the period remained remarkably consistent.

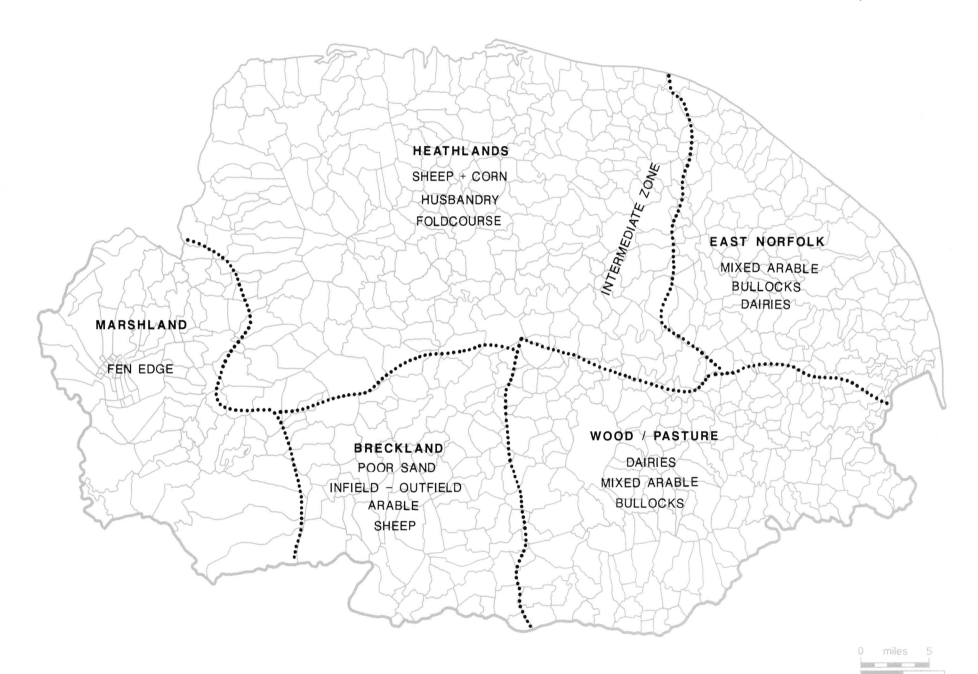

HEATHLANDS

SHEEP + CORN

HUSBANDRY

FOLDCOURSE

INTERMEDIATE ZONE

EAST NORFOLK

MIXED ARABLE

BULLOCKS

DAIRIES

MARSHLAND

FEN EDGE

BRECKLAND

POOR SAND

INFIELD – OUTFIELD

ARABLE

SHEEP

WOOD / PASTURE

DAIRIES

MIXED ARABLE

BULLOCKS

0 miles 5

0 km 10

47. THE DRAINAGE OF THE NORFOLK FENS

Bob Silvester

Never more than a few metres above, and now in some places even below, sea level, the Fens have inevitably required drainage to convert them to the rich farmland apparent to anyone heading westwards out of Norfolk. The chronicle of attempts to turn bog and marsh to pasture and arable spans nearly two millennia, from the small-scale operations of Roman settlers colonising the silts edging the coast to the major engineering project known as the Murdoch Macdonald scheme that was completed less than thirty years ago. We should not, however, see drainage as an invariable objective of those who cut new lodes and diverted existing waterways. Other functions - flood prevention, transport facilitation and, most recently, water transfer to reservoirs - have frequently been of equal or greater importance.

The Norfolk Fens are divided between the siltlands bordering the Wash and the peat levels further inland. Each area has its own characteristic settlement history, resulting in very different patterns of land use and drainage. The exploitation of the silts occurred first. Although the Roman colonisation was short-lived, the siltlands were re-settled in the Saxon period and witnessed sustained development after the Norman Conquest. Marshland, as this region came to be known, was drained by a multitude of dykes that separated the small individual holdings. These dykes discharged into larger drains which delivered the waters either into the great rivers that edged the silts, the Nene in the west and the Great Ouse to the east, or seawards through culverts beneath the great sea bank that protected Marshland. The drainage systems expanded in tandem with the reclamation of the silts, reflecting a pragmatic approach to a perennial problem and in marked contrast to the grand designs imposed on the neighbouring peat fens in later centuries.

The peat fens of the Middle Ages were utilised but not tamed. They offered a range of natural resources, but there were few attempts to transform the landscape. Slow-moving rivers meandering across the peat levels were straightened as much to ease transport problems as to improve drainage. The Little Ouse, the Great Ouse and the Nar all took up new courses and it is tempting to see in these changes the hand of the major monasteries that thrived on the higher reaches.

At the beginning of the 17th century a new wave of entreprenurial enthusiasm threatened the Fens. The potential profits of draining and farming blocks of fenland appealed to wealthy individuals. Various schemes were proposed. All ultimately failed, but relics of these enterprises remain: London Lode running into the Well Creek at Nordelph was probably constructed by London merchants at the beginning of the century and only a few years later the cutting of Popham's Eau from the Old River Nene to the Well Creek was financed by the Lord Chief Justice and others.

But it was the ambitious project devised by the Earl of Bedford and the engineer Vermuyden that marked the first unitary attempt to drain the southern peat fens. Between 1630 and 1653 existing rivers were straightened and new cuts made to carry water more rapidly to the outfalls. The outstanding achievements of this phase were the Old and New Bedford Rivers, parallel channels that confined a gigantic 'reservoir' for winter floodwater known as The Washes. Other new watercourses have lasted less well. Sam's Cut, which took the waters of a Feltwell stream directly to the Great Ouse, is now largely obsolete although its course is still maintained by a secondary road.

Drainage of the peat fens initiated a cycle of events that could not have been foreseen by the early drainers. The removal of water led to the drying out of the peat and the consequent fall in the level of the land. Within a century windmills were universally adopted to pump water from the field dykes into the main drains which remained at a higher level. In the 19th century the windmill gave way to steam engines housed in pumping stations. These too have now been superseded by electrically driven pumps. Relics of these earlier methods of drainage are rare, but Nordelph can still boast the shell of a windmill beside the Well Creek, and near Hilgay on the south bank of the Wissey is a derelict pumping station.

The 18th and 19th centuries brought improvements to the outfalls of the Nene and the Great Ouse. In the estuaries the channels of these rivers were straightened and below King's Lynn a loop of the Ouse was removed with the opening of the Eau Brink Cut in 1821. A few years later in 1848, waters from the Isle of Ely were channelled across Marshland along the Middle Level Drain to the Great Ouse.

For the moment the picture of fenland drainage is completed by the Murdoch Macdonald scheme of the post-war years. In times of flood the waters of the Lark, Little Ouse and Wissey can be diverted into the Cut-off Channel which runs around the eastern fringe of the Suffolk and Norfolk Fens, and thence into the Relief Channel which follows a direct course to the Eau Brink Cut. In times to come further major drainage works may be required, for with the seemingly inevitable rise in sea level the Fens will be one of the largest coastal regions in this country under threat.

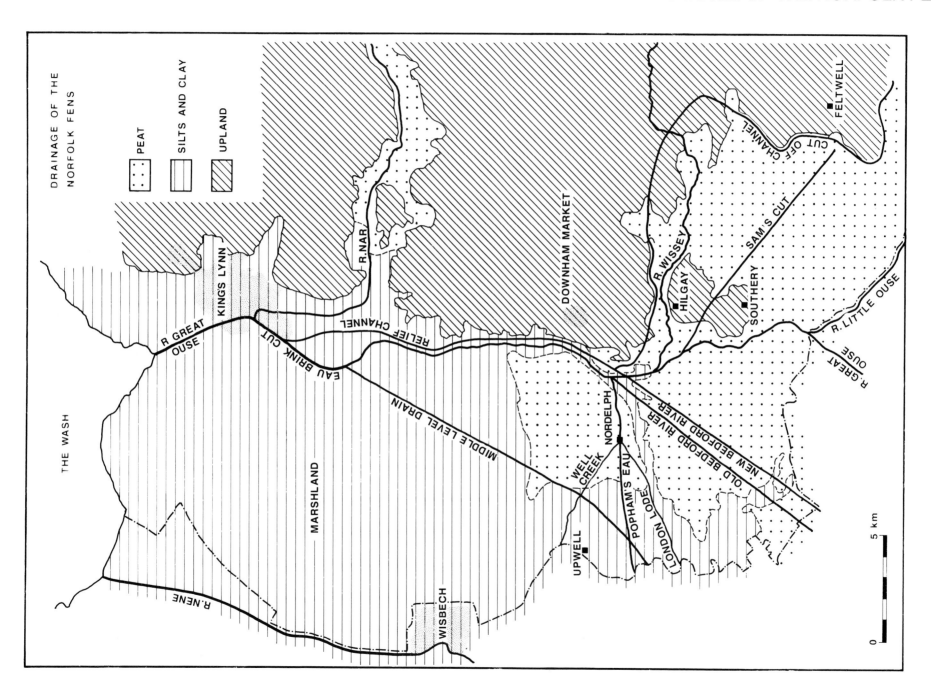

DRAINAGE OF THE NORFOLK FENS

PEAT

SILTS AND CLAY

UPLAND

THE WASH

R GREAT OUSE

KINGS LYNN

R. NAR

DOWNHAM MARKET

FELTWELL

CUT OFF CHANNEL

R. WISSEY

SAM'S CUT

HILGAY

SOUTHERY

R. LITTLE OUSE

R.GREAT OUSE

RELIEF CHANNEL

EAU BRINK CUT

MIDDLE LEVEL DRAIN

MARSHLAND

NORDELPH

NEW BEDFORD RIVER

OLD BEDFORD RIVER

WELL CREEK

POPHAM'S EAU

LONDON LODE

UPWELL

WISBECH

R. NENE

5 km

0

48. THE GENTRY OF NORFOLK DURING THE CIVIL WAR

Gordon Blackwood

The gentry of Norfolk were those landowners *consistently* described in official documents as baronets, knights, esquires and gentlemen, and recognised as such by their contemporaries. Were they predominantly Royalist or Parliamentarian during the Civil Wars of 1642-48? They were neither, and probably mainly neutral. Of the 633 gentry families of Norfolk in 1642, only 186 (29%) participated in the conflict. This is, of course, a conservative estimate, yet many of the other 447 families (71%) must have been neutral because Norfolk was not one of the major theatres of war, and most gentlemen were not forced to choose sides.

Two other general points must be mentioned. First, unlike the situation in Lancashire, the allegiance of local gentry owed little to the influence of nobles. The three Royalist peers named on the map - the Earl of Dorset, Lord Abergavenny and Lord Maltravers - were neither influential nor resident in the county. Secondly, few gentry families in Norfolk were 'by the sword divided'. The 21 families who did split, or whose members changed sides (shown on the map by two-coloured symbols), formed only 11% of the combatant families.

The map opposite shows those gentry families of Norfolk who between 1642 and 1648 served either Charles I or Parliament in a military or civil capacity. A cursory glance reinforces the current view that the Parliamentarians had an overwhelming majority over their opponents. 106 gentry families supported Parliament but only 59 the king. But if we look more closely and concentrate on the activists (i.e. brave or high-ranking soldiers and/or conscientious civilian officials), a different picture emerges. Both Parliamentarian and Royalist activist families numbered 48. Perhaps, then, Norfolk should be seen as an evenly divided county rather than a Roundhead heartland - at least as regards the gentry.

The map shows that both Parliamentarian and Royalist gentry (active and passive alike) were widely dispersed and not concentrated in particular areas, as was the case in Lancashire. But, in all the main agricultural regions (Map 46) the Parliamentarian gentry were in a majority. In the Broadland hundreds of East Flegg, West Flegg, Happing and Walsham the Parliamentarian gentry families literally outnumbered their opponents by two to one. In the Fenland district - comprising Freebridge Marshland hundred and western Clackclose and western Grimshoe - there were five Parliamentarians and two Royalist families. In the sheep-corn region - embracing Brothercross, Erpingham North, Erpingham South, Eynesford, Freebridge Lynn, Gallow, Greenhoe North, Greenhoe South, Holt, Launditch, Smithdon, Taverham and Tunstead hundreds, East Clackclose, East Grimshoe and the western parts of Guiltcross, Shropham and Wayland - the Roundhead gentry overwhelmed the Cavaliers by 65 families to 32. In the wood-pasture region - comprising Blofield, Clavering, Depwade, Diss, Earsham, Forehoe, Henstead, Humbleyard, Loddon and Mitford hundreds and the eastern parts of Guiltcross, Shropham and Wayland - there were 23 Parliamentarian gentry families but as many as 18 Royalist. This strong Royalist presence among the gentry may have been partly a hostile reaction to the independence of the common people, as it was in some other wood-pasture areas (in Derbyshire, Durham and Warwickshire for example).

In the textile manufacturing districts the strength of the two parties varied. In the main worsted weaving areas - comprising the City of Norwich and the hundreds of South Erpingham and Tunstead - the 22 Parliamentarian gentry families swamped the eight Royalist. But in the linen-producing hundreds of south Norfolk - Depwade, Diss, Earsham and Loddon and the eastern parts of Guiltcross and Shropham - there were 11 Parliamentarian families but as many as eight Royalist.

The Parliamentarian gentry had a predominance over their opponents in two of the three main urban centres. In Great Yarmouth there was one Parliamentarian gentleman - Miles Corbett, a future regicide - but no upper class Royalist, apart from the absentee Earl of Dorset. In Norwich the Parliamentarians comfortably outnumbered the Royalists by nine families to three. In King's Lynn on the other hand there were three Cavalier families as against only one Parliamentarian, perhaps because of the influence of the neighbouring Royalist gentry.

Finally, the Norfolk gentry, unlike their brethren in many other counties, do not seem to have been seriously divided by religion. Of the 59 Royalist families 46 were Anglicans, but how many were sincere or lukewarm is impossible to say. Only two (3%) of the Royalist families were Puritan and just 11 (19%) were Roman Catholic, though nine of those were activists. Even so, Norfolk contrasts with Lancashire where over 65% of Cavalier families were Papist. Moreover, the Parliamentarian gentry of Norfolk differed from their counterparts in Suffolk where a majority were Puritan. In Norfolk only 36 (34%) of the 106 Parliamentarian families were Puritan - the kind of people whom Percival Wiburn called 'the hotter sort of protestants'. Even among the 48 activist Parliamentarian families Puritans were in a minority - only 22 (46%). Only among the small number of urban Parliamentary gentry families were Puritans in a majority, comprising eight (73%) out of 11 such families. The urban gentry were exceptional. The map suggests that from a purely statistical standpoint Puritanism was not the main driving force among the Parliamentarian gentry and that religion was probably not the key issue in the Civil War in Norfolk.

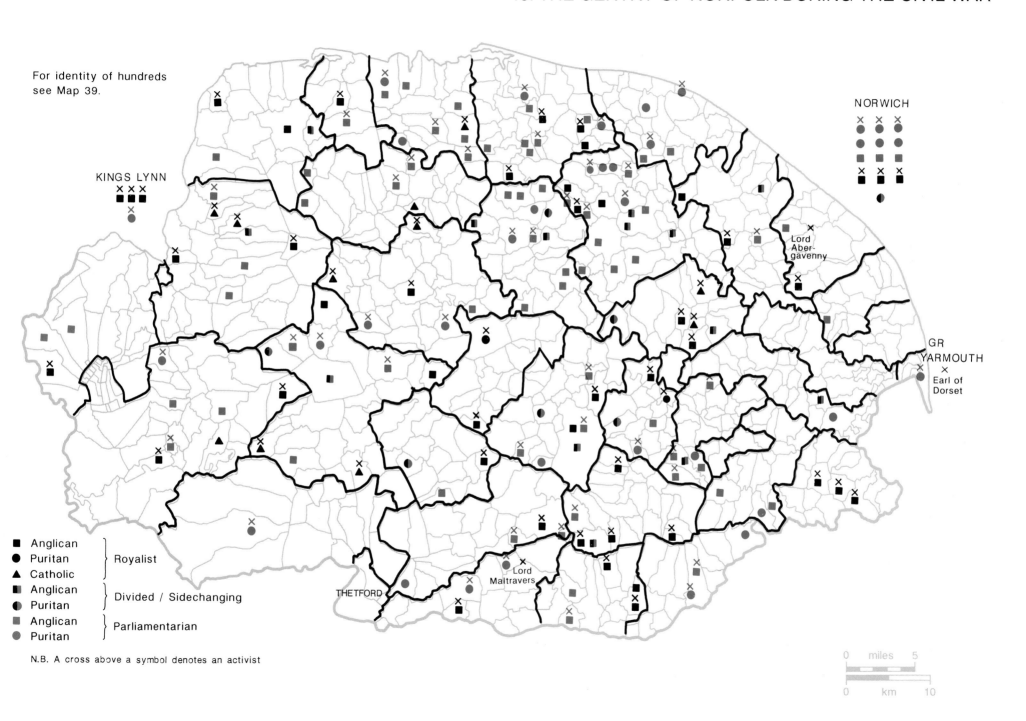

For identity of hundreds
see Map 39.

NORWICH

KINGS LYNN

Lord Aber-gavenny

GR YARMOUTH
Earl of Dorset

Lord Maltravers

THETFORD

■ Anglican } Royalist
● Puritan
▲ Catholic

◧ Anglican } Divided / Sidechanging
◑ Puritan

■ Anglican } Parliamentarian
● Puritan

N.B. A cross above a symbol denotes an activist

0 miles 5

0 km 10

49. COUNTRY-HOUSE BUILDING IN NORFOLK, 1700-1900

Alan Mackley

The map shows the location and building history of the main seats of Norfolk's resident owners of estates of at least 1,000 acres in the 1870s. Five notable houses on smaller estates have been added: Elsing, Halvergate, Narborough, Rainthorpe, and Raveningham. Two family houses are shown for five estates: the Earl of Orford's Mannington and Wolterton; the Bulwer's Quebec Lodge, East Dereham, and Heydon; the Gurney's Keswick and Northrepps; the Mills's Clermont Lodge, Little Cressingham, and Hilborough; and the Newcome's Feltwell and Hockwold.

The quarter century in which 18th and 19th-century building or alteration started is shown, or an indication given where less precise information is available, 'Georgian' or '19th century', for example. 'Late-Georgian' houses have been assigned to the first quarter of the 19th century.

The mapped data signify the culmination of two centuries of estate enlargement and concentration, founded on post-Restoration political stability, economic growth, and agricultural improvement, reflecting the high political value and social status of landownership. However, the relationship between landholding and housebuilding is not simple: land-rich often meant cash-starved. Non-landed sources of income were very important.

The geographical distribution of the houses follows that of the estates, of which the largest are concentrated on the less fertile and cheaper soils of the north and west, where manorial holdings were relatively large, and the smallest are to the east and south of Norwich, where land was more expensive and the prevalence of small freeholders inhibited the accumulation of large consolidated holdings. Greater houses are scarce in Broadland, on the fens of the extreme west, and on the boulder clay of mid-Norfolk.

Many of Norfolk's hundreds of medieval estates lost their separate identity when absorbed by others, through inheritance, marriage, or sale. Their houses may have survived as secondary seats or dower houses, or may have declined into farmhouses or tenements, or been let, sold, or demolished. Oxnead and West Dereham were among the largest houses listed in the 1660s tax returns, but were demolished without replacement. Among prominent seats shown on Faden's map of the 1790s, West Tofts was later combined with Lynford, Buckenham with Didlington, and Hethel with Ketteringham. Therefore, any attempt to construct a generalised building chronology from the mapped data, will risk the under-representation of building activity, increasing in degree with distance in time from 1870.

Many of the mapped houses have long histories. Well over half of the houses of estates of over 2,000 acres originated before 1700. One quarter survived the next 200 years without being completely rebuilt, although some were radically altered: Didlington and Shadwell Park for example. A landowner without the means to rebuild could still improve the function and comfort of his house, and present a fashionable facade to the world, by periodic alteration and extension.

Survivors from earlier periods range from Elsing, Mannington and Oxburgh of the 15th century, to Blickling, Felbrigg and Raynham of the earlier 17th century.

Hoveton, Melton Constable, Narford and Ryston represent the post-Restoration revival of building activity and were followed by the great early-18th century Palladian symbols of the dominant landowners: Houghton financed by the rewards of public office, and Holkham, reflecting the more prudent spending of estate income over 30 years. Smaller landowners also built new houses or altered and extended old ones, to identify stylistically with the leaders of national and county society, and to satisfy new demands in function, comfort and privacy. However, in the lean years of the earlier 18th century, Hockham, Langley, Sculthorpe, and West Harling, were sold. Few of the new early-18th-century houses on the smaller estates were still in the hands of the builders' families by the 1870s.

The smaller estates were strongly represented in the surge of activity from the 1790s through to the 1820s, stimulated by rising rent-rolls in the boom years of the Napoleonic war period. Many of the so-called 'Georgian' houses will date from this period. Established families dominated building; only two of the 13 datable houses started in the first quarter of the 19th century, Letheringsett and Sheringham, were built by new estate owners, and the rate of turnover of ownership was much lower than a century before. Beeston St. Laurence led the fashion change of the Gothic revival, into the eclecticism of Victorian architecture. The building of Bylaugh and Haveringland in the depressed 1840s illustrates that builders' personal circumstances, inheritance and marriage were often more important than prevailing economic conditions in determining decisions to build.

Twenty-one houses were built in the second half of the century, including six for men new to the county, reflecting not only the golden age of 'High Farming' but also the march of business and other fortunes into the countryside, and the importance of sporting estates in the west and south west, including the Green family at Ken Hill, Stephens at Lynford, and the Prince of Wales at Sandringham.

Mansion building was halted by the agricultural depression of the late 19th century, but seven houses were rebuilt in the 20th century, five by new owners: non-landed money was more important than ever. The end of the age of the landed estate and the country house was fast approaching, and other new houses at Overstrand, Happisburgh, and Home Place, Holt typified the desire of the rich businessman for a small recreational retreat rather than a power base.

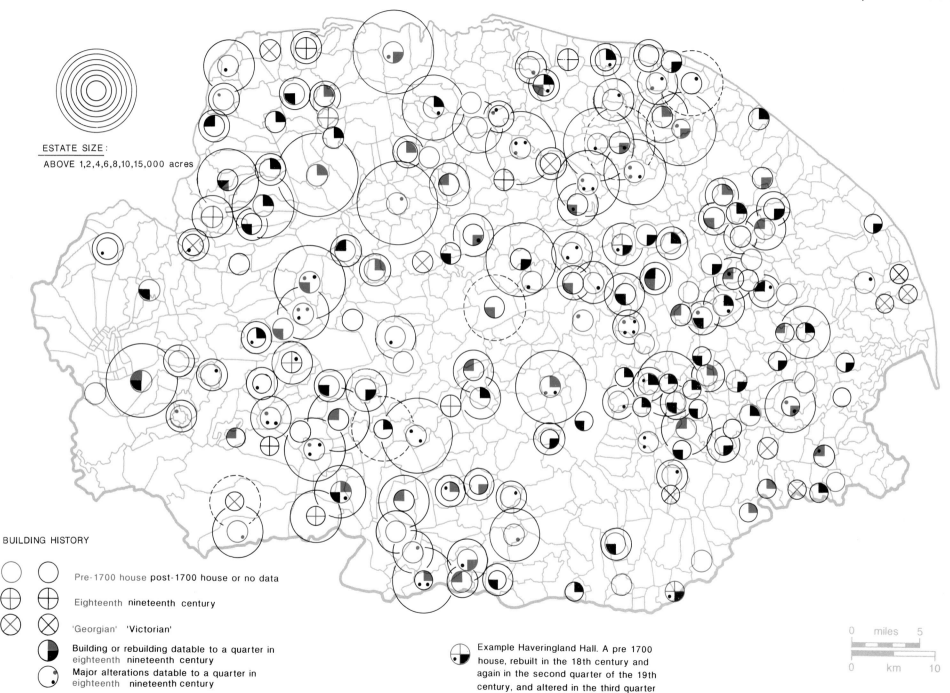

49. COUNTRY-HOUSE BUILDING IN NORFOLK, 1700-1900

ESTATE SIZE:

ABOVE 1,2,4,6,8,10,15,000 acres

BUILDING HISTORY

○ ○ Pre-1700 house post-1700 house or no data

⊕ ⊕ Eighteenth nineteenth century

⊗ ⊗ 'Georgian' 'Victorian'

◑ Building or rebuilding datable to a quarter in
eighteenth nineteenth century

◔ Major alterations datable to a quarter in
eighteenth nineteenth century

⊕ Example Haveringland Hall. A pre 1700
house, rebuilt in the 18th century and
again in the second quarter of the 19th
century, and altered in the third quarter

0 miles 5

0 km 10

50. PARKS IN THE 18TH AND 19TH CENTURIES

Tom Williamson

Parkland made an important contribution to the landscape of Norfolk in the eighteenth and nineteenth centuries, and many of the great landscapes created during this period are still prominent features of the countryside.

The first map attempts to show the distribution of parkland in 1750. It is unsatisfactory for a number of reasons. During the first half of the eighteenth century, the meaning of the word 'park' was changing. Johnson's *Dictionary* might, in 1755, still define park in traditional terms - as 'A piece of ground enclosed and stored with wild beasts of chase' - but in practice a looser definition had become established. An area was often considered a park if it lay next to, or surrounded, a gentleman's residence, and had an appearance which, in some way, corresponded to that of a traditional deer park: i.e., it consisted of pasture, with a number of trees scattered across it. But the fully-developed, 'landscape' park did not yet exist, and contemporary cartographers were unsure about whether such areas could really be considered as parks, or whether that term should be restricted to areas which actually contained deer, or which were so extensive that their status as distinctive elite landscapes could hardly be doubted. Even parks which had previously been stocked with deer, and which continued to have a park-like appearance, had an uncertain status. Ornamental parks are thus unevenly recorded on large-scale county maps, such as that surveyed by James Corbridge in 1730, and our knowledge of their existence depends on their chance appearance on estate maps, or in references in letters or estate documents. The map, therefore, is an incomplete representation. It does, however, clearly show that the largest parks were associated, as we would expect, with the leading county families: the Walpoles, Townshends, Harboards, Astleys, Wodehouses, and Hobarts: and also (even when we have allowed for numerous omissions) that parks were comparatively rare in the Norfolk landscape.

The second map shows the distribution of different sizes of park at the end of the century. It is based on William Faden's map of Norfolk, published in 1797. This, too, needs to be treated with a measure of caution. Much of the area distinguished as 'park' at Langley, or at Holkham, for example, was actually under the plough at the time the map was surveyed. The surveyors classified such areas as 'park' because they lay within a continuous belt of trees, and were crossed by drives separated from the public roads by lodges. There are also some cases where the map unquestionably depicts the size or outline of a park inaccurately. Nevertheless, despite such deficiencies, Faden's map is correct in its broad outlines. It shows that in the second half of the century there was a massive increase in the number of parks; but that these were mainly small or medium-sized landscapes. Almost all the largest parks which it depicts - those extending over more than 150 hectares - had already been in existence, in some form, by 1750. Parks were widely distributed across the county, but with some marked concentrations, and some corresponding *lacunae*. They tended to cluster in the area around Norwich, largely on the loam soils to the north of the city but also, to some extent, on the lighter clays of the south. There was another concentration further to the south east, on or beside the Waveney valley, in the vicinity of Beccles. Elsewhere, parks were less prominent. In the north and west, this was probably because the dominance of estates like Holkham, Houghton, and Raynham left little room for the creation of landed holdings large enough to support a park. But in addition, there were few parks of any size in Broadland, in the Fens, or on the more level parts of the boulder clay plateau in the south of the county. This could, in part, reflect the aesthetic preferences of the gentry, and in particular, a dislike of flat land as a location for a residence. But it is mainly a manifestation of landholding patterns, and of the survival in these areas of large numbers of small freeholders.

Parks proliferated during the nineteenth century, and by the time that the second edition of the Ordnance Survey 6": 1 mile maps were surveyed (mainly 1905 - 1912); the third map shows that they could be found almost everywhere in the county. Most of the new arrivals seem to have come into existence in the first three decades of the nineteenth century. Most were comparatively small. There was only one entirely new park in the largest size category (i.e., 150 hectares or more) - that at Bylaugh, created in 1848 - although several existing parks expanded to this size, including Hunstanton, Wolterton, Barningham and Ketteringham.

The overwhelming majority of parks in existence at the time of Faden's map still existed in the early twentieth century; of these, the majority had either remained the same size, or had grown. Only a minority had dwindled, and fewer still had disappeared altogether. There is a slight tendency for these to be located in the area around Norwich, and on the clay soils to the south east, but this may reflect no more than the particular density of eighteenth century parks in these areas.

PARKS c1750
(VARIOUS SOURCES)

● Deer park, or large park without deer

● Small parks without deer, or sites of uncertain status.

PARKS IN THE LATE EIGHTEENTH CENTURY
(BASED ON WILLIAM FADEN'S MAP OF THE COUNTY OF NORFOLK, 1797)

PARKS EXTENDING OVER:

● 150+ hectares

● 75–150 hectares

· 15–74.9 hectares

+ Less than 15 hectares

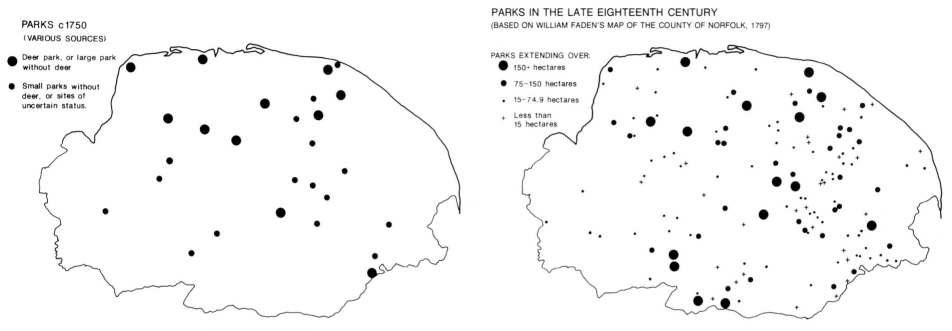

PARKS IN THE EARLY TWENTIETH CENTURY
(BASED ON THE SECOND EDITION ORDNANCE SURVEY 6IN:1 MILE MAPS, MAINLY 1905–1912)

PARKS EXTENDING OVER

● 150+ hectares

● 75–150 hectares

· 15–74.9 hectares

+ Less than 15 hectares

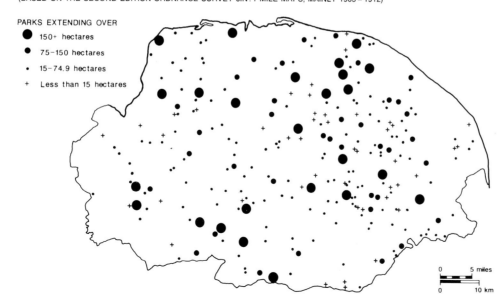

0   5 miles
0   10 km

Brickmaking in East Anglia, which was reintroduced in the 13th century, reached its finest expression in the Elizabethan and Jacobean periods, made possible by its prosperous trade links with the Low Countries and the availability of good brick earth. Although brick was being used in some Norwich undercrofts by the late 14th century, it was only with the advent of the Tudors that it became fashionable. Early examples at Red Mount Chapel (Kings Lynn), Middleton Towers and Oxburgh Hall suggest that brick-making techniques were introduced separately into west Norfolk up the River Ouse, while the great halls at Shelton and Kenninghall in south Norfolk were near major overland routes.

The great re-building of the late 16th century, financed by trade and the redistribution of monastic land, enabled the *nouveau riche* to express their wealth in terms of the latest architectural style when old manorial sites were often too cramped and the buildings dilapidated. The courtyard plan at Oxburgh and Shelton was abandoned in favour of a standard E plan at Thelverton, Rainthorpe, Kirstead, Morley and Channonz Halls in south Norfolk and at Salle and Heydon Halls in north Norfolk. This important group displays the full range of details which epitomise Tudor brickwork.

The most emphatic feature was the three-storey porch complete with four-centred arch and polygonal angle shafts. Arranged around it were a series of pedimented mullion and transom windows with stepped gable cross wings. The brickwork, still in English bond, was often distinguished by diaper patterning. Clusters of tall chimney stacks enabled the bricklayer to indulge in intricate chevron and rope twist patterns to dazzling effect as at East Barsham Manor.

These features soon appeared on more ambitious vernacular buildings. Where an elaborate brick feature was added to a timber frame building the results were sometimes bizarre - the gable end to Methwold Rectory or the shafts at Chimneys Farm, Topcroft are memorable exam-ples. Most examples are less spectacular, a two-storey porch and stepped gable were all that most farmers could afford. The number of chimney stacks was a clear indication of wealth, usually two or three lozenge shaped shafts on the main stack inserted into an earlier open hall house.

The stepped gable is the most characteristic feature of Elizabethan and Jacobean brickwork. Introduced from the continent it is found all along the east coast of England and Scotland. Pevsner quotes it as an example of a 15th-century motif carried through into the early 18th century without being adapted to Renaissance taste. Its distribution gives a valuable indication of wealth in late 16th and early 17th century Norfolk.

Of the 164 examples, most are in eastern Norfolk, the greatest concentration being south west of Norwich. The absence of early Tudor brickwork is surprising considering the examples in Norwich, but here in the fertile Tas, Wensum and Yare valleys merchants, lawyers and financiers built an impressive range of brick halls (Great Witchingham, Great Melton, Barnham Broom, Gowthorpe, Tharston etc.). Whereas most houses with stepped gables were built of brick (63%), a further 24% are on timber frame houses in south-east Norfolk, such as Blo Norton and Banham Halls, a clear status symbol.

Because of the structural problems posed by stepped gables, the tumbled brick parapet was the preferred gable end finish on most flint buildings, but in north-east Norfolk stepped gables are spread thinly from a small cluster around Wood Norton Hall. The important Fen group of early Tudor brickwork close to main waterways at the Wiggenhalls and Outwell/Upwell and along the Fen edge at Denver, Wallington, Fordham, Hilgay and Foulden, is noticeable for the absence of both the stepped gable and its successor the 'Dutch' gable.

The 'Dutch' gable became the hallmark of late 17th and early 18th century brickwork. In its original form, as a series of concave and convex curves separated by steps and capped by a pediment, it is restricted to a few advanced early 17th-century buildings eg. Blickling and Raynham Halls, Scole Inn. On most examples the Renaissance pediment is replaced by a rounded top and on some smaller houses and barns the simple bell shape was used, the result of a persistent tradition in English architecture to adapt foreign influence.

The distribution of 'Dutch' gables in eastern Norfolk is part of a broader belt, 10-15 miles inland round East Anglia and south-east England. The 148 recorded examples in Norfolk is the largest concentration but few occur near the coast where the tradition of flint construction persisted. Although broadly coincident, the distribution of stepped and 'Dutch' gables reveals an important economic shift from south-east Norfolk (60% stepped 35% Dutch) to north-east Norfolk (29% stepped 53% Dutch) and towards the market towns (4% stepped 20% Dutch) many being rebuilt in brick following disastrous fires and emphasising the importance of waterborne transport.

The largest concentration along the Bure Valley including Coltishall, together with the Aylsham/Cawston grouping, represents a small but significant shift of wealth south eastwards from the Heydon/Salle group of late 16th/early 17th century brickwork. In south-east Norfolk clusters of Dutch gables grew up around the earlier concentration of stepped gables south west of Norwich, in the Tas valley and along the Wymondham-Hingham axis. The more even scatter on the Loddon peninsula was part of a more general movement south eastwards onto lighter soils and the drained marshes of the Waveney valley.

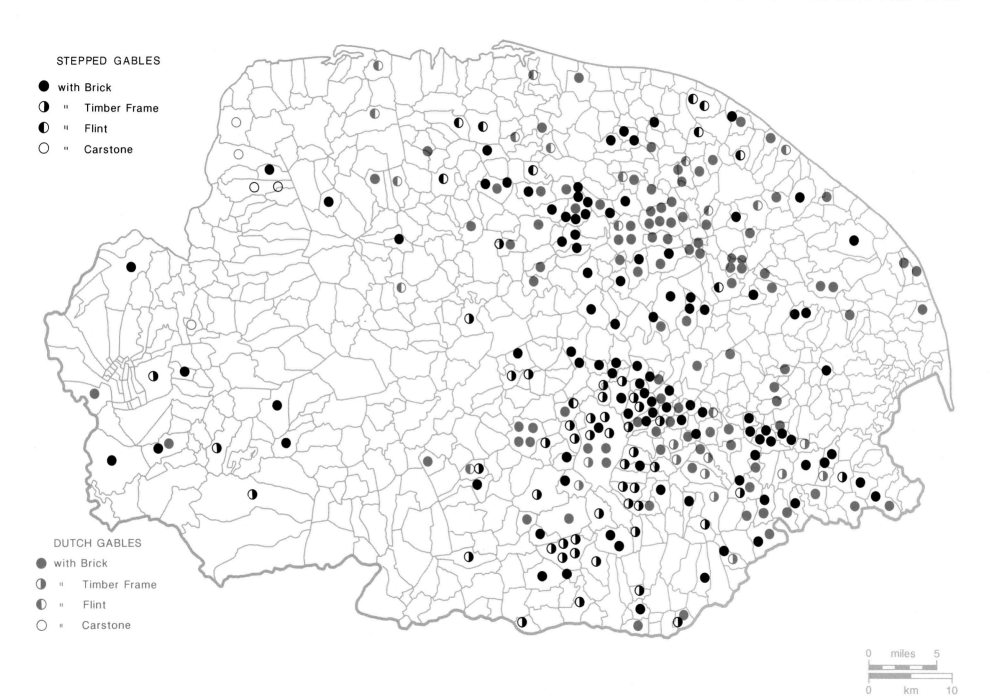

51. BRICK AS AN INDICATOR OF WEALTH 1450-1750

STEPPED GABLES

● with Brick
◑ " Timber Frame
◐ " Flint
○ " Carstone

DUTCH GABLES

● with Brick
◑ " Timber Frame
◐ " Flint
○ " Carstone

0 miles 5

0 km 10

Descriptions of the building materials of parsonage houses which may be found within glebe terriers provide an unequalled source of information, stretching across the county and relating to a series of different dates from the late 18th century onwards, for the vernacular architecture of Norfolk. Before the 19th century parsonage houses were not characteristically different from other dwellings and the map presented here, based on information taken from the terriers, fairly represents the range and geographical distribution of traditional walling materials. The materials mentioned were timber, fashioned as a frame and usually described as studwork; clay, by which was meant any sticky mud which would stand up when dry; stone, comprising flint, carstone and chalk but rarely, if ever, imported freestone; and brick, used in association with other materials but also by itself.

Timber construction in the county has a long history and, indeed, a prehistory. The all-timber system inherited from the medieval period of supporting the roof with a series of bay-trusses rigidly secured by wall- and roof-plates and intervening horizontal rails was continued in the 16th to 18th centuries, albeit as a less sophisticated level and with a less than adequate supply of hardwood eked out with imported softwood for positions in which the timber was not exposed.

Running parallel to timber-frame construction in those areas where it predominated, especially in the south of the county, was what was a much cheaper if ruder alternative. Puddled clay with a straw additive was built up into walls with a fork - cob as it is called today in south-west England - or it was slopped down between shutters. Excavations and field surveys on deserted village sites within the parishes of Pudding Norton, Rougham and Tittleshall show that clay construction was extensive in the medieval period. A valuation of the Blickling estate made in 1756 reveals that 12 out of 83 buildings in Blickling itself had mud or clay walls. Cob and shuttered-clay construction continued into the 19th century, although it would seem at a much reduced level than formerly because in this year, 1992, there survive in the county only 25 sites with identified examples of construction of this type, referred to as buildings of 'solid clay' so as to distinguish them from those buildings raised in clay lump.

The fact that clay-built parsonages were, at the end of the 18th century, concentrated in mid-south Norfolk, in that socio-geographical and agricultural zone termed the wood-pasture region, demonstrates the existence of a close link between solid-clay construction and construction in clay lump, similarly concentrated in the same region but having no specific reference in 18th-century documents. In clay-lump construction the clay was not laid solid but was laid in blocks or lumps, using clay slurry as a mortar and also, commonly, as a plaster, having been stabilized with lime and other substances. The method had a number of advantages over that employed in solid-clay construction and by the end of the 19th century buildings raised in clay lump accounted for the overwhelming majority of clay buildings in the county.

With few exceptions houses were not, in the medieval period, constructed of stone and the later construction of stone houses and other stone buildings in coastal and inland western districts might well be related to the pressing deficiency of building hardwoods in those parts. Stone construction with flint, carstone or chalk, was invariably accompanied with dressings in brick, producing a variety of patterned effects. Flint, which was mined but which was also available from field surfaces, gravel-beds and the sea-shore, was the most commonly used of all Norfolk stones. Construction in carstone and chalk followed in a north-south corridor located very generally between Swaffham and King's Lynn, where such deposits came close to the ground surface. At Snettisham where, according to William White's *Directory of Norfolk*, three quarries were being worked for carstone in 1836, a carstone mine remains in operation at Norton Hill. As a walling material chalk was often not visible, as in the vicarage at Martham described by the 1834 terrier as 'built with Chalk, fronted with white brick'.

From the outset of the medieval use of brick (dating, at the earliest, from the end of the 12th century), the cost-factor operated as a limit to its spread. The very restricted range of buildings in which brick was used came only slowly to include domestic premises: whilst some great all-brick houses were built from the 15th century onwards (with a notable early group sited in Fenland and on the Fen-edge), it was usual in the post-medieval period for a new building involving brick to have a front, a chimney-stack or end gables of brick, with other parts raised in less costly materials. It is not without significance that, at the end of the 18th century, the parsonage houses which were built wholly or largely of brick were most numerous in the districts where land values and land-generated incomes were also high. The ports of Lynn and Yarmouth led the countryside in the use of brick but Norwich, whilst it can demonstrate much medieval use of brick, especially in its remarkable range of surviving undercrofts, did not noticeably develop as a brick city until the 18th century.

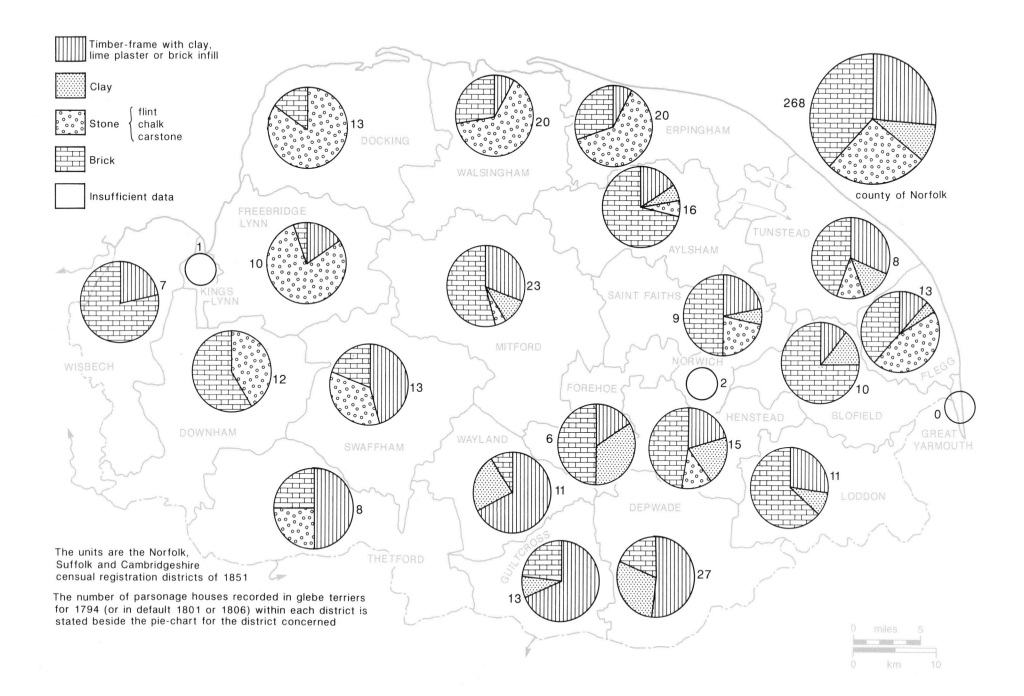

52. WALLING MATERIALS OF PARSONAGE HOUSES, 1794

Timber-frame with clay, lime plaster or brick infill

Clay

Stone { flint, chalk, carstone }

Brick

Insufficient data

DOCKING

WALSINGHAM

FREEBRIDGE LYNN

ERPINGHAM

TUNSTEAD

AYLSHAM

268

county of Norfolk

KINGS LYNN

WISBECH

SAINT FAITHS

NORWICH

FLEGG

MITFORD

DOWNHAM

SWAFFHAM

WAYLAND

FOREHOE

HENSTEAD

BLOFIELD

GREAT YARMOUTH

LODDON

DEPWADE

THETFORD

GUILTCROSS

The units are the Norfolk, Suffolk and Cambridgeshire censual registration districts of 1851

The number of parsonage houses recorded in glebe terriers for 1794 (or in default 1801 or 1806) within each district is stated beside the pie-chart for the district concerned

miles   5

km   10

Glebe terriers, which provide valuable evidence for the materials with which parsonage houses (and by extension other houses) were built from the 18th century onwards, are specific not only regarding the materials for walling but also for the materials for roof coverings. Roof coverings were far less permanent than walls.

As with many other counties of England, the overwhelming majority of buildings in Norfolk in the medieval period were thatched, with only monasteries, some churches and a small proportion of public and private buildings having higher-status roof coverings. What changed the situation in the post-Reformation period was the introduction of pantiles, which were imported from the Netherlands in considerable quantity for use in new building or in replacement of thatch. But thatch was not ousted in a day, and Sir Philip Skippon's diary of a visit to Norfolk in the 1670s has left the comment that the houses of Norfolk were generally thatched, and so were many of the churches. Thatch continued to be the predominant roof covering in Broadland and in south Norfolk until well into the 19th century, although by this date it was clear the practice of thatching was in retreat. Thatch gave place not only to tile but also to slate, which from the late 18th century onwards was being brought on a regular basis by schooner from North Wales. Censual returns for occupations show the local strength of thatching as it existed in 1851, at which date Norfolk enjoyed a ratio of one thatcher to 295 houses, occupying the tenth most favourable position for thatching amongst 39 English counties. In towns the move from thatch to tile reflected an awareness of the ever-present fire hazards posed by thatch: it is doubtful, however, whether anti-thatch legislation played a major rôle in mobilizing the change. The strength of thatching in Broadland can, of course, be attributed to the celebrated Norfolk reed, said to have had a life of 60 to 80 years and greatly praised in the 18th century by the agricultural writers William Marshall and Nathaniel Kent. In other areas reliance was placed upon the shorter-lasting long-wheat straw, although rye straw is stated to have been the most prized thatching straw in the medieval period. Outbuildings were, in some marshy areas, roofed with gladden or reed-mace. Sedge, employed generally for ridges, was a common overall covering for thatched buildings in Fenland Norfolk.

The success of the pantile, as a tile and as a roof covering, was due to two factors. First was the proximity of the English east coast to the Netherlands, where the tiles were originally made and from where they were exported as a desirable return commodity to England's export of corn and woollen cloth. Second was the suitability of the pantile, which in roofing squares was half the weight of plaintile, to be laid on the lightly-timbered roofs of the eastern counties, some of which were originally constructed to take thatch. Pantiles were made in England from the late 17th century, in Norfolk from the 1740s, but contemporaries considered them inferior to those of Dutch manufacture. Only when the pattern of Anglo-Dutch trade changed in the second half of the 18th century was the Norfolk market supplied in bulk with pantiles of local production. By this date, however, the Norfolk pantile had a rival in the form of pantiles imported from Humberside, where the techniques of production resembled those which were applied in the Netherlands.

There can be no doubt that pantiles provided the principal form of roof coverings for Norfolk buildings in the 19th century: in 1820 67% of parsonage houses in the county were tiled, and 51% of the barns or principal outbuildings. The tiling, however, also included plaintiling, although plaintiles were used within a far narrower range of buildings than pantiles and were strong only in particular areas. The main such area, adjoining the river Great Ouse and reaching from Downham Market to King's Lynn, would seem to have benefited in the 16th and 17th centuries from plaintiles made in the substantial tileyards of Ely. The introduction of pantiles, and more especially the beginning of pantile manufacture in Norfolk, appears to have adversely affected the use of plaintile which may once have been general, although restricted to a modest total of roofs through the county. Amongst buildings surviving today raised and roofed before 1860 it is on the roofs of the small number of high-status buildings raised and roofed before 1740 that the plaintile may be most commonly observed. Such buildings include the naves and chancels of churches. Plaintiles, like pantiles, have obviously been replaced from time to time, in continuation of a conservative tradition which has bound both builder and client over centuries. The use of plaintiles, and especially those with decorative profiles, in the later Victorian and Edwardian periods can be attributed to the design ideas of 'polite architecture'.

The roofing of Holkham Hall with slate in the mid 18th century set a fashion for the material which, because of the costs and hazards of shipping at a time of recurrent wars with the French, could have few adherents before 1815. Between that date and 1865 the proportion of parsonage houses roofed with slate rose from less than 5% to 44.19%, but this extension of slate cover was not followed by the county at large.

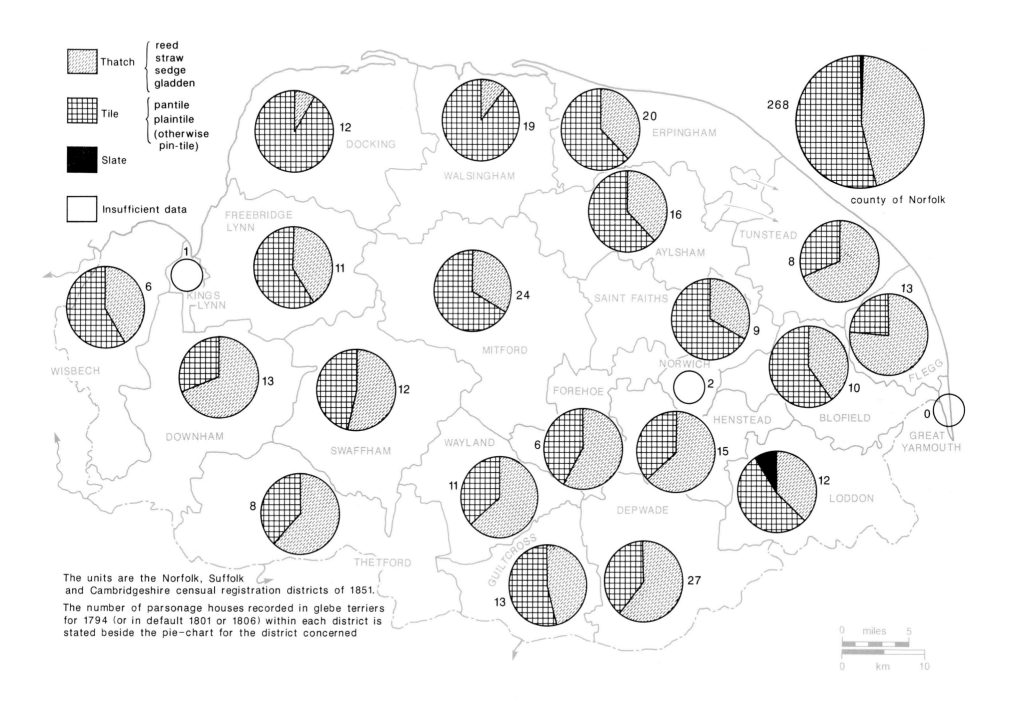

Thatch { reed / straw / sedge / gladden }

Tile { pantile / plaintile / (otherwise pin-tile) }

Slate

Insufficient data

DOCKING 12
WALSINGHAM 19
ERPINGHAM 20
county of Norfolk 268
FREEBRIDGE LYNN 11
KINGS LYNN 1
WISBECH 6
MITFORD 24
AYLSHAM 16
TUNSTEAD 8
SAINT FAITHS
NORWICH 9
FLEGG 13
DOWNHAM 13
SWAFFHAM 12
WAYLAND
FOREHOE 2
HENSTEAD
BLOFIELD 10
GREAT YARMOUTH 0
THETFORD 8
GUILTCROSS 11, 6, 15
DEPWADE 13, 27
LODDON 12

The units are the Norfolk, Suffolk and Cambridgeshire censual registration districts of 1851.

The number of parsonage houses recorded in glebe terriers for 1794 (or in default 1801 or 1806) within each district is stated beside the pie-chart for the district concerned

miles 0 5
km 0 10

54. EDUCATION BEFORE 1750

Pamela Warren

There was, of course, no system of education in this period and the majority of children had no opportunity to attend school. Generally, education was for more privileged children whose parents could afford to pay; girls usually received little education before the mid 17th century whatever their social background.

'Free' Grammar schools and 'English' schools were usually founded to provide free education for a particular number of poor children. Fee payers would also be admitted in order to supplement the masters' income. Cromer Grammar School was founded in 1505 under the will of Sir Bartholomew Rede for 'gentlemens' sons and goodmens' children and especially poor mens' children' (sic). Little Walsingham Grammar School was founded in 1639 for 30 free scholars; poor boys were to be accepted before rich men's children. Grammar school education was designed to prepare boys for university; thus, emphasis was placed upon the teaching of Latin and Greek. Vocational training was not usually given although the endowment of Little Walsingham required boys to be taught navigational skills. In the course of time the character and instruction in some of these schools changed from that intended by the founder. From the late 17th century free boys were taught separately from fee payers at Scarning School and the number of free scholars entering the school declined in favour of more fee paying pupils despite ample funds being available. From 1733 to 1750, when 165 boys were admitted, only 22 were free scholars. Fee payers also increased in other grammar schools in the county and free places declined, which meant that poorer children for whom these schools were intended were excluded. Some schools ceased to function as grammar schools. An Enquiry held in 1643 heard that at Cromer school classical instruction was no longer given and masters appointed were incompetent. The inhabitants considered that the lack of grammar was not a disadvantage so long as a skilled master was employed to concentrate on the teaching of reading, writing and arithmetic, subjects they felt were more beneficial to the type of boys attending the school. Classical instruction was not, therefore, re-instated. Aylsham, Feltwell and Great Yarmouth Grammar Schools also discontinued classical instruction either through lack of demand or lack of funds.

Endowments for grammar schools declined after the mid-17th century, whereas those for non-classical schools increased significantly. Most of the endowed non-classical schools provided education for a small number of children, although at Wells provision was made for 60 children to be taught by two poor widows. Instruction in these schools might consist of basic reading, writing and arithmetic, although some taught only reading, as at Kettlestone where six poor boys could stay until they could read their Bibles. Most endowments stressed the importance of religious learning and moral behaviour. Knitting, sewing and spinning were sometimes taught and occasionally apprenticeships were given on leaving, as at Anguish's School in Norwich. Unlike the endowed grammar schools it seems that generally free places were maintained in these schools and in some cases they increased as further donations were received.

A few poor children in Norwich received some form of teaching in the late 16th century. Under the city's revised Poor Laws, 12 children in St Giles Hospital were to be taught their letters. A survey made of the poor of Norwich in 1570 discloses that whilst the majority of poor children began work at a very early age, about 16% of those between five and 12 years attended a school. Some of these would have been industrial schools but it is not believed they were all of this type.

Small fee-paying schools were set up from time to time in a number of Norfolk market towns. Some were run by graduates who prepared boys for university. Others instructed at an elementary level. Most of these schools were ephemeral and few records are extant. Clergymen might sometimes take pupils to augment a small living; at Whissonsett in the late 16th century it was suggested the proposed incumbent supplement the living by teaching. Others might teach a few boys 'out of charity'.

The Society for the Promotion of Christian Knowledge founded in 1699 encouraged the formation of schools, which became known as Charity Schools. The earliest in Norfolk were opened in Norwich in 1708. By 1719 there were 12 schools in the city teaching about 400 boys and girls. Fees of 1d. or 2d. a week were usually charged in the Norwich schools and some clothing was provided. Whilst Charity Schools were set up in rural areas, the lack of active support prevented them from becoming widespread in the county. Reading was taught with emphasis upon the Bible and sometimes instruction in writing and arithmetic was given. Financial aid came from donations and subscriptions. Four schools were also opened by the Dissenters in Norwich in the early 18th century and one in King's Lynn.

By 1750 the number of schools in Norfolk had increased, but numerically they were few and unevenly distributed. Illiteracy remained widespread, although there had been a slight decline in particular groups. It was increasingly felt that education should be designed around one's rank in life. Many held the belief that 'too much learning' would render the poor dissatisfied and unfit for laborious employment and that schools for poor children should concentrate on teaching industry and subordination. This belief persisted into the 19th century.

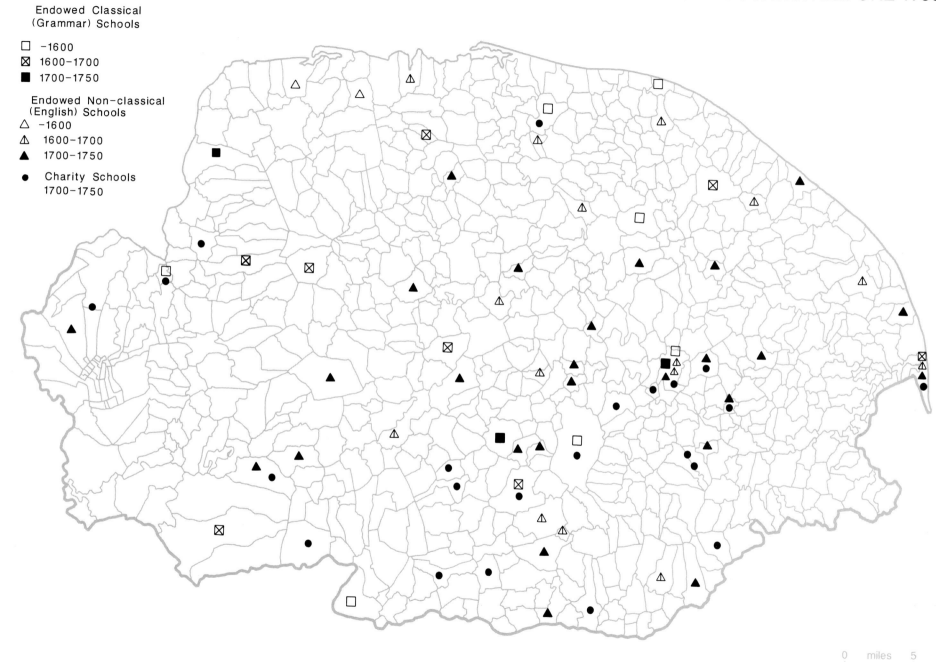

54. EDUCATION BEFORE 1750

Endowed Classical
(Grammar) Schools

□ –1600
⊠ 1600–1700
■ 1700–1750

Endowed Non-classical
(English) Schools
△ –1600
△ 1600–1700
▲ 1700–1750

● Charity Schools
1700–1750

0 miles 5

0 km 10

Susanna Wade Martins

The voting system of the late-18th century bore little resemblance to that with which we are familiar today. Not only were electors restricted to those male freeholders with land worth more than forty shillings (£2), but the elections in which they participated were often manipulated by others.

In Norfolk there were over 5,000 forty-shilling freeholders who made up about an eighth of the adult male population, including the clergy, gentry, yeomanry, many farmers and some craftsmen. Yet even this large group of apparently independent voters were not as free as they might seem. As voting took place in public at the hustings, there could be no secret over who voted for whom. Many of the farmer-freeholders also rented some land and so would vote to please their landlords. Tradesmen, too, depended on a good relationship with the gentry, although they might themselves be able to influence the votes of others. In 1788 James Lee, a shopkeeper in Upwell had 'a great deal of money out in small sums' and so could command most of the voters in three parishes. (There were 36 voters in Upwell alone.).

Two other less tangible influences on votes were 'gratitude' and 'obligation' which many of the smaller freeholders felt towards one candidate or his supporters, and it was generally local and family interests rather than party loyalties that determined the way the electorate voted.

However, national parties did have a role to play. By the 1780s political news took up a large part of the space in the three county newspapers, and it was Thomas William Coke's support for the hated Fox-North coalition that lost him his seat in 1784.

In 1788 rumours of a dissolution of parliament were rife and Coke was determined to regain support. Lists were prepared stating the districts and persons to be canvassed and Humphrey Repton, soon to be better known as a landscape gardener, was employed to compile a map entitled, 'A general view of the Influence operating in the elections for the County of Norfolk', resulting in what is perhaps the first example of a piece of market research produced for political ends; its findings are reproduced here.

The map was compiled by hundreds and the number of voters in each was given. Occasionally the numbers in the larger villages and towns is given separately. Not surprisingly, there were more freeholders in the more populous centre and east than in the west. The sparsely populated Breckland area is particularly lacking in voters. More significantly, the names of those with an income of more than £1,000 a year and who were supposed to influence more than 20 voters were given, with the candidate they were likely to support. The map shows that although the dozen or so major county names are included, the 150 landowners who influenced the other 4,850 voters were mainly plain country squires. That there were so many indicates the wealth and potential political independence of the county. Although these men of capital were well spread across the county, there is a noticeable lack of influence in the Broads and the most southerly hundreds. There do not appear to be any clear centres of support for individual candidates, although Edward Astley, who had been elected in 1780 and 1784, had most support around his family seat at Melton Constable in Gallow Hundred.

From this group of 150 emerged the very few families who provided the candidates for the county seats. As well as the two members for Norfolk, the boroughs of Norwich, Yarmouth, Kings Lynn, Thetford and Castle Rising all elected two M.P.s. In Norwich by 1831 there were 4,000 voters out of a total population of just over 61,000, in Yarmouth 1,700 out of 24,115 inhabitants and in Kings Lynn 300 out of 13,370. The two boroughs of Thetford and Castle Rising were far smaller and their elections were entirely controlled by the major landowners.

The families who provided the M.P.s for these various seats were small in number and had to possess some distinctive characteristics.

Firstly, they needed a great deal of money. Because of the expense, many elections were uncontested. If a vote was necessary, freeholders needed feasting and taking to the hustings in Norwich. In 1768 the four candidates and their friends probably spent £40,000 whilst Coke on another occasion spent £20,000; the equivalent of a year's income from rent.

Secondly, was 'county standing'. This could only be attained after long years of ownership of a great estate. The county M.P.s between 1750 and 1820 were provided by the Townshend, Wodehouse, de Grey, Astley, Coke and Wyndham families, all of which had owned extensive lands in the county for 400 years.

An indication of the independence and honour felt by the elected member is summed up by Thomas William Coke's statement to the electors in 1806, 'The situation of being the representative of the freeholders of Norfolk is certainly the proudest that an independent man can be placed in', and he followed this in 1820 by saying, 'Kings make peers, but they do not make County Members'.

The election for which this map was drawn did not in fact take place until 1790. In the event, it was uncontested. Edward Astley withdrew so Thomas William Coke and his rival John Wodehouse, were elected.

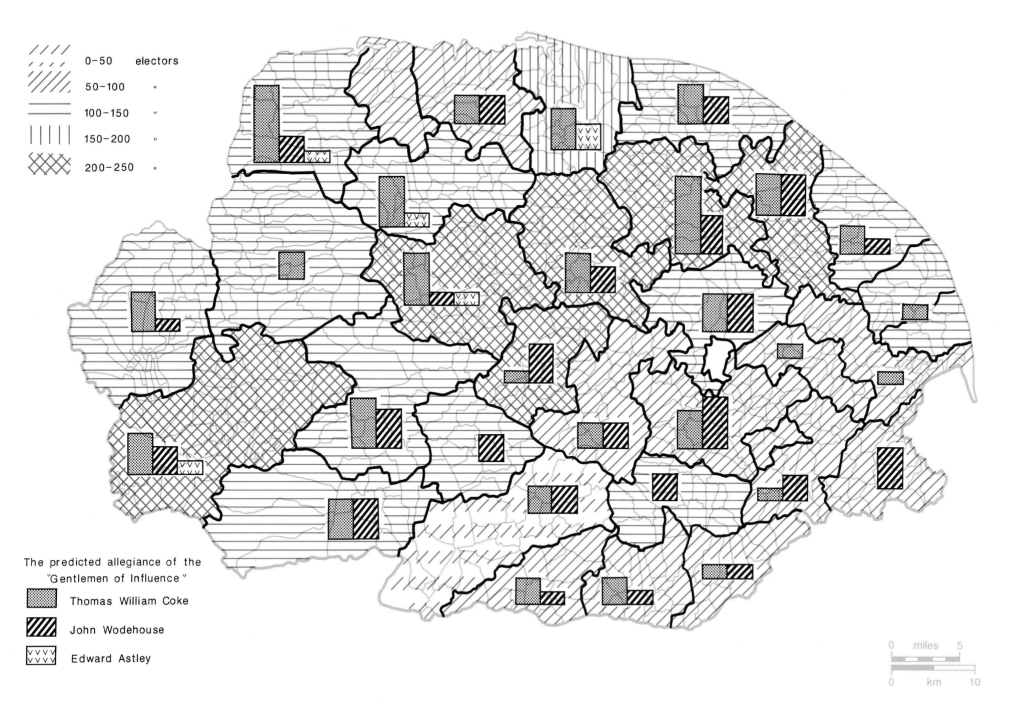

0–50 electors

50–100 "

100–150 "

150–200 "

200–250 "

The predicted allegiance of the
"Gentlemen of Influence"

Thomas William Coke

John Wodehouse

Edward Astley

miles 5

km 10

By 1880 over half of Norfolk was owned by landowners with more than one thousand acres, and much of the landscape of the county was dominated by their houses, parks, farms and villages.

Estates varied enormously in size and therefore in wealth, and so it is almost impossible to consider the landed gentry as a homogeneous group. They ranged from those who were little more than gentlemen farmers to those controlling estate offices and huge workshops with 40 or 50 farms on their rent roll.

The owners of all the Norfolk estates over 15,000 acres by 1880 were members of the aristocracy, with Lord Leicester's Holkham estate, covering 43,000 acres, by far the largest. His near neighbours were two other families who had risen to political eminence in the late 18th century, the Walpoles and the Townshends at Houghton and Raynham with between 15,000 and 18,000 acres under their control.

Below these giants were a further eight estates with more than 10,000 acres, most of which were also in the north-west of the county.

Also shaded on this map are the areas in estates of between 5,000 and 10,000 acres, 25 in all, and it can be seen that most of these are in the same parts of the county as their larger counterparts. It is difficult to explain why the densely populated area of small farmers in the eastern part of the county should have remained independent while so much of the west was estate dominated. It has been suggested that this can be traced back to Domesday Book and perhaps to the Danish settlements before. It was in east Norfolk that the 'freeman', a social group possibly of Scandinavian origin, are recorded in their largest numbers in 1086.

The contrast between the freehold and leasehold areas of the county was noticed by 18th-century observers. The owner-occupiers of the small and medium sized farms on the rich soils of north-east Norfolk were credited with the introduction of 'Norfolk husbandry' which only spread to the great estates later. Nathaniel Kent was worried by the 'numerous little places of the yeomanry (which) have fallen into the hands of men of fortune'. Although there is evidence for an increase in the size of many estates in the late 18th century, it is clear from the map that much of east Norfolk remained outside estate influence.

The difference this has made to the landscape and buildings in estates areas is obvious. Only on the great estates did the complete reorganisation of farmland follow on enclosure, and until recently the south and east areas of small irregular fields dating back to 16th century enclosure strips, or even, sometimes, far earlier. On the great estates entire farmsteads were replaced and farm houses rebuilt, whilst in the owner-occupier areas, medieval houses and barns are far more likely to survive.

Villages too were rebuilt, churches restored and schools founded. Although a few early examples of estate villages, such as that at Houghton, survive, most are late 19th century often near the gates to the great house.

The most popular pastime of the landowners was field sports. The strict preservation of game became an important estate activity in the 19th century and has resulted in a very distinctive estate landscape with ancient woodland surviving and clumps being planted as cover. By the end of the century shooting alone ensured the survival of estates, particularly in the poor Breckland soils. These were bought by industrialists who did not rely on agriculture to provide them with an income.

Some Norfolk estates can trace a continuous ownership in the same family back to the Middle Ages. The LeStranges were established at Hunstanton by 1200 whilst Sir Thomas De Grey became the owner of Merton in 1306 and the Duke of Norfolk owned land in south Norfolk and a palace at Kenninghall in the 16th century. Many dynasties were either founded or greatly added to at the time of the Reformation and the later troubles of the Civil War. The fortunes for these purchases were often made through political activities or the legal profession. Sir Nicholas Hare was a Privy Councillor and Keeper of the Great Seal for Mary 1st before he bought Stow Bardolph in 1553. Queen Elizabeth's Chief Justice, Sir Edward Coke, bought up land around his home in Mileham and Tittleshall before expanding into the Holkham area. Sir Charles Harbord, Surveyor General to Charles 1st and 2nd began accumulating the Gunton estate in the 17th century and William De Grey, later Baron Walsingham, was able to add to the family estate around Merton as a result of his spell as Lord Chief Justice beginning in 1771.

There were some comparative late comers. The accumulation of the large Evans-Lombe estate around Marlingford and later Bylaugh did not begin until the middle of the 18th century using money made in the manufacture of silk in Derbyshire.

The 19th century was undoubtedly the hey-day of the great estate based on an opulance provided by buoyant agricultural rents which began to fall after 1870. The temporary recovery of agriculture during the first world war led to mass sales after 1918 when a third of England changed hands. The great estate and the landlord-tenant system which had dominated society across so much of Norfolk was finally broken.

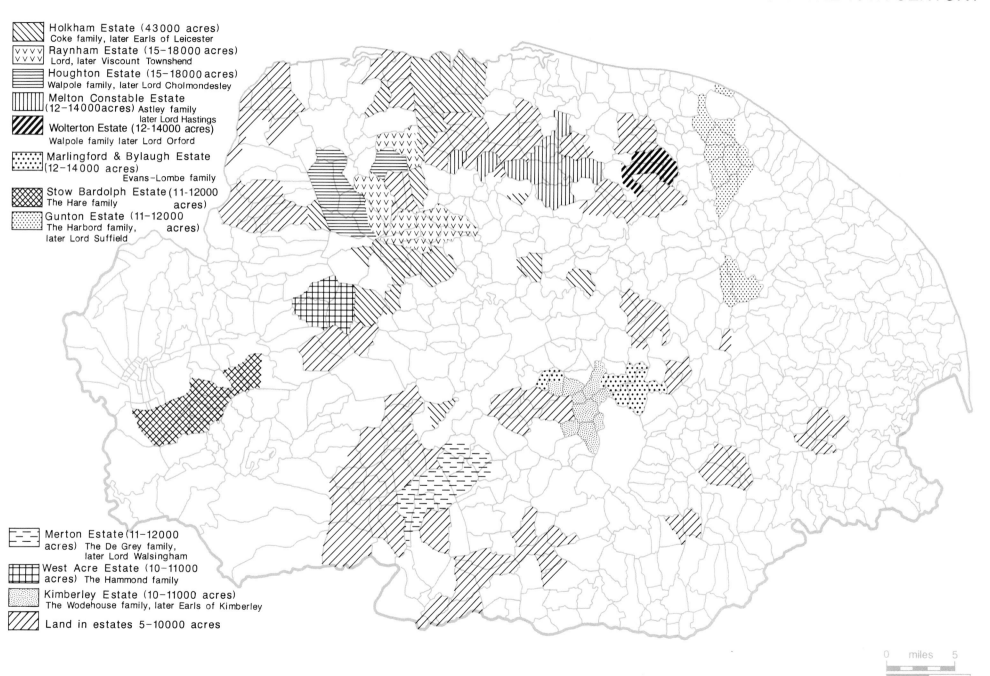

Holkham Estate (43000 acres)
Coke family, later Earls of Leicester

Raynham Estate (15-18000 acres)
Lord, later Viscount Townshend

Houghton Estate (15-18000 acres)
Walpole family, later Lord Cholmondesley

Melton Constable Estate
(12-14000 acres) Astley family
later Lord Hastings

Wolterton Estate (12-14000 acres)
Walpole family later Lord Orford

Marlingford & Bylaugh Estate
(12-14000 acres)
Evans-Lombe family

Stow Bardolph Estate (11-12000 acres)
The Hare family

Gunton Estate (11-12000 acres)
The Harbord family,
later Lord Suffield

Merton Estate (11-12000
acres) The De Grey family,
later Lord Walsingham

West Acre Estate (10-11000
acres) The Hammond family

Kimberley Estate (10-11000 acres)
The Wodehouse family, later Earls of Kimberley

Land in estates 5-10000 acres

0   miles   5

0   km   10

57. PARLIAMENTARY ENCLOSURE

Michael Turner

This section is entirely concerned with enclosures by parliamentary acts, and for Norfolk there were over 300 such acts. This places the county third in order of importance behind the West Riding of Yorkshire and Lincolnshire in terms of the number of acts. Over 400,000 acres were enclosed in the 18th and 19th centuries putting it third in a ranked list. In other ways Norfolk was important. If we view the accompanying maps simply as locational indicators then we see that a huge area was touched in some way by an enclosure act, and sometimes by more than one. And yet Norfolk is rarely regarded in the literature as a premier county of parliamentary enclosure. Why is this? The map of density of enclosure partly explains the problem. Over large areas the acts tidied up a process of abandoning open-field agriculture which had been ongoing for some centuries, or they finally brought small commons and wastes into cultivation, sometimes for the first time, or they led to the improvement of heaths and fens. In total only about 31% of the county area was affected by enclosure acts, thus placing it not third but fourteenth in a list of English counties. The national average was about 21%.

The first Norfolk act was for 'draining, improving and inclosing the Common' at Stokesby in 1720, but the enclosure award appears not to have survived (according to Tate's *Domesday*). Many acts before the mid-18th century were for confirming existing enclosure agreements or existing enclosures. In these cases formal awards were not always necessary. The last Norfolk enclosure act was for enclosing 47 acres of Saxlingham Common in 1863 (but under the umbrella of the 1845 General Act).

The great majority of Norfolk villages were involved yet there were only 300 or so acts for a county of about 700 parishes. This brings out one feature which was particularly prevalent in Norfolk, the incidence of parishes sharing enclosure acts. Enclosure was an expensive business and it made sense to share some of the legal and parliamentary costs. It was quite usual for parishes or villages in England which shared some common ground such as a heath, fen or common and waste to enclose that ground and therefore become mutual parties to the legal procedures, but rarely on the scale we see in Norfolk. In addition, in Norfolk, there was also a lot of this legal co-operation even where common facilities were not present. On closer inspection we find parishes enclosing under the umbrella of the same act which were not even contiguously located. For example, an act of 1808 was passed to enclose Bawdeswell and Lyng in north central Norfolk, but these are by no means contiguous places. Probably the most extreme example of this practice was the enclosure between 1818 and 1823 of the last remnants of open fields in Wood Dalling and of the heaths and waste grounds in Itteringham, Oulton, and Wickmere. Only two of these parishes are adjacent.

The accompanying maps show two features: the chronology of enclosure; and the density of that enclosure. The chronology has been simplified because the time profile of parliamentary enclosure at the national level had a distinctive shape. Eighty per cent of English parliamentary enclosure took place in two narrow windows of time of about 20 years each - essentially the 1760s and 1770s, and then during the period of the French revolutionary and Napoleonic Wars. The relatively heavy soils of the English Midland counties were enclosed mainly in the first period and were followed by conversion of arable to pasture. The wartime enclosures included heavy soils, but they were dominated by lighter soils and the enclosure and reclamation of various types of commons, wastes, heaths and fens. Essentially this was a period of extending and improving the arable during high wartime prices and of bringing otherwise unused or ill-used land into cultivation. Norfolk was very much a county of wartime enclosures. The pre-1793 enclosures were mainly on the west of the county and were mainly for the enclosure of the open-field arable. A prominent feature was the coincidence of open-field arable with high density of enclosure, whether pre-1793

or during the war. The lower density and dominantly common and waste enclosures occurred in the east. There were enclaves which upset this generalisation, especially the fen enclosures on the Lincolnshire/Cambridgeshire border. Given the high incidence of common and waste enclosures depicted on the chronological map, it may come as some surprise to learn that upwards of three quarters of the land involved in Norfolk enclosures was in fact open-field arable.

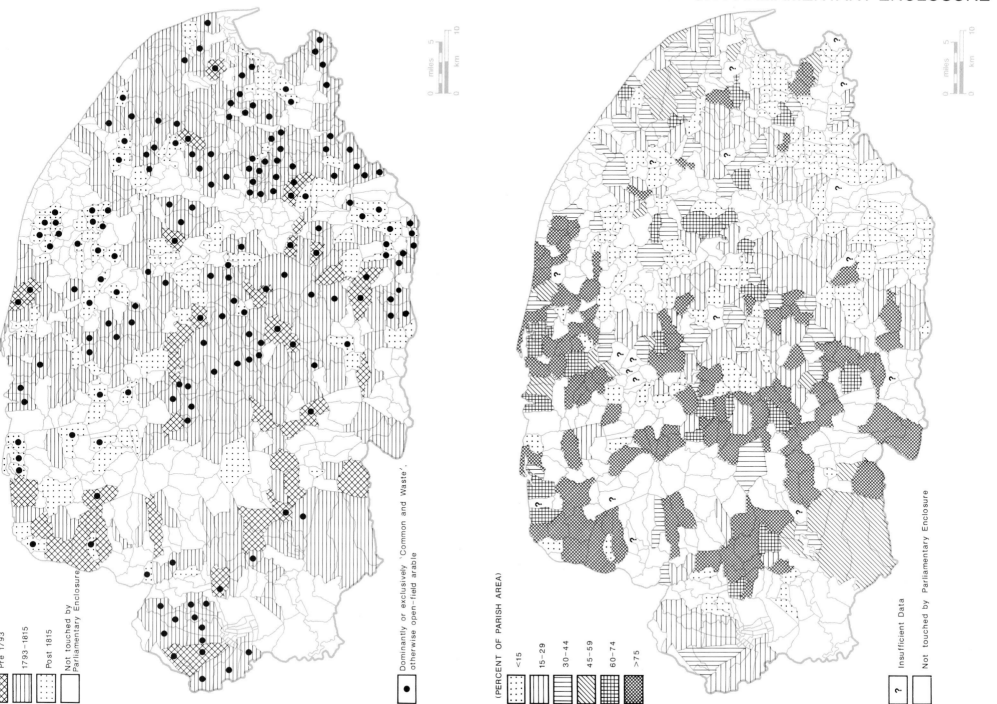

57. PARLIAMENTARY ENCLOSURE

Pre 1793

1793–1815

Post 1815

Not touched by
Parliamentary Enclosure

● Dominantly or exclusively 'Common and Waste',
otherwise open-field arable

(PERCENT OF PARISH AREA)

<15

15–29

30–44

45–59

60–74

>75

? Insufficient Data

Not touched by Parliamentary Enclosure

Rumbling discontent and suspicion between employer and employed had been typical of relations between farmers and labourers since the main phase of parliamentary enclosure during the Napoleonic Wars, and Norfolk was the most troubled area of Britain through the first 30 years of the 19th century. Chronic underemployment meant wages could be kept near starvation levels, and as corn prices rose during the war the fear of famine was very real indeed. The peace of 1815 did not bring the much hoped for fall in prices, because a farmer-landowner dominated parliament passed the Corn Laws, which prevented the importing of grain until the price of British corn reached 80 shillings a quarter. This resulted in the first wave of riots amongst agricultural labourers, in the west of the county around Littleport and Southery on the Norfolk-Cambridgeshire border. These were, first and foremost, food riots with starving labourers attacking corn mills as well as farmers. Wage increases, to bring weekly earnings up to ten shillings a week were the usual demand. After order was restored smouldering discontent remained and the danger of both rick burning and machine breaking was never far away.

The most hated machines were the threshing machines which deprived the labourer of an important source of winter employment, the hand-flailing of cereal crops. Although threshing machines were available from the 1780s, low wages and their unpopularity with the labourers meant that they spread across East Anglia only slowly. There was an outbreak of machine-breaking in south Norfolk in 1822, which further discouraged farmers from buying them.

In 1830 discontent again surfaced in the far more widespread 'Swing' riots which affected much of southern Britain. For eight weeks from the middle of November 1830 trouble swept through just over 150 Norfolk parishes. Arson and machine breaking was often preceded by letters signed by 'Swing', addressed to individual farmers threatening action if machines were not dismantled by the farmers themselves. The identity of 'Captain Swing' has never been established and the origin of this code name is obscure. It is unlikely that there was any central planning or control of the riots; rather, they spread spontaneously from neighbouring villages.

Evidence for the riots comes mainly from the local press which records not only the riots, but also the trials of those trouble-makers brought to justice. Hobsbawm and Rude collected much of this information for their book published in 1970, and later J.E. Archer made a more extensive search of local papers. This map has been drawn from both these sources.

The Swing riots took several different forms. Firstly there were incidents of machine breaking and arson. Machine breaking was confined mainly to the central and eastern parts of the northern half of the county and did not occur in those parishes affected in 1822. Perhaps the farmers here had learnt their lesson and abandoned attempts at mechanisation.

There was some support for the labourers' cause amongst the magistrates. Those in North Walsham printed a notice urging farmers to dismantle threshing machines and increase wages. This attitude was endorsed by a committee of magistrates set up in Norwich for the preservation of the peace. In a few instances, industrial as well as agricultural machinery was attacked. A paper mill in Lyng and looms in Norwich as well as a saw mill at Catton, near Norwich, were broken.

Secondly there were wage riots which seem to have been confined to the Diss area in the south and to the north-east of the county. The clustering of certain types of riot suggests a local ring leader active in a group of parishes, but it is difficult to suggest any reasons for the regional differentiation other than local personalities and grievances.

Thirdly, and usually associated with wage demands, were the tithe riots. Tithes had long been a source of grievance to farmers who decided to turn the wage protests to their benefit by responding to workers' demands with an offer of increased wages made conditional on a reduction in tithes. The labourers were encouraged to go to the local tithe owner, usually the parson, and continue their demonstration there, often with some success. This uniting of farmer and labourer against a common grievance was short-lived. A Norfolk witness to a Select Committee on Agriculture in 1833 claimed that feelings were so unpleasant between farmers and labourers that it deterred newcomers from taking a farm. To the question, 'Is there the same good feeling between farmers and labourers that there was formerly?', the answer was 'Nothing like there was before the fires.'

As the map shows, there is no clear geographical pattern behind the parishes where riots occurred. Tithe riots were more frequent in the south, although there were isolated examples in the fens, whilst wage riots were clustered in the north and machinery breaking in the middle of the county. The west of the county on the whole fared better, with fewer disturbances in the less populated areas of the large estates. Elsewhere riots occurred in all types of village; estate and non-estate, large and small. Much more work on local communities and the loyalties and stresses within them is needed before there can be an adequate explanation of the geography of unrest in this last wave of riots before the beginnings of trade union activity in 1870.

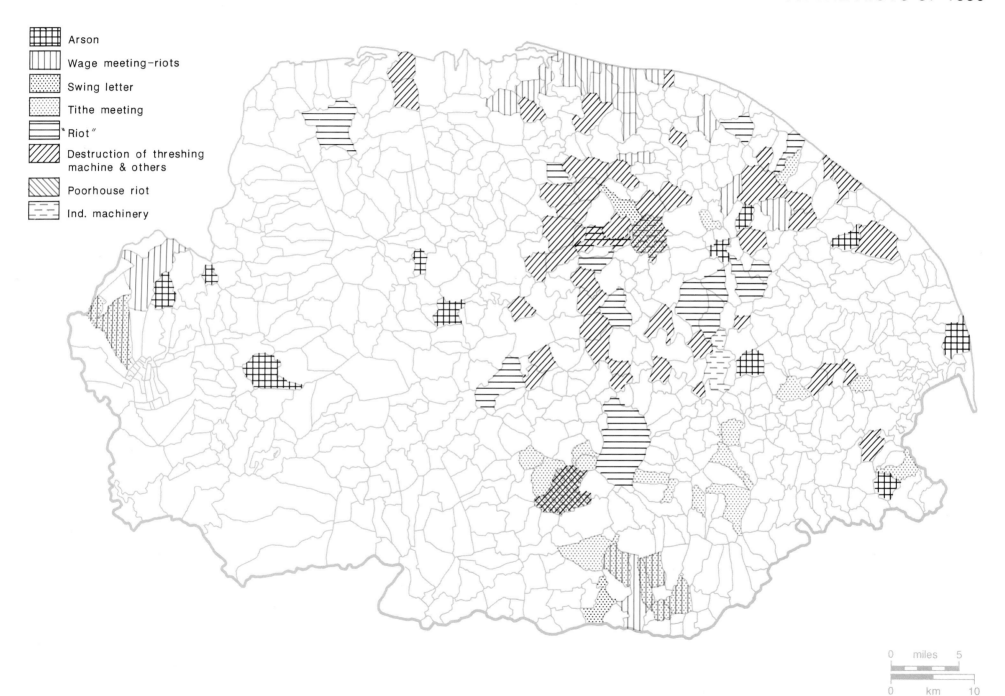

Arson

Wage meeting-riots

Swing letter

Tithe meeting

"Riot"

Destruction of threshing machine & others

Poorhouse riot

Ind. machinery

0   miles   5

0   km   10

Norfolk in 1850 had for 200 years been in the forefront of agricultural improvement. The signs of the prosperity this had brought were to be seen everywhere; hedges and ditches were well kept, fields were weed-free and farm buildings, particularly on the estate farms, were large, up-to-date and in good order. It was only the labourers' cottages that fell below this generally high standard.

The set of maps drawn here are compiled from a major source of information for this period; the statistics collected by Sir John Walsham, a Norfolk inspector for the Poor Law Board in 1853-4 for which the Poor Law Union was used as the unit of collection.

The first map shows the proportion of land in each union under various crops, and it can be seen that only in the Breckland Union of Thetford did grain account for as little as 6.5% of the crop. Elsewhere a mixed system predominated. Very often grain crops took up about the same area as that under roots and artificial grasses put together, suggesting that the classic four-course rotation was being practised. The other two unions that did not follow this pattern are Blofield and Downham. Rather than growing grass, Blofield relied on the permanent pasture of the Broadland marshes for animal feed, whilst in the recently drained and cultivated fertile Fenland area of Downham, 45.6% of the land was under grain, the highest percentage for any of the Norfolk unions.

The second map shows the type of grain being grown. Wheat, although the most profitable crop, was not ideally suited to Norfolk soils, and Norfolk was famous as a barley county. Enough oats was grown on all farms to feed the horses, but on the poorest soils it was grown as a cash crop. Similarly, rye is found mainly on the poor Breckland soils of Thetford Union. The largest areas of wheat were grown in the fertile fens and the rich loams of Blofield Union. Only in Thetford and the heavy southern clays of Guiltcross Union was wheat less than 40% of the cereal acreage. Elsewhere in the south there

must have been considerable drainage of the clays to allow sizeable wheat acreages to be planted.

The third map shows the various crops such as roots and pulses that could be grown as break crops in a crop rotation. Roots included turnips, mangolds and carrots, whilst pulses were either peas or beans. It is here that the differences between the heavy and light soils of the county show most clearly. Roots were more suited to the light soils, and peas and beans to the heavier ones. Turnips still made up over 90% of the root crop in Aylsham, Docking, Erpingham and Walsingham Unions. R.N. Bacon an editor of the Norfolk Chronicle and author of *The Agriculture of Norfolk*, published in 1844, went so far as to say, 'The prosperity of the Norfolk farmer depends principally on his successful cultivation of the turnip, and consequently on no other crop is so large an outlay made, either in manure or labour, or so much care or attention bestowed.'

The final map shows the number of animals kept. The number of horses per acre is both a reflection of the heaviness of the soil and of the level of mechanisation. Both the heavy lands of Loddon and Clavering and the rich loams of East and West Flegg kept one horse for every 19-20 acres, whilst in the little cultivated soils of Thetford, there was only one horse for every 56 acres. Dairy cattle were of little importance in Norfolk but in contrast, sheep were particularly numerous on the light soils, where it was claimed the folding of sheep on the turnip crop had made the land strong enough for wheat cultivation. Sheep, therefore were found in the light soils, in the intensively farmed areas of Docking and Walsingham as well as in the sandy areas bordering on Breckland, in Swaffham and Wayland.

These statistics are particularly valuable because they show the regional differences within the county. The most striking is the poorness of the Thetford area with very little grain grown and a third of that being oats or rye. Very few horses were needed in a region where rab-

bits and game were the most important crops. It is surprising that more sheep are not recorded, as there were some large flocks kept on the open land. In contrast, the fens were very fertile and intensively farmed with a high percentage of land under grain, much of which was wheat. On the light soils, we see a careful rotation system depending on the folding of sheep on the turnip fields. On the heavier soils of the south, more barley was grown than wheat, and beans were more important than root crops. In the marshland areas, permanent pasture was more important, with wheat on the good loams. The average yield of wheat across the county was 30 bushels an acre, which Sir John Walsham thought was impressive considering the unsuitability of most Norfolk soils to the crop. The yields of barley were better (34 bushels per acre). There can be no doubt that many of the farms away from Breckland and the very heavy clays of the extreme south were intensively farmed mid-century and that Norfolk farming was still a model for the rest of the country to follow.

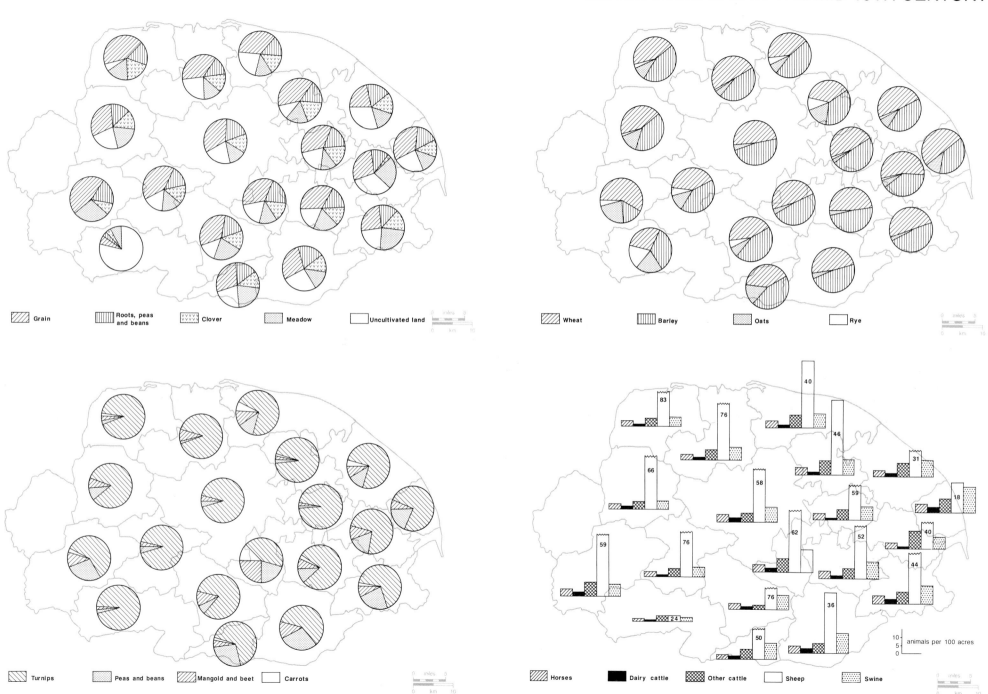

Grain
Roots, peas and beans
Clover
Meadow
Uncultivated land

Wheat
Barley
Oats
Rye

Turnips
Peas and beans
Mangold and beet
Carrots

Horses
Dairy cattle
Other cattle
Sheep
Swine

animals per 100 acres

Christopher Barringer

The changing relative importance of market centres is of great interest and it results from the operation of many factors: the Norman conquest, for example, by leading to the move of the seat of the Bishop of East Anglia from Thetford to Norwich, resulted in a steady decline of Thetford: the dissolution of the monasteries resulted in the collapse of many small market centres such as Shouldham and Binham and the changes in the means of transport emphasised some centres at the expense of others. Hingham, for example, had no railway station whereas Wymondham and Watton did. As movement became easier so the journey to market could be increased; the daily journey possible by horse and cart to market limited the service areas of market towns to some four or five miles i.e. a ten mile round trip. The more specialised a market the larger its hinterland - the Stourbridge Fair where cloth, butter and earthenware were sold and which was held just outside Cambridge is perhaps the most famous East Anglian example, but the Norwich cloth market and the King's Lynn barley and corn markets also drew traders from all over Europe.

The great markets of Norfolk were in the four major towns, Norwich, Great Yarmouth, King's Lynn and Thetford. The gap in market towns around Norwich is noticeable (as in earlier periods: Map 33), and whilst as far as is known there was no prevention of nearby markets, as there was around Bury St. Edmunds, it was never worth anyone's while to attempt competition with the drawing power of the 'Second City' with its need to feed its large population.

Lynn had its two medieval market places - the earlier Saturday Market and the slightly later and more spacious Tuesday Market Place. The Tuesday Market's February 'mart' lasted for 12 days and drew traders to it from a very wide area, but by the 1840's it was a 'pleasure fair' only.

Thetford's market was moved in the 1870's from its earlier site next to the castle ramparts, a situation not unlike that of Norwich, to a new site on the north edge of the new town that had evolved north of the Little Ouse in the post Norman period. It still had four fairs in 1845, one for cattle, two for sheep and one for wool - these three reflecting the influence of the Breckland economy.

Yarmouth has always been primarily a fishing port. However its market place is impressive and covers two and three quarter acres. The former medieval herring fair survived there until 1844 when a new fish market was opened. Its market day of Saturday was the general market for Yarmouth and East Norfolk.

After the four major towns the scatter of lesser markets was relatively evenly spaced across the county but the process of adjustment to new influences was always at work. Downham Market was long famous for 'Cambridge' butter but by 1809 Swaffham had replaced it as a butter market and was itself in decline by 1845. A more obvious shift in importance stemmed from the building of turnpikes and railways and in one or two cases the improvement of waterways. Aylsham's market place lies near the church but the completion of the Bure Navigation in 1773 led to the development of granaries and maltings in Millgate and building between the mill and White Horse Street became virtually continuous. Watton, also known for its butter market, had benefited from the construction of the turnpike from Norwich by 1770.

The fairs often occupied a different site within a market town from the market as at Wymondham, Hingham and Diss. Several important fairs such as those at Hempton, Cawston and Horsham St. Faiths survived after the markets had gone and in one or two cases existed in villages where no market charter had ever been granted.

By the mid-19th century the following markets were noted in White's Directory as obsolete, though fairs had in some cases survived: Acle, New Buckenham, Cawston (long obsolete), Great Massingham (reduced to two pleasure fairs), Methwold (long obsolete and almost disused by 1809); and Snettisham, said to have been a market town: Wells market survived only until 1854.

Of the surviving markets, Swaffham, Downham, Diss, Fakenham, Aylsham, North Walsham, Holt, Wymondham and Harleston were probably the most important. In every case they were served by the railways.

A typical market town had a population of about 1,000 in 1845 and had acquired, apart from its market place, a number of activities that distinguished it from a 'village'. These usually included academies, perhaps including a grammar school; banks, fire and life insurance offices; several inns; lawyers; booksellers; brewers and maltsters; cabinet makers; clock and watch makers; chemists; china dealers; grocers and drapers; gunsmiths; iron founders and engineers; surgeons; surveyors; wine and spirit merchants; coachbuilders and stonemasons.

Norfolk villages had fewer people in 1881 than they had in 1841. However, while the market towns held their own, when compared with the new industrial towns of the midlands, the north of England and London and Birmingham, they grew slowly. It is this lack of 19th century growth that led to Diss, Wymondham, Swaffham, Hingham and Holt, for example, maintaining their characters and charm as small market towns, at least until the new expansion in the period since 1960.

60. MARKETS AND FAIRS IN THE 18TH AND 19TH CENTURIES

+   Market in 1845

F   Fair in 1845

H   Hiring Session

Burnham Market
FF +

Wells +
F

Cromer +(extant 1722)
F

+ Holt
FF (Stock)

Walsingham
F H +

+ Snettisham (extant
H   in 17th c.)

North Walsham
F H +

Fakenham +
H

+ Aylsham
FFH

Hempton
FF(Cattle)

Cawston
FFF (Sheep)

• Castle Rising
F

+ Reepham
HF (Stock)

+ + + KINGS LYNN
F (Cattle)

FF • Great Massingham

FF • Castle Acre

Horsham
+ St Faiths
F(Cattle)

FF + East Dereham

NORWICH
+ + +
F (Cattle)

Acle
F •

Great
Yarmouth
+
FF(Fish)

Swaffham (Butter)
FFF +
Races

Downham Market (Butter)
+
FFFH

Watton (Butter)
+
FFF (Cattle)
F (Sheep)

Hingham
FFF

Wymondham
+ FFFH

+ Loddon
FFH

• Northwold
F

Attleborough
+ FFFF

• Methwold
FH

New Buckenham
FFH+

• Feltwell
F

THETFORD
+
FF(Sheep) F (Wool)
F (Cattle)

East Harling
+
HFF (Cattle)
F (Sheep)

Harleston
+
FF (Lambs)
F(Scotch Cattle)

Diss
+
FF (linen
1736)

0   miles   5

0   km   10

John Wright

Population change in the first half of the 19th century was characterised by rapid growth, continuing a trend that had been taking place since about 1740. In 1801 there were 273,000 people in Norfolk; by 1851 the total had grown by 62% to 443,000. The peak rate of growth, as measured by census counts, was between 1811 and 1821 when the population increased by 18% at an average of 5,200 per year. Although migration into and out of the county was certainly taking place, the primary reason for the substantial increase in population was that there were many more births than deaths. In the early years of the century, before civil registration, the Registrar General asked for counts of baptisms and burials for every parish. The 1820 totals for Norfolk came to over 11,000 baptisms and 6,000 burials. The baptism figure, even without adjusting for possible omissions, represents a high birth rate (over 30 per 1,000 people) but such figures were typical of rural England. However, the effect of high birth rates was reduced somewhat by high rates of infant mortality. Between 1813 and 1830, one quarter of all deaths in the county were of children under the age of one, but mortality rates were declining. The early censuses, beginning in 1801, have nothing to say about the age structure of the population, but they do show that occupancy rates were declining steadily. The housing stock almost doubled between 1801 and 1851, a faster rate of increase than that for population, and the average occupancy rate for the county declined from 5.7 to 4.8 people per dwelling.

The map shows the percentage population change in each civil parish, using 'best fit' figures from relevant census volumes. To permit easy comparisons with population change in later periods, the map shows the parish boundaries as they were in 1981. Since 1851 there have been many parish amalgamations and some new parishes have been created (namely, Nordelph, Marshland St. James, West Downham, Hunstanton, Sheringham and West Caister). For these parishes rates of growth have been estimated. Other, more minor, boundary changes have not been taken into account.

The dominant feature of the map is population growth, especially in the west and north west of the county, in the vicinity of Norwich and Great Yarmouth, and in some coastal areas. Slower rates of growth are apparent in the north, east and south of the county. Actual decline is rare. The three main centres, Norwich, Great Yarmouth and King's Lynn, all increased faster than the county average. Together they had nearly 18,000 more people in 1851 than had they grown at the average rate. To that extent, it can be said that the county became more urbanised. Moreover, Sprowston and Thorpe grew very rapidly during this period, as did Clenchwarton, close to King's Lynn, and Walsoken, next to Wisbech. On the other hand, the 'top ten' market towns, ranging from Wymondham with 3,600 people in 1801 to Harleston with 1,500, together increased by exactly the average rate for the county. At the other end of the scale, the 100 smallest parishes, with South Wootton, Spixworth and Hellesdon well down the list, increased in total by only 48%.

The pattern of change depicted on the map only hints at some of the reasons for population change in individual parishes. Then, as now, it was the larger towns which offered the best prospects for work. Conversely, the smallest villages could offer fewer opportunities and therefore had less potential for growth, unless there was work available in another parish close by. Some villages remained small because of the control exercised by the dominant landowners, some of whom prevented house-building in order to minimise the number of people who might need relief from parish rates. In any event, few parishes with large estates had significant population growth. Blickling, Felbrigg and Melton Constable are among the few parishes which declined in population and there was relatively little growth at Holkham, Raynham, Heydon and Houghton. In contrast to these 'closed' parishes were the 'open' villages with more opportunities for new housing. The best known example is probably Castle Acre, where the gang system was employed to take workers out to farms in neighbouring parishes. Many villages, however, did not fall easily into either category.

The seaside was just beginning to be an important factor. Great Yarmouth and Cromer had both begun to function as resorts before 1800 and continued to develop thereafter (Map 83). Fishing and maritime trade boosted population growth in some coastal villages (Map 82). The widespread enclosure of open fields also provided some opportunities for growth, and the census volumes contain reminders that census counts do not necessarily represent 'normal' conditions. Some figures, for example, are inflated by migrant workers building railways (Map 71), embankments or mansions, or even by 'strangers' attending a fair. More important, however, is the frequent reference to emigration, particularly in the latter part of the period. Some people moved to the industrial areas of the country, while many others went overseas, especially to North America, sometimes with the assistance of the parish.

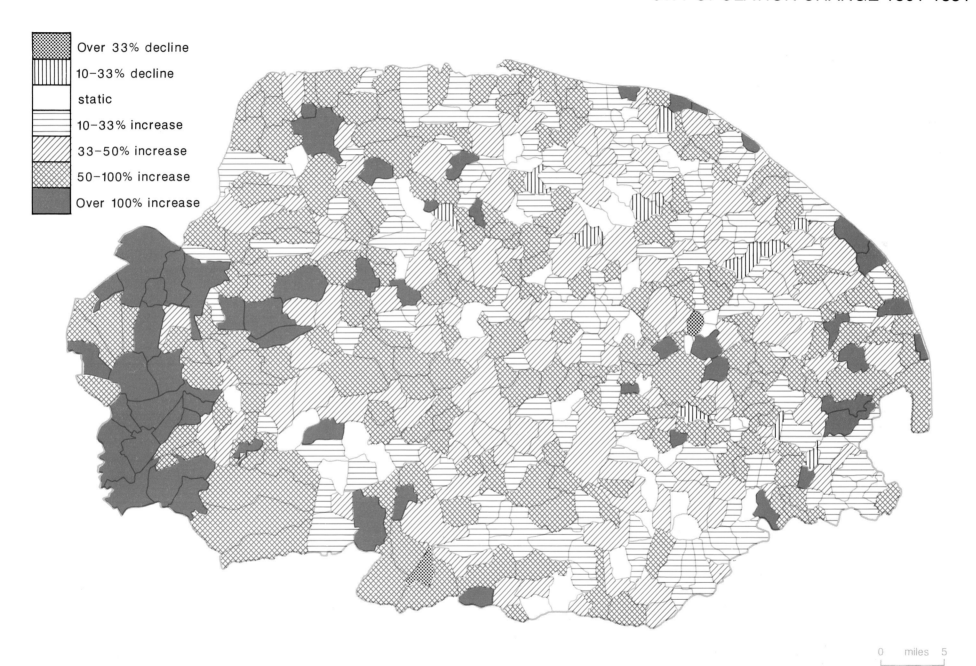

61. POPULATION CHANGE 1801-1851

Over 33% decline
10-33% decline
static
10-33% increase
33-50% increase
50-100% increase
Over 100% increase

0   miles   5

0   km   10

62. POPULATION CHANGE 1851-1951

John Wright

Following rapid growth of population in the early 19th century there was a decrease after 1851 and it was not until about 1880 that the population of the county returned to the 1851 total of 443,000. Thereafter there was continual growth on a relatively modest scale, quickening after the turn of the century, fading during the inter-war years and picking up again after 1945. By 1951 the population had increased in total by 24% to 548,000. Boundary changes, principally the transfer of Gorleston from Suffolk to Norfolk in 1894, added nearly 14,000 to the population, but other growth represents the balance between natural change and migration. The high birth rates of the mid 19th century declined steeply after 1900 to about 15 per 1,000 people in 1951. Death rates decreased from about 22 to 12 per 1,000 people over the whole period. In consequence natural growth declined from a peak of around 6,000 per year to only about 2,000. Comparing these rates with total population growth shows that there was a continual, and substantial, net emigration from the county.

The age structure of the population changed significantly over the 100 year period. In 1851, 45% of the population were aged under 20; by 1951 this had decreased to 29% - and there were only four people in this age group in 1951 for every five 100 years earlier. Conversely, the proportion of older people in the population increased: 12.6% were over 65 in 1951 compared with 9.2% in 1851. Occupancy rates continued to decrease, due in part to the increase in older people living separately from the younger generation. The average occupancy rate declined from 4.8 people per occupied dwelling in 1851 to 4.3 in 1901 and 3.5 in 1951.

The map shows percentage population change for all the civil parishes which existed in 1981. Six were created during this period and their 1851 populations have been estimated. Many parish amalgamations have taken place and there have been other boundary changes, mostly minor, but some quite large, such as the gains by Norwich from Catton and Sprowston and by Cromer from Overstrand. It has not been possible to assess the 1851 populations of areas transferred (for comparison with 1951) but there are only a few cases where a parish would have been in a different category had it not been for the boundary change.

Population decline is the dominant feature of the map and the contrast with the map for 1801 - 1851 is clear. Two thirds of all parishes lost population, despite the overall growth in the county total. This implies an increasing concentration of people in fewer locations. Norwich, combined with adjacent parishes, doubled in size and Great Yarmouth increased by two thirds, while King's Lynn grew at the average rate for the county. The result is that the population living in the three largest urban areas increased from 29% to 42% of the county total. The remainder of the county grew at much less than the county average. The 'top ten' market towns, ranging from Wymondham with 5,200 people in 1851 to Attleborough with 2,300, grew by only 5%, with large increases in East Dereham and North Walsham partly offset by declines in Swaffham and Wells. In the rest of the county there was an overall decline, despite substantial gains in individual parishes.

In the pattern of change across the county there are some similarities with the 1801-1851 map. Growth is most in evidence around the largest centres and in certain coastal locations, while the decline in south Norfolk and in parts of central and north Norfolk is reminiscent of those areas which previously had lower rates of growth. There are a number of parishes with large percentage increases in areas where population decline is predominant. Some, of course, are market towns (Watton) or adjacent parishes (Pudding Norton next to Fakenham). One or two (Choseley) were very small in 1851 and a doubling of the population still represents only a small number of people. The growth at Melton Constable is due to the 'planned' expansion of the former small village to accommodate railway workers - leaving a unique townscape in rural Norfolk. In other villages (Stiffkey, Raynham, Wretham etc.) the apparent growth was due to the construction of airfields or other military installations and the consequent presence of servicemen in 1951. If the service population were excluded there would have been an even more continuous swathe of population decline throughout rural Norfolk.

The reasons for decline lie mainly in the loss of jobs in agriculture, but many villages also lost some of the trades which had made them more self sufficient in the mid 19th century. Population growth around the main urban areas shows the influence of increased commuting to work, while the expansion in holidays and tourism brought population growth to many coastal areas. Sheringham and Hunstanton, for example, were still very small in 1851. Wells did not share in this growth because of its decline as a port. Some Broads villages have grown, not only because of their attractive surroundings but also because of their proximity to Norwich and Great Yarmouth. Within the 100 year period other trends have been masked by time including, for example, the rise in the population of market towns as the railways arrived.

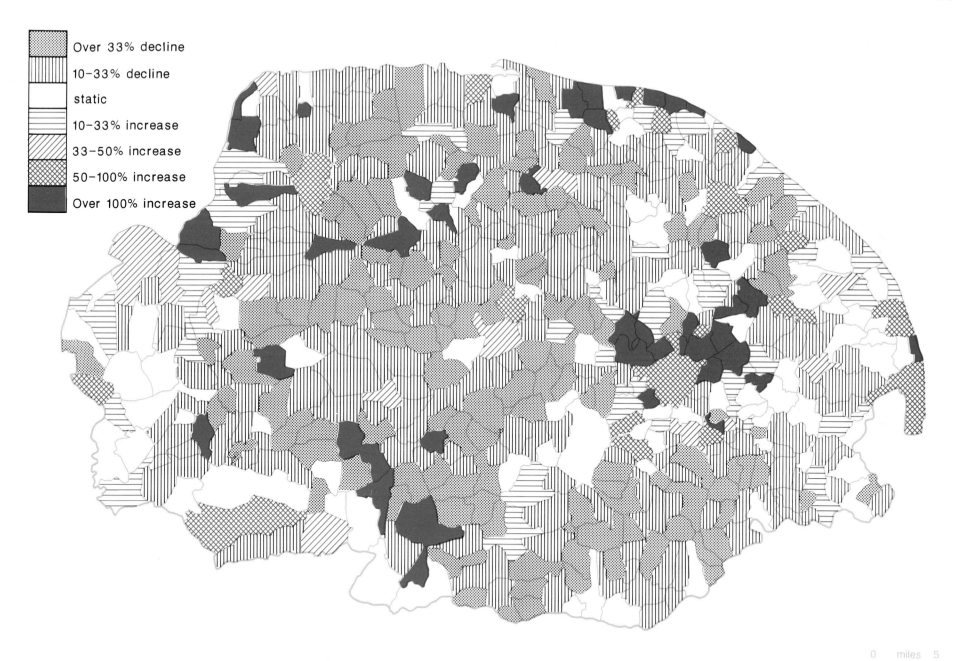

Over 33% decline
10–33% decline
static
10–33% increase
33–50% increase
50–100% increase
Over 100% increase

0 miles 5

0 km 10

63. ARMADA AND 17TH-CENTURY DEFENCES

Peter Kent

In the 16th century coastal fortifications, previously a local responsibility, became a major concern of the Crown. Henry VIII, fearing invasion from France and the Low Countries, in 1539 ordered a survey of the entire coastline of England.

In Norfolk, King's Lynn, Weybourne and Yarmouth were deemed in need of defences, the last two having sheltered deep-water anchorages close to the shore. But the only defences to be built then were two gun batteries at Yarmouth.

Half a century later, when the Armada threatened, the same vulnerable places were noted, but King's Lynn now had a small fort, St Anne's, there was a small earth fort at Weybourne and several cannon along the coast. At Yarmouth the batteries of 1540 had gone but the town wall had been backed with earth and strengthened with a large mound, the Mount.

Men and money were collected from the county to work on defences and Captain York, a skilled military engineer, drew an elaborate scheme to enlarge the fort at Weybourne and build a new fort at the mouth of Cley Haven, with a line of rampart running between the two. He planned to strengthen Yarmouth by adding ravelins to the walls, an outwork to defend the bridge, and two small forts at the river mouth.

At King's Lynn a new fort was planned half a mile downstream and the town walls were repaired. Further plans were made to block river crossings inland and build a citadel on Mousehold Heath above Norwich. Most of these plans remained on parchment, as the Armada was defeated when only a part of the Weybourne scheme had been carried out and at Yarmouth earthworks had been built around the south of the town with a brick bastion added to the wall below the Mount.

When the Civil War broke out in 1642 Norfolk declared for Parliament and looked to its defences. At Norwich this only entailed blocking up some of the gates and placing guns on the castle mound, but King's Lynn, guarding the entry into Norfolk from Lincolnshire, had strategic importance and was converted into a strong fortress by earthwork extensions to its medieval walls. Ironically, they were only of use against a Parliamentary army, for the town changed allegiance by declaring for the King and endured a three week siege before surrendering. The medieval walls and Armada defences at Yarmouth were repaired, a new line of earthworks built and batteries sited to defend the Roads and the river. None of these Norfolk defences were put to the test by the King's forces. The three Dutch Wars that were fought intermittently between 1652 and 1672 caused occasional panic but only a small brick fort by the river mouth at Yarmouth was built.

64. NAPOLEONIC FORTIFICATIONS

Peter Kent

For most of the 18th century the main naval threat to England was from France, so most attention was paid to the defences of the south coast. Norfolk was left with its forts at Yarmouth and King's Lynn and a few cannon at seaside villages.

The situation changed in 1778 when the war with the American Colonies broadened into a more serious conflict as France, then Spain and Holland, joined in. The east coast was in danger of attack from across the North Sea. In response, St. Anne's Fort at King's Lynn was rearmed, a small battery placed at Cromer and five forts, mounting 64 guns, built at Yarmouth to command the Roads, which were important as a safe anchorage; three were sited along the beach, one by the old fort and another on the heights at Gorleston. They had just been completed when the war ended in 1782, but they were

reactivated when war with France began in 1793. The coast was then surveyed and Weybourne, as before, was regarded as the most vulnerable spot, but still no fortifications were built there.

The most acute fear of invasion was in 1803. Although it was thought unlikely that the French would land a main invasion force, diversionary raids were considered possible, and, to counter these, batteries were proposed for the likely landing places. Weybourne was again first on the list, followed by other places in north Norfolk. The natural obstacles of the Wash were thought defence enough for the coast between Hunstanton and King's Lynn, and the official view taken of the section between Hunstanton and Sheringham was that it was best to rely on flooding the saltmarshes behind the beaches and to defend the few roads leading inland.

Of all the proposed works only those at Cromer, Mundesley and one, or possibly two, on Holkham beach were built. To supplement them obstacles were placed at the exits from the beaches. At Cromer, cliff paths were destroyed and other gaps in the cliffs blocked with palisades, thorn bushes and barricades of fishermen's boats.

The defences were maintained until 1815. St. Anne's Fort was disarmed in the 1820s and the harbour fort at Yarmouth was undermined by the scour of the river and demolished in 1833, leaving only the three beach batteries, with 21 guns. By the middle of the century they had all been disarmed, and, as St. Anne's Fort was left 100 yards inland after a change in the course of the river, Norfolk had no effective coastal defences at all.

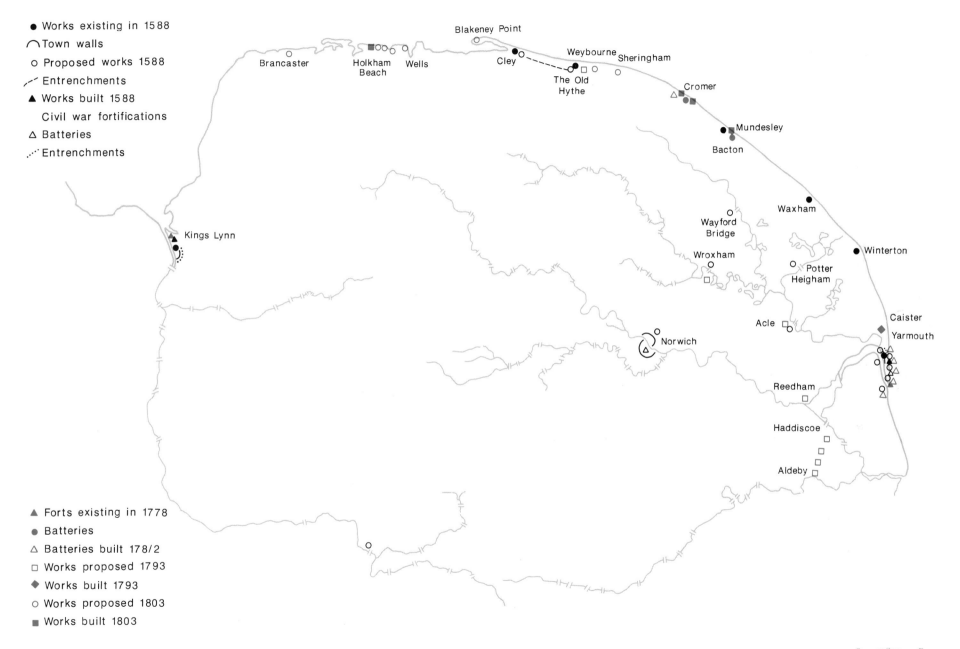

63. ARMADA AND 17TH-CENTURY DEFENCES

64. NAPOLEONIC FORTIFICATIONS

- ● Works existing in 1588
- ⌒ Town walls
- ○ Proposed works 1588
- ⌐ Entrenchments
- ▲ Works built 1588

Civil war fortifications

- △ Batteries
- ⋯ Entrenchments

Blakeney Point

Brancaster

Holkham
Beach

Wells

Cley

Weybourne Sheringham

The Old
Hythe

Cromer

Mundesley

Bacton

Waxham

Wayford
Bridge

Wroxham

Winterton

Potter
Heigham

Kings Lynn

Acle

Caister
Yarmouth

Norwich

Reedham

Haddiscoe

Aldeby

- ▲ Forts existing in 1778
- ● Batteries
- △ Batteries built 178/2
- □ Works proposed 1793
- ◆ Works built 1793
- ○ Works proposed 1803
- ■ Works built 1803

0   miles   5

0   km   10

'In the beginning of the eleventh year of her reign (1569) Cornwallis, Bedingfeld and Sulyard were the first recusants, they absolutely refusing to come to our churches, and until they in that sort began, the name of Recusant was never heard of among us.'

This term was applied to Protestant as well as Catholic non-conformists and in some early lists and indictments the two groups can only be differentiated when additional evidence is available. Catholics were later singled out for heavier penalties than the fine of one shilling imposed for non-attendance at the parish church. For the Catholic, the Mass and union with the Pope were the touchstone of faith; the role of the priest was essential to the practice of the Christian life. The role of the laity was to shelter and provide for the priest and so make the sacraments of the Church available to the Faithful. Statutes in 1581 and 1585 raised the penalty for non-attendance to 20 shillings a month (calculated on a 13 month year) brought in the death penalty for all priests ordained abroad, threatened all those who aided priests in any way with imprisonment the confiscation of goods and up to two-thirds of their estates and, in some cases, with death. Although Catholics repeatedly declared their temporal loyalty to the Crown, the excommunication of Elizabeth, plots real and imagined, to replace her by Mary, Queen of Scots and finally, the threats of foreign invasion, culminating in the Armadas, provoked an even more severe statute in 1593. Nevertheless, Catholicism remained alive, and in Norfolk as elsewhere gained ground in the first decade of the 17th century.

Until 1574 when the first 'seminary' priests trained in English colleges abroad arrived in England, Catholicism had been kept alive by 'old' priests ordained in the reigns of Henry VIII and Mary, who had not conformed to the Church of England. The seminaries were staffed by exiles who taught and wrote for an English audience. In 1580 a small number of English Jesuit priests also joined the English Mission. The Norfolk coast provided excellent landing places, and friendly houses sheltered and provided centres to which neighbours could come to hear Mass. The work of these priests was reflected in the number of recruits to the seminaries overseas. Between 1574 and 1616, 49 students were ordained from the county, of whom 21 joined the Jesuits, 20 were secular priests, four Benedictines, two Franciscans and one each Carthusian and Carmelite. Most of them returned to England, though not necessarily to Norfolk. They faced great risks: many were imprisoned for long periods and some were executed. Lay Catholics suffered too, bearing the financial penalties of the Mulct, the confiscation of lands and long terms of imprisonment. The loss to a celibate priesthood of a high proportion of men, the numbers of girls entering convents abroad, both established houses and new foundations for English women, and the attrition of the penal statutes all led to the ruin of a number of gentry families. But Catholicism in Norfolk was never confined to an elite: the Quarter Sessions indictments reflect a wide social mix in which a high proportion were women.

In 1633 the Jesuits set up their College of the Holy Apostles to establish a network in Essex, Suffolk and Norfolk. Chaplaincies were established and Fr. Francis Sankey lived as Jesuit Superior in Norwich from 1647-55, where he was joined by Fr. James Mumford, himself a Norfolk man. He was arrested there in 1650 but freed on bail and succeeded Fr. Sankey until his death in 1666. The Jesuit chapel and school were established briefly in a granary between St. Andrew's Hall and the river. The Catholic Dukes of Norfolk made additional provision for the secular clergy at their old Palace. But Catholicism was becoming increasingly difficult to practise in the countryside. The Compton Census of 1676 indicates a dwindling number of Catholics except where a gentry house provided a chaplain to serve the neighbourhood. Further evidence is to be found in the once prominent names absent from the 1717-77 *Returns of Papists' Estates*.

Norwich City returned in the Compton Census 50 Catholics from 16 parishes, 0.25% of the total population.

By the time the 1767 *Return of Papists* was made the numbers in the city had risen to 419 in 28 parishes. Although it was illegal to build a Catholic chapel until the second Catholic Relief Act of 1791 Norwich Catholics were able to attend Mass at a variety of locations. One tradition puts the Jesuit chapel in Chapel Fields, before Fr. Edward Galloway S.J. made a chapel in his house in St. Swithin's Lane, financed by the sale of property in Ringland and by a donation of £280 from College funds. When the Duke of Norfolk conformed to the established Church in 1780 the chapel in the Palace was no longer available and the congregation led by Fr. Beaumont moved to three garret rooms in Willow Lane. In 1791 this congregation was able to build a licensed chapel behind Strangers Hall, on the Dancing Master's Estate. The building still stands as the Maddermarket Theatre, although the congregation has moved to St. John's Cathedral. The principal obstacles for Catholics were thus removed; they were now free to worship openly and to take a full part in the life of the city and the countryside.

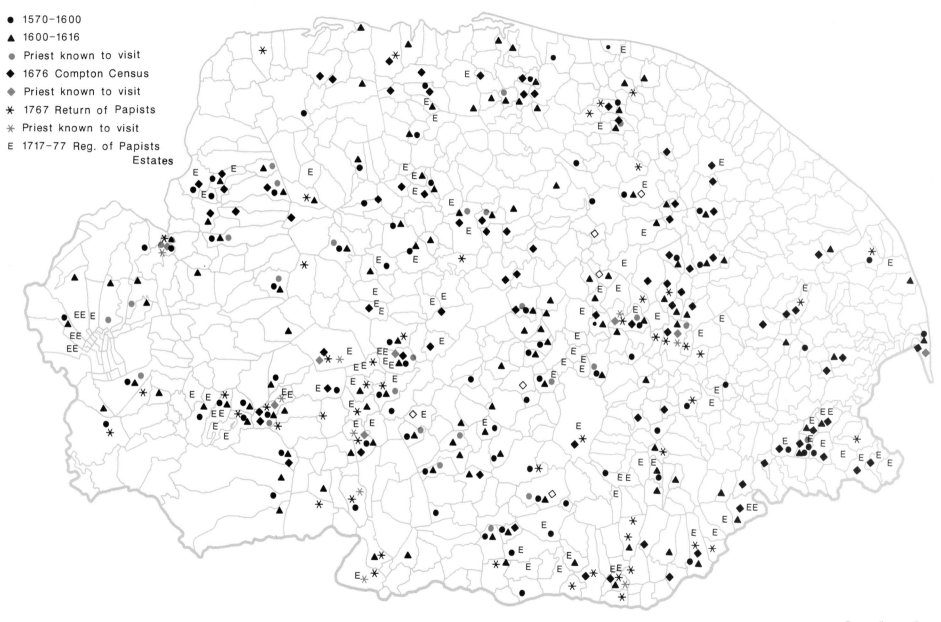

- ● 1570–1600
- ▲ 1600–1616
- ● Priest known to visit
- ◆ 1676 Compton Census
- ◆ Priest known to visit
- ✴ 1767 Return of Papists
- ✳ Priest known to visit
- E 1717–77 Reg. of Papists Estates

Janet Ede and Norma Virgoe

Dissent from the teaching of the Established Church has occurred in Norfolk as elsewhere since the time of the Lollards. In the 16th and early 17th centuries upheavals in religious affairs both in England and on the Continent led to the formation of nonconformist sects, most notably Independents, Baptists, Presbyterians and Quakers.

During the Civil War and Commonwealth the hierarchy of the Church of England was abolished. Attempts were made to make Presbyterianism the established church, but during these years all the nonconformist congregations flourished, often worshipping in the parish church, though a few purpose-built meeting houses were erected such as that at Guestwick of 1652. After the Restoration hopes of religious toleration were quickly dashed; following the Act of Uniformity of 1662 large numbers of clergy were ejected from their livings for refusing to comply with the Revised Book of Common Prayer and dissenters suffered much persecution. There was a brief respite in 1672 when the Declaration of Indulgence temporarily relaxed the penal laws against nonconformists and Catholics and allowed worship in licensed buildings, but then persecution was resumed until the Toleration Act of 1689 permitted freedom of worship for all Protestant dissenters in licensed premises. With the subsequent relaxation of persecution, purpose-built meeting houses began to be erected, one of the earliest being the Old Meeting House in Norwich built in 1693 by the Independents.

In the mid 18th century there was a new upsurge of evangelism most notably led, at first from within the Anglican Church, by John and Charles Wesley. The Methodist movement finally broke away from the Anglican Church following John Wesley's death in 1791. A feature of the late 18th century and early 19th centuries was the foundation of minority sects such as the Countess of Huntingdon's Connexion, Plymouth Brethren and Swedenborgians, as well as the splitting of existing sects - for instance the Primitive Methodists, formed in 1811, and the Wesleyan Reform Methodists who broke away in 1849. Although as the century progressed groups continued to break away, other minority groups united and this trend towards unity has continued into this century.

Although the incidence of nonconformity has been changing constantly, the map demonstrates two periods - the later 17th century and 1851. The documentary sources for these dates are reliable and make for effective comparison with the Historical Atlas of Suffolk. Quaker meetings do not appear in the list of 1672 licences, but there is a record of their gatherings in 1667 and these two documents provide the earlier source of material. The 1851 entries are from the Religious Census of that year which recorded all religious meeting places, their denominations and the attendance at services on Sunday 30th March. Even with these documents no map could claim to be a complete record of nonconformity in the county since congregations may have continued to meet secretly without licences, or refused or failed to complete the census record; also, congregations may have existed between the two dates; for example it is known that Quaker meetings were held at Hingham. Moreover, the 1851 Census predated the formation of some nonconformist groups such as the Salvation Army. Congregations also occasionally changed their denominational allegiance with a change of minister or when quarrels within congregations led to new foundations as in 1818 when a section of the Countess of Huntingdon's Connexion at the Norwich Tabernacle broke away with the minister and in 1819 founded Princes Street Congregational Chapel.

The map sources record the existence of congregations not their buildings. Many early nonconformist congregations met discreetly in cottages and private houses to avoid hostility from magistrates or the ravages of the mob. Later, when numbers increased and dissent was more tolerated, barns and workshops were used; usually it was long after a congregation was gathered that a chapel was built.

Apart from the areas of river marsh south east of Norwich, the thinly populated heathland near the north Norfolk coast and in Breckland, there were relatively few parishes without nonconformist congregations by 1851. The Presbyterian groups recorded in 1672 had disappeared; Congregationalists had increased by half as many again, mostly concentrated in areas where an early congregation had met; Baptists had spread from the handful of early groups on the Suffolk border; at Norwich and near the north east coast to a generous spread throughout the eastern half of the county and in a broad band in the centre west; Mormon congregations clustered in south central Norfolk and reached the peak of their 19th-century popularity in 1851. However, most startling is the universality of Methodist congregations, with numbers far greater than in Suffolk. Wesleyan and Primitive Methodists flourished throughout the County, often both types of congregation existing within a single parish, as at North Creake and Dickleburgh. Wesleyan Reformers were grouped in north west and west central Norfolk and isolated congregations of Bible Christian and Independent Methodists occur; but all the Methodist sections differed in organisation and administration rather than theology, and so it is the ubiquity of Methodism by 1851 which so dominates the map.

Dissent was a significant feature throughout eastern England from the 17th century. Baptist and Congregational membership was strong in Norfolk, though less so than in surrounding counties, but by 1851 Methodism was the dramatic force in the county with Primitive Methodism attracting exceptional support.

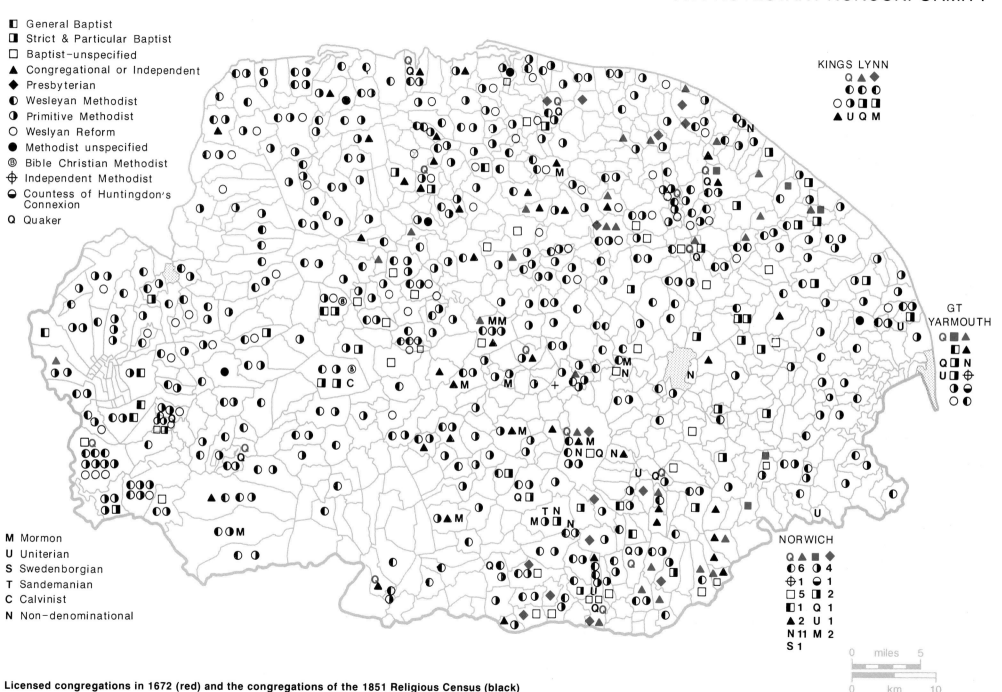

General Baptist
Strict & Particular Baptist
Baptist-unspecified
Congregational or Independent
Presbyterian
Wesleyan Methodist
Primitive Methodist
Weslyan Reform
Methodist unspecified
Bible Christian Methodist
Independent Methodist
Countess of Huntingdon's Connexion
Q Quaker

M Mormon
U Uniterian
S Swedenborgian
T Sandemanian
C Calvinist
N Non-denominational

KINGS LYNN

Q ▲ ◆
◑ ◑ ◑
○ ◑ ▣ ▣
▲ U Q M

GT YARMOUTH

Q ▣ ▲
▣ ◑ ▲
Q ◑ N
U ⊕
◑ ◑
○ ◑

NORWICH

Q ▲ ■ ◆
◑ 6 ◑ 4
⊕ 1 ◒ 1
□ 5 ▣ 2
▣ 1 Q 1
▲ 2 U 1
N 11 M 2
S 1

miles 5

km 10

Licensed congregations in 1672 (red) and the congregations of the 1851 Religious Census (black)

67. WORKHOUSES BEFORE 1834

David Dymond

From 1598 the relief of poverty was made the responsibility of individual parishes. Normally the poor were given 'out-relief' in their own homes: money, clothing, food, fuel or medical services. However, the problems of unemployment and poor housing also worried contemporaries. An Act of 1576 had ordered towns to acquire 'a competent store' of materials to provide work, while another of 1597 encouraged the provision of 'Abiding and Working Houses'. Thus parishes gradually acquired institutions such as 'poor houses', 'town houses' and 'workhouses'. In 1580-82 King's Lynn constructed a workhouse from a medieval chapel, while in 1719 the inhabitants of Watton subscribed towards 'a dwelling house...for the use of the poor'. Certain major towns went further, obtaining Acts to set up Corporations of the Poor with centralised workhouses. This was done at King's Lynn in 1701 and at Norwich in 1711.

Strictly, workhouses provided both accommodation and work. They became more common after the 'Workhouse Test Act' of 1722-3. This encouraged individual parishes to found workhouses without further resort to Parliament, and also allowed two or more parishes to combine. Returns made in 1776 show that Norfolk was slow to use this Act. Only 24 workhouses are listed, yet Suffolk had 89. Several of the main towns, such as Swaffham and Aylsham already had workhouses; the main rural concentrations were in the extreme south and west of the county.

In the last quarter of the 18th century, as the costs of relief soared, Norfolk embraced the workhouse principle with alacrity. By 1803 when more returns were made, the county was spending £45,000 a year on 4,000 residents in about 130 workhouses. Around 120 of them had been created by individual parishes, including market towns and large villages which had not featured in 1776. However, many other parishes had chosen, in various ways, to join forces.

Firstly, before Gilbert's Act of 1782, a small number of parishes, not necessarily contiguous or in the same hundreds, seemingly chose to associate without any further sanction. Thus, although they were separated by the town of Wells, the parishes of Holkham and the two Warhams combined to run a workhouse.

Secondly, some administrative hundreds, singly or in pairs, sought local Acts to form 'Incorporated Hundreds', each running a large central House of Industry. First in 1763 came Loddon and Clavering, an area of 41 parishes with its House at Heckingham. Five such bodies representing about 176 parishes appeared in eastern and central Norfolk between 1763 and 1785. These, with nine parallel institutions in eastern Suffolk, formed one of the earliest attempts in rural England to find a cheaper and more efficient way of relieving poverty. However, long-term success was elusive for three of Norfolk's Incorporated Hundreds were later dissolved as individual parishes resumed their traditional autonomy.

Gilbert's Act of 1782 provided a third alternative. It gave magistrates the power to sanction new combinations, and to appoint guardians running centralised Houses of Industry for 'the aged, infirm and impotent poor'. This option (ignored in Suffolk) was favourably regarded in Norfolk, partly no doubt because it saved the cost of obtaining a special Act. Thus, mainly in the eastern half of the county and filling gaps between Incorporated Hundreds, a further nine unions appeared under Gilbert's Act. They varied considerably in size, were oddly shaped, changed their names, and grew as new parishes joined. For example, in 1788 a House of Industry was set up in Acle supported by six parishes; by 1832 about 18 parishes were involved. Against the trend, nine parishes using Buxton workhouse were incorporated by a special Act in 1806, but were later absorbed into a larger Gilbert union called Taverham.

The map opposite shows workhouses created in parishes, early urban incorporations, incorporated hundreds and Gilbert unions. Despite defects in the sources, it seems that over 350 parishes were involved in the running of about 150 workhouses, but they still spent more on relieving paupers outside. For example, in 1832 Denton had a workhouse containing 26 paupers; simultaneously it paid out-relief to another 108 men, women and children. Blank areas on the map show that many parishes never did create workhouses, especially where villages were small and the pressures less intense. With or without workhouses, all communities in the early-19th century came to rely heavily on various forms of out-relief - giving payments according to need, supplementing wages, providing menial work, arranging work by contract, or adopting scales of relief according to family size and the price of flour.

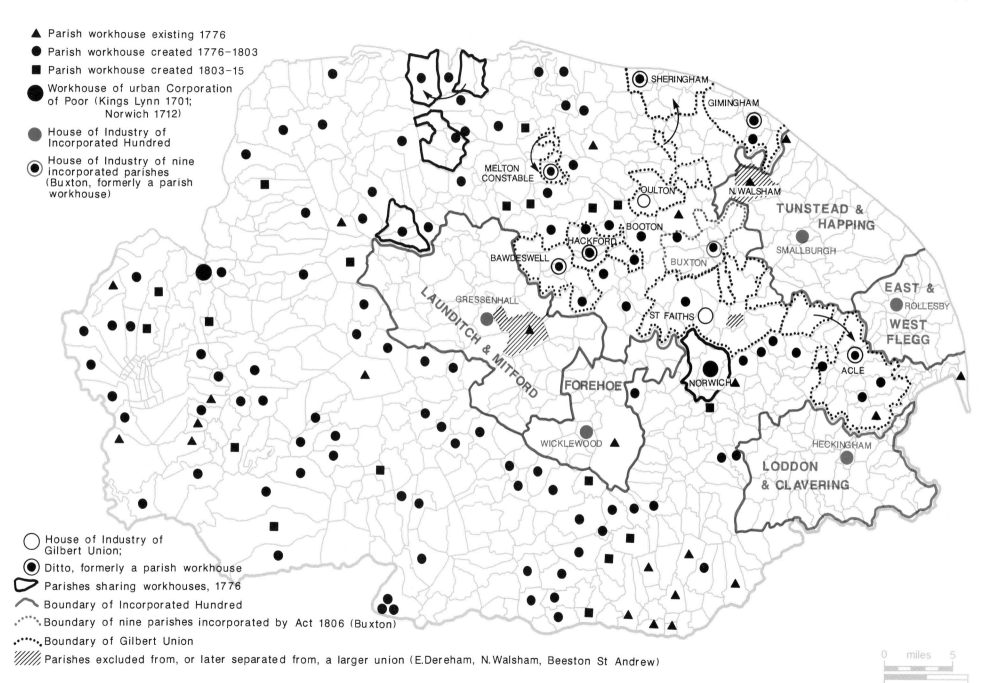

▲ Parish workhouse existing 1776

● Parish workhouse created 1776–1803

■ Parish workhouse created 1803–15

⬤ Workhouse of urban Corporation of Poor (Kings Lynn 1701; Norwich 1712)

⬤ House of Industry of Incorporated Hundred

◉ House of Industry of nine incorporated parishes (Buxton, formerly a parish workhouse)

SHERINGHAM

GIMINGHAM

MELTON CONSTABLE

OULTON

N. WALSHAM

TUNSTEAD & HAPPING

SMALLBURGH

BOOTON

HACKFORD

BAWDESWELL

BUXTON

EAST & WEST FLEGG

ROLLESBY

LAUNDITCH & MITFORD

GRESSENHALL

ST FAITHS

NORWICH

ACLE

FOREHOE

WICKLEWOOD

HECKINGHAM

LODDON & CLAVERING

○ House of Industry of Gilbert Union;

◉ Ditto, formerly a parish workhouse

⬗ Parishes sharing workhouses, 1776

〜 Boundary of Incorporated Hundred

∷∷ Boundary of nine parishes incorporated by Act 1806 (Buxton)

•••• Boundary of Gilbert Union

▨ Parishes excluded from, or later separated from, a larger union (E.Dereham, N.Walsham, Beeston St Andrew)

0 miles 5

0 km 10

In creating the geography of the New Poor Law, priority was given to convenience in the formation and operation of the new unions. The administrative ideal of uniformity enshrined in the Poor Law Amendment Act of 1834 should have resulted in equal-sized areas centred on market towns but, in practice, unions were created that could use existing workhouse accommodation and which found favour with landowners. As a result, some unions were based on a nucleus of a single hundred whilst others included two or three. Unions therefore varied in size from 21 parishes in Guiltcross to 60 in Mitford and Launditch, and from an 1841 population of 11,965 in the former to 28,493 in the latter. Union boundaries coincided with the county boundary except that 14 of the 34 parishes in the Thetford Union were in Suffolk; and seven of the 18 parishes in the Wisbech Union were Cambridgeshire ones.

Eighteen new unions were formed between 1835 and 1838. Of the six former Incorporations under Local Act, two were dissolved shortly after 1834 (Loddon and Clavering, Mitford and Launditch), and a further two (Norwich, Smallburgh) were dissolved in 1863 and 1869 respectively. Forehoe and East and West Flegg continued legally as Incorporations under Local Act, although in the administration of poor relief they differed to a decreasing extent from surrounding unions as time went on. This framework of unions continued with remarkably few changes. There were marginal amendments to union boundaries in the three western unions of King's Lynn, Swaffham and Thetford between 1835 and 1837. Later, in 1869, the sole remaining Gilbert Union was dissolved and the two parishes of Brinton and Melton Constable were added to Walsingham Union. The only major change came in 1902, when the Guiltcross Union was dissolved, and its parishes divided between the three neighbouring unions of Thetford, Wayland and Depwade.

One important reason for the formation of parishes into unions after 1834 was their joint financing of a union workhouse. The map shows workhouses for each union under the New Poor Law. Where there were several workhouses between 1834 and 1930 the location shown in each union is that which was utilised for the longest period. Between 1835 and 1838 12 unions built new workhouses. These were at Lingwood, Pulham St. Mary Magdalene, Docking, Downham Market, Gayton, Kenninghall, Swainsthorpe, Swaffham, Thetford, Great Snoring, Rockland All Saints and Yarmouth. These continued to be used until the end of our period, except in the case of Kenninghall. Accommodation sanctioned by the central body, the Poor Law Commissioners, for paupers in these workhouses varied from 150 at Gayton to 450 at Docking, whilst authorised expenditure ranged from £4,128 at Rockland to £9,700 at Pulham.

In the remaining eight unions earlier buildings from Gilbert Unions or Incorporations under Local Act continued to be used either temporarily or permanently as workhouses after 1834. The Aylsham Union used Gilbert Union houses at Buxton and Oulton until a new union workhouse was built at Aylsham in 1849. Similarly, the Erpingham Union used Gilbert Union accommodation at Sheringham (until 1848), and Gimingham (until 1851), when a new workhouse was opened at West Beckham. The St. Faith's Union never abandoned its Gilbert Union accommodation at Horsham St. Faith, despite its obvious inadequacies. In the incorporations that survived temporarily or permanently under Local Act (Tunstead and Happing, East and West Flegg, and Forehoe), existing buildings of the houses of industry at Smallburgh, Rollesby, and at Wicklewood continued in use. And in both the Mitford and Launditch, and the Loddon and Clavering, Incorporations (legally dissolved after 1834 but formed into New Poor Law unions under the same name), previous houses of industry at Heckingham and at Gressenhall also continued to be employed. In the urban centres of King's Lynn and Norwich new workhouses were opened in 1856 and 1859 respectively.

During the later phase of Norfolk workhouse construc-tion numbers of paupers authorised for each union or incorporation were larger than in the 1830s (all being for over 400 inmates), whilst expenditures were also greater (having in each case a minimum of £12,000 spent). Large sums could also be sanctioned for alterations and extensions to existing houses of industry; in some cases these could amount to as much - or more - than the expenditure on a small, new workhouse. This was the case in Mitford and Launditch which spent £6,300 between 1834 and 1870.

Norfolk workhouses were often less utilitarian than those found elsewhere since the tradition of the well-built houses of industry - the pauper palaces - lived on. Architects of the New Poor Law workhouses in the county built in a variety of styles - classical, Tudor and Jacobean. They most frequently used a linear grid-iron plan, but occasionally employed an octagonal design, as at Great Snoring or at Pulham. Workhouses were formally designated as poor law institutions in 1913, although in popular use the old name continued. The Local Government Act of 1929 (which abolished unions and boards of guardians) encouraged local authorities to take over these poor law institutions as hospitals. Many still survive today, some employed in the NHS, although others find varied use as a museum, as farm buildings, as offices, as private housing, or as stores. For a short time the Pulham workhouse even figured as The Bumbles Hotel!

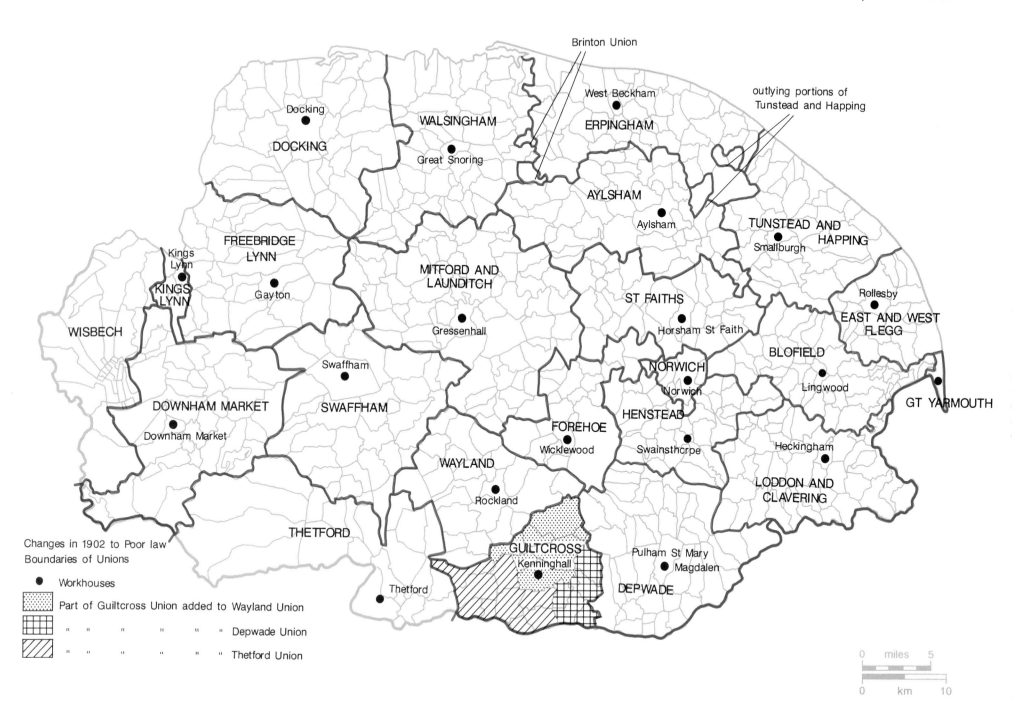

68. POOR LAW UNIONS AND WORKHOUSES, 1834-1930

Brinton Union

outlying portions of
Tunstead and Happing

West Beckham

Docking

WALSINGHAM

ERPINGHAM

DOCKING

Great Snoring

AYLSHAM

Aylsham

TUNSTEAD AND
HAPPING

Smallburgh

FREEBRIDGE
LYNN

Kings
Lynn

KINGS
LYNN

Gayton

MITFORD AND
LAUNDITCH

ST FAITHS

Rollesby

WISBECH

Gressenhall

Horsham St Faith

EAST AND WEST
FLEGG

BLOFIELD

Swaffham

NORWICH

Lingwood

Norwich

GT YARMOUTH

DOWNHAM MARKET

SWAFFHAM

HENSTEAD

Downham Market

FOREHOE

Heckingham

Wicklewood

Swainsthorpe

WAYLAND

LODDON AND
CLAVERING

Rockland

Changes in 1902 to Poor law
Boundaries of Unions

THETFORD

GUILTCROSS

Pulham St Mary

Kenninghall

Magdalen

● Workhouses

Thetford

DEPWADE

Part of Guiltcross Union added to Wayland Union

"   "   "   "   "   " Depwade Union

"   "   "   "   "   " Thetford Union

0   miles   5

0   km   10

69. TURNPIKES AND ROADS

Richard Joby

Road surfaces were not systematically improved outside towns until the Turnpike Acts were passed from the 1660s onwards. Thenceforth, capital was raised by local trusts to improve sections of major routes, and money for maintenance and servicing the debt was raised by means of tolls on most traffic.

The first Act covered the Wymondham to Attleborough section of the present A11, followed by Thetford to Newmarket in 1768. Over the next seven years a flood of Acts covered most of the roads radiating from Norwich and King's Lynn. This was followed by another group of Acts in the 1790s covering Norwich to North Walsham and Aylsham, and Yarmouth to Blythburgh (A12). One of the last was the Acle New Road (A47) in 1820, a straight causeway road across the drained Bure Marshes which shortened the distance of the Norwich to Caister road of 1769 by some five miles.

From the 1780s onwards the macadamised cambered road was introduced and provided a harder and drier surface, which together with improvements in coach construction allowed average speeds of up to 10mph in most weather conditions. London mail coaches were scheduled to take 12 to 14 hours against two days or more in the 1750s. Non-turnpike roads were also often improved by landowners keen to reap the benefits of enclosure and despatch their increased harvests quickly to market.

The railway age returned roads to local use only; turnpikes were wound up and local road boards formed, taken over by the county council in 1889. The next major improvement was the tar-sealing of roads which largely took place between 1919 and 1939. Motor buses, private cars and trucks increased tenfold in that period, but few

by-passes, let alone improved alignments were constructed, until the 1960s. An early exception was the Norwich Ring Road, built in part to relieve unemployment in the inter-war period.

Thenceforth most market towns acquired by-passes (Map 86); the A11 and A47 became strategic trunk roads and had short sections of dual carriageway included. Plans have recently been announced to complete dualling of these roads and also the A140 to Ipswich. Bus routes have declined as private vehicles have increased. Almost all freight is now moved by road in Norfolk.

70. WATERWAYS

Richard Joby

Tributaries of the Great Ouse, Waveney, Yare and Bure were used extensively for navigation until Late Saxon times when many were blocked by the erection of watermills, extensively listed in Domesday. Artificial cuts made in the late Middle Ages through to the 17th century greatly increased navigations in the Fens. From the 17th century onwards Acts of Parliament were used to raise capital for river navigation improvements to build locks to bypass mills, embank rivers, make cut-offs and to dredge. The Nar, Little Ouse, upper Bure to Aylsham and Waveney from Beccles to Bungay all benefited.

There were few artificial waterways, the most important being the North Walsham and Dilham Canal from Dilham on the Ant to Antingham, opened in 1826, and

the Norwich and Lowestoft Navigation whose New Cut from Reedham to Haddiscoe linked sections of the Yare and the Waveney to the new harbour at Lowestoft by 1833 allowing seagoing ships to reach Norwich avoiding Breydon Water's mudbanks and the costly port tolls of Yarmouth.

Navigation by shallow draft keelboats, clinker-built rowing boats and punts allowed tonnages of up to 30 tons to be moved extensively in east and west Norfolk systems. Grain, hay, peat, marl and dung, lime and consumer goods were traded, especially between King's Lynn and Great Yarmouth and inland centres. In the 19th century the wherry in east Norfolk increased loads on the Yare and Waveney to 60 tons and could sail into the wind

thanks to a yacht-type sail. Despite the arrival of the railways, water transport played a large part in local goods traffic well into the 20th century, with leisure traffic, especially in the Broads, seasonally increasing traffic to historical maxima, with over 12,000 registered pleasure vessels now using the Broads waterways. Commercial traffic has almost completely ceased.

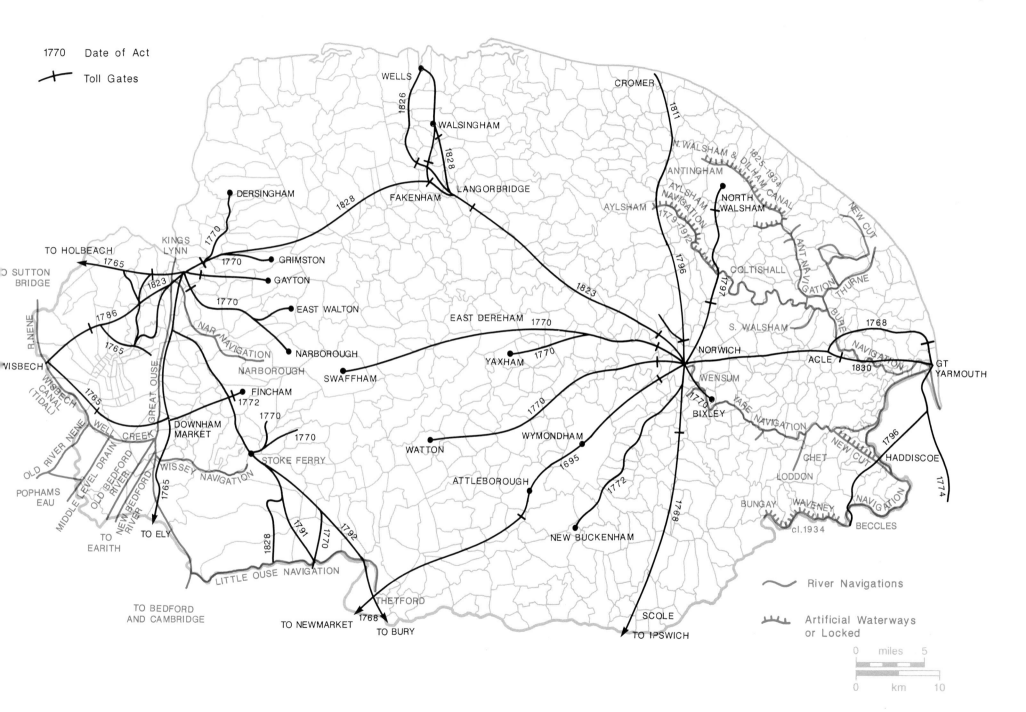

1770   Date of Act

✕   Toll Gates

WELLS

CROMER

WALSINGHAM

LANGORBRIDGE

1826

1828

FAKENHAM

N. WALSHAM & DILHAM CANAL

1825-1934

1811

ANTINGHAM

AYLSHAM
NAVIGATION
1779-1912

AYLSHAM

NORTH
WALSHAM

NEW CUT

DERSINGHAM

1828

KINGS
LYNN

1770

1770

GRIMSTON

GAYTON

1770

EAST WALTON

EAST DEREHAM

1770

COLTISHALL

ANT NAVIGATION

THURNE

BURE

S. WALSHAM

1768

1797

TO HOLBEACH

1765

O SUTTON
BRIDGE

1823

R. NENE

1786

1765

NAR NAVIGATION

NARBOROUGH

NARBOROUGH

SWAFFHAM

YAXHAM

1770

1823

NORWICH

WENSUM

ACLE

1830

NAVIGATION

GT
YARMOUTH

VISBECH

WISBECH CANAL (TIDAL)

1765

GREAT OUSE

FINCHAM
1772

1770

1770

DOWNHAM
MARKET

STOKE FERRY

WATTON

WYMONDHAM

1770

BIXLEY

1770

YARE NAVIGATION

NEW CUT

1796

HADDISCOE

CHET

LODDON

OLD RIVER NENE

WELL CREEK

MIDDLE LEVEL DRAIN

OLD BEDFORD RIVER

NEW BEDFORD RIVER

WISSEY NAVIGATION

1765

ATTLEBOROUGH

1695

1772

1768

BUNGAY

WAVENEY

cl.1934

NAVIGATION

1774

POPHAMS
EAU

TO
EARITH

TO ELY

1828

1791

1770

1792

NEW BUCKENHAM

BECCLES

LITTLE OUSE NAVIGATION

TO BEDFORD
AND CAMBRIDGE

THETFORD

1768

SCOLE

River Navigations

TO NEWMARKET

TO BURY

TO IPSWICH

Artificial Waterways
or Locked

0   miles   5

0   km   10

Norfolk was one of the last English counties to establish a railway system, starting in 1844 with the Yarmouth and Norwich Railway, followed by the Norfolk Railway from Norwich to Brandon in 1845 which linked it to London. Thenceforth several local railway systems, the East Anglian Railway centred on King's Lynn, the Eastern Union Railway based on Ipswich and the Norfolk Railway, now merged with the Yarmouth and Norwich, spread out from Thorpe station to serve Fakenham and Lowestoft as well. Thus, by about 1850 the major centres were linked but the north coast was not yet connected to the system. The Eastern Counties Railway merged all the lines serving Norfolk by 1854 and fully absorbed them in 1862 to become the Great Eastern Railway.

Only three new lines were built in the 1850s, from Wells to Fakenham, the Waveney Valley line from Tivetshall to Harleston, and the continuation of this in the early 1860s to Bungay and Beccles. Yarmouth acquired a second station in 1859 when the East Suffolk line opened a service from Ipswich to South Town station. Shortly afterwards, in 1861, the Lynn and Hunstanton Railway raised capital locally to develop the railway and its attendant resort. An extension from Heacham to Wells was built three years later, again with local capital.

The parlous financial condition of the Eastern Counties Railway prevented capital expenditure on any scale; it was buttressed by a regional monopoly only broken in the 1870s, when independent railways were built from Lynn to Fakenham and from Yarmouth to North Walsham, eventually joining at Melton Constable in 1883 and extending to Norwich and Cromer. These lines then formed the Midland and Great Northern Joint Railway from 1893 after four years of receivership. Faced with competition, the resident Great Eastern Railway put in hand a range of extensions to improve their system. The East Norfolk line from Norwich to Cromer added a branch to Aylsham and across to North Elmham on the Dereham to Fakenham line. Dereham in turn got a faster connection to London via Wymondham and Forncett,

avoiding Norwich. A more direct route from Norwich to Yarmouth via Acle was completed in 1883, whilst a branch line from Denver to Stoke Ferry opened up Methwold Fen to commercial agriculture.

The final touches to the system were aimed at developing the coastal resorts. The doubling of lines from Norwich to North Walsham and from Lynn to Wolferton increased line capacity. As a new joint venture between the GER and M&GNJR, the Norfolk and Suffolk Joint Railways built a coastal loop from North Walsham to Mundesley and on to Cromer via Overstrand and a direct line between Yarmouth and Lowestoft, which served the newly developed resort of Gorleston. Mundesley station had four through platforms and direct expresses to London for a village of under 1000 souls. Yarmouth had the great Breydon viaduct to connect Beach station with South Town, but for a brief summer season this was never profitable and the lines closed between 1953 and 1970.

The other lines to note were the tramways linking the quays and docks at King's Lynn, Wells, Yarmouth and Norwich with the main systems, providing direct loading from vessels to railway wagons. A rather different tramway was completed in 1883 on the western border of Norfolk from Wisbech to Upwell, an attempt at cheap construction of a roadside line into a fruit growing area.

By 1906 the system was complete and Blakeney was the only town of any size which was more than five miles from a railway station. The coming of local buses in the 1920s ended the rail monopoly, and passenger services on the Upwell and Stoke Ferry lines ceased in 1927 and 1931 respectively. Many other services were abandoned in the 1950s, the largest being the M&GN in 1959. Further cuts in the Beeching rationalisation of 1964-8 resulted in only a skeleton being left. Local freight stopped in 1964; then lines were torn up and stations often adapted to residential purposes.

The remaining railways in Norfolk lost most of their staff in 1966. Only Norwich, Yarmouth, Lynn, Thetford and Downham remained as staffed stations, while others became unstaffed halts. Improvements only came from the mid-1980s, when first the Ipswich to Norwich line was electrified and its signalling system updated; then the Ely to King's Lynn line was similarly upgraded, with services starting in 1992. Cross country express services provided by Regional Railways have been speeded up as new railcars and signalling have been introduced, whilst local services are gradually being re-equipped with newer railcars.

Re-opening of abandoned lines and stations by preservation groups and commercial tourist operators has also become significant in the last two decades. The North Norfolk Railway has brought back services between Sheringham and Holt. A narrow gauge railway between Wells and Walsingham uses the trackbed of a line abandoned in 1964, whilst most recently the Bure Valley Railway has converted nine miles of the East Norfolk Railway between Aylsham and Wroxham into a narrow gauge tourist railway. An even larger project is being started from County School to Wymondham via Dereham, which also intends to run a service for commuter and other passengers all the year round when re-opened. Trackbed of abandoned lines is used for long distance footpaths such as Weavers Way, and rail and footpath are combined on the Bure Valley Railway.

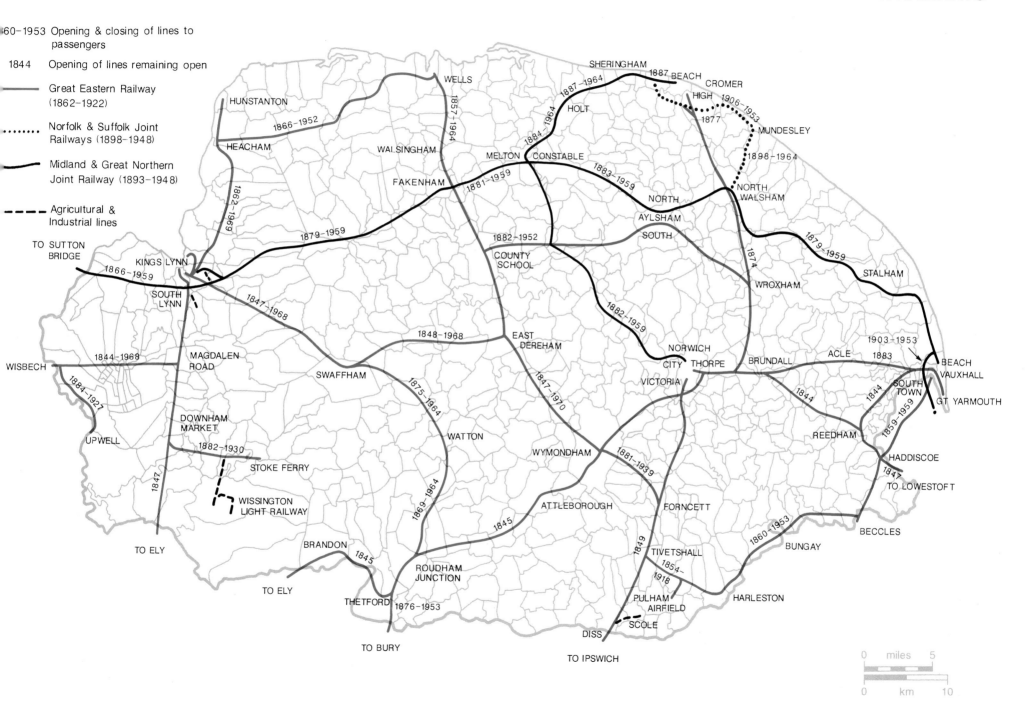

Legend:

60–1953 Opening & closing of lines to passengers

1844 Opening of lines remaining open

——— Great Eastern Railway (1862–1922)

········· Norfolk & Suffolk Joint Railways (1898–1948)

━━━ Midland & Great Northern Joint Railway (1893–1948)

- - - Agricultural & Industrial lines

SHERINGHAM 1887 BEACH
CROMER
HIGH 1906–1953
1877
MUNDESLEY
1887–1964
1884–1964
1898–1964
HOLT
WELLS
1857–1964
HUNSTANTON
1866–1952
HEACHAM
WALSINGHAM
MELTON CONSTABLE
1883–1959
NORTH
NORTH WALSHAM
FAKENHAM
1881–1959
AYLSHAM
SOUTH
1882–1952
1879–1959
COUNTY SCHOOL
1874
STALHAM
TO SUTTON BRIDGE
1862–1969
WROXHAM
1866–1959
KINGS LYNN
1882–1959
SOUTH LYNN
1847–1968
1848–1968
EAST DEREHAM
1903–1953
ACLE
1883
BEACH
WISBECH
1844–1968
MAGDALEN ROAD
SWAFFHAM
NORWICH CITY THORPE
BRUNDALL
VAUXHALL
1884–1927
1847–1970
1875–1964
VICTORIA
SOUTH TOWN
1844
GT YARMOUTH
UPWELL
1844
1847
DOWNHAM MARKET
1882–1930
STOKE FERRY
WATTON
WYMONDHAM
1881–1939
REEDHAM
1859–1959
HADDISCOE
1847
TO ELY
WISSINGTON LIGHT RAILWAY
1869–1964
ATTLEBOROUGH
FORNCETT
TO LOWESTOFT
1860–1953
BECCLES
BRANDON
1845
TIVETSHALL
BUNGAY
TO ELY
ROUDHAM JUNCTION
1849
1854–1918
HARLESTON
THETFORD 1876–1953
PULHAM AIRFIELD
TO BURY
DISS SCOLE
TO IPSWICH

0 miles 5
0 km 10

Nesta Evans

The manufacture of textiles was for many centuries the most important industry in Norfolk and Norwich. The map opposite shows four groups of weavers: those undifferentiated by their thread, worsted weavers, linen weavers and all other types of weavers.

For all the weavers, probate records from 1370 to 1857 were the main source in compiling the map but, for those making linen, a wider range was used. The 2,256 weavers plotted on the map are only a fraction of the real total, as the sources used are unavoidably biased towards the better-off.

All kinds of weavers were to be found in most of the county, except the western third where they only appear on the edge of the Fens. This distribution is related to farming regions. The area where virtually no weavers are known to have lived was predominantly a district of large estates, concentrating on corn growing and sheep rearing.

The main centre of linen weaving was the valleys of the Waveney and Little Ouse, where most hemp, the fibre generally used for linen in East Anglia, was grown; this is also true for Suffolk. As most of its production was sold locally, unlike worsteds which were exported as well as having a national market, the linen industry of East Anglia is little known. It was certainly not insignificant, for the second largest group of weavers is that making linen.

The production of woollens and worsteds, especially the latter, had two main centres: Norwich and villages near it, and a block of parishes in the north east of the county around Aylsham and North Walsham. It is possible that some men described simply as weavers, but living where the production of linen or worsteds predominated, may have been making these cloths.

An industry cannot grow without a workforce, and this was provided by the increasing population of east and central Norfolk, which farming alone could not support. Textile production was labour intensive, needing the support of many ancillary trades such as spinning, dyeing, bleaching, combing and fulling. Most of these provided employment for women and children, and combined well with part-time farming. Manorial control was usually weak in areas where textile production flourished, and the prospect of work attracted immigrants.

Cheap linen and woollen cloth was made all over England for purely local markets, but in certain regions, notably the West Country and East Anglia, a commercial textile industry developed in the Middle Ages. The production, for outside markets, of both linen and worsted in Norfolk goes back to at least the 13th century, and possibly much earlier. In the 17th century Norfolk linen manufacture grew into an industry and continued to flourish in the 18th century, but it only produced cheap quality cloth for local markets.

Of the 69 worsted weavers known from wills made between 1370 and 1550, all but 16 lived in Norwich. An alnager was appointed to measure worsteds made in the city in 1315, well before Flemish weavers arrived during the reign of Edward III. Sixty-two percent of the known worsted weavers lived in Norwich; in the industry's heyday a considerable number were to be found elsewhere in the county, but in its last years from 1819 to 1857 virtually all lived in the city.

Norwich weavers bought yarn produced in Suffolk and elsewhere, thus providing work for spinners over a wide area. Commercially by far the most important of the textiles made in Norfolk were the Norwich stuffs, whose history has been admirably described in a recent book by Ursula Priestley. After 1660 a wide variety of stuffs were created to cater for the new fashion market for dress and furnishing fabrics. An enormous range of these materials was made in the 17th and 18th centuries; some of pure worsted and others mixed with silk.

In the 17th century most of the weaving workshops in Norwich were small scale, but by the 1770s only about 30 firms in the city were making stuffs. Between 1660 and 1800 the wealth of Norwich was based on its textile industry, which had important export markets in the 18th century, and its collapse in the 1790s was disastrous for the city. At the same date the Norfolk linen industry virtually disappeared as its low quality product could not compete with factory-produced cottons.

The 1840 report of the Commission on Hand-Loom Weavers shows that in rural Norfolk all kinds of textile production had virtually come to an end. The one bright spot was the two Lopham villages near Diss, where the making of high quality hand-woven linen continued until 1925. The Lopham firm of Buckenham was awarded a royal warrant in 1837. Most of its customers lived in Norfolk, London and the Home Counties, and included a number of masters at Eton College.

In Norwich new specialities were introduced in the early 19th century, but were copied more cheaply in Yorkshire. The only success was the manufacture of shawls, which in turn declined in the 1860s. The textile industry struggled on in the city until the end of the century, but it never recovered the position it had enjoyed before 1800.

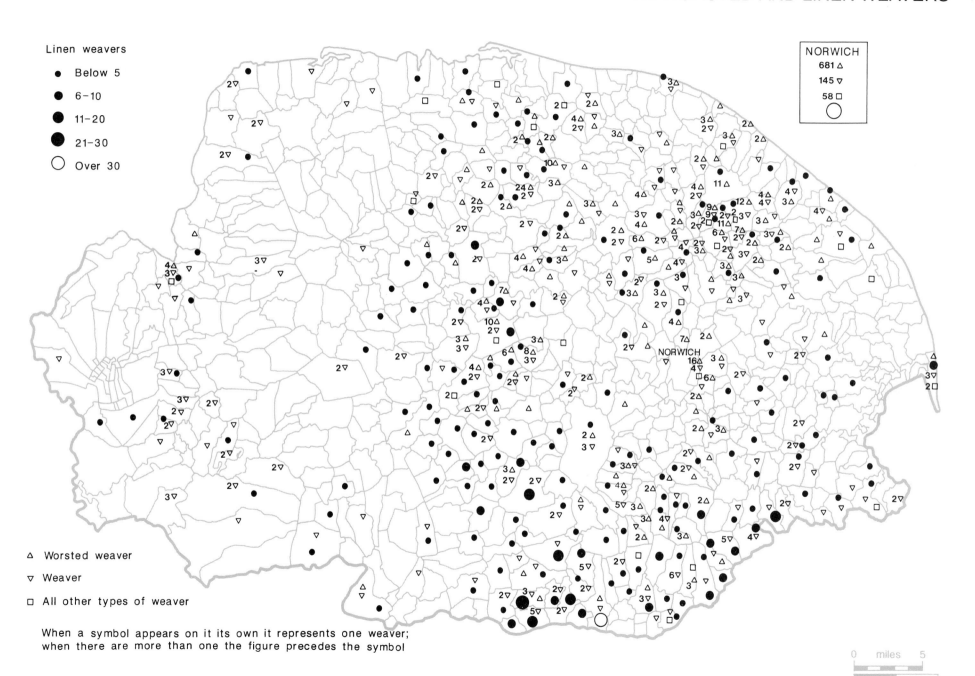

Linen weavers

- ● Below 5
- ● 6–10
- ● 11–20
- ● 21–30
- ○ Over 30

NORWICH
681 △
145 ▽
58 □
○

△ Worsted weaver

▽ Weaver

□ All other types of weaver

When a symbol appears on it its own it represents one weaver;
when there are more than one the figure precedes the symbol

0 miles 5

0 km 10

73. TANNERS AND TANNING

Christopher Barringer

The map opposite represents a sample of the information on those engaged in tanning within Norfolk between 1500 and 1850. The trades of currier, fellmonger, glover and leather cutter have been omitted because of the apparent lack of consistency in their definitions. The sampling has depended on the extent to which the Diocesan and Archdeaconry will registers for Norfolk have been indexed by occupation. As the table below shows, only sample periods are available for the two Archdeaconries of Norfolk and Norwich, so that the map is primarily drawn from the evidence of Consistory Court wills. As the Archdeaconry of Norwich includes Norwich, Great Yarmouth, Kings Lynn and Thetford, it is likely more tanners did exist. Whether the pattern of distribution would have been different is more debatable. Similarly, the other leather trades as listed by Dr. Pound for 17th century Norwich, for example, would probably have emphasised the patterns that appear on the map.

It is accepted that wills proved in the Bishop's Court tend to reveal greater prosperity of the testators than those proved in the Archdeaconry Courts. The relative wealth of tanners might therefore determine in which court the bulk of wills is likely to have been proved. No examination of Norfolk wills proved in the Canterbury Court has been made but a small group of Dean and Chapter wills does have an occupational index for the 17th century.

The will evidence for tanners before 1500 is minimal, but tanning is an ancient process. In Norwich the medieval tanning district was Conesford, presumably near the river. In Thetford in 1066 the borough made an annual payment of ten goat skins and four ox hides to the King and Tanner Street was an early place name in the town. In Lynn there were tanners in Heukwalds Fleet in the 12th century, tanners were fined in 1167 and by the 14th century raw hides were coming into Lynn from Newcastle. The lack of tanneries in rural areas before about 1600 is explained in part in that Norfolk

Consistory Court inventories show that farms had one or two hides in their own tan pit rather than being specialist tanners. The market towns would provide the main markets for the many leather workers dependent on cured hides for their raw material and were the main butchery centres.

The two main essentials for tanning were a supply of bark, usually oak, for the tan pits and of fresh water for washing the hides and for replenishing the pits. Lime was also necessary for slaking the raw hides initially. The need for water was reflected in Lynn in 1423 when barkers (tanners) petitioned the corporation to be allowed a channel of water through the community's land for their processing. The pollution of streams and the stench of tan pits made tanning an unpopular activity in towns and this may have led to a movement of tanneries out of the towns in the 17th and early 18th centuries as the processes became more specialised and the units larger in scale. Specialised buildings and space for a run of tan pits became necessary to allow a steady progression of hides through the long curing processes. The development of a banking system allowed capital investment by this date.

Demand for leather steadily increased as the population grew and the need for horse harness and leather clothes, together with leather covers for carriages and for domestic wall hangings, increased. The improvements in road transport increased the number of horses greatly. The later arrival of the railway reduced the demand for post horses and carriages however.

The map shows the dominance of Norwich and its adjoining parishes of Heigham and Thorpe as the centres of tanning in the 16th century. As the city grew the initial tanning area in Conesford became unsuitable and meadow sites outside the city were chosen. As late as 1850 the pollution map of the Wensum produced for the enquiry into the sanitary conditions of Norwich showed seven fellmongers in Heigham upstream of the city.

The next two centuries saw tanning develop in more rural centres, especially in the Waveney valley in Diss and Earsham near where large herds of cattle were fattened on the marshes. In mid-Norfolk the boulder clay uplands had much grazing land on them. Toftwood in Dereham and Hindolveston wood would have yielded a lot of bark for tanning; the Bunting family of Hindolveston produced five tanners between 1640 and 1696 and this suggests that local expertise was another factor in the location of tanneries.

In the 19th century, as with brewing, economies of scale reduced the numbers of tanneries and by the end of the century imported hides from South America began to undercut the home supplies. Many tanneries closed around the end of the century such as those run by the Leaman and Leeds families at Whitwell. By 1900 two tanneries survived in Norwich; one in Dereham, one in Whitwell and one in Thetford. After the first world war one only survived at Thetford.

Numbers of Tanners Listed in Indexes by Centuries

Period	N.C.C.	Norfolk Archdeaconry	Norwich Archdeaconry	Dean and Chapter
1500-1599	29	13	-	
1600-1699	51	-	19 (56 years)	5
1700-1799	38	-	-	-
1800-1857	11	-	-	-

The help of Diana Spelman in tabulating the tanners' wills is gratefully acknowledged.

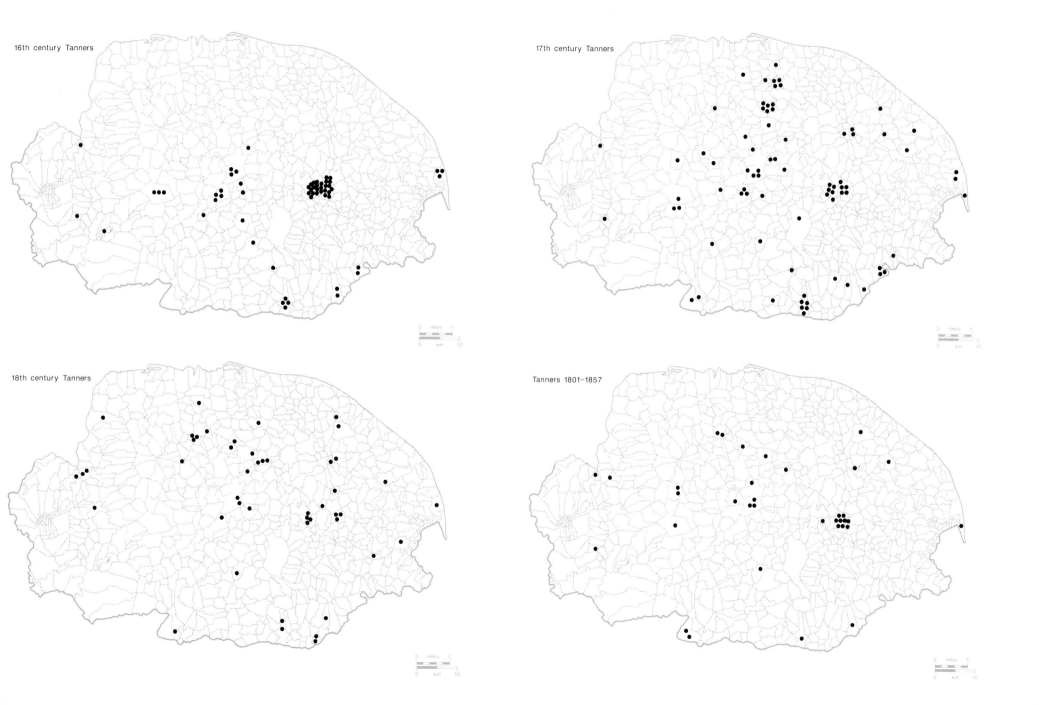

73. TANNERS AND TANNING

16th century Tanners

17th century Tanners

18th century Tanners

Tanners 1801–1857

A conflation of figures drawn from the *Mineral Statistics* of 1858 and the *Census of England and Wales* for 1861 reveals that Norfolk was at that time, with 114 brickyards, fourth amongst 36 English counties in the number of brickyards, sixth in its ratio of brickyards to houses, but 14th in the value of output and 29th in the ratio of brickmakers to brickyards. What determined for Norfolk such an impressive number of brickyards was not the physical extent of the county, but rather the traditional development of the industry, with small productive units spread out over a large area so as to minimise the transport of heavy materials. Indeed, the actual siting of many yards, close to waterways, serviceable roads and, later, railways, or set either within or adjacent to heath and woodland from which firing fuel could be obtained, make clear the determining influence of transport facilities on site location. The existence of clay, the prime material of the brickyard, was a crucial but not controlling factor. The reality is that Norfolk has, or had, brickearth of different description, quality and suitability over most of its extent, and all these earths were exploited.

Limited demand, a small number of brickmakers, and the desire to minimise transport costs meant that in the medieval and early modern periods much of the business was carried on by itinerant brickmakers, a not insignificant number of whom were also bricklayers. Changing conditions allowed, from the 17th century, the establishment of a small number of longer-lived brickyards where, instead of the temporary clamp, a permanent kiln could be used for firing, fuelled by furze and wood faggots and, from the late 18th century (and sometimes earlier), coal. The kilns included the open-topped East Anglian box kiln with under-floor or replaceable fire-channels, the conical kiln, which was a circular variant of the same with a tall overhead chimney, and the Dutch or Scotch kiln, with firing apertures set along the long sides of an oblong rectangle. These were all intermittent-firing kilns holding between 20,000 and 50,000 bricks. After 1860 the multi-chambered, continuous-firing Hoffman kiln made its appearance in the brickyards

of Sprowston, Upper Hellesdon and Old Catton where deep 'jambs' (seams) could yield the clay and vigorous demand provide the market to sustain and finance its vastly-increased productive capacity.

Many brickyards, and perhaps the majority of small, single-kiln brickyards, were in the hands of farmers who were themselves, or who employed, brickmakers: as the farming year permitted, field labour was diverted to those brickyard tasks for which the skill required was modest. In traditional brickmaking, which before the introduction of the pug-mill and water-pump lacked any mechanical aid, extraction of the clay took place in the late autumn and winter: tempering in the late winter and early spring; moulding and drying in the late spring and early summer; and firing throughout the summer into the autumn. A clamp could take up to six weeks to fire whereas a kiln could be fired in less than a week.

It was not, of course, simply red brick which was produced in the brickyard. The white brick was a 'special' in Norfolk, just as it was in Suffolk. Roofing-tiles, floor-tiles, drainage-ware, flowerpots and other special wares, some of which were glazed, were fired very often in the same kiln as the bricks, in positions selected for heat and safety. Brickmakers, working closely with bricklayers, developed a repertoire of structural forms and decorative motifs, for chimneys, gables, cornices, door- and window-hoods, string-courses and plinths. The most elaborate brickwork can be attributed to the Victorian and Edwardian periods when a choice and contrast of colours and textures were added to what was already a wide range of ornamental devices.

Through the 18th and 19th centuries localities were known for the number of brickyards, the size of the workforce and the quality of the wares produced. Banham, Costessey, Lakenham, Reedham, Rockland St. Mary, Surlingham, Swanton Novers and Welborne were some of these. In terms of the quantity of persons employed, censual returns show that the manufacture of

bricks and tiles in Norfolk reached its peak in 1861. After that time the business re-organised itself into fewer and larger productive units coming increasingly into the hands of builders and builders' merchants, a not unprecedented association of production and use. Bricklayers, particularly in Norwich and King's Lynn, had long been involved in production, partly, no doubt, so as to secure their own supply of building materials. A force behind the re-organisation of these years was the introduction of rail transport (Map 71), the first effects of which were, through its own construction needs and through a reduction of the cost of coal, to stimulate production. The railway, however, made it possible to bring bricks into the county from areas such as Northamptonshire and Bedfordshire where they could, for a variety of factors, be produced more cheaply. From the 1880s, as these out-of-county yards became highly capitalised, productive capacity in Norfolk dwindled to the point that Kelly's *Directory of Norfolk* for 1937 listed no more than 24 brickmaking concerns. All brickyards within the county were closed for the duration of the second world war and of the handful which opened afterwards, it was only the yards at Barney, Old Catton and Upper Hellesdon which survived to the mid 1960s, when all three were closed.

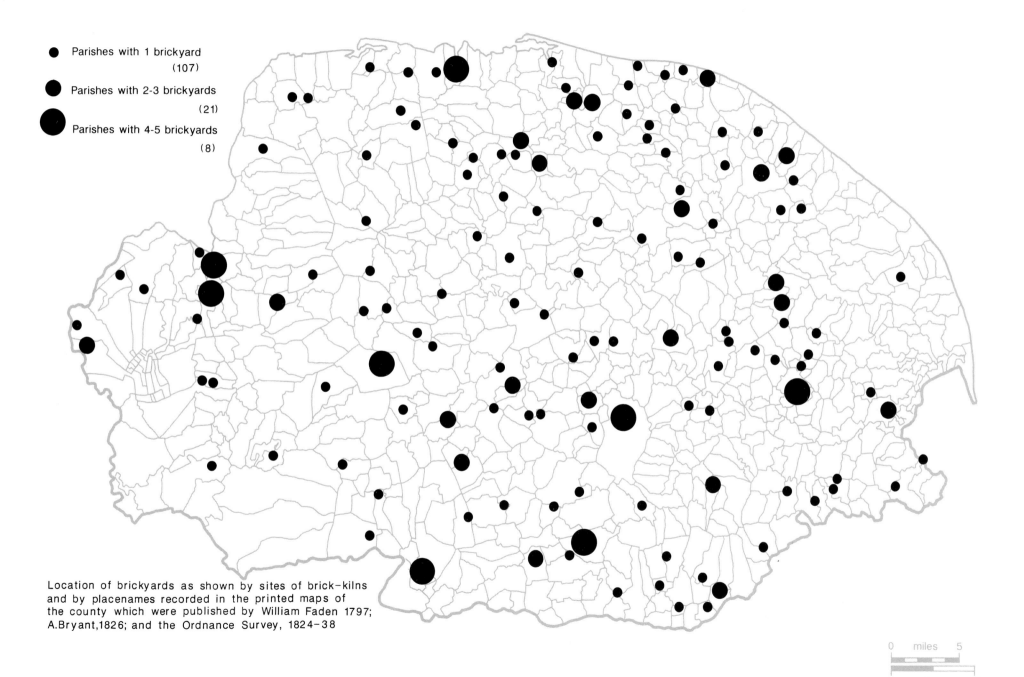

● Parishes with 1 brickyard
(107)

● Parishes with 2-3 brickyards
(21)

● Parishes with 4-5 brickyards
(8)

Location of brickyards as shown by sites of brick-kilns
and by placenames recorded in the printed maps of
the county which were published by William Faden 1797;
A.Bryant,1826; and the Ordnance Survey, 1824-38

0   miles   5

0   km   10

75. MALTING AND BREWING

Andrew Davison

Malting and brewing are of considerable antiquity, and there is evidence to suggest that both have been important locally for over a millennium. Until the later 18th century both industries were carried out on a largely domestic scale. Maltings were generally farm-based, producing only for the local market. Many householders brewed on a seasonal basis for their families, landlords for their public houses, and farmers for their labourers. An ignorance of brewing science, and the difficulties of transporting a bulky and perishable product, meant that the operations of 'common brewers', brewing for both public houses and the domestic trade, were generally small in scale.

This pattern began to change towards the end of the 18th century, with the emergence of large-scale common breweries, supplying larger areas and populations. The rise of the common brewers was due to a number of factors, including the production of beers of increasing quality through a better understanding of the science of brewing, improved communications (initially by water, but increasingly by rail as the 19th century progressed) and control of retail outlets through the 'tying' of public houses. The rise of the common brewers was balanced by a decline in the numbers of small-scale 'retail brewers', brewing for individual public houses or for a limited household trade, who increasingly found that they could not compete with the larger concerns for quality or for price. During the course of the 19th century retail brewers virtually disappeared; brewing by individual householders also vanished, for few could be bothered with the trouble and expense of producing their own beer, when a superior product could be readily obtained elsewhere.

By the early 1850s a number of major breweries had emerged. Norwich alone boasted seven sizeable firms, whilst Yarmouth, Lynn, and a number of smaller towns also supported significant concerns. While most supplied a relatively restricted geographical area, several of these firms enjoyed a much wider trade. Lacon's of Yarmouth, for example, sent over 30,000 barrels of beer annually to London, Newcastle-upon-Tyne and Plymouth. Nevertheless, much brewing was still on a modest scale; in 1852, there were 88 common breweries operating in the county, whilst a further 212 licensed houses still brewed their own beer.

The second half of the 19th century saw a rapid acceleration of the trend towards production in fewer, large-scale breweries. Partly as a result of the increasing effectiveness of the Temperance Movement, with a consequent decline in the available market for beer, a premium was placed upon the acquisition of 'tied' public houses, which guaranteed outlets for the product. Considerable sums were expended by the larger brewers on the purchase of public houses, and as the number available diminished smaller breweries were purchased solely to gain control of their tied estate. Towards the end of the century there was a move towards incorporation as Limited Liability Companies, to raise additional capital, through share issues, for the purchase of public houses or for the enlargement of brewing premises. Morgan's was the first of the Norwich brewers to take this course in 1887, but its major local competitors soon followed. The extent of the consolidation of the brewing industry was such that, by 1900, the number of breweries operating in the county had been reduced to 25, and public house breweries had virtually disappeared.

There were also changes in the structure of the malting industry during the course of the 19th century. Individual maltings became larger in size, and by the end of the century tended to be sited in those towns with good rail connections, since Norfolk malt found a ready market with brewers elsewhere. Diss, Dereham, Fakenham and Thetford, in addition to Lynn, Norwich and Yarmouth, were particularly noted for malting. Unlike brewing, there was little tendency to concentrate malting on a small number of sites, perhaps because the available technology changed little during the course of the century. Whilst in the early years of the century individuals or firms usually operated only a single site, by its end the majority of firms were operating maltings in more than one location. Thus, while there were still 104 maltings in 1900, compared with 139 in 1845, they were operated by only 53 concerns compared with the 134 a half century earlier.

The process of concentration in the brewing industry continued throughout the 20th century, until the county's three surviving companies fell to take-over bids from London-based brewers in the mid 1960s; the last major brewery in Norfolk, that in King Street, Norwich, closed in 1985. However, in recent years a number of new, small-scale operations have emerged.

The number of maltings in the county has also diminished during the last 90 years, although here the stimulus has been technological, with improved machinery allowing the production of larger quantities of malt, more rapidly, on a smaller number of sites. A number of maltings still operate within the county.

The map illustrates the process of concentration in both industries, showing the distribution of maltings and breweries in 1845 on the eve of the arrival of the railways (although the location of the majority of retail brewers, who left no record of their activities, is not shown), and in 1925, when the number of breweries had been reduced to 12 and maltings to 45.

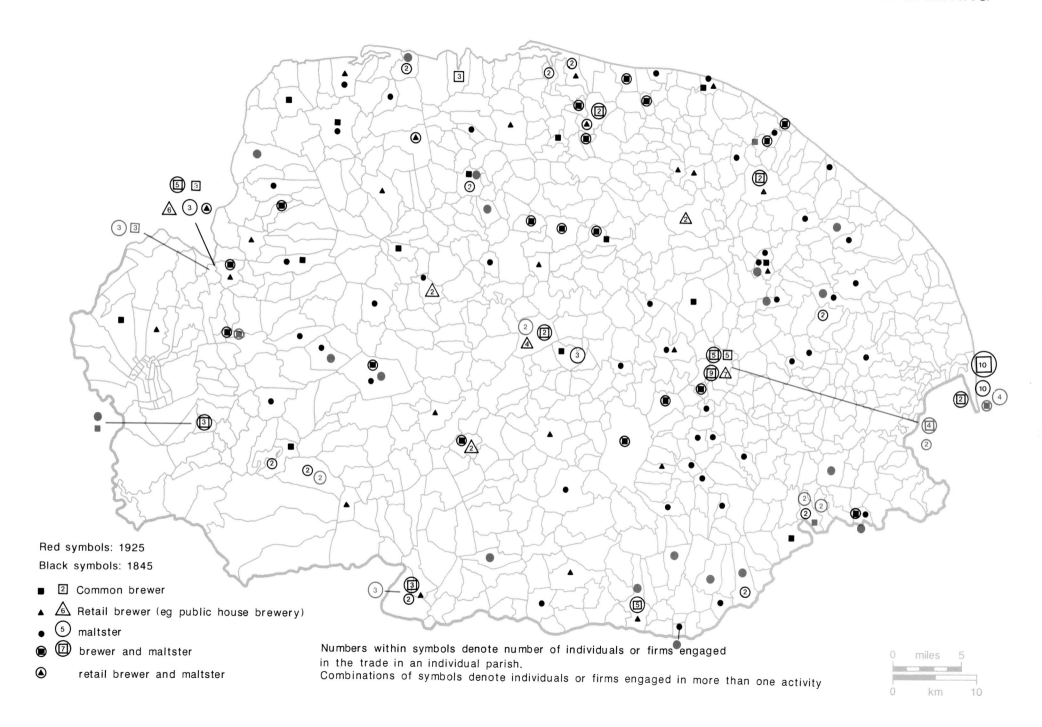

75. MALTING AND BREWING

Red symbols: 1925

Black symbols: 1845

■ ② Common brewer

▲ ⬠6 Retail brewer (eg public house brewery)

● ⑤ maltster

⬛ ⑦ brewer and maltster

⊕ retail brewer and maltster

Numbers within symbols denote number of individuals or firms engaged in the trade in an individual parish.
Combinations of symbols denote individuals or firms engaged in more than one activity

0 miles 5

0 km 10

76. PAPER MILLS

Mary Fewster

The use of watermills for the manufacture of paper began in Norfolk in the late 17th century. The processes of papermaking required quantities of pure water, and in the 18th century water power was also needed, steam only being introduced in the early 19th century. The mills were therefore sited where there was sufficient strength of current. There is a concentration on the Wensum above Norwich, but otherwise they are isolated.

A number of factors encouraged the development of papermaking: the increased expense of imported paper from France, the immigration of Huguenot papermakers, the lapse of the Licencing Acts in 1695, making possible the printing of papers in the provinces, and the expansion of the worsted industry. Different types of paper were required to meet these needs, and most mills produced several varieties. Paper mills were not necessarily custom-built, nor was papermaking always their sole business. The first recorded mill, at Castle Rising, was a converted fulling mill. Some millers were farmers, and also ground corn at the mill. In the early 19th century Stoke Holy Cross became a corn mill, returned briefly to papermaking, and then became a mustard mill. Papermaking machinery could be moved from mill to mill; in the 1860s R.G. Bagshaw purchased the machinery from the Nar Mills, King's Lynn, to set up a mill in St. Miles parish, Norwich.

Taverham Mill had the longest and perhaps the most distinguished history. It was in operation in 1701, being mentioned by Francis Burges, the Norwich printer, as providing paper fit for printing at a cheap price. In the early 19th century a partnership of Norwich businessmen invested large sums in modernising the mill, including the installation of the newly patented Foundrinier papermaking machines, costing more than £1,000, and producing a continuous roll of paper instead of separate sheets. In 1846 Taverham and Bawburgh Mills, by then in common ownership, were taken over in the interests of *The Times* by J.H. Walter, and produced about a third of the paper required for the London *Times*, as well as paper for the Oxford Dictionary. The closure of these mills in 1899 signalled the end of the industry. The number of mills employed in paper manufacture reached a peak of about nine at the end of the 18th century. It subsequently fell off as mills were converted to other uses, and then revived to its former number, but with greater production, in the mid-19th century.

77. WATERMILLS

Martin Scott

Watermills are mentioned in connection with 302 settlements in the Domesday Book. Milling continued on the sites of most of these until the Industrial Revolution.

The change to imported wheat milled at roller mills at, or near, the ports of entry spelt the death of local mills. The use of water power declined sharply in the 20th century. In 1906, 72 mills were working but by 1956 there were 21, and by 1969, only one was still using water power.

Hellesdon had two Domesday mills, one being for fulling, but both ceased by the 16th century. Other industrial uses included bone crushing for fertiliser (Antingham, Narborough), mustard making (Bawburgh, Stoke Holy Cross), tanning (Whitwell), sewage pumping (Blickling), water pumping (Little Cressingham, King's Lynn, Norwich), worsted and mohair spinning (Lakenham) and sawing (Gunton).

At Kettle Mills, King's Lynn, a new drinking water pump was constructed in 1578 by a carpenter, Richard Brown. There were six pumps made of elm sunk in a pit specially dug for the purpose. Many watermills succumbed to fire: Lakenham (1908), Gressenhall (1914), Cringleford (1916), Costessey (1924), Mundesley (1956), Burnham Overy (1959), Horstead (1963), Hardingham (1966) and Buxton (1991).

There were two bone mills at Antingham, both shown on the Ordnance Survey First Edition of 1838. The mill on the lower pond was erected by Lord Suffield and worked until 1937. Jeremia Colman, great uncle of Jeremia James Colman, began milling mustard at Bawburgh but only a few years before moving to Stoke Holy Cross.

Mills were often replaced by new ones on the same site. At Costessey, in 1857, Henry Utting Culley demolished the old mill and built a new one of white brick five storeys high. He employed 16 people, supplying flour to Price Bros. bakeries at Norwich, Gorleston and Ipswich.

Elsing Mill, when paper-making ceased, became a corn and seed-crushing mill in 1854. Water power was used there until shortly before the last war, when electricity took over. The stones continued in use for a while, eventually being replaced by a hammer mill. Elsing ceased working in 1969 and was converted into a house.

The Catchment Boards destroyed some waterwheels, including Fakenham and Goggs Mill, Hempton, to ease the flow of the river and Shotesham Mill was demolished in 1949 to prevent flooding. This provoked considerable local argument and similar controversy arose over the proposal to burn Hardingham Mill for a scene in the film "The Shuttered Room".

Some 111 watermill sites can still be seen, but only 19 mills still have their waterwheels and some machinery intact, whilst 38 have been converted and 54 are just ruins or foundations.

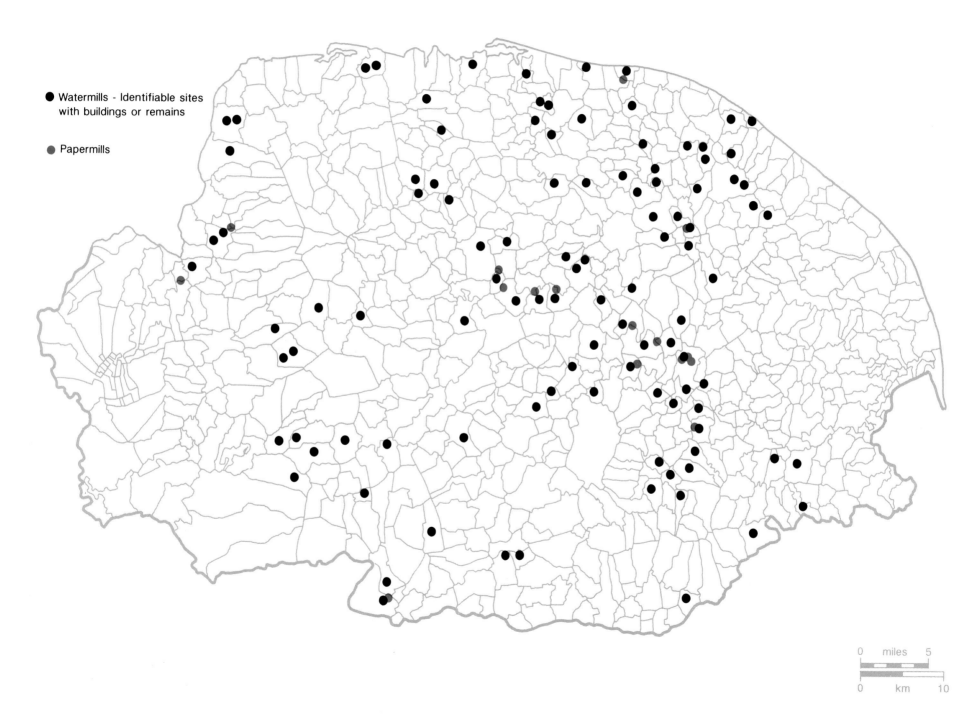

● Watermills - Identifiable sites
  with buildings or remains

● Papermills

0   miles   5

0   km   10

78. IRON FOUNDERS AND AGRICULTURAL ENGINEERS

David Alderton

The first foundry in Norfolk was probably that set up by Robert Ransome in Norwich in 1779. Although Ransome moved to Ipswich ten years later, other founders established themselves and by the turn of the century there are known to have been three founders in Norwich and at least another three in Norfolk. Thereafter numbers expanded rapidly, so that by 1845 there were no less than 44 ironfounders listed in White's Norfolk Directory. Frequently other trades were associated with founding, most commonly engineering and agricultural implement making, though a substantial number were also iron-mongers. Many firms had their own specialities, like Charles Barnard of Norwich who was an 'iron hurdle and self rolling mangle manufacturer'.

Agricultural implement manufacture was obviously of considerable importance in a county which was in the van of agricultural improvement. Many firms listed only as agricultural implement manufacturers, millwrights or engineers are known also to have had foundries. In some cases, such as England's, the Ludham millwrights, these may have produced castings solely for their own use, but others, like Tidman and Son of Norwich, described in 1888 as 'engineers, millwrights, machinists and boiler-makers', undoubtedly undertook general casting. Over the years firms developed new specialisations and shifted location: both happened to Smithdale's who in Norwich were 'Ironfounders and Steam-engine builders', before moving to Panxworth as 'Millwrights and engineers', and finally to Acle as specialists in marsh drainage.

There were take-overs: when Cubitt at North Walsham closed, the goodwill and patterns went to the Northrepps foundry and the name remained in use. Unlike Suffolk, no agricultural machinery maker in Norfolk seems to have had much of a national market, though in heavy steam engineering Dodman's and Savage's had a national and Burrell's an international reputation.

The number of foundries seems remarkably large when Norfolk is compared with Leicestershire, a county which had much the same population as Norfolk and was rather more industrialised. In the Trades section of Kelly's Directories for the two counties for 1888, Leicestershire has 17 ironfounders listed and Norfolk 44, and there is no reason to think any underestimate would be greater in Leicestershire. There is another marked difference between the counties: in Leicestershire 11 foundries were in Leicester and the remaining six in rail served industrial areas, whereas in Norfolk only six were in Norwich and 21, almost half the total, were in what were indubitably rural areas. In defiance of what might seem to be obvious geographical imperatives, many long-lived Norfolk foundries flourished in villages well off the beaten track, without easy access to turnpikes, navigable waterways or railways.

The map suggests an answer: there is a fairly even distribution of foundries across the county, and the problems of bringing in the necessary raw materials, pig or scrap iron, foundry coke and limestone, were probably less than those of distributing fragile castings and bulky farm machinery. There is certainly evidence that the great majority of firms made their living by supplying castings, implements and machinery to meet local requirements. Thus the stock of patterns at Northrepps foundry not only included parts for the firm's locally popular ploughs and wagons, but also covered a wide range of domestic needs, such as drain covers, fire grates, gate posts and bench ends as well as crabpot bases for the local fishing industry. Great Walsingham foundry produced grave crosses and provided castings for the local council. Cubitt's at North Walsham supplied the lock gear and, presumably, the unusual iron balance beams used on the North Walsham and Dilham Canal.

The Norfolk firms had diverse origins. Some, such as Hunton's at Carbrooke, grew from a blacksmith's.

Joseph Burrell, founder of the Thetford firm, was probably a whitesmith. Plowright's of Swaffham started as ironmongers, while family tradition had it that Thomas Smithdale walked to Norwich from Lancashire before settling down and taking over the existing firm of Blyth, Francis and Buttifant. This is more likely than it may seem: research into census records in other parts of the country has shown that it was not uncommon for skilled foundrymen to move frequently, often over considerable distances, to obtain work or betterment. The Holkham estate set up its own engineering works and foundry at Longlands Farm and other estates may have followed suit. The recurrence of names suggests the possibility of family connections, for example the Huntons in both Carbrooke and Swaffham.

The main sources of evidence used for the map have been the previously mentioned Directories. Unfortunately, neither is necessarily comprehensive. Not all foundries or agricultural engineers were listed, estate works being a notable omission, and entries often inadequately reflected the range of a firm's activities. For example, in the 1888 directory the major Norwich firm of Barnard, Bishop and Barnard has a lengthy entry which never mentions ironfounding, but also listed are three individual Barnards, all described as ironfounders and with the subscription 'See Barnard, Bishop and Barnard'. Thus different Directories produce apparent anomalies: 67 ironfounders have been identified from White's 1883 Norfolk Directory and a decline of 23 in the five years to 1888 seems unlikely. The six inch Ordnance Survey maps can help identify actual sites but provide little new information. Oral and archaeological evidence have added to these sources. The presence of a foundry in a particular parish in both 1845 and 1888 does not, of course, necessarily imply continuity either of firm or exact location.

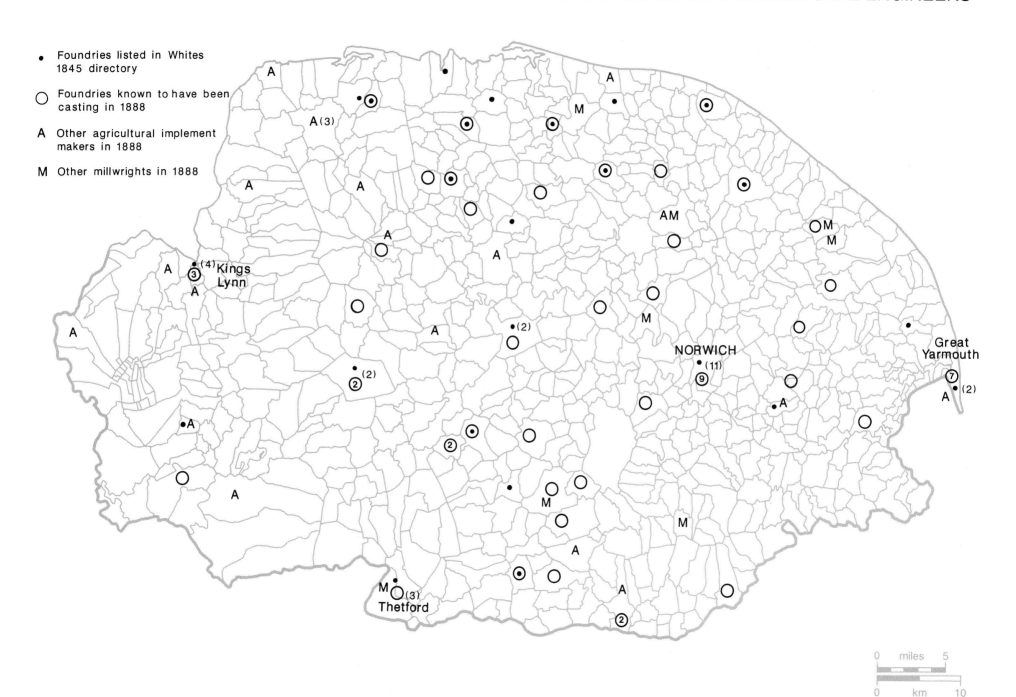

78. IRON FOUNDERS AND AGRICULTURAL ENGINEERS

- Foundries listed in Whites 1845 directory
- ○ Foundries known to have been casting in 1888
- A Other agricultural implement makers in 1888
- M Other millwrights in 1888

Kings Lynn

NORWICH

Great Yarmouth

Thetford

0 miles 5

0 km 10

79. LIME BURNING AND EXTRACTIVE INDUSTRIES

John Jones and Mary Manning

Lime Burning

Lime has been an important material ever since its introduction to this country during the Roman period.

Its principal uses are in agriculture, for correcting acidity in soil and for making mortar and plaster for building. Other uses include tanning and making limewash for coating walls.

The manufacture of lime requires calcium carbonate as a raw material. Normally limestone was used but in East Anglia none occurs naturally and instead, chalk, a softer from of the same compound, was burnt into lime. The chalk strata tilt from west to east and over much of the county are overlaid by glacial deposits. In Great Yarmouth, a well had to be sunk over 500 feet before reaching the chalk: in the west of the county it is accessible close to the surface over a considerable area.

Lime was difficult to transport over long distances before the introduction of the railways, since it was extremely vulnerable to damage by rain or even atmospheric moisture. Therefore it should ideally be made as close as possible to the place where it is to be used. However, a significant weight loss occurs when chalk is burnt into lime and for this reason transport is easier if the lime is made at, or adjacent to, the chalk pit. Consequently chalk pits were normally established as close as possible to the market for their lime.

Thus the geology of the county principally determines the distribution of lime-burning sites. The other major factor is the market for the product and it is not surprising, therefore, that Norwich, with its large number of buildings constructed with lime mortar, should have been surrounded by lime kilns. Many of the now disused pits in and around the city are of very great size indicating what quantities of chalk have been extracted over the years.

The map shows the lime kiln sites believed to have been in operation around 1840. The main sources of information have been the first series 1 inch Ordnance Survey, published in 1838, and White's 1845 *Directory of Norfolk*. A number of other sources were used. Many other sites were in operation for periods before or after 1840 but their omission from the map does not significantly alter the pattern of distribution. The county can be divided into four areas:-

In west Norfolk west of a line running roughly from Thetford through East Dereham to Holt, the chalk deposits are on or close to the surface and can be extracted wherever the need arises. The northerly part contains the preponderance of sites, probably reflecting the need to improve the sandy soils in this region.

In central Norfolk the chalk is covered by glacial deposits which become deeper towards the east. Very often the pits are found where river valleys have eroded the overlying layers and a series of such sites can be seen following the course of the rivers Yare, Wensum, Glaven and Tas.

In south-east Norfolk, apart from a cluster at East Harling, Quidenham and Banham, the lack of accessible chalk has prevented extraction in this area. An interesting exception is at Kimberley where a pit makes use of what is probably an 'erratic', a large deposit included in the glacial material.

In Broadland, despite the lack of chalk, there was a group of lime kilns in the villages around Barton Turf and other sites are at Acle, Reedham and Great Yarmouth. What they have in common is water transport. The large riverside pits at Whitlingham, Thorpe and Horstead produced chalk which was carried by wherry to these kilns.

Extractive Industries

Since the surface of Norfolk is mixed glacial sands, clays and gravels overlying chalk, extraction pits exist over the whole of the county, having been opened as need arose, often by local builders.

Clay for daub and pottery has been used from earliest times; it has been puddled with straw and animal hair to make clay lump building blocks and fired to make bricks, tiles and land drainage pipes. As well as for lime burning, chalk has been quarried to make blocks (clunch) for building, to extract flint, and for roadbuilding. Flint, also picked by hand from the beaches of Norfolk, was sent to glassmakers for its silica content whilst being a building material in itself. Carstone, a hard but brittle sandstone from north-west Norfolk has been quarried for building material. Gravels were quarried for road-making and mending, small deposits being exploited formerly by village communities, but today vast pits are producing graded gravels for by-passes and other road construction uses. Sands have been utilised for building work and also, in the Leziate area near Kings Lynn, a large deposit of fine and high grade sand has been quarried for glass for the chemical industry.

For soil improvement, marl was spread, the practice originating at least as far back as the 13th century and its increased use in the late 18th and 19th centuries led to pits being made on most farms where this chalky clay could be found.

Today, ploughed-out hollows mark the position of extraction pits or they may be landscaped and water-filled to create reserves for fishing, wild life and recreation. Between 1918 and the 1930's crude oil was extracted in the Setch area for paraffin production, a forerunner of the offshore oil and gas fields in the North Sea. So many pits and quarries survive in Norfolk that mapping is impracticable.

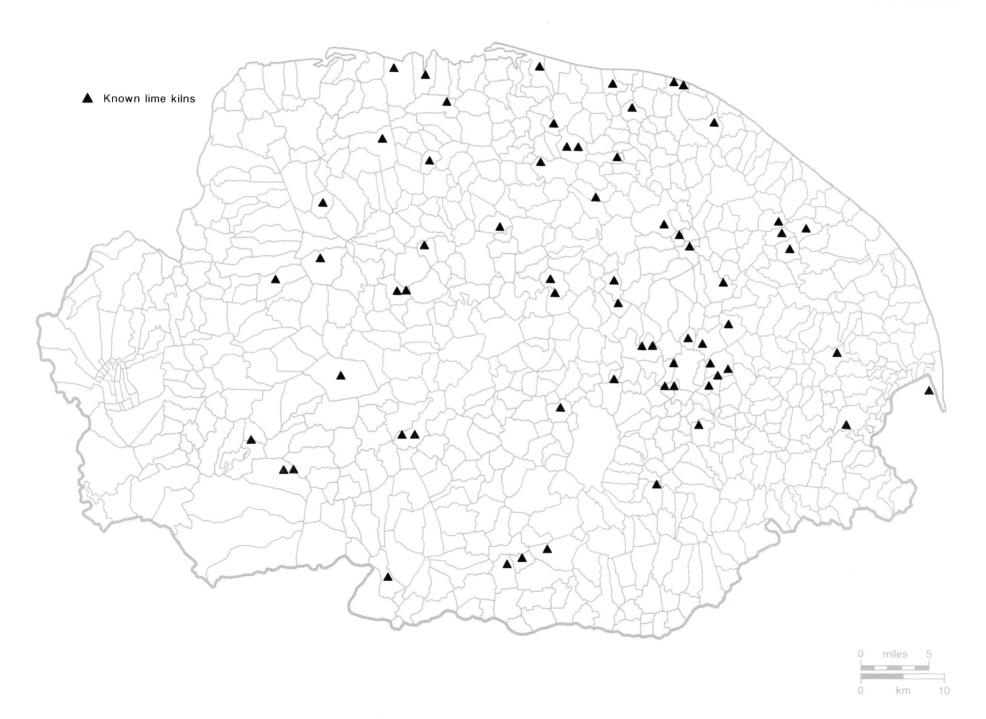

▲ Known lime kilns

80. CORN WINDMILLS

Martin Scott

Processing grain from Norfolk's farms, for human and animal consumption, required mills. There were many of these, both windmills and watermills. Windmills also provided power for other purposes, including bone-crushing, sawing, cement grinding, bark grinding, starch milling, drawing water, threshing clover seed, crushing cole seed for oil, snuff milling, driving cotton mill machinery and spinning yarn.

There never was a 'typical' Norfolk windmill, each being different in size and shape. This is true of the tower mills, now the commonest remaining windmills, although most people may think of them being five storeys high with a boat-shaped cap, four sails and six or eight-bladed fantail. Previously, Norfolk had many post mills and smock mills. Now the only surviving post mill is Garboldisham Mill, although there are many remains and Thrigby Mill has been reconstructed. The last remaining smock mill was the North Mill at Wymondham, which burnt to the ground in 1950. There are over 40 known 13th-century references to windmills, from Stiffkey in the north to Kenninghall in the south and from West Walton across to Great Yarmouth on the east coast. A mill 'outside the City ditch' at Norwich is recorded in 1235 and, like all 13th century windmills, would have been an open trestle post mill.

William Faden's map of 1797 was the first to depict windmills Norfolk-wide and shows 256. Henry Bell's 'Lynn Regis Prospects from the West', of about 1683, shows the South Lynn Oil Mill, reputedly built by the Dutch in 1638, also St. Ann's Starch Mill, the Kettle Mill and Greyfriars 'Oyle' Mill. All of these were smock mills on brick or stone bases.

Briningham smock mill was built in 1721 and later that century was converted into Belle Vue Tower. The brick base is the oldest remaining portion of a windmill in Norfolk. In the 19th century, there were 38 windmills in Norwich, 34 in Yarmouth, 17 in King's Lynn and, in 1854, 423 throughout Norfolk. This number fell to around 100 in 1912 and to 11 in 1937. The last to work was Billingford in 1956.

Once the windmills ceased working, there was little use for them. Wicklewood, Denver, Billingford, Little Cressingham and Old Buckenham are in the care of the Norfolk Windmills Trust. Worsted, Ringstead, Weybourne and Cley are amongst those converted to residential. Over 50 of the remaining windmills are derelict, stumps or foundations.

The map shows the location of 120 windmill remains: 93 tower mills; five smock mills; 20 post mills; and two composite mills. These last two were post mills mounted on a round-house at Thornham and on the two-storey stump of a tower mill at Banham.

81. WINDPUMPS

Stephen Earl

Drainage windpumps have long been a distinctive feature of the Norfolk Broads. In their heyday during the 19th century over 120 windpumps drained the marshes, with over 1,000 being used in the Fens area of Cambridgeshire, Lincolnshire and Norfolk. Steampumps quickly superseded the Fens windpumps leaving only two remaining at Nordelf. The Broads with 69 remains have the greatest concentration in the country. The only evidence for the drainage of the Broads marshes is a stray reference to embanking near St. Benet's Abbey. At Haddiscoe Church organised drainage is indicated by a tombstone dated 1525 to Barbele, wife of Pier Piers, a Dutchman, who was 'Master of the dykes'.

In the 18th and 19th centuries, comprehensive schemes were implemented following technical improvements in windpump design and construction. It seems that the first windpumps were timber-built smock windpumps, with scoopwheels and 'common sails' which involved spreading cloth across the sail frames, and the caps were turned by hand using a tailpole. The fantail, invented by Edmund Lee in 1745, ensured that the sails could always be automatically turned into the wind. In 1807, William Cubitt's Patent sails, fitted with automatically-adjusting shutters, which spilled the wind in strong gusts, did away with the need to spread cloths or alter the shutters manually. This with the development of improved cast-iron techniques, developed during the late 18th century, enabled the building of taller and more powerful windpumps while many existing towers were heightened.

Only one complete smock windpump remains in the Broads area. Most of the windpumps in the area are brick tower windpumps, with Norfolk boat-shaped caps, fantail and patent sails. Two other types of windpump were built in great numbers on the Broads, the 'trestle' and the 'hollow post'. Variations included those with boarded trestle, scoopwheel, turbine and plunger pump. All were built principally from timber and only five examples have survived. The early windpumps all lifted water from the marsh dykes by scoop wheels. In 1851 Appold's invention of the turbine pump enabled windpumps to drain greater areas than before. In a steady wind the turbine could lift half as much water again as the scoop wheel.

During the late 1920s, about 30 windpumps were still working draining the Halvergate area, but by 1953, the last windpump ceased work. They were superseded by steam, diesel and most recently, electrically-driven machinery. The more modern pumps were easier to operate and maintain, and more efficient than the windpumps, and the new sources of power proved more certain than the vagaries of the wind.

● Identifiable sites with
  buildings or remains

miles 5

km 10

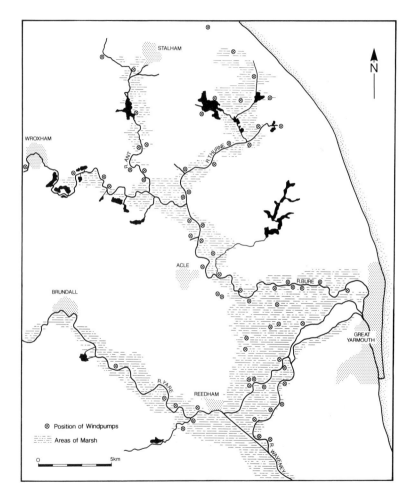

STALHAM

WROXHAM

R. ANT

R. THURNE

ACLE

R. BURE

BRUNDALL

GREAT
YARMOUTH

R. YARE

REEDHAM

R. WAVENEY

⊗ Position of Windpumps

Areas of Marsh

0 5km

82. FISHING AND MARITIME INDUSTRIES, POST 1600

Charles Lewis

Merchant trade and fishing were the principal contributors to the economies of Norfolk's coast. The rich fisheries of the North Sea and the county's position opposite continental Europe and along the east coast shipping routes were the keys to prosperity (see also Map 34).

The autumn herring fishery from Great Yarmouth was of international importance, attracting fishermen from far afield, particularly the Dutch in the 17th century and the Scots from the late 19th century. After the peak years of the early 1900s, market problems, followed by overfishing, saw a steady decline which brought the industry to an end in the late 1960's. During the 17th century, vessels from King's Lynn and Great Yarmouth engaged in the Icelandic cod fishery. Both ports also sent whaling vessels to the Arctic in the mid 17th and late 18th centuries, and this trade continued at Lynn into the late 19th century. A major trawl fishery for sole and turbot was introduced at Yarmouth in the mid 18th century but came to an abrupt end at the turn of the century. Cockles, mussels, oysters, whelks, shrimps, crabs and lobsters were all fished commercially along the coast, particularly in the 19th century. Many such fisheries have vanished but small inshore fleets still land shrimps and cockles at King's Lynn, whelks at Wells and crabs at Cromer and Sheringham.

Great Yarmouth and King's Lynn, serving extensive agricultural hinterlands, have always been Norfolk's major trading ports, but Blakeney/Cley and Wells once served north Norfolk, and smaller vessels traded from beaches and creeks elsewhere. Economic and physical factors brought about the decline of the smaller ports by the early 20th century and only Wells can still handle the occasional small coaster.

Norfolk's principal foreign trades have been the export of agricultural products, particularly grain, across the North Sea and the import of timber products from Scandinavia and the Baltic. Herring was also an important export from Yarmouth, particularly to the Mediterranean up to the late 19th century and then to northern Europe into the 20th century. The largest bulk import, however, was coal from the north-east, a trade eventually killed by the railways.

Shipbuilding yards were once active at Wells, King's Lynn and, particularly, Great Yarmouth, the industry reaching its peak in the mid-19th century. Only one shipyard now survives, at Yarmouth. The most recent maritime industry has been the search for North Sea gas which saw Great Yarmouth develop as an important supply and service port from the early 1960s. Gas from three offshore fields is now piped to a terminal at Bacton.

83. SEASIDE RESORTS

Martin Warren

In the 18th century fashionable society and county gentry sought the coastline of Norfolk in search of leisure, the picturesque and sea-water bathing. The port of Great Yarmouth, with excellent beaches and proximity to Norwich, was among the first to grow and a Bath House was built in 1759. Despite early opposition, building began along the shore early in the 19th century and Yarmouth eventually became a mass holiday resort.

The picturesque scenery of Cromer brought a select band of visitors to the little fishing village, and a bathing machine was available as early as 1779. A Bath House was built on the beach in 1814 and the watering place was considered amongst the most fashionable in the kingdom. Late Georgian Mundesley too was a minor watering place.

Lodgings were scarce at first but gradually these watering places catered for the visitors and a distinctive brand of seaside architecture and entertainment grew up, including, of course, the seaside piers. Several factors combined to stimulate the holiday trade - a rising middle class, the creation of Bank Holidays in 1870 and the desire to escape from urban drudgery. Royal or aristocratic patronage helped too. The growth of resorts reached a crescendo in the last quarter of the 19th century. By the First World War they had reached their zenith.

Resorts could only be reached by road or by sea until railways opened up new opportunities (Map 71). The line to Yarmouth from Norwich opened in 1844. There was not the economic incentive to push into north or west Norfolk at first. Indeed there were influential people who were reluctant to allow select Cromer to be spoiled by the railway, but no resort could be successful without connection to the railway system. New Hunstanton, for instance, was created to a grand design by a rich estate owner but the project was only completed once a railway connected it to King's Lynn and beyond. Villages such as Sheringham and Mundesley and the seaport of Wells only developed as resorts once connected to the railway.

In the 1880s and 1890s the writer Clement Scott stimulated trade by coining 'Poppyland' for the area around Cromer. At once he conveyed romance on a coast ripe for exploitation. Overstrand grew as a high class suburb of Cromer. Sometimes the anticipated growth failed to materialise, as at Weybourne and to an extent at Mundesley.

Tourism today is economically important but large hotels have been disappearing in favour of caravans, holiday camps and self-catering. Residential development has often come in the wake of the holidaymakers.

82. FISHING AND MARITIME INDUSTRIES, POST 1600

83. SEASIDE RESORTS

Wells
TSD I

Blakeney Cley
TD I

Sheringham
T I

Cromer
T I

Hunstanton

△ Minor Victorian Resorts

✳ Major Victorian Resorts

Bacton
O

Kings Lynn
TSD I

Great
Yarmouth
TSD IO

FISHING AND MARITIME
INDUSTRIES POST 1600
■ MAIN CENTRES

	Past	Present
Merchant trade	T	T
Shipbuilding	S	S
Deep sea fisheries	D	
Inshore fisheries	I	I
Offshore industry		O
Port facilities		

0   miles   5

0   km   10

84. POPULATION CHANGE 1951-1981

John Wright

The population of Norfolk (as defined by the 1981 boundary) was about 550,000 in 1951. Growth has been rapid since the early 1960s and the 1991 census is expected to show a population approaching 755,000. All this growth has been due to inward migration. On average, some 18,000 people leave the county each year but even more move in. Births and deaths have relatively little impact on the total population. There are about 9,000 deaths each year and the trend is upward. Births are more variable. A peak of 9,600 in 1970 was followed by a steep decline to 7,500 in 1977, giving rise to the recent fall in the number of school leavers. Births have increased again during the 1980s, reaching 9,000 in 1990. The age structure of the population has continued to change. The proportion of people aged 65 and over, for example, has increased from 12.6% in 1951 to about 19.6% in 1990, and there are now more than twice as many people in this age group as there were in 1951. Occupancy rates continue to decrease. Taking account only of people in private households, the average number of people per occupied dwelling dropped from 3.2 in 1951 to 2.6 in 1981. This fall is due largely to the increasing numbers of households containing one or two people, which now form 56% of all households.

Most people moving into Norfolk have come from the South East, or from other parts of East Anglia, either to retire or to take up jobs locally. The scale of migration depends in part on the state of the national economy. More people of working age moved into Norfolk during the 'boom' conditions of the early 1970s and later 1980s than during intervening recessions. These movements have been accompanied by a more constant retirement migration, not just to the coast but throughout the rural area.

The map shows the percentage change in population in each civil parish between 1951 and 1981, using the actual numbers present on census night and making allowance, where necessary, for boundary changes. The pattern of change has not remained constant over the whole period.

During the 1950s population growth concentrated around the main urban areas, with population decline dominating the rest of the county. Since then growth has spread to areas further afield, although decline is still prevalent in the smaller villages; of the 100 smallest villages in 1951, 80 had lost population by 1981. The map shows an amalgam of all these features: population decline in the north of the county, more remote from employment centres, and in parts of the south west, and population growth in the Norwich area and around King's Lynn, and across the centre of the county. There are hints that growth is associated with the trunk roads, which normally provide the best access to employment centres. Yet even static population totals can mask significant local changes. In 1951 the rural areas were still heavily dependent on jobs in agriculture, but as these became fewer many young people moved out, either to the towns or out of the county altogether. Many of those who subsequently moved in were older people, either retired, or else able and willing to commute to jobs elsewhere.

Despite the broad trends illustrated by the map, changes at parish level still depend upon particular local factors. One such is the deployment of the armed forces. Since 1951 the closure of many war-time establishments has contributed to population decline. The closure of Sculthorpe as an active American base in the early 1960s, for example, had a considerable impact on the surrounding area. Landowners and developers have played their part through decisions about whether, where and when to provide new housing. These decisions have been made in relation to local authority planning policies which have encouraged development in some locations and inhibited it in others. An extreme example is the Town Development Scheme at Thetford which brought in people (and jobs) from London with the result that the small market town of 4,400 in 1951 had a population approaching 20,000 by 1981. A similar scheme took place at King's Lynn. Other towns and villages have been selected for development on a smaller scale according to their location in relation to employment centres, their capacity in terms of service provision and the needs of the surrounding area. Most of the market towns had population increases of between 60% and 90% between 1951 and 1981. By comparison, the population in the built up area of Norwich increased by 17%.

Although there is no simple correlation between house-building and population change, planning policies have had a major impact on individual parishes and they will continue to do so in the future. Yet planning policies can only shape the way that development pressures are accommodated. The demand for new housing is a potent factor and there is almost certain to be further population growth over the next 10 to 15 years, much of it in the smaller towns and villages.

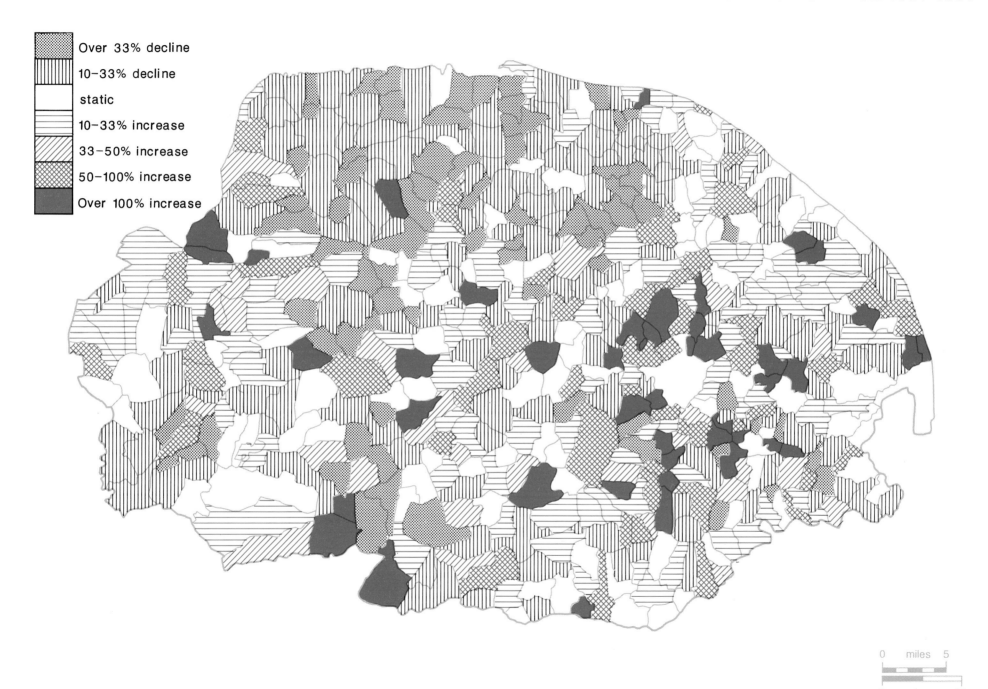

84. POPULATION CHANGE 1951-1981

Legend:
- Over 33% decline
- 10–33% decline
- static
- 10–33% increase
- 33–50% increase
- 50–100% increase
- Over 100% increase

0 miles 5

0 km 10

85. RURAL PRIMARY SCHOOL CLOSURES, 1947-1990
John Wright

One of the features of rural areas since the Second World War has been the loss of facilities and services, such as shops, pubs and buses. This section looks at the changing distribution of one particular service: the primary school.

The Education Act of 1944 required every Local Education Authority to prepare a development plan for the provision of education needs. The Norfolk plan was prepared in 1947 and contained far-reaching proposals for primary school closure and new building. The County Council, as Education Authority for all of Norfolk apart from the City of Norwich and the County Borough of Great Yarmouth, had many problems to consider. Most Norfolk schools were old: of 464 primary schools 200 had been built before 1870 and 405 before 1900. New regulations from the Ministry of Education had set out minimum standards for school accommodation which were, in the words of the plan, 'probably above that of any existing school and certainly far beyond that of the vast majority of Norfolk schools at the present time'. A detailed survey undertaken in 1946 had shown that in most cases it would not be practicable to bring the existing schools up to the new standards. Many of the schools were small, both physically and in the number of children attending: exactly half had fewer than 51 pupils. Some schools were not in convenient locations, and it was evident that new schools would be needed for the population increase anticipated in the Norwich 'fringe' (the built-up area beyond the City boundary). In the rest of the county, however, relatively little growth in pupil numbers could be expected in the foreseeable future, beyond that implied in the already apparent post-war bulge in the birth rate.

Turning to the educational issues, the plan set out clearly some of the arguments which have pertained to school closures ever since. The value of close association between school and local community was acknowledged, but much greater weight was given to the need for bigger schools so that a larger complement of teachers could provide a better standard of education than was possible in small schools with only one or two teachers. The plan was therefore based on providing wherever possible schools large enough to have at least three teachers, for which the Ministry's minimum standard was 51 pupils. The proposals involved closing 358 schools, retaining 105 and building 164 new ones. Of the 270 schools thereby provided, only 26 would have fewer than 51 children. Some small schools would still be necessary in areas where travelling distances would otherwise be too great.

An 18-year programme was drawn up to carry out the proposals but it proved to be much too ambitious. However, the basic principles of the plan have been maintained in successive programmes of the County Council up to the present time, and some 170 primary schools have been closed since 1947.

The map portrays the closure of village schools but does not record new building and therefore represents only a partial picture of events since 1947. Unshaded parishes are those which had at least one primary school in 1990, including infant and junior, and first and middle schools, as well as the more traditional primary schools with children aged 5 to 11/12. All these parishes also had schools in 1946, except for Brundall, Spixworth and South Wootton, where there were none. In the remaining parishes either there were no schools in 1946 or else those schools which did exist have been closed. In most cases it is the only school which has gone, but sometimes two have been closed. In a few cases a closure has left at least one school open. The map does not show exact locations within the modern (1981) civil parishes, some of which contain more than one settlement.

Because schools need to be accessible to all children there are no significant disparities in the distribution of closures. In the west of the county, for example, there are relatively few parishes without schools, but here parishes are larger than in north Norfolk, where villages tend to be small and closely spaced. The area north of Thetford contains the 'battle area' where three schools were closed during the last war.

For comparison with the 1946 figures, there were 352 primary schools in the county in 1990, excluding those in Norwich and Great Yarmouth, of which 73 had fewer than 51 full-time pupils. Over the years since 1947 the number on roll at the time of closure has changed very little - few such schools have had more than 30 children. Many smaller villages have decreased in population, and school age children have declined as a proportion of the total population. More schools have therefore dropped into the 'small' category.

Over the next few years the same broad trends seem likely to continue. The number of children in the vicinity of the smaller rural schools will not increase significantly and the Local Education Authority may conclude that more should be closed. The present guidelines are that schools should have at least three teachers and 60 pupils.

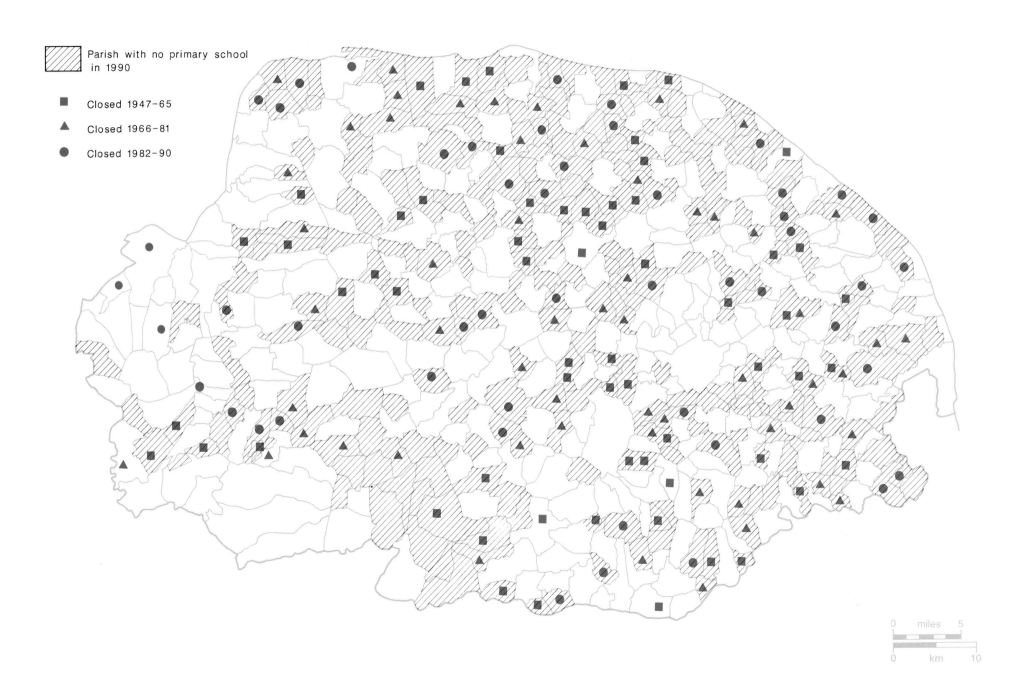

Parish with no primary school
in 1990

■ Closed 1947–65

▲ Closed 1966–81

● Closed 1982–90

0   miles   5

0   km   10

86. THE PATTERN OF ROADS IN THE 20TH CENTURY

John Ayton

The pattern of the road network in the county changed little over the first half of the century. So far as the highway authorities were concerned, it was essentially a matter of maintaining the structure of the road network to cope with increasing traffic and the change from horses to motors. Road works were confined to localised changes to junctions or bends to improve safety.

Before the Second World War, the only significant change to the county road network was the creation of most of the outer ring road at Norwich, linking country lanes with new sections through new housing estates.

Between 1939 and 1945 roads across the airfields and the Stanford 'battle area' were closed - and many have remained closed. Diversion routes were gradually improved (some over 30 years after the original diversion), including Syderstone, Marham and Scottow and the Bodney-Little Cressingham road. (One surviving curiosity is the rural dual carriageway between Tunstead and Scottow, reputedly constructed for heavy lorry traffic to Coltishall airfield.)

Changes to the network since the end of the Second World War have been carried out either by the Department of Transport, who are responsible for the 'trunk roads' - (A.10, A.11, A.47, A.140 and A.134) and the County Council who are responsible for all other public highways. Before 1974 Norwich and Great Yarmouth were separate highway authorities. In Norwich, the major changes to the road network were the building of Rouen Road and the western and northern sections of the Inner Ring. The Trunk Road programme reflected national priorities and resources - and a central government view that Norfolk was a low priority. County schemes reflected a more local view of the need to relieve towns and villages of through traffic, and the shorter, easier schemes tended to be implemented before the longer and more expensive bypasses. The routes between settlements on both trunk roads and the principal county roads were straightened and widened throughout the 1960s and 1970s.

On the trunk roads, the earlier schemes were short 'relief' roads designed to relieve the worst bottle necks - such as Damgate Street and Market Street, Wymondham and Bridge Street, Thetford. (These were still trunk roads until the late 1950s.) As a result the provision of a full 'outer' bypass was given a low priority and Thetford only achieved an outer bypass in 1990 - Wymondham is still (1991) only a line on a map.

The southern bypass to King's Lynn was an early 1960s priority; on the A.47 village bypasses (Honingham, Hockering) were done before the towns (Swaffham and Dereham). For some, unexplained, reason the A.10 was given a higher priority with both an inner and outer bypass at Downham Market. The new A.17 from King's Lynn to Sutton Bridge followed the former railway line.

On the 'county' roads, the first major new road was the King's Lynn eastern bypass and in the 1970s included bypasses to Caister, Harleston, Aylsham and Loddon, and of special note, a number of schemes built on former railway lines, including North Walsham, Stalham to Potter Heigham, Wortwell to Earsham (and Bungay) and Holt. (The East Dereham trunk road bypass followed the former railway through Scarning and Wendling.) Villages bypassed where the 'old' road followed a tortuous route through the village included Bawdeswell, Stoke Ferry and Attlebridge. Where villages 'straddled' the road, the temptation to take the cheaper direct route, severing the village, was too much at Garboldisham, Thurton, Foxley and Wereham.

The 1980s saw an acceleration in new road building, with more attention to the A.11 - Attleborough bypass, the Wymondham-Cringleford section and (at last), the Thetford bypass; to the A.47 east of Norwich (Blofield and Acle and the Great Yarmouth Western Bypass; the A.10 at Hilgay and Southery and to the A.140 (Dickleburgh). On the 'county' roads the major schemes were at Fakenham (north), Dersingham to Snettisham, Downham Market (south) and Great Hockham (a 'battle area' diversion).

Currently the Norwich Southern Bypass, the biggest single road scheme ever undertaken in the county and the Trowse Bypass, are under construction. In Norwich, major road proposals include the completion of the Inner Ring, and new roads on the old rail lines to City and Victoria stations.

The trunk road programme envisages straightening and dualling all the trunk roads before the end of the century, and major bypasses are proposed at Narborough, North Tuddenham (A.47), Larling and Wymondham (A.11), Scole and Long Stratton (A.140) and West Winch (A.10).

On the county roads, in addition to straightening (including some notorious bends like Ovington), the programme provides for bypasses on the principal roads including Wroxham-Hoveton, Ormesby, Letheringsett, Brockdish and Needham, the Rudhams, Kirstead, and Guist and, in the longer term, Haddiscoe, Thurton, Bodham, Diss/Roydon, Lopham, Shipdham, Outwell and Fincham.

The greater part of the rest of the network is not programmed for change and as a consequence although the character of many of the roads will be different, the pattern of roads between the trunk and principal roads in 2000 will be very similar to that in 1900. They won't be suitable to carry large volumes of traffic, or heavy lorries, and the challenge will be to devise methods of traffic management geared to the conservation of the character of the routes in the countryside and through towns and villages.

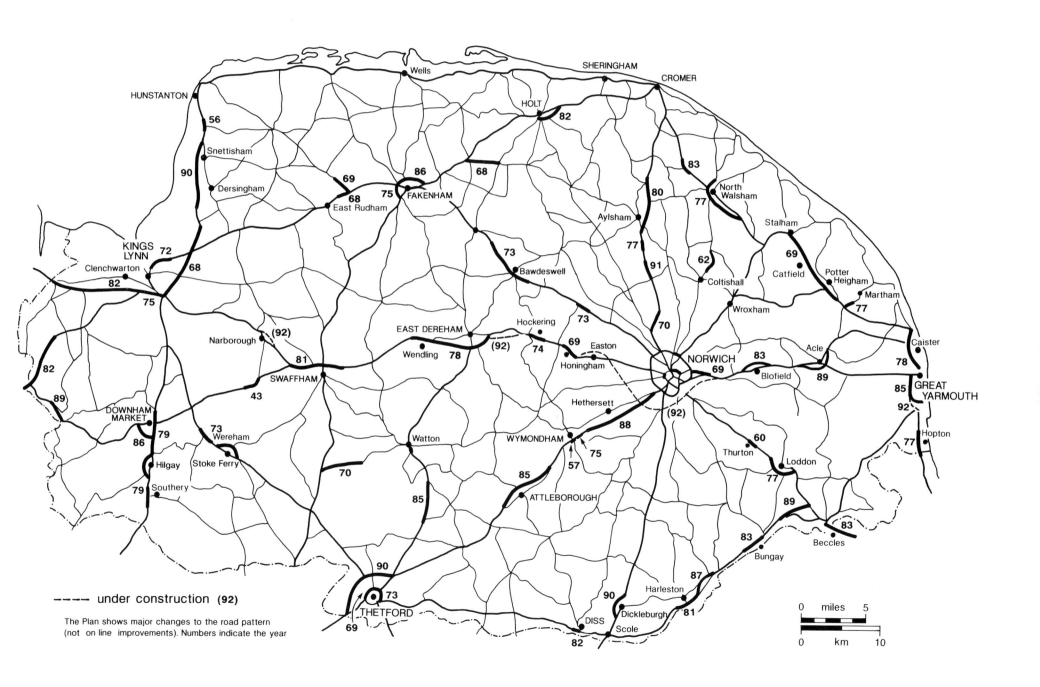

- - - - under construction (92)

The Plan shows major changes to the road pattern
(not on line improvements). Numbers indicate the year

The rise of German naval power at the beginning of the 20th century refocussed attention on the defences of the east coast. By this time all the Norfolk forts had been dismantled except the South Battery at Yarmouth, and this was obsolete. A plan to install modern artillery was opposed by the town, and when the First World War broke out in 1914 there were no effective defences in the whole of Norfolk.

On the declaration of war troops were quickly concentrated at Weybourne, but little was done to provide defences until the German fleet dashed across the North Sea to bombard Yarmouth in November. Damage was slight but the incident inflamed fears of invasion and stimulated a frantic bout of trench digging. Sheringham golf links were desecrated by a complex system of field defences reinforced by reserve lines of defence inland between Hunworth and Briston. Two batteries, each of six heavy field-guns, were stationed at Weybourne and Mundesley, two 4.7-inch guns at Cromer and five 15-pounders in small open emplacements along the coast. Curiously, Yarmouth, a minor naval base with a sea-plane station, had no fixed guns until after a second German bombardment of April 1916, when a 4.7-inch gun was emplaced on the cliffs at Gorleston.

Fears of a sudden German descent on the coast lasted throughout the war and the defences were strengthened by concrete pillboxes, some in a line inland from Weybourne to Sea Palling and others defending the landward side of Yarmouth. Pillboxes had first been encountered on the Western Front where they formed formidable additions to the German defences, and British engineers were quick to realise their worth. Those in north Norfolk were circular, made of concrete blocks, with steel-shuttered loopholes and doors. Another type, at Yarmouth, was the prototype of the common hexagonal pillbox of the Second World War. After the armistice in 1918, when all the field works and temporary batteries were abandoned, only the pillboxes remained.

Rearmament in the 1930s brought the establishment of two anti-aircraft artillery practice camps at Stiffkey and Weybourne. On the outbreak of war in 1939 a battery of two 6-inch guns was immediately installed at Yarmouth but nothing more was done as invasion was considered a remote prospect. Then complacency turned to alarm following the fall of France in June 1940. Although it was deemed most probable that the Germans would land on the south coast, it was thought that a diversionary assault might be attempted on East Anglia, and this prompted the most extensive programme of fortification undertaken in the region. The coast and small ports were again fortified and for the first time since the Civil War extensive defences were constructed inland.

The overall plan was simple: a crust of fortifications, consisting of pillboxes, trenches, anti-tank obstacles, barbed wire and mines along the coast, further lines of defence inland, and extra defences at important junctions and airfields. First World War tactics had envisaged meeting the enemy with 'vigorous counterstrokes' but the army in the summer of 1940 had neither tanks nor transport and was forced to adopt a static role.

The most formidable defences were the coastal batteries. Nine were quickly installed in June 1940, each armed with two elderly ex-naval guns, mostly 6-inch, and two searchlights. The guns were bolted onto base-plates fixed in a slab of concrete and each were protected by a framework of steel girders covered in sandbags, later replaced by brick and concrete gun-houses. These were linked by a semi-underground corridor lined with magazines and shelters. The batteries were ingeniously camouflaged with foliage, nets, hayricks and false roofs, which had an unfortunate tendency to blow off when the guns fired. By 1942 there were 14 batteries with a total of 28 guns.

These were not the only defences of the shoreline. Miles of scaffolding lined the water's edge, thousands of concrete blocks marched along the beaches and tens of thousands of anti-tank mines were buried in the sand. On the cliff tops and in the dunes were lines of trenches supported by pillboxes.

Inland there were five successive lines of defence. The first three were based on the rivers Ant, Bure and Wensum, the fourth on the Yare and the fifth on the River Ouse, fortified at Thetford and Brandon. Norwich was surrounded by a ring of anti-tank obstacles stiffened by half a dozen pillboxes. As an illustration of the continuity of defensive strategy, all those places recommended for fortification during the Armada were fortified in 1940.

The coast defences reached a peak in extent and efficiency in 1943; from then there was a gradual reduction as regular troops were replaced by the Home Guard and many batteries were closed and occupied by 'care and maintenance' parties. By early 1945 only the Pier Battery at Yarmouth remained operational and that closed as soon as the war ended.

Work had begun on clearing the beaches before the German surrender and after VE day the whole system was quickly dismantled. All the guns were scrapped in the winter of 1945/6 although the emplacements were only demolished if they interfered with civic amenities. Clearing the mines and beach obstacles took much longer and even today the odd piece of rusty military steelwork occasionally surfaces from the sand.

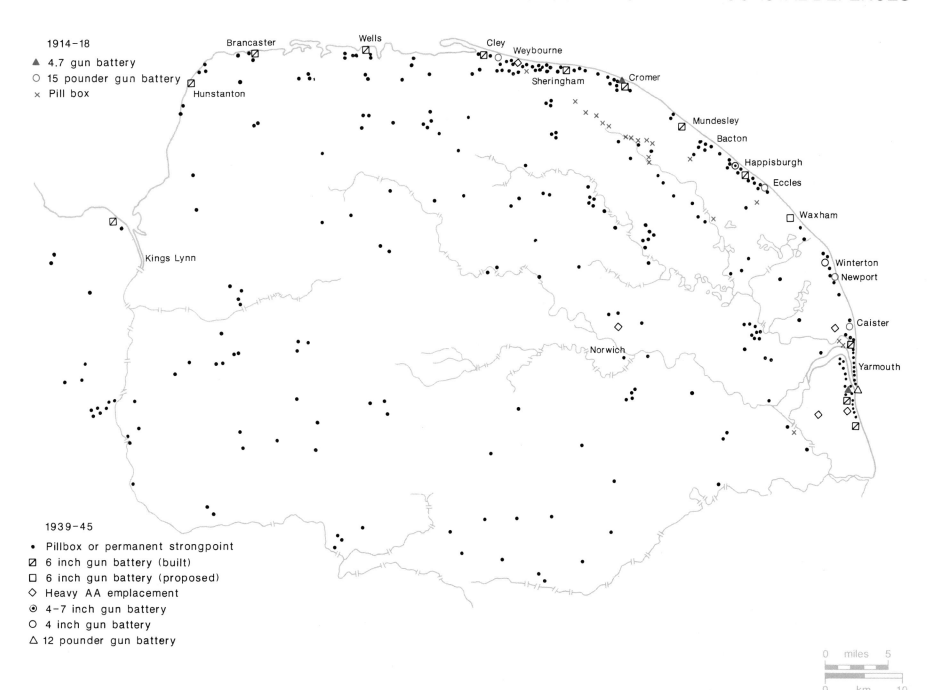

1914–18

▲ 4.7 gun battery

○ 15 pounder gun battery

✕ Pill box

Brancaster

Wells

Cley

Weybourne

Hunstanton

Sheringham

Cromer

Mundesley

Bacton

Happisburgh

Eccles

Waxham

Kings Lynn

Winterton

Newport

Caister

Norwich

Yarmouth

1939–45

● Pillbox or permanent strongpoint

▨ 6 inch gun battery (built)

▢ 6 inch gun battery (proposed)

◇ Heavy AA emplacement

◉ 4–7 inch gun battery

○ 4 inch gun battery

△ 12 pounder gun battery

0   miles   5

0   km   10

In 1914 the pattern of Norfolk farming had hardly changed in four generations. By 1972, the eve of entry to the European Economic Community, it had been revolutionised. The charts suggest a few of the many changes over this 60-year period and how the pattern of farming has always been influenced by the diversity of Norfolk soils.

At the turn of the century Norfolk agriculture could be divided broadly between the east, where wheat and pulses flourished on the stronger land and the lighter soils to the west, where barley production predominated and the finest malting quality was grown. Similarly, there was a broad division in livestock enterprises. In the east farmers wintered fattened rangy Irish store cattle for the London market on the heavy crops of fodder roots. In the west great flocks of sheep maintained the fertility of the light soils. But throughout the county farming was based on the traditional Norfolk four-course rotation of roots and green crops alternating with corn. Fodder roots for the yarded cattle or folded sheep on which the farm depended for fertility, were followed by barley. This was undersown with grass and clover for hay, particularly for the farm's horses. On the ploughed-under sward the second cereal crop of wheat or oats was autumn drilled. This simple, self-contained system kept the land clean and in good heart and, although they were allowed some latitude, farmers were bound to it both by their leases and by tradition.

Following the First War, the chill winds of foreign competition sent first cereal and then livestock prices tumbling. The traditional Norfolk four-course rotation was no longer economic and one glaring weakness was the root shift. Not only were mangels, swedes and turnips expensive to grow but they generated no cash until the livestock on which they were fattened were finally sold, and little enough then. Sugar beet, introduced by the Dutch who built the first factory at Cantley in 1912, proved the answer. First, it was grown under contract to the factories. Secondly, it was a cash crop. Growers

therefore had an assured market, guaranteed prices and were paid promptly. Furthermore, experiments at the Norfolk Agricultural Station proved that the beet pulp remaining after the sugar extraction process, and the beet tops, could be used for feeding livestock in place of the traditional roots. From the mid 1920s sugar beet quickly became the pre-eminent break crop for Norfolk farmers. As the long inter-war agricultural depression dragged on farmers diversified into other new crops. In central and west Norfolk, for example, vegetable production, especially carrots and brassicae, developed into a profitable alternative to traditional break crops.

The period between the Wars saw two important changes in livestock production. The first stemmed from the immigration of many farmers from dairying districts, where land was dear and farms hard to find, to Norfolk, where land was cheap and plentiful. Until their arrival 'cow keeping' had been looked down upon as an inferior, peasant type of occupation but the newcomers expertly developed winter milk production on the arable farm, especially on the heavier soils of central and south Norfolk. By 1939 the county had become a major milk producing area. The second major change was the decline year by year in the number of sheep as the cost of folded flock became increasingly uncompetitive against the flood of imported lamb.

During the Second War, every effort was made to increase arable production. Agriculture was placed under tight control and the pump was primed with grants for farm improvement. The worst ravages of the depression years were repaired, derelict land reclaimed and permanent pastures brought under the plough. Farm advisory services were expanded. By the time agriculture was finally de-controlled in 1954 some prosperity had returned to the industry and Norfolk farmers began to tool up for mechanisation. Indeed, investment in machinery was, in real terms, higher in the decade after de-control than at any subsequent period. At the same time, improved crop varieties and the chemical revolu-

tion - herbicides, fungicides, insecticides and more artificial fertilisers - were raising yields and transforming farming practice. Farmers no longer needed livestock, nor needed to follow a strict rotation to maintain fertility.

Nevertheless, as the pie chart for 1972 suggests, the tradition and basic principles of good husbandry epitomised in the old four-course rotation had not been forgotten. (The figure of permanent pasture is exaggerated because farmers included leys of more than three years. The only extensive area of permanent pasture in the county lay in the estuaries of the east Norfolk rivers). Upland Norfolk was still being farmed on sound rotational principles with cash break crops in place of the old fodder roots and a higher proportion of cereals in barley, partly since oats were no longer needed for farm horses.

Each year, as mechanisation increased in range and scale, there were fewer farms requiring fewer farmworkers. In the late 1950s the number of holdings under 100 acres, and the number of workers, had hardly altered since the beginning of the century. In little more than a decade the numbers of both were almost halved. There was also a radical restructuring in the pattern of land ownership. In 1914 fewer than one farmer in six owned the land he farmed. By the early 1970s two out of three were owner-occupied.

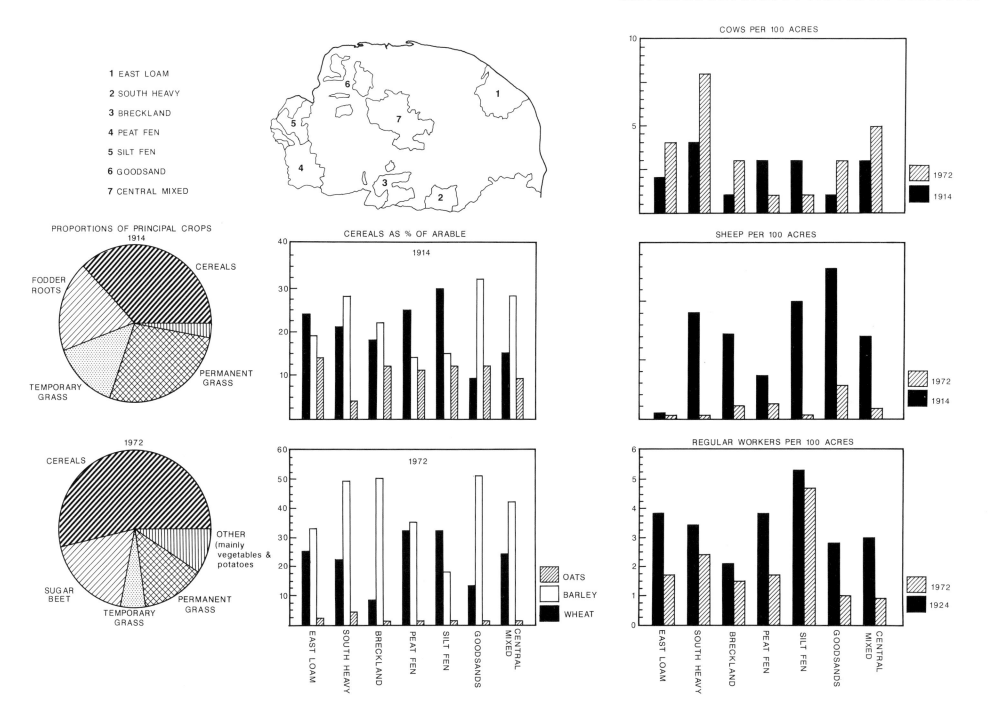

1 EAST LOAM

2 SOUTH HEAVY

3 BRECKLAND

4 PEAT FEN

5 SILT FEN

6 GOODSAND

7 CENTRAL MIXED

PROPORTIONS OF PRINCIPAL CROPS

1914

CEREALS
FODDER ROOTS
TEMPORARY GRASS
PERMANENT GRASS

1972

CEREALS
SUGAR BEET
TEMPORARY GRASS
PERMANENT GRASS
OTHER (mainly vegetables & potatoes)

COWS PER 100 ACRES

1972
1914

CEREALS AS % OF ARABLE

1914

1972

OATS
BARLEY
WHEAT

EAST LOAM
SOUTH HEAVY
BRECKLAND
PEAT FEN
SILT FEN
GOODSANDS
CENTRAL MIXED

SHEEP PER 100 ACRES

1972
1914

REGULAR WORKERS PER 100 ACRES

1972
1924

EAST LOAM
SOUTH HEAVY
BRECKLAND
PEAT FEN
SILT FEN
GOODSANDS
CENTRAL MIXED

89. LANDSCAPE AND NATURE CONSERVATION

Steve Harris

Far from being the flat and visually dull countryside imagined by many, Norfolk encompasses a very wide variety of lowland landscapes, each with definable characteristics. This character often derives from natural or semi-natural habitats with distinctive associated wildlife. The scenery and wildlife of the Broads, Brecks and north Norfolk coast are well known. Recognition of their great natural history interest goes back many years, although widespread appreciation of their scenic qualities has been gained rather more recently. Other areas too have characteristic landscape and wildlife: the rolling chalk-based Goodsands of north west Norfolk with their rectilinear network of late enclosure thorn hedges around large fields; the 'ancient' countryside of central and south Norfolk characterised by patchwork field systems, sinuous mixed hedges, and woodland whose history is measured in centuries; Fenland, with the Ouse Washes as a clue to the 'natural' landscape of the area; the well-wooded country of the Greensand scarp of west Norfolk; and the fertile loam landscapes of the north east, its fields separated by grassy banks and a thinning population of senescing oaks. Superimposed on all these are the river valleys, corridors of visual interest and high wildlife value.

The pressures on this resource seem relentless. Post-war agricultural policy led to much destruction, while pollution from many sources increased. More subtly, changing economic circumstances caused the death of traditional rural activities that created and conserved valuable habitats such as coppiced woodland, meadows and heaths. Now local population growth and associated development pressure, combined with likely climatic change threaten further erosion.

Landscape and wildlife conservation have for many years been treated separately both at national and local level. Increasingly however, a more holistic approach is discernible, incorporating the wider undesignated countryside and those responsible for its management, particularly farmers.

Norfolk has long been highly regarded for its natural history interest and as a result several important conservation initiatives have arisen in the county. 1888 saw the founding of the Breydon Water Birds' Protection Society. In 1912, Blakeney Point, wardened since the turn of the century, became Norfolk's first non-privately-owned nature reserve. The purchase of Cley Marshes in 1926 presaged the founding of the Norfolk Naturalists' Trust, the first County Trust. 1954 saw Scolt made the first of Norfolk's now ten National Nature Reserves and the first of currently (1991) 138 Sites of Special Scientific Interest. Until the 1981 Wildlife and Countryside Act, SSSI status only ensured that the nature conservation value of such sites was considered in the planning process. Since 1981 SSSI's have been protected from operations outside planning control, but despite this improvement, deterioration has continued due to lack of appropriate management. During 1983-5 the NNT co-ordinated a survey of the county's undesignated land. The resulting c.1500 best wildlife sites ('C' sites) represent habitats of county significance, some of which may warrant SSSI status. Local government's policy document, the Structure Plan, provides for the protection of specific habitats from development, and seeks to safeguard the 'C' site network.

Landscape conservation historically has largely been the by-product of function; trees were a raw material, hedges contained stock. Today the conservation of landscape and its features is assisted by government action, first manifested in Norfolk in 1968 with the declaration of the coastal Area of Outstanding Natural Beauty. Interestingly the Broads, since 1990 virtually a National Park, were first proposed for National Park status in 1947. The Brecks, suggested as an AONB, also in 1947, are only now being put forward again for national recognition. The creation of the Countryside Commission in 1968 gave landscape conservation more emphasis, and in partnership with local authorities and private landowners the Commission has facilitated many advances. The Heritage Coast was declared in 1974 followed by three countryside management projects in the 1980's.

Dramatic changes in the landscape have prompted government action. The loss of elms to disease produced the Amenity Tree Planting Scheme, funded by a partnership between the Countryside Commission and the County Council. Recent storms have seen incentives to restore affected landscapes by the same partnership. The landscape impact of ploughing Broadland pastures produced the Broads Grazing Marshes Conservation Scheme, the success of which, by subsidising less profitable but environmentally-benign farming, led to the EC's Environmentally Sensitive Area designations. In the Structure Plan significant landscapes are identified for enhancement and protection from inappropriate development.

The conservation of nature and landscape may now be becoming better integrated, with mechanisms to promote appropriate management of key areas, including those in the wider undesignated countryside. Whilst some SSSI's are reserves, managed by conservation organisations, many are not, and may be helped by new grants from English Nature for positive management. Several SSSI's have higher designations, conferring greater protection, but not necessarily facilitating appropriate management. ESA's promote conservation of landscape and wildlife together, and Norfolk has two of the UK total of 18. The success of the ESA principle of financially supporting traditional practices has led to the latest initiative, Countryside Stewardship, designed to give owners of appropriate areas payment for conservation management. The Amenity Tree Planting Scheme has broadened into grants for a wider range of landscape conservation measures. In part this has been prompted by the significant take-up of woodland planting grants from the Forestry Commission and the Ministry of Agriculture and MAFF grants for hedge planting and management. The latest structure plan combines landscape and nature conservation into a single topic of 'countryside' conservation.

89. LANDSCAPE AND NATURE CONSERVATION

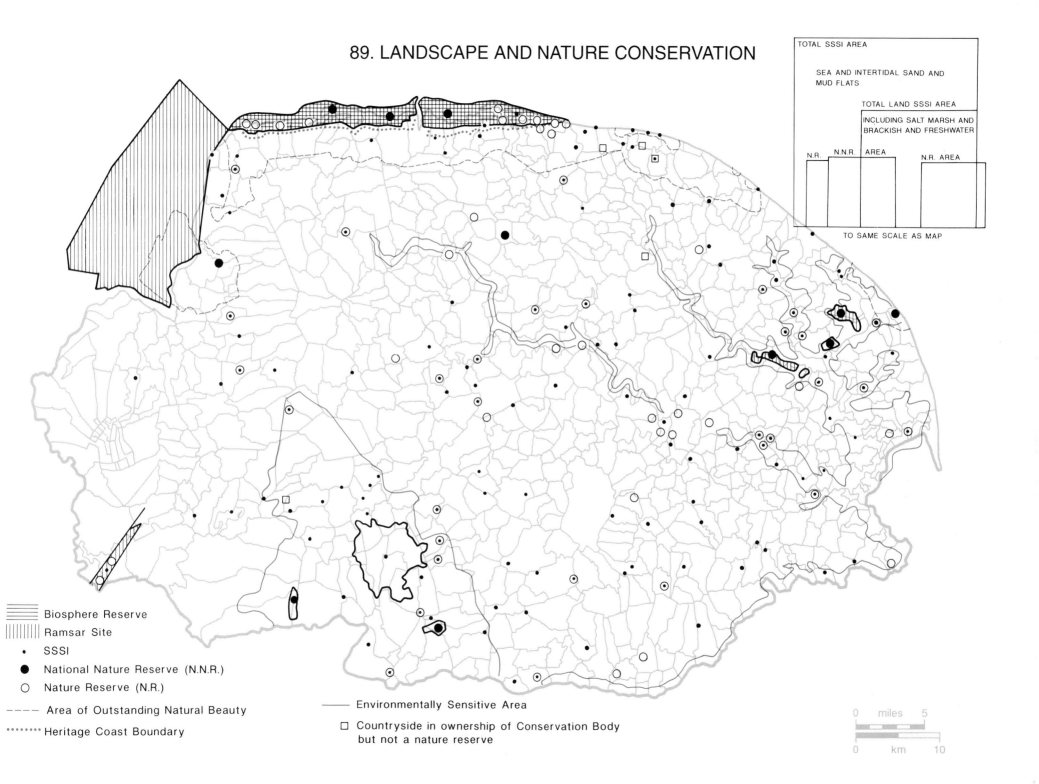

TOTAL SSSI AREA

SEA AND INTERTIDAL SAND AND
MUD FLATS

TOTAL LAND SSSI AREA

INCLUDING SALT MARSH AND
BRACKISH AND FRESHWATER

N.R. N.N.R. AREA N.R. AREA

TO SAME SCALE AS MAP

Biosphere Reserve

Ramsar Site

• SSSI

● National Nature Reserve (N.N.R.)

○ Nature Reserve (N.R.)

– – – Area of Outstanding Natural Beauty

•••••••• Heritage Coast Boundary

—— Environmentally Sensitive Area

☐ Countryside in ownership of Conservation Body
but not a nature reserve

0 miles 5

0 km 10

The purpose behind the designation of Conservation Areas is to preserve and enhance the character of chosen *areas* rather than individual buildings. Pleasant groups of buildings together with open spaces, trees, historic street patterns, village greens or features of historic or archaeological interest can all contribute to the special character of an area making it eligible for designation by the Local Authority.

Initially, Conservation Areas were based around town and city centres. The first in Norfolk was the Camperdown area in Great Yarmouth designated in 1969, followed by six areas in the centre of Norwich. These were followed by rural village centres, as at Heydon in 1971 and New Buckenham in 1973. In recent years the designation of less populated areas of important landscape value has become more widespread. Some are centred around large country estates as at Gunton or Melton Constable. Others are in areas of particular natural beauty and landscape importance. The Glaven Valley Conservation Area, stretching from Cley and Blakeney on the coast inland to Stody and Edgefield, is an unusually large example of this type of Conservation Area. In total, there are now well over 200 designated Conservation Areas, including 19 in market towns, eight in major towns and 18 in the city of Norwich.

There are two main controls on development in Conservation Areas. Firstly, consent is required from the local authority for demolition in the designated area with only a few minor exceptions. Secondly, applications for planning permission for development which would effect the character or appearance of the area have to be advertised by the local planning authority. The definition of development which would effect the character or appearance of the area is open to fairly wide interpretation. For example, the proposed development may be outside the designated area, but visible from it. Planning authorities are also required to pay special attention to the desirability of preserving or enhancing the character or appearance of a Conservation Area when processing planning applications. Some permitted development (that is, work which does not require planning permission) is more restricted within designated areas. For example, consent is needed for the cladding of buildings with stone or artificial materials, the permitted size of extensions is smaller and permission is needed for satellite dishes to be sited on chimneys or fronting a road or footpath. There is also a limit on the size of the dish. In addition, the cutting down, lopping or topping of trees has to be advertised six weeks in advance, and non-compliance can carry large fines.

The main threat to the quality of a Conservation Area is the cumulative effect of permitted development such as the replacement of traditional timber windows with UPVC, the use of off-the-shelf doors, concrete roofing tiles and unsympathetic extensions. In some cases control can be increased if the planning authority issues an Article 4 Direction. This specifies the removal of particular permitted development rights such as alterations to windows, or new paint work. They are only issued either where the Authority can make a strong case to the Secretary of State that the Direction would help establish a positive policy towards improvement of the area as part of an overall scheme of enhancement initiatives, or where there is a known threat to the character of the area. For example the estate village of New Houghton which was built with perfect symmetry in the 18th century was suffering from the encroachment of new fencing, the erection of sheds and altered windows before a Direction was issued.

Local planning authorities should also take positive steps to improve the appearance of Conservation Areas through enhancement schemes. The main emphasis is on devising and implementing paving schemes, and the best examples use traditional materials and well designed street furniture. For instance, the Purfleet Quay enhancement scheme in King's Lynn has transformed a former car park into an appropriate setting for the fine 17th century Customs House. The quayside has been paved mainly with York stone and granite setts and salvaged anchor chains are used to prevent traffic encroachment. The scheme was commended in the 1990 Civic Trust Awards.

In order to encourage public support and enthusiasm for conservation, Local Authorities sometimes set up Conservation Area Advisory Committees drawn from local amenity societies, architects, surveyors, planners and other interested local residents. These committees are invited to advise and comment on applications for development within Conservation Areas. In Norwich the Conservation Area Advisory Committee meets every month to comment on proposals in the city whilst in King's Lynn a regular C.A.A.C. meeting discusses proposals for the whole district. In South Norfolk there is a Conservation Forum every six months. Other districts rely on active local amenity societies to monitor development proposals.

North Norfolk District Council has been the most active in designating Conservation Areas but the process in other districts still continues. In South Norfolk around 20 new Areas are under consideration, while in Breckland four new Areas are being considered. In 1991, in line with the move towards designating larger areas of countryside, two rural Conservation Areas were designated in Broadland, one at Blickling centred around Blickling Hall and one at Heydon extending the earlier village Conservation Area to encompass Heydon Park and part of Salle parish. Maps showing the extent of Conservation Areas are available for viewing at District and County Planning Departments.

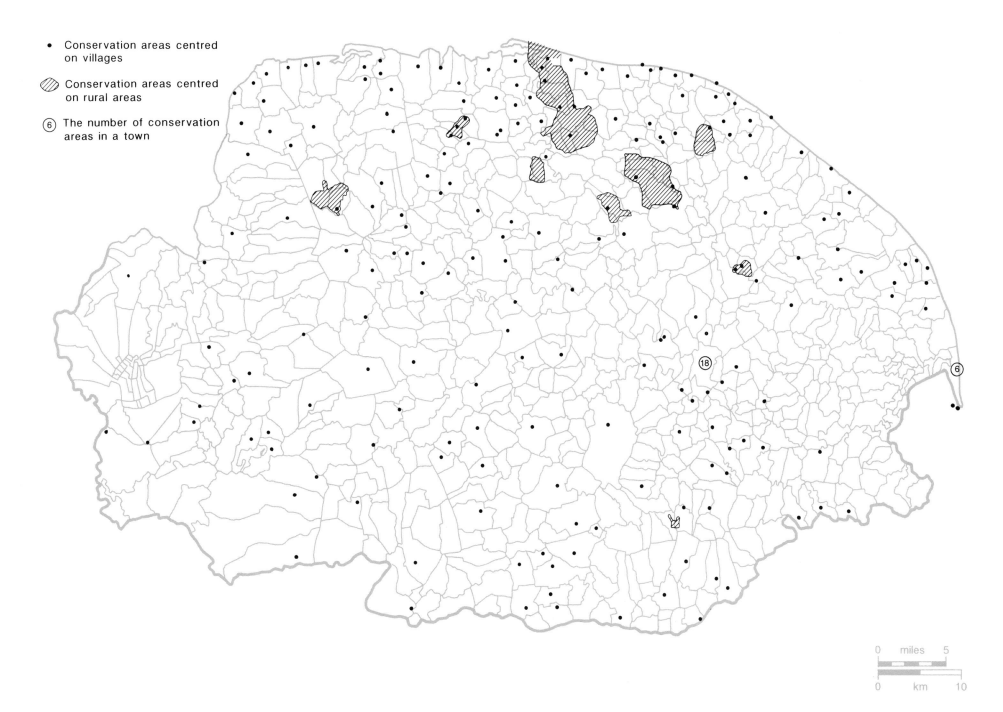

- Conservation areas centred on villages
- Conservation areas centred on rural areas
- (6) The number of conservation areas in a town

Listed Buildings provide the legislative framework for protecting our architectural heritage. Lists of buildings of Special Architectural or Historic Interest are compiled by the Secretary of State on the advice of English Heritage and there are just over 10,000 in Norfolk. The principles of selection are:

(i) Those buildings constructed before 1700 which survive in anything like their original form.

(ii) Most buildings constructed between 1700 and 1840.

(iii) Between 1840 and 1914 only buildings of definite quality, including works by principal architects such as Teulon at Shadwell Court and Lutyens at Overstrand Hall.

(iv) Between 1914 and 1939 a few selected buildings of high quality such as Norwich City Hall and King Edward VII Grammar School in King's Lynn.

(v) From 1939 to 1961 a few outstanding buildings are listed.

In choosing buildings, attention is paid to their social, economic or technological importance. Included in this category are almshouses, workhouses, Fakenhan Gas Works and the early concrete bridge at Homersfield. Association with well-known historic events or famous people may also be taken into account, and this explains the listing of Burston Strike School. Some buildings may also be listed for group value in a street whilst not necessarily of listable quality in their own right. As part of the listing process, buildings are categorised as follows:

Grade I - Buildings of exceptional national importance. There are 539 in Norfolk or 5.4%.

Grade II* - Particularly important buildings, mostly of national importance. There are 722 or 7.2% mostly, either medieval churches, monastic ruins or Country Houses.

Grade II - Buildings of special interest; and by far the largest category - 8740 or 87.4% They cover a fascinating range of buildings. Predominantly farmhouses, barns, cottages, townhouses and commercial premises, this grade also includes some of the more obscure and bizarre structures - the Shell House at Merton, dog kennels at Costessey Park, and turnstiles at Whissonsett, some 18th-century gravestones, 1930's telephone kiosks, dovecots, obelisks and milestones.

The first lists prepared in the 1950s omitted many important buildings and others were described inaccurately. Although Norwich and most of the market towns were resurveyed in the early 1970s the lists for the rural areas continued to concern conservationists for many years until eventually, the Secretary of State allocated resources for a national resurvey which in Norfolk ran from 1982 to 1986. This resulted in a doubling of listed buildings to 10,000.

The urban resurvey in the 1970s has since proved inadequate and as a result the Department of the Environment is now undertaking a review of these lists. This is unlikely to result in a significant increase in numbers but a more detailed and accurate assessment of those already listed.

There will, however, always be a few new additions to the lists as eligible buildings are identified following the discovery of important new evidence during the course of renovation work. If such buildings are in imminent danger, their immediate protection can be secured by a Building Preservation Notice served by the local authority. Other additions may result from the extension of the current listing criteria to include more 20th-century examples.

Once listed, the owner has a responsibility to ensure that the building is maintained in good repair. Failure to do so, following prolonged neglect, may result in the local authority serving a Repairs Notice which, if not complied with, could result in compulsory acquisition. To draw attention to the problems of neglect and redundancy the County Council has, in conjunction with the Districts, published a 'Buildings at Risk' register which identifies those buildings in urgent need of attention. Prominent among those 236 buildings in the current edition are redundant barns, ruined churches and estate buildings such as dovecots and orangeries. By giving wide publicity to their plight and by identifying sources of grant aid, the register is encouraging the sale or repair of an increasing number of problem buildings.

The obligations which come with owning a Listed Building are considerable, but do allow for changes. There may be modern additions which spoil the building's appearance and should be removed, but any demolition, alteration or extension work must firstly receive Listed Building Consent. The insertion of UPVC windows in place of traditional wooden sashes; the painting or rendering of brickwork; the replacement of thatch or clay pantiles with concrete tiles; the removal of internal features such as fire places, panelling and plasterwork are amongst the worst abuses which, if carried out without consent, will almost certainly result in prosecution.

Of the 10,000 Listed Buildings in Norfolk, one third are concentrated in the market towns including 10% in Norwich alone. The distribution of the remainder reflects general variations in the rural settlement pattern. West of a line from Blakeney through Dereham to Thetford, 15% are spread thinly over the Fens, the light Breckland soils, the Greensand and chalk ridges of west Norfolk.

East of that line 50% is concentrated in the more fertile valley loam area of north east Norfolk and the timber frame boulder clay area of south Norfolk. The density only drops off significantly in the Broads. In south Norfolk the picture is somewhat exaggerated by the figure for Depwade R.D. (12.3% of the total and twice as great as the next highest district). This area was resurveyed in the late 1970s before the listing criteria was applied so rigorously.

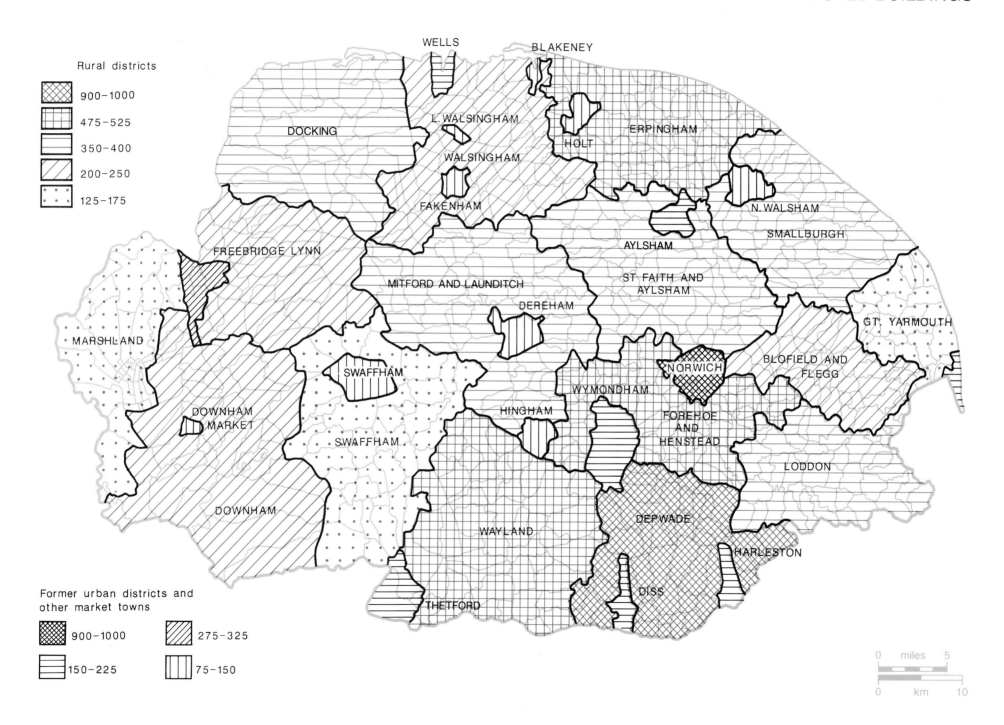

Rural districts

- 900–1000
- 475–525
- 350–400
- 200–250
- 125–175

Former urban districts and other market towns

- 900–1000
- 150–225
- 275–325
- 75–150

WELLS

BLAKENEY

DOCKING

L. WALSINGHAM

WALSINGHAM

FAKENHAM

HOLT

ERPINGHAM

N. WALSHAM

SMALLBURGH

FREEBRIDGE LYNN

MITFORD AND LAUNDITCH

DEREHAM

AYLSHAM

ST FAITH AND AYLSHAM

GT. YARMOUTH

MARSHLAND

SWAFFHAM

SWAFFHAM

HINGHAM

WYMONDHAM

NORWICH

FOREHOE AND HENSTEAD

BLOFIELD AND FLEGG

DOWNHAM MARKET

DOWNHAM

WAYLAND

DEPWADE

LODDON

HARLESTON

THETFORD

DISS

miles 0 5

km 0 10

92. SCHEDULED ANCIENT MONUMENTS

Caroline Davison and Stephen Heywood

Ancient Monuments are historic sites or monuments of national importance, roughly comparable with Grade I or II* listed buildings. However, the statutory controls for scheduled monuments are more rigorous than those controlling listed buildings. To be included on the Schedule of Monuments the site or monument has to be of national importance, although it cannot be an occupied dwelling or a church in ecclesiastical use. Scheduled monuments range from sites which are known to contain archaeological remains of historic importance but of which there is no permanent visible evidence above ground, such as cropmark patterns, to extensive monastic ruins such as Castle Acre Priory and from prehistoric burials mounds to an early gas works at Fakenham.

There are 329 scheduled items in Norfolk covering approximately 340 monuments; the map shows the different types and their distribution. There are 13 categories of monuments on the schedule. 58% of the monuments are field monuments or underground archaeological sites. 42% are standing masonry ruins.

There are 10 'camps and settlements', principally prehistoric earthwork monuments, including the famous flint mines at Grimes Graves. Prehistoric 'burial mounds' feature well in the schedule with 78 entries, although many have been destroyed by the plough over the years. There are 24 'Roman remains' but only 10 'Anglo-Saxon remains', including eight protected urban areas just within Thetford. There are 8 entries under 'linear earthworks', 5 of these refer to Devil's Dyke and 2 to Bunn's Bank. There are 23 'castles and fortifications', mainly the town walls at Norwich, King's Lynn and Yarmouth, but also ruinous castles from the 12th to 16th centuries and 11th and 12th century motte and bailey earthworks. There are 66 items under 'ecclesiastical buildings' covering monastic sites and some ruined churches. Under the category 'deserted villages' there are 14 protected sites. Under the category of 'moated sites' there are only 18 scheduled sites out of the many which survive in the county (Map 28).

There are 26 market and wayside 'crosses', 41 'other secular sites and buildings', which include buildings such as medieval vaulted undercrofts and guildhalls. There are 11 'bridges', mostly of medieval date and only three 'industrial monuments', consisting of two windpumps and the Fakenham gasworks.

The first statutory protection for monuments was introduced in 1882, and over the last 100 years items have been added to the schedule in a piecemeal and unsystematic way. Therefore it would be wrong to use the map as an indication of where there are, for example, greater numbers of moated sites or ruined churches. On the other hand monastic sites, medieval crosses and burial mounds are relatively well covered in the schedule.

The inadequacy of the existing schedule has been recognised by the Department of the Environment and English Heritage. In order to improve and regularise the schedule, English Heritage has embarked on a full-scale review entitled the Monuments Protection Programme. The Norfolk review began during the summer of 1991 and it involves the thorough use of the County's Sites and Monuments Record at Gressenhall and consultation with local authorities. It is expected that it will result in a large increase of scheduled monuments, although some buildings, which are at present listed as well as scheduled, will be de-scheduled. Many monuments such as ruined churches and monastic remains have tightly drawn schedule boundaries around the upstanding fabric only. It is expected that the scheduled areas will be increased to include the potential archaeological evidence which surrounds these monuments.

The control of works to Scheduled Monuments is very comprehensive and involves applications for Scheduled Monument Consent which have to specify in detail all proposals.

English Heritage is able to offer grants under Section 24 of the 1979 Ancient Monuments and Archaeological Areas Act. These relate only to the costs of repairs, archaeological recording and consolidation of monuments. As a general rule private owners tend to receive offers of 40% grant aid.

The necessity of obtaining Scheduled Monument Consent does not protect monuments from neglect. As most scheduled monuments have negative economic value it is not surprising that neglect is the greatest threat to their survival. Deep ploughing can also be very damaging to below-ground remains. Ruins require as much, if not more, maintenance than a building in use. Thus, much of the work of the Inspectors of Ancient Monuments and Field Monument Wardens is to arrange management agreements with owners which may involve payments under Section 17 of the 1979 Act to facilitate good site management.

In 1991 Norfolk County Council in association with the Country Landowners Association, The National Farmers Union, English Heritage and the Countryside Commission commissioned a pilot study of scheduled field monuments in the north west corner of the county. Twelve earthworks were identified as being seriously at risk from erosion due to lack of appropriate management and it was resolved by the County Council's Planning and Transportation Committee in June 1991 to take action to protect these sites. This action takes the form of negotiations with owners and the allocation of grant aid from English Heritage in some cases. Whilst in the past the protection of scheduled monuments has been left to central government through English Heritage the committee resolution marks an important step towards a fruitful co-operation between English Heritage, local authorities and other interested institutions.

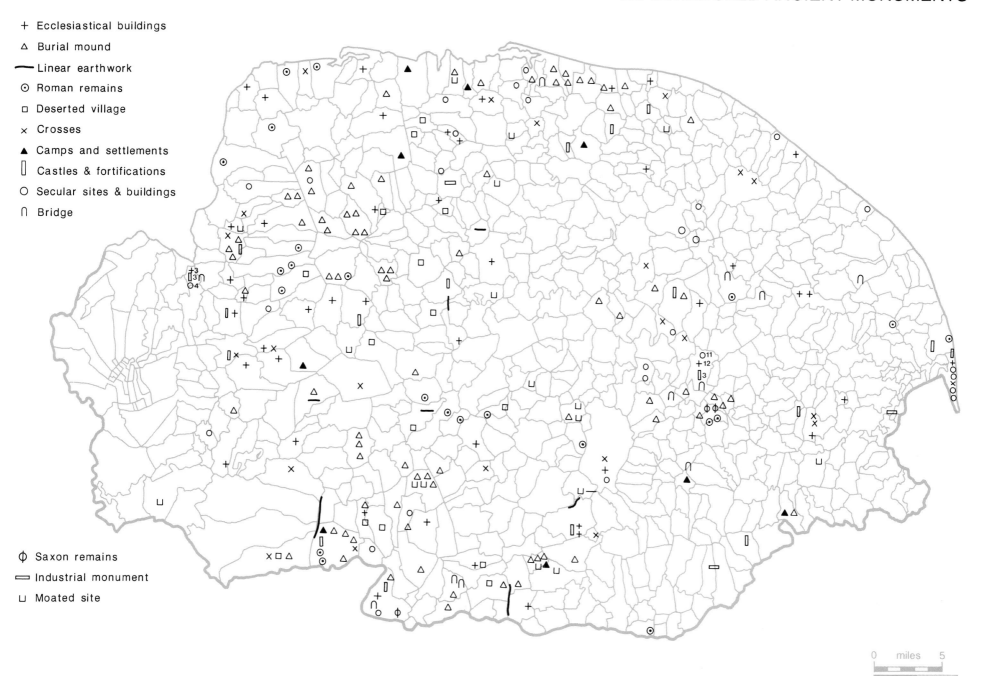

+ Ecclesiastical buildings
△ Burial mound
— Linear earthwork
⊙ Roman remains
□ Deserted village
× Crosses
▲ Camps and settlements
▯ Castles & fortifications
○ Secular sites & buildings
∩ Bridge

φ Saxon remains
⊏⊐ Industrial monument
⊔ Moated site

miles 5

km 10

A new pattern of local government was established in April 1974, based primarily on two tiers of operational authorities, counties and districts, with parish and town councils continuing to provide some services. The administrative functions of the new Norfolk county authority were greatly increased to provide education, social services, planning and transportation, highways, police and fire services, museums and libraries. Responsibility for personal health was transferred to regional and area health authorities, and for water, sewerage and land drainage to the Water Authority. The eighty-four members of the County Council are elected for a 4-year term, and serve on 7 main committees, each of which is backed by various sub-committees. Major questions of policy are dealt with at meetings of the full Council, which take place 5 times a year. All decisions of the Council and its committees are implemented and executed by its staff under the supervision of the Chief Executive and Clerk and his officers.

Norfolk is divided into 7 district councils, which replaced 15 rural district councils, 10 urban district councils, the municipal boroughs of King's Lynn and Thetford, and the county boroughs of Norwich and Great Yarmouth. The 7 new districts are Breckland, Broadland, Great Yarmouth, King's Lynn and West Norfolk, North Norfolk, Norwich, and South Norfolk. Each district council has the responsibility in its own area for housing, public health, conservation of ancient buildings, recreation and promotion of the arts. They also administer the development control aspect of planning, car parks, markets, and refuse collection. The boroughs retain their civic status and traditions.

This was the first major change in local government since county councils were established in 1889. A series of reports after the 1939-45 War influenced the government to initiate reform in local government and set the pattern for the administrative structure which followed, encouraged by the findings of the Redcliffe-Maud Commission. The local Government Act was passed in 1972, and re-organisation was achieved by April 1974. Although changes in Norfolk were less sweeping than in several other counties, there were inevitable differences stemming from apportionment of services. Norwich, for purposes of local government and administration, had formerly been separate unit, not only a County Borough with responsibility for all services in its area, but also an historic city which had enjoyed independence andautonomy since 1194, when King Richard I sealed the Charter which granted to the City the freedom of self-government. After re-organisation, however, the City Council lost control of some services to the County Council. Generally, however, the transition has been achieved smoothly. A County Liason Committee, upon which the County Council and all District Councils have representatives, discusses and seeks to give guidance upon issues of common interest. The Museums of Norfolk and the County Records Office are run by Joint Committees involving all councils, while the County Council and the NOrwich City Council combine for administering Norwich Airport (through a P.L.C.). Districts can take over responsibility from the County for various aspects of administration in their area: for example, Norwich City Council acts as the County's agent for maintaining Highways.

Administration in Norfolk is made more demanding because of the size of the county and diversity of settlement. Norfolk is the fifth largest of the English counties, containing an area of 536,777 hectares; 60% of hte population lives in villages with fewer than 600 residents. In the districts of Breckland, West and North Norfolk the density is less than 1 person per hectare. In contrast , the City of Norwich comprises an area of 3,989 hectares and the population in 1987-8 was 118,600. The Norwich district is wholly urban, Great Yarmouth is largely so with 75% of the population in the built-up area, and half of Broadland's population live within the built-up area of Norwich.

Re-organisation coincided with the oil crisis of the early 1970s and the consequent impact of world-wide inflation. Whereas from 1946 onwards the whole culture of local government had been associated with an era of growth and reconstruction, finance was no longer available to expand local authority services at the same rate. For the first time party political issues became identified with spending priorities.

Subsequently, during the 1980s, an unprecedented amount of government legislation has been enacted. Some fifty Acts affecting local government have placed a whole new set of demands on the services of the counties. This has increased the pressures on the resources of local authorities, whose income and expenditure have at the same time become subject to greater control from Whitehall. A special problem facing Norfolk during the present decade arises from increase in population, caused almost entirely by inward migration. Between 1987-88 the population of Norfolk increased by 57,000 (8.4%), which is twice the rate of increase for the counties generally, and this growth is forecast to continue for the remainder of the 20th century. Population growth generally, and in particular the continued inward movement of people nearing retirement age, adds further to demands on the services provided by local authorities. Other problems arising from this growth rate include the increase of traffic on the road system, the continuing pressure to develop agricultural land, and threats to the county's enviromental heritage, both in towns and in the countryside.

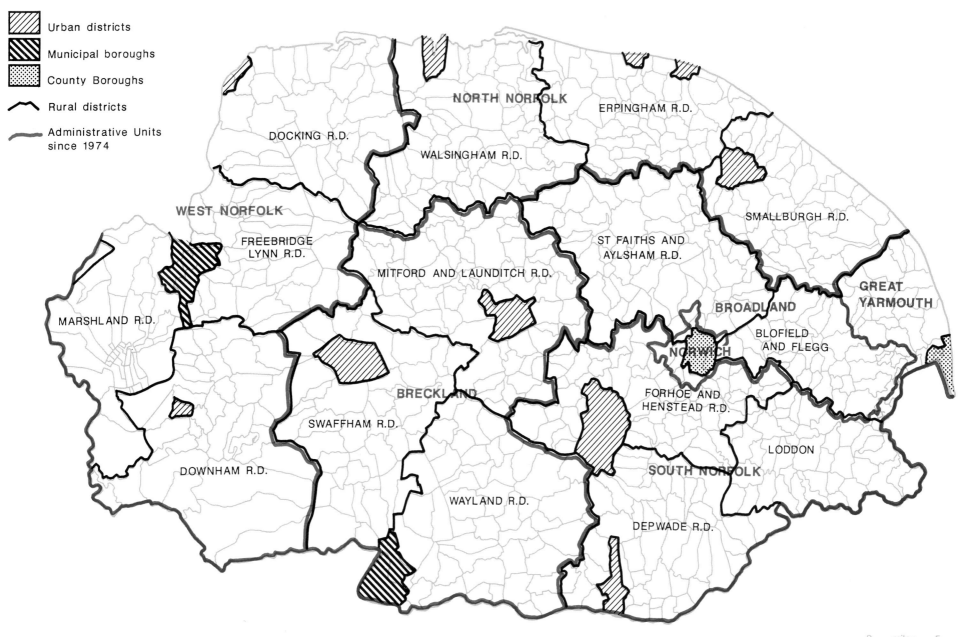

Urban districts

Municipal boroughs

County Boroughs

Rural districts

Administrative Units
since 1974

NORTH NORFOLK

ERPINGHAM R.D.

DOCKING R.D.

WALSINGHAM R.D.

SMALLBURGH R.D.

WEST NORFOLK

FREEBRIDGE
LYNN R.D.

ST FAITHS AND
AYLSHAM R.D.

GREAT
YARMOUTH

MITFORD AND LAUNDITCH R.D.

MARSHLAND R.D.

BROADLAND

BLOFIELD
AND FLEGG

NORWICH

BRECKLAND

FORHOE AND
HENSTEAD R.D.

SWAFFHAM R.D.

LODDON

DOWNHAM R.D.

SOUTH NORFOLK

WAYLAND R.D.

DEPWADE R.D.

0   miles   5

0   km   10

Further Reading and Sources

1. Solid Geology

Bulletins of the Geological Society of Norfolk, Index to Bulletins Nos. 1-35, in Bulletin No.36 (1986) (Norwich)

Chatwin, C.P., 1961 (reprinted 1982). *East Anglia and adjoining areas* (4th edition), British Regional Geology (London)

Funnell, B.M., 1976. 'Past environments of East Anglia', in Washbourn, R. (ed.), *Nature in Norfolk a Heritage in Trust*, 29-47 (Norwich)

Sources

Map 1 compiled by Mrs.P.A.Funnell, based on British Geological Survey Sheet: 52°N - 00° East Anglia, Solid Geology 1:250,000 Series (1985).

2. Glaciers Change the Landscape

Boulton, G.S., Cox, F., Hart, J. and Thornton, M., 1984. 'The glacial geology of Norfolk', *Bulletin of the Geological Society of Norfolk* 34, 103-122 (Norwich)

Harmer, F.W., 1909. 'The Pleistocene Period in the Eastern Counties of England', *Jubilee Volume of the Geologists' Association*, Part I, 103-123 (London)

Larwood, G.P and Funnell, B.M., 1961. 'The Geology of Norfolk' in Briers, F. (ed.), *Norwich and its Region*, 18-30 (Norwich)

Sources

Map 2 compiled by Mrs.P.A.Funnell, based on the Institute of Geological Sciences Hydrogeological Maps of Northern and Southern East Anglia, Sheet 1: Regional Hydrological characteristics and explanatory notes, 1:125,000 (1976 and 1981).

3. Recent Geology

Coles, B.P.L. and Funnell, B.M., 1981. 'Holocene palaeoenvironments of Broadland, England', *Special Publications of the International Association of Sedimentologists*, 5, 123-131 (Oxford)

Funnell, B.M. and Pearson, I., 1989. 'Holocene sedimentation on the North Norfolk barrier coast in relation to relative sea-level change', *Journal of Quaternary Science* 4, 25-36 (Chichester)

Godwin, H., 1978. *Fenland: its ancient past and uncertain future* (Cambridge)

Lambert, J.M., Jennings, J.N., Smith, C.T., Green, C. and Hutchinson, J.N., 1960. *The Making of the Broads*, Royal Geographical Society, Research Series 3 (London)

Sources

Map 3 compiled by Mrs.P.A.Funnell, based on the Institute of Geological Sciences Hydrogeological Maps of Northern and Southern East Anglia, Sheet 1: Regional Hydrological characteristics and explanatory notes, 1:125,000 (1976 and 1981).

4. The Soil Landscapes

Hodge, C.A.H., Burton, R.G.O., Corbett, W.M., Evans, R. and Seale, R.S., 1983. Soils of England and Wales, Sheet 4 Eastern England, scale 1:2500,000

Hodge, C.A.H., Burton, R.G.O., Corbett, W.M., Evans, R. and Seale, R.S., 1984. Soils and their use in Eastern England, Soil Survey of England and Wales Bulletin 13 (Harpenden)

Young, A., 1804. General view of the agriculture of the County of Norfolk (London)

5. Pre-Norman Vegetational Change and Woodland Clearance

Bennett, K.D., 1983. 'Devensian Late-Glacial and Flandrian vegetational history at Hockham Mere, Norfolk, England: 1. Pollen percentages and concentrations', *New Phytologist* 95, 457-487

Dimbleby, G.W. and Evans, J.G., 1972. 'The pre-enclosure environment' in Wainwright, G.J., 'The excavation of a Neolithic settlement on Broome Heath, Ditchingham, Norfolk', *Proceedings of the Prehistoric Society* 38, 1-97

Healy, F., 1988. 'The Anglo-Saxon cemetery at Spong Hill, North Elmham, Part VI. Occupation during the seventh to second millennia BC', *East Anglian Archaeology* 39

Lambert, J.M. and Jennings, J.N., Smith, C.T., Green, C. and Hutchinson, J.N., 1960. *The Making of the Broads*, Royal Geographical Society Research Series 3 (London)

Murphy, P., 1984. 'Prehistoric environments and economies' in Barringer, C, (ed.), *Aspects of East Anglian Prehistory*, 13-30 (Norwich)

Murphy, P., 1984. 'Environmental Archaeology in East Anglia' in Keeley, H.C.M. (ed.), *Environmental Archaeology: A Regional Review*, 13-42, Directorate of Ancient Monuments and Historic Buildings Occasional Paper No.6 (DoE, London)

Peglar, S.M., Fritz, S.C. and Birks, H.J.B., 1989. 'Vegetation and land-use history at Diss, Norfolk, U.K.', *Journal of Ecology* 77, 203-22

6. The Palaeolithic Period

Roe, D.A., 1981. *The Lower and Middle Palaeolithic Periods in Britain* (London)

Wymer, J.J., 1984. 'East Anglian Palaeolithic sites and their settings' in Barringer, C. (ed.), *Aspects of East Anglian Prehistory* (Norwich)

Wymer, J.J., 1985. *Palaeolithic sites of East Anglia* (Norwich)

7. Late Glacial and Mesolithic Hunters

Jacobi, R.M., 1984. 'The Mesolithic of Northern East Anglia and Contemporary Territories' in Barringer, C. (ed.), *Aspects of East Anglian Pre-history* (Norwich)

Wymer, J.J., 1977. *Gazetteer of Mesolithic Sites in England and Wales* (Norwich and London)

8. The Neolithic Period

Healy, F., 1984. 'Farming and Field Monuments: the Neolithic in Norfolk' in Barringer, C. (ed.), *Aspects of East Anglian Pre-history* (Norwich)

Mercer, R.J., 1981. *Grime's Graves, Norfolk, excavations 1971-72 1* (London)

Wainwright, G.J., 1972. 'The excavation of a Neolithic settlement on Broome Heath, Ditchingham, Norfolk, England', *Proceedings of the Prehistoric Society* 38, 1-97

9. Early Farming in Norfolk

Reports on plant and animal remains from excavations in the county will be found in published and forthcoming volumes of the series *East Anglian Archaeology*, as parts of excavation reports. Some of the more significant published reports are in the following:

Atkin, M., Carter, A. and Evans, D.H., 1985. 'Excavations in Norwich 1971-78. Part II', *East Anglian Archaeology* 26 (Norwich)

Ayers, B., 1987. 'Excavations at St. Martin-at-Palace Plain,

Norwich 1981', *East Anglian Archaeology* 37 (Gressenhall)

Ayers, B. and Murphy, P., 1983. 'A waterfront excavation at Whitefriars Street Car Park, Norwich, 1979', *East Anglian Archaeology* 17 (Gressenhall)

Healy, F., 1988. 'The Anglo-Saxon cemetery at Spong Hill, North Elmham,Part VI: Occupation during the seventh to second millennia BC', *East Anglian Archaeology* 39 (Gressenhall)

Mercer, R., 1981. *Grime's Graves, Norfolk. Excavations 1971-2* I (London)

Rogerson, A., 1977. 'Excavations at Scole, 1973', *East Anglian Archaeology* 5, 97-224 (Gressenhall)

10. The Bronze Age

Lawson, A., 1980. 'The evidence for Later Bronze Age settlement and burial in Norfolk' in Barrett, J., and Bradley, R. (eds), *Settlement and Society in the British Later Bronze Age*, British Archaeological Reports 83, 271-294 (Oxford)

Lawson, A., 1984. 'The Bronze Age in East Anglia with particular reference to Norfolk' in Barringer, C., (ed.) *Aspects of East Anglian Prehistory*, 141-177 (Norwich)

Lawson, A., 1986. 'Barrow excavations in Norfolk, 1950-82', *East Anglian Archaeology* 29

Norfolk Museums Service, 1977, 2nd edition. *Bronze Age Metalwork in Norwich Castle Museum*

11. The Iron Age

Allen, D.F., 1970. 'The Coins of the Iceni', *Britannia* 1, 1-33

Davies, J.A. et al., 1992. 'The Iron Age Forts of Norfolk', *East Anglian Archaeology* 54

Gregory, A.K., et al., 1992. 'Excavations at Thetford, 1980-1982, Fison Way', *East Anglian Archaeology* 53

Gregory, A.K. and Gurney, D., 1986. 'Excavations at Thornham, Warham, Wighton and Caistor St. Edmund, Norfolk', *East Anglian Archaeology* 30

Silvester, R.J., 1991. 'The Fenland Project Number 4: The Wissey Embayment and the Fen Causeway, Norfolk', *East Anglian Archaeology* 52

Stead, I.M., 1991. 'The Snettisham Treasure: excavations in 1990', *Antiquity* 65, 447-464

Sources

Information on the map comes from the Sites and Monuments Record. The record of stray finds is so large that only presence in any parish could be recorded. Each symbol therefore can represent one or many find-spots.

12. The Roman period

Clarke, R.R., 1950. 'Roman Norfolk since Haverfield', *Norfolk Archaeology* 30, 140-155

Gregory, A.K., 1982. 'Romano-British Settlement in West Norfolk and on the Norfolk Fen Edge' in Miles, D. (ed.), 'The Romano-British Countryside: Studies in Rural Settlement and Economy', *British Archaeological Reports* 103, 351-376

Knowles, A.K., 1977. 'The Roman Settlement at Brampton, Norfolk: Interim Report', *Britannia* 8, 209-221

Robinson, B. and Gregory, T., 1987. *Norfolk Origins 3: Celtic Fire and Roman Rule* (North Walsham)

Robinson, B. and Rose, E.J., 1983. *Norfolk Origins 2: Roads and Tracks* (North Walsham)

Wacher, J., 1974. *The Towns of Roman Britain*, 226-238 (London)

Webster, G., 1978. *Boudica* (London)

13. Early Saxon Settlement

Bond, R., Penn, K. and Rogerson, A., 1990. *The North Folk: Angles Saxons and Danes* (North Walsham)

14. The Middle Saxon Period

Andrews, P., forthcoming. 'Middle Saxon Norfolk - evidence for settlement, 650-850', *Norfolk Archaeological and Historical Research Group "Quarterly"*

Ayers, B.S. forthcoming. 'Excavations on Fishergate, Norwich, 1985' *East Anglian Archaeology*

Davison, A., 1990. 'The Evolution of settlement in three parishes in South-East Norfolk', *East Anglian Archaeology* 49

Rogerson, A., forthcoming. 'A late Neolithic, Saxon, and medieval site at Middle Harling, Norfolk', *East Anglian Archaeology*

Rogerson, A., and Silvester, R.J., 1986. 'Middle Saxon Occupation at Hay Green, Terrington St Clement', *Norfolk Archaeology* 39, 320-22

Wade-Martins, P., 1980a. 'Excavations in North Elmham Park, 1967-1972', *East Anglian Archaeology* 9

Wade-Martins, P., 1980b. 'Village sites in Launditch Hundred', *East Anglian Archaeology* 10

15. Late Saxon Social Structure

Darby, H.C., 1952. *The Domesday Geography of Eastern England* (Cambridge)

Davis, R.H.C., 1955. 'East Anglia and the Danelaw', *Transactions of the Royal Historical Society* 5th series, 5, 23-39

Dodwell, B., 1941. 'Free Peasantry of East Anglia in Domesday', *Norfolk Archaeology* 27, 145-157

Finn, R.W., 1967. *Domesday Studies: The Eastern Counties* (London)

16. Late Saxon Population Densities

Darby, H.C., 1952. *The Domesday Geography of Eastern England* (Cambridge)

17. Place-name Patterns

Sandred, K.I., 1987. 'The Vikings in Norfolk: some observations on the place-names in Norfolk', *Proceedings of the Tenth Viking Congress*, 309-24 (Oslo)

Schram, O.K., 1961. 'Norfolk Place Names' in Briers, F. (ed.), *Norwich and its Region* (Norwich)

18. Saxon Thetford

Crosby, A., 1986. *A History of Thetford* (Chichester)

Dunmore, S. with Carr, R., 1976. 'The Late Saxon Town of Thetford', *East Anglian Archaeology* 4

Rogerson, A. and Dallas, C., 1984. 'Excavations in Thetford, 1948-59 and 1973-80', *East Anglian Archaeology* 22

19. Medieval Land Use and Land Values

Campbell, B.M.S., Galloway, J. and Murphy, M., 1992. 'Rural landuse in the metropolitan hinterland, 1270-1339: the evidence of *Inquisitiones Post Mortem*', *Agricultural History Review*, 40, 1-22

Campbell, B.M.S., 1990. 'Rural society and economy 1066-1500' in Dodgshon, R.A. and Butlin, R.A. (eds), *An Historical Geography of England and Wales*, 69-121 (London)

Darby, H.C., 1952. *The Domesday Geography of Eastern England* (Cambridge)

Raftis, J.A., 1974. *Assart Data and Land Values: Two Studies in the East Midlands, 1200-1350* (Toronto)

Other Sources

Calendar of Inquisitions Post Mortem *and Other Analogous Documents in the Public Record Office, Henry III-Henry IV*, 18 vols. (London, 1904-87)

Notes

Given the frequent survival of more than one IPM extent per manor/township and their tendency towards understatement, the maps are based on those extents which provide the highest valuations and fullest information per location.

20. Medieval Arable and Pastoral Husbandry, 1250-1349

Bailey, M., 1989. *A Marginal Economy*? *East Anglian Breckland in the Later Middle Ages* (Cambridge)

Campbell, B.M.S., 1983. 'Agricultural progress in medieval England: some evidence from eastern Norfolk', *Economic History Review* 2nd series, 36, 26-46

Campbell, B.M.S., 1988. 'Towards an agricultural geography of medieval England', *Agricultural History Review* 36, 87-98

Campbell, B.M.S. and Power, J.P., 1989. 'Mapping the agricultural geography of medieval England', *Journal of Historical Geography* 15, 24-39

Campbell, B.M.S., 1992. 'Commercial dairy production on medieval English demesnes: the case of Norfolk' in Grant, A. (ed.), *Animals and their Products in Trade and Exchange, Anthropozoologica, 16*, 107-18

Campbell, B.M.S., forthcoming 1992/93. 'Intensive pastoral husbandry in medieval England: a Norfolk perspective' in Dewindt, E.B. (ed.), *Festschrift for Professor J.A. Raftis*

Campbell, B.M.S. and Overton, M., 1993. 'A new perspective on medieval and early modern agriculture: six centuries of Norfolk farming c.1250-1850', *Past and Present, 141*

Notes

The manorial accounts upon which these maps are based are preserved in the following public and private archives: Norfolk Record Office; North Yorkshire Record Office; Nottinghamshire Record Office; Public Record Office; West Suffolk Record Office; Bodleian Library, Oxford; British Library; Cambridge University Library; Canterbury Cathedral Library; Chicago University Library; Harvard Law Library, Cambridge, Mass.; John Ryland's Library, Manchester; Nottingham University Library; Christ's College, Cambridge; Elveden Hall; Eton College; Holkham Hall; King's College, Cambridge; Magdalen College, Oxford; Pomeroy and Sons, Wymondham; Raynham Hall; St George's Chapel, Windsor.

The seven crop and seven livestock combinations have been derived by means of the technique known as Cluster Analysis. The resultant typology should not be regarded as definitive, since it is in part an artefact of the actual clustering technique employed (Relocation Method), of the range of variables to which this has been applied, and of the method - percentages of acres and livestock units - by which these have been measured. The method and its limitations are discussed in Campbell and Power (1989).

21. Medieval Manorial Structure

Blake, W.J., 1952. 'Norfolk manorial lords in 1316', *Norfolk Archaeology* 30, 235-86

Campbell, B.M.S., 1986. 'The complexity of manorial structure in medieval Norfolk: a case study', *Norfolk Archaeology* 34, 225-61

Dodwell, B., 1939. 'The free peasantry of East Anglia in Domesday', *Norfolk Archaeology* 27, 145-57

Douglas, D.C., 1927. *The Social Structure of Medieval East Anglia* (Oxford Studies in Social and Legal History), 9

Hudson, Rev. W., 1895. 'The Assessment of the Townships of the County of Norfolk for the King's Tenths and Fifteenths, as settled in 1334', *Norfolk Archaeology* 12, 243-97

Kosminsky, E.A., 1956. *Studies in the Agrarian History of England in the Thirteenth Century* (Oxford Studies in Medieval History), 8

Notes

For a fuller discussion of the classification scheme employed in the first map and its method of derivation, see Campbell 1986. The Hundred Roll returns of 1279 undoubtedly offer the best single opportunity to reconstruct the manorial structure of individual townships. The Hevingham return is by no means a sole Norfolk survivor, see also Greenway, D.E., 1982, 'A newly discovered fragment of the Hundred Rolls of 1279-80', *Journal of the Society of Archivists* 7, 73-7

22. Medieval Deer-Parks

Shirley, E.P., 1867. *Some Accounts of English Deer Parks* (London)

Yaxley, D.C., 1980. 'The documentary evidence' in Wade-Martins, P., 'Norfolk Elmham', *East Anglian Archaeology 9*, 526.

Sources

The map is based on the Revd. E. Farrer's ms History and gazetteer of Norfolk Deer Parks in the Norfolk Record Office. The author has checked most of Farrer's references and made over a score of additions, mainly from 16th and 17th century references.

23. Round-towered Churches

Dehio, G., 1971. *Handbuch der Deutschen Kunstdenkmaler. Hamburg, Schleswig Holstein*, Deutscher Kunstverlag

Dehio, G., 1977. *Handbuch der Deutschen Kunstdenkmaler. Bremen/Niedersachsen*, Deutscher Kunstverlag

Ehl, H., n.d. *Norddeutsche Feldsteinkirchen*

Gage, J., 1831. 'On the Ecclesiastical Round Towers of Norfolk and Suffolk', *Archaeologia* 23, 10-17

Goode, W.J., 1982. *East Anglian Round Towers and their Churches* (Lowestoft)

Heywood, S.R., 1988. 'The Round Towers of East Anglia' in Blair, J. (ed.), *Minsters and Parish Churches, the Local Church in Transition 950-1200*, 169-177 (Oxford)

Merhautova, A., 1974. *Romanische Kunst in Polen, der Tschechoslowakei, Ungarn, Rumanien, Jugoslawien* (Vienna)

Oswald, F., Schaefer, L. and Sennhauser, H.R., 1966-1971. *Vorromanische Kirchenbauten* (Munich)

Taylor, H.M. and J., 1965. *Anglo-Saxon Architecture* (Cambridge)

24. Medieval Masons

Cattermole, P. and Cotton, S., 1983. 'Medieval parish church building in Norfolk', *Norfolk Archaeology* 38, 235-279

Coulton, G.G., 1953. *Art and the Reformation* (Cambridge)

Harvey, J., 1984. *English medieval architects* (London)

Fawcett, R., 1975. *Later Gothic architecture in Norfolk* (Unpublished PhD Thesis, University of East Anglia)

Fawcett, R., 1979. 'Sutton in the Isle of Ely and its architectural context', *Medieval art and architecture at Ely Cathedral* (Conference transactions of the British Archaeological Association for 1976), 78-96

Fawcett, R., 1980. 'A group of churches by the architect of Great Walsingham', *Norfolk Archaeology* 37, 277-294

Fawcett, R., 1982. 'St. Mary at Wiveton in Norfolk, and a group of churches attributed to its mason', *Antiquaries Journal* 57, 35-56

Knoop, J.T. and Jones, D., 1967. *The medieval mason* (Manchester)

Salzman, L.F., 1967. *Building in England down to 1540* (Oxford)

25. Medieval Churches in Use and in Ruins

Batcock, N., 1991. 'The Ruined and Disused Churches of Norfolk', *East Anglian Archaeology* 51

Blair, J. (ed.), 1988. *Minsters and Parish Churches, The Local Church in Transition 950-1200* (Oxford)

Dymond, D., 1985. *The Norfolk Landscape* (London)

Hudson, W., 1910. 'The 'Norwich Taxation' of 1254 so far as relates to the diocese of Norwich', *Norfolk Archaeology* 17, 46-157

Jessop, A., 1888. 'The condition of the Archdeaconry of Norwich in 1603', *Norfolk Archaeology* 10, 1-49,166-84

Lunt, W.E., 1926. *The Valuation of Norwich* (Oxford)

Morris, J. (ed.), 1984. *Domesday Book: Norfolk* 2 vols. (Chichester)

Rogerson, A., et al., 1987. 'Three Norman Churches in Norfolk', *East Anglian Archaeology* 32

26. Vicarages and Appropriated Livings

Barton, T.F. (ed.), 1964. 'The Registrum Vagum of Anthony Harrison, Pt.II', *Norfolk Record Society*, 33

Ecton, J., 1728. *Liber Valorum et Decimarum* (London)

Harper-Bill, C., 1990. *English Episcopal Acta, VI: Norwich 1071-1214* (Oxford)

Lunt, W.E., 1926. *Valuation of Norwich* [1254] (Oxford)

Ransford, R., 1989. *The Early Charters of Waltham Abbey, 1062-1230* (Woodbridge)

Spelman, Sir H., 1616. *De Non Temerandis Ecclesiis: A Tract of the Rights and Respect due unto Churches...* (London)

Spelman, Sir H., 1698. *The History and Fate of Sacrilege...* [written 1632] (London)

Kennett, W., 1704. *The Case of Impropriations and of the Augmentation of Vicarages...* (London)

Sources

Ecclesiastical Taxation of Pope Nicholas [1291], (Record Commissioners, 1802)*Valor Ecclesiasticus* [1535], Vol.III, (Record Commissioners, 1817)'

Report on Ecclesiastical Revenues', *Brit.Parl. Pap.*, 1835, 22

Hood, C.M. (ed.), 1938. *The Chorography of Norfolk* [1600-05], (Norwich)

27. Monastic Houses

Cook, G.H., 1969. *English Monasteries in the Middle Ages* (London)

Coppack, G., 1990. *Abbeys and Priories* (London)

Dugdale, W., 1655-1673, reprinted 1846. *Monasticon Anglicanum* 3 volumes (Oxford)

Doubleday, H.A. (ed.), 1901. *The Victoria History of the Counties of England - Norfolk* (London)

Johnson, S., 1983. 'Burgh Castle, Excavations by Charles Green 1958-61', *East Anglian Archaeology* 20

Knowles, D. and Hadcock, R.N., 1971. *Medieval Religious Houses, England and Wales* (London)

Wilton, J.W., 1980. *Monastic Life in Norfolk and Suffolk* (Fakenham)

28. Moated Sites

Aberg, F.A. (ed.), 1978. *Medieval Moated Sites*, Council British Archaeology Research Report 17 (London)

Dollin, B.W., 1986. 'Moated Sites in North-East Norfolk', *Norfolk Archaeology* 39, 262-277

29. Castles

Armitage, E.S. 1912. *Early Norman Castles of the British Isles* (London)

Brown, R. Allen, 1976. *English Castles* (London)

Coad, J.G. and Streeten, A.D.F., 1982. 'Excavations at Castle Acre Castle, Norfolk, 1972-77', *Archaeological Journal* 139, 138-301

Coad, J.G., Streeten, A.D.F., and Warmington, R., 1987. 'Excavations at Castle Acre Castle, Norfolk, 1975-82', *Archaeological Journal* 144, 256-307

King, D.J.C., 1983. *Castellarium Anglicanum* 2, 305 (New York)

Renn, D.F., 1968. *Norman Castles in Britain* (London)

30. Early Unplanned Towns

Aston, M. and Rowley, T., 1974. *Landscape Archaeology* (Newton Abbot)

Hindle, B.P., 1990. *Medieval Town Plans* (Princes Risborough)

31. Planned Towns

Norwich

Blomefield, F., 1805-10. *An Essay Towards a Topographical History of the County of Norfolk 3 and 4* (London)

Campbell, J., 1975. 'Norwich' in Lobel, M.D. (ed.), *Historic Towns* (London)

Green, B. and Young, R., 1981. *Norwich: the growth of a city* (Norwich)

Planted Towns

Bereford, M., 1967 *New Towns of the Middle Ages* (London)

Blomefield, F., 1805-10. *An Essay Towards a Topographical History of the County of Norfolk* (London)

Saunders, H., 1939. 'First Register of Norwich Cathedral Priory', *Norfolk Record Society* 11

32. Norwich

Blomefield, F., 1805-10. *An Essay Towards a Topographical History of the County of Norfolk* 3 and 4 (London)

Campbell, J., 1975. 'Norwich' in Lobel, M.D. (ed.), *Historic Towns* (London)

Green, B. and Young, R., 1981. *Norwich: the growth of a city* (Norwich)

33. Medieval and Later Markets

Blome, R., 1673. *Britannia* (London)

Blomefield, F., 1805-1810. *An Essay Towards a Topographical History of the County of Norfolk* (London)

Britnell, R.H., 1981. 'The Proliferation of Markets in England, 1200-1349', *Economic History Review*, 2nd Series, 34, 209-21

Camden, W., 1607. *Britannia* (London)

Dymond, D.P., 1985. *The Norfolk Landscape*, 147-64 (London)

Everitt, A., 1967. 'The Market Town' in Thirsk, J. (ed.), *Agrarian History of England and Wales*, 467-506 (Cambridge)

Hood, C.M. (ed.), 1938. *Chorography of Norfolk* [1600-05] (Norwich)

Scarfe, N., 1989. *An Historical Atlas of Suffolk*, 60-61,143 (Ipswich)

Sources

Brit.Parl.Pap. 1888. LIII (Report of Royal Commission on Market Rights)

Index of Market Grants, Public Record Office, Chancery Lane, London Various medieval calendars (eg. Patent Rolls, Hundred Rolls, etc.)

34. Medieval and later ports, trade and fishing up to 1600

Calender of Close Rolls, 1413-1419, 297

Calender of Patent Rolls, 1292-1301, 583

Carus-Wilson, E., 1962-3. 'The medieval trade of the ports of the Wash', *Medieval Archaeology* 6-7, 182-201

Clarke, H., 1979. 'Archaeology, history and architecture of the medieval ports of the east coast of England, with special reference to King's Lynn' in McGrail, S. (ed.), *The archaeology of medieval ships and harbours in Northern Europe*, British Archaeological Reports, internat.ser. 66, 155-165

Cozens-Hardy, B. (ed.), 1936. 'The maritime trade of the port of Blakeney - 1587 to 1590', *Norfolk Record Society* 8, 17-37

Owen, D.M. (ed.), 1984. *The making of King's Lynn: a documentary survey* (London)

Poole, A.L., 1951. *From domesday book to Magna Carta*, 96 (Oxford)

Saul, A., 1981. 'The herring industry at Great Yarmouth *c.*1280 - *c.*1400', *Norfolk Archaeology* 38, 33-43

Saul, A., 1982. 'English towns in the late middle ages: the case of Great Yarmouth', *Journal Medieval History* 8, 75-88

Scammell, G.V., 1961. 'English merchant shipping at the end of the middle ages: some east coast evidence', *Economic History Review* 13, 327-341

Smith, A., Hassell and Baker, G.M. (eds), 1983. *The papers of Nathaniel Bacon of Stiffkey* II, 143-150 (Norwich)

Williams, N.J., 1988. *The maritime trade of the East Anglian ports, 1550-1590* (Oxford)

35. Heaths and Commons

Bailey, M., 1989. *A Marginal Economy, East Anglian Breckland in the Late Middle Ages*, chapter 2 (Cambridge)

Manning, M. (ed.), 1988. *Commons in Norfolk*, Norfolk Research Committee (Norwich)

Mosby, J.E.G., 1938. *The Land of Britain Part 70, Norfolk* (London)

Young, A., 1969. *General View of the Agriculture of Norfolk 1804* (Newton Abbott)

Texts relevant to the article in sequence:

Davison, A., 1990. 'The Evolution of Settlement in three Parishes in South-East Norfolk', *East Anglian Archaeology* 49

Faden's Map of Norfolk, 1796, Larks Press Edition (Dereham), 1989

Barringer, J.C., 1977. *Towards a History of Mattishall* (Mattishall)

Barringer, J.C., 1984. 'The Commons of Attleborough', *Norfolk Research Committee Bulletin*

36. The Broads

Broads Authority, 1982. *Report of the Ecology Working Group* BASMP 5 (Norwich)

Ellis, E.A. (ed.), 1965. *The Broads* (London)

George, M., 1992. *The land Use, Ecology and Conservation of Broadland* (Chichester)

Green, C. and Hutchinson, J.N., 1960. 'Archaeological evidence' in *The Making of the Broads* 113-145, Royal Geographical Society Research Series No.3 (London)

Lamb, H.H., 1977. *Climate: present, past and future Vol.2*, 'Climatic History and the Future' (London)

Lambert, J.M., Jennings, J.N., Smith, C.T., Green, C. and Hutchinson J.N., 1960. 'Stratigraphical and associated evidence' in *The Making of the Broads* 1-61, Royal

Geographical Society Research Series 3 (London)

Moss, B., 1983. 'The Norfolk Broadland: experiments in the restoration of a complex wetland', *Biological Review* 58, 521-561

Smith, C.T., 1960. 'Historical evidence' in *The Making of the Broads* 63-111, Royal Geographical Society Research Series 3 (London)

37. Deserted Villages and Rural Depopulation

Allison, K.J., 1955. 'The Lost Villages of Norfolk', *Norfolk Archaeology* 31, 116-162

Butler, L. and Wade-Martins, P., 1989. 'The Deserted Medieval Village of Thuxton, Norfolk', *East Anglian Archaeology* 46

Cushion, B. et al., 1982. 'Some Deserted Village Sites in Norfolk', *East Anglian Archaeology* 14, 40-101

Davison, A., 1980. 'West Harling: a village and its disappearance', *Norfolk Archaeology* 37, 295-306

Davison, A., 1983. 'The distribution of medieval settlement in West Harling', *Norfolk Archaeology* 38, 329-336

Davison, A. et al., 1988. 'Six Deserted Villages in Norfolk', *East Anglian Archaeology* 44

Davison, A. with Fenner, A., 1990. 'The Evolution of Settlement in Three Parishes in South-east Norfolk', *East Anglian Archaeology* 49

Hatcher, J., 1977. *Plague, Population and the English Economy 1348-1530* (London and Basingstoke)

Wade-Martins, P., 1975. 'The Origins of Rural Settlement in East Anglia' in Fowler, P.J. (ed.), *Recent Work in Rural Archaeology* (Bradford-on-Avon)

Wade-Martins, P., 1980. 'Village Sites in Launditch Hundred', *East Anglian Archaeology* 10

Other Sources

Apart from works cited above the following were consulted: translations of the Norfolk part of Domesday Book in the *Victoria History of the County of Norfolk*, Volume 2 (1906) and '*Domesday Book: Norfolk*' edited by Philippa Brown (1984); 'Norfolk Manorial Lords in 1316' by W.J. Blake, *Norfolk Archaeology* 30 (1951-2) for the "Nomina Villarum"; 'The assessment of the townships of the County of Norfolk for the King's tenths and fifteenths as settled in 1334' by W.

Hudson *Norfolk Archaeology* 12 (1895) for the Lay Subsidies of 1334 and 1449; Blomefield's *History of Norfolk* (1739-75) and Dr. Tanner's *Indexes to the Bishop's Registers* (Norfolk Record Office, REG 30, 31) for institutions of beneficed clergy 1348-50; *Feudal Aids* III for parishes with less than ten households in 1428; and the volumes of *Norfolk Archaeology* and original maps and documents in the Norfolk Record Office for details of specific places.

38. The Uprising of 1381

Cornford, B., Edwards, W.F., Leake, G.F. and Reid, A.W., 1984. *Studies Towards a History of the Rising of 1381 in Norfolk* (Norwich)

Dobson, R.B. (ed.), 1970. *The Peasants' Revolt of 1381* (London)

Hilton, R.H., 1973. *Bond Men Made Free* (London)

Hilton, R.H. and Aston, T.H. (eds), 1984. *The English Rising of 1381* (London)

Powell, E., 1896. *The Rising in East Anglia in 1381* (Norwich)

Reville, A. and Petit-Dutaillis, C., 1898. *Le Soulevement des Travailleurs d'Angleterre en 1381* (Paris)

Presentments of Hundred Juries established under a Commission headed by William de Ufford, Earl of Suffolk, June-July 1381: Public Record Office, KB9 166/1

John Capgrave, *Liber de Illustribus Henricis* Rolls Series No.7, 1858, London

Thomas de Walsingham, *Historia Anglicana* 2, Rolls Series No.28, 1864, London

39. Norfolk Hundreds

Barringer, J.C., 1979. 'Some remarks on the early administration geography of Norfolk', *Bulletin of Norfolk Research Committee* 22

Cam, H., 1930. *The Hundred and the Hundred Rolls* (London)

Cam, H., 1944. *Liberties and Communities in Medieval England*, Chapters V and VI (Cambridge)

Darby, H.C., 1952. *Domesday Geography of Eastern England*, fig.20 (Cambridge)

Jones, G.R.J., 1976. *Medieval Settlement*, Chapter III (London)

Miller, E., 1969. *The Abbey and Bishopric of Ely*, 33 (Cambridge)

Rye, W., 1926-8. *Some Historical Essays Chiefly relating to*

Norfolk; Part III (Norwich)

40. Ecclesiastical Jurisdiction

Heywood, S., 1982. 'The Ruined Church at North Elmham', *Journal of the British Archaeological Association* 135, 1-10

Hudson, W., 1910. 'The Norwich Taxation of 1254', *Norfolk Archaeology* 17, 46-158

Landon, L., 1928. 'The Early Archdeacons of Norwich Diocese', *Proceedings of the Suffolk Institute of Archaeology* 20, 11-35

Palgrave-Moore, P., 1983. *National Index of Parish Registers* (London), 7

Wade-Martins, P., 1980. 'North Elmham 1', *East Anglian Archaeology* 9, 3-11

Whitelock, D., 1972. 'The pre-Viking Age Church in East Anglia' in Clemoes, P. (ed.), *Anglo-Saxon England* Vol.I (Cambridge), 1-22

Youngs, F.A., 1979. *Guide to the Local Administrative Units of England* I, Southern England (Royal Historical Society)

The map is redrawn from that by Dr. A.G. Crosby in the Norfolk Record Office *Guide to Genealogical Sources* (1985).

41. Parish Registers

Folland, H. Rev. Deanery Inventory Books, Ms Norfolk Record Office

Norfolk Record Office, Listings of registers held, Ts.

Palgrave-Moore, P., 1983. *National Index of Parish Registers Vol.VII, Cambridgeshire, Norfolk and Suffolk*, Society of Genealogists (London)

Palgrave-Moore, P., 1986. *Tracing Ancestors* (Norwich)

Palgrave-Moore, P., 1987. *Understanding the History and Records of Nonconformity* (Norwich)

Additional Map Information

A   Norwich
All Saints 1573, St. Andrew 1558, St. Augustine 1559, St. Benedict 1562, St. Clement 1538, St. Edmund 1550, St. Etheldred 1665, St. George Colegate 1538, St. George Tombland 1538, St. Giles 1538, St. Gregory 1571, St. Helen 1708, St. James 1556, St. John Maddermarket 1558, St. John de Sepulchre 1632, St. John Timberhill 1559, St. Julian 1589, St. Lawrence 1558, St. Margaret 1559, St. Martin at Oak 1560, St. Martin at Palace 1538 St. Mary Coslany 1557, St. Mary in the Marsh 1591,St. Michael at Coslany 1558, St. Michael at Plea 1538, St. Michael at Thorn 1833, St. Paul 1785, St. Peter Hungate 1596, St. Peter Mancroft 1538, St. Peter Mountergate 1538, St. Peter Southgate 1558, St. Saviour 1555, SS. Simon and Jude 1539, St. Stephen 1538, St. Swithin 1700, Cathedral 1697.

B
Kirby Bedon St. Andrew 1558, Kirby Bedon St. Mary 1561.

C
Saxlingham Thorpe 1560, Saxlingham Nethergate 1537.

D
Tivetshall St. Margaret 1673, Tivetshall St. Mary 1672.

E
Bradeston 1731.

F
King's Lynn St. Margaret 1559, King's Lynn St. Nicholas   1562.

42. Population in the 16th Century

Cornwall, J.C.K., 1970. 'English Population in the Early Sixteenth Century', *Economic History Review* 23

Palliser, D.M., 1983. *The Age of Elizabeth: England under the Later Tudors, 1547-1603* (London)

Patten, J., 1979. *Pre-Industrial England*, 81 (Folkstone)

Patten, J., 1979. 'Population distribution in Norfolk and Suffolk during the Sixteenth and Seventeenth Centuries' in Patten, J. (ed.), *Pre-Industrial England*, 71-92 (Folkestone)

Pound, J.F., 1988. *Tudor and Stuart Norwich*, 127 (Chichester)

Wrigley, E.A. and Schofield, R.S., 1981. *The Population History of England, 1541-1871: A Reconstruction* (London)

43. The Distribution of Wealth in the Early 16th Century

Cornwall, J.C.K., 1988. *Wealth and Society in Early Sixteenth Century England* (London)

Pound, J.F. (ed.), 1971. 'The Norwich Census of the Poor', *Norfolk Record Society* 40

Pound, J.F., 1986. *Poverty and Vagrancy in Tudor England* (London)

Pound, J.F. (ed.), 1986. The Military Survey of 1522 for

Babergh Hundred, *Suffolk Records Society* 28

Pound, J.F., 1986. 'Clerical Poverty in Early Sixteenth Century England: some East Anglian Evidence', *Journal of Ecclesiastical History* 37, 389-96

Pound, J.F., 1988. *Tudor and Stuart Norwich* (Chichester)

Schofield, R.S., 1965. 'The Regional Distribution of Wealth in England, 1334-1641', *Economic History Review* 17

Sheail, J., 1979. 'The Distribution of Taxable Population and Wealth in England during the Early Sixteenth Century' in Patten, J. (ed.), *Pre-Industrial England*, 55-70 (Folkestone)

44. Kett's Rebellion, 1549

Bindoff, S.T., 1949. *Kett's rebellion 1549* (London)

Carter, A., 1984. 'The site of Dussindale', *Norfolk Archaeology* 39, 54-62

Fletcher, A., 3rd ed., 1983. *Tudor rebellions* (London)

Land, S., 1977. *Kett's rebellion: the Norfolk rising of 1549* (Ipswich)

MacCulloch, D., 1979. 'Kett's rebellion in context', *Past and Present* 84, 36-59

Russell, F.W., 1859. *Kett's rebellion in Norfolk* (London)

Other Sources

A typescript list of rebels, with references, is available in the Local Studies Library at the Norwich Central Library, Bethel Street, Norwich. The data was compiled by members of a Cambridge University Extra-mural Board class led by Fiona Macdonald and Elizabeth Rutledge during the winter of 1983-84.

The incidents indicated on the map are taken from printed sources, except for that at New Buckenham for which the reference is Norfolk Record Office, PD 254/171.

45. The Communicant Return of 1603

Sources

Whitgift's and Jegon's letters and the returns for the archdeaconry of Norwich are in Jessop, A., 1888, 'The Condition of the Archdeaconry of Norwich in 1603', *Norfolk Archaeology* 10, 1-49,166-184.

The figures for the archdeaconry of Norfolk are taken from Blomefield, F., 1805-1810, *History of Norfolk*, passim.

46. Farming Regions, 1500-1750

Allison, K.J., 1957. 'The Sheep-Corn Husbandry of Norfolk in the Sixteenth and Seventeenth Centuries', *Agricultural History Review* 5

Holderness, B.A., 1985. 'East Anglia and the Fens' in Thirsk, J. (ed.) *The Agrarian History of England and Wales, 1640-1750* 5 (Cambridge)

Overton, M., 1980. 'Agricultural Change in Norfolk and Suffolk, 1580-1750' (PhD dissertation, University of Cambridge)

Postgate, M.R., 1969. 'The Field Systems of East Anglia' in Baker, A.R.H. and Butlin, R. (eds), *Studies in the field system of the British Isles* (Cambridge)

Spratt, J., 1939. 'Agrarian conditions in Norfolk and Suffolk, 1600-1650' (MA dissertation, University of London)

Thirsk, J., 1988. *Agrarian regions and agrarian history in England, 1500-1750* (London)

47. The Drainage of the Norfolk Fens

Darby, H.C., 1956. *The Drainage of the Fens* (Cambridge)

Darby, H.C., 1983. *The Changing Fenland* (Cambridge)

Silvester, R.J., 1988. 'The Fenland Project, Number 3: Marshland and the Nar Valley, Norfolk', *East Anglian Archaeology* 45

Silvester, R.J., 1991. 'The Fenland Project, Number 4: The Wissey Embayment and the Fen Causeway', *East Anglian Archaeology* 52

Summers, D., 1976. *The Great Level* (Newton Abbot)

48. The Gentry of Norfolk During the Civil War

Allison, K.J., 1957. 'The Sheep-Corn Husbandry of Norfolk in the Sixteenth and Seventeenth Centuries', *Agricultural History Review*, 5, 12-30

Allison, K.J., 1960 and 1961. 'The Norfolk Worsted Industry in the Sixteenth and Seventeenth Centuries', *Yorkshire Bulletin of Economic and Social Research* 12, 73-83; 13, 61-77

Blomefield, F., 1805-10. *An Essay Towards a Topographical History of the County of Norfolk*, 11 vols (London)

Clarke, A.W.H. and Campling, A., 1934. 'The Visitation of Norfolk 1664', *Norfolk Record Society*, 4 and 5

Evans, J.T., 1979. *17th Century Norwich* (Oxford)

Evans, N., 1985. *The East Anglian Linen Industry: Rural Industry and Local Economy 1500-1850* (Aldershot)

Ketton-Cremer, R.W., 1985. *Norfolk in the Civil War* (Norwich)

Mason, R.H., 1884. *History of Norfolk*

Newman, P.R., 1981. *Royalist Officers in England and Wales 1642-1660: A Biographical Dictionary* (New York)

Rye, W. (ed.), 1891. *Visitations of Norfolk 1563, 1589 and 1613*, Harleian Soc., 32

Rye, W., 1913. *Norfolk Families*, 2 vols. (Norwich)

Schofield, B. (ed.), 1949. 'The Knyvett Letters 1620-1644', *Norfolk Record Society* 20

Shipps, K., 1971. *Lay Patronage of East Anglian Puritan Clerics in Pre-Revolutionary England* (Yale Univ. Ph.D., copy in Norwich Central Library)

Other Sources

For lists of Norfolk gentry in Charles I's reign see Public Record Office, London: E 178 (knighthood composition lists 1631-32); E 179 (lay subsidy rolls, 1628 and 1641); E 377/49 (recusant roll, 1641). For gentry allegiancies in the Civil War see P.R.O., E 113 (Exchequer, Bills and Answers against defaulting accountants); SP 19 (Committee for Advance of Money); SP 23 (Committee for Compounding); SP 28 (Commonwealth Exchequer papers); SP 29/68, fols.48-87 (*A List of Officers claiming to the Sixty Thousand Pounds*, 1663); British Library, Additional MSS. 5508 (Accounts and papers relating to sequestered estates 1642-48); 15,903 (Original letters relating to Norfolk 1557-1732).

49. Country House Building in Norfolk, 1700-1900

Bateman, J., 1883. *The Great Landowners of Great Britain and Ireland* (London)

Barringer, J.C. (ed.), 1975. 'William Faden's Topographical Map of Norfolk, 1797', *Norfolk Record Society* 42 (Norwich)

Frankel, M.S., Seaman, P.J. and Palgrave-Moore, P.T.R. (eds), 1983. 'Norfolk Hearth Tax Assessment Michaelmas 1664', *Norfolk Genealogy* 15

Pevsner, N., 1977. *The Buildings of England: North-West and South Norfolk* (Harmondsworth)

Pevsner, N., 1979. *The Buildings of England: North-East Norfolk and Norwich* (Harmondsworth)

Return of Owners of Land, 1872-3 (England and Wales), *Parliamentary Papers*, 1874, 72, Part I

Sayer, M., 1981. 'Norfolk' in *Burke's and Savills Guide to Country Houses III East Anglia*, 81-210 (London)

Seaman, P. (ed.), 1988. 'Norfolk and Norwich Hearth Tax Assessment Lady Day 1666', *Norfolk Genealogy* 20

Winkley, G., 1986. *The Country Houses of Norfolk* (Lowestoft)

Note

This work has drawn upon unpublished research by the author to be submitted to the University of East Anglia for the degree of PhD.

50. Parks in the 18th and 19th Centuries

Williamson, T. and Taigel, A. (eds), 1990. *Gardens in Norfolk 1550-1900* (Norwich)

Williamson, T. and Taigel, A., 1990. 'Some Early Geometric Gardens in Norfolk', *Journal of Garden History* 11, 1-2,1-111

51. Brick as an Indicator of Wealth 1450-1750

Moore, M.J., 1968. 'Development of Brick Architecture 1300-1600', *East Anglia*, Royal Commission on Historical Monuments for England

Pevsner, N., 1962. *The Buildings of England: North East Norfolk and Norwich* (Harmondsworth)

Pevsner, N., 1962. *The Buildings of England: North West and South West Norfolk* (Harmondsworth)

Simpson, A., 1968. 'The Wealth of the Gentry, 1540-1660', *East Anglian Studies*

Tolhurst, P.D., 1982. *The Vernacular Architecture of Norfolk*, M.A. Thesis, Manchester University

Yaxley, D., 1978. *The Manor House in Norfolk* (Ipswich)

52. Walling Materials of Parsonage Houses, 1794

Bouwens, D., 1988. 'Clay lump in south Norfolk: observations and recollections', *Vernacular Architecture* 19, 10-18

Lucas, R., 1995 (forthcoming). 'Clay-lump construction in Norfolk', *Transactions of the Association for Studies in the Conservation of Historic Buildings*

McCann, J., 1987. 'Is clay lump a traditional building material?', *Vernacular Architecture* 18, 1-16

Messent, C.J.W., 1967. *A thousand years of Norfolk carstone, 967-1967* (Fakenham)

O'Neil, B.H.St.J., 1953. 'Some seventeenth-century houses in Great Yarmouth', *Archaeologia* 95, 141-80, pl.LII-LXVI

Orna, B. and A., 1984. *Flint in Norfolk building* (Norwich)

Smith, R. and Carter, A., 1983. 'Function and site: aspects of Norwich building before 1700', *Vernacular Architecture* 14, 5-18

Tolhurst, P.D., 1982. *The Vernacular Architecture of Norfolk*, M.A. Thesis, Manchester University

Sources

Information for the map has been taken from the Norwich diocesan holdings of glebe terriers for parishes within the county of Norfolk. The terriers form a deposit in the Norfolk Record Office under the reference DN/TER 1-180, which embraces about 25,000 separate documents. Of more than 700 terriers inspected for the year 1794, 268 yielded descriptions of the materials with which parsonage houses were constructed. The figure includes a number of descriptions taken from the terriers for 1801 and 1806 in cases where no returns at all, or no sufficiently descriptive returns, were made for 1794. A high proportion of the houses described were walled or roofed in more than one material and in such cases the first two materials named have been entered into the district totals as half units. Apart from the glebe terriers, the text also made use of reports of excavations at deserted village sites published in *East Anglian Archaeology*, and of estate papers deposited in the Norfolk Record Office.

53. Roof Coverings of Parsonage Houses, 1794

Boardman, H.C., 1933. 'Reed thatching in Norfolk', *Architects' Journal* 77, 563-7

Ladbrooke, R., 1823-36. *Views of churches in Norfolk* 7 vols. (Norwich)

Tolhurst, P.D., 1982. *The Vernacular Architecture of Norfolk*, M.A. Thesis, Manchester University

Winder, T., 1908. *Hand-book of Farm Buildings* (London and Glasgow)

Sources

Information for the map is taken from the same set of documents as served to create the map for walling materials. It is subject to the same qualifications. The text, which is concerned with the delivery at Norfolk ports of pantiles and slates, has made use of customs accounts (Exchequer papers E122, covering the 16th and 17th centuries) and port books (E190, covering the 18th century), held by the Public Record Office. Entries in accounts of estate disbursements, notably those relating to Stiffkey (16th century), Felbrigg (17th and 18th centuries), Langley (18th century) and Stradsett (19th century), have proved important sources: most of these are held by the Norfolk Record Office. More useful still have been notices from the 18th and 19th centuries in county newspapers referring to the arrival of sea-cargoes at King's Lynn and Great Yarmouth. Similarly useful have been contemporary sale notices for stock entered by brickmakers, auctioneers and merchants. Reference has also been made to occupational data extracted from the *Census of Great Britain, 1851*.

54. Education before 1750

Barclay, P.S., 1989. *A History of Sir Bartholomew Rede, The Goldsmith's Free Grammar School and the Cromer Exhibition Foundation* 3 (Cromer)

Cressy, D., 1977. 'Levels of Illiteracy in England 1530-1730', *History Journal* 20, 1-23

Feyerham, W., 1976. 'The status of the schoolmaster and the continuity of education in Elizabethan East Anglia', *History of Education* 5, 103-115

Jones, M.G., 1964. *The Charity School Movement* (London and Edinburgh)

Lloyd-Pritchard, M., 1965. 'The Education of the Poor in Norfolk 1700-1850', *Norfolk Archaeology* 33, 321-31

Pound, J., 1988. *Tudor and Stuart Norwich*, 133 (Chichester)

Other Sources

Report of the Charity Commissioners, County Norfolk, 1815-1839

Cox, T., 1724. *Magna Britannia* (London)

Minute Book of the Norwich Charity Schools, 1711-1759 N.R.O.

Charity School Account, 1709, N.R.O.

55. Voting in the Late 18th Century

Hayes, B.D., 1957. *Politics in Norfolk, 1750-1832* Unpublished Ph.D. Thesis

Ketton-Cremer, R.W., 1908. 'The County Election of 1806', *A Norfolk Gallery*, 215-37 (London)

Stirling, A.M.W., 1908. *Coke of Norfolk and His Friends* 2 vols. (London)

Wade Martins, S., 1988. *Norfolk, a Changing Countryside* 1780 - 1914 (Chichester)

56. Great Estates in the 19th Century

Robinson, J.M., 1989. *The English Country Estate* (London)

Thompson, F.M.L., 1962. *English Landed Society in the Nineteenth Century* (London)

Wade Martins, S., 1980. *A Great Estate at Work* (Cambridge)

Wade Martins, S., 1988. *Norfolk, a Changing Countryside* 1780 - 1914 (Chichester)

57. Parliamentary Enclosure

Tate, W.E., 1978. *A Domesday of English Enclosure Acts and Awards*, 178-90 (Reading)

Turner, M., 1980. *English Parliamentary Enclosure*, 176-81 (Folkestone)

Turner, M., 1984. *Enclosures in Britain 1750-1830*, 11 (London)

58. The Riots of 1830

Archer, J.E., 1981. *Rural Protest in Norfolk and Suffolk 1830-1870*, University of East Anglia PhD Thesis

Hobsbawm, E.J. and Rude, G., 1970. *Captain Swing* (London)

Peacock, A.J., 1965. *Bread or Blood* (London)

Wade Martins, S., 1988. *Norfolk, A Changing Countryside* 1780 - 1914 (Chichester)

59. Agriculture in the mid 19th Century

Bacon, R.N., 1844. *The Agriculture of Norfolk* (Norwich)

Dodd, J.P., 1976. 'Norfolk Agriculture in 1853-4', *Norfolk Archaeology* 36, 253-264

Kain, R.J.P., 1986. *Tithe Atlas* (Cambridge)

Wade Martins, S., 1980. *A Great Estate at Work* (Cambridge)

Wade Martins, S., 1988. *Norfolk, A Changing Countryside* (Chichester)

60. Markets and Fairs in the 18th and 19th Centuries

Britton, J. and Brayley, A.W., 1809. *A Topographical and Historical Description of the County of Norfolk*

Crosby, A., 1986. *A History of Thetford* (Chichester)

Defoe, D., 1971. *A Tour Through the Whole Island of Great Britain 1724-6* (Harmondsworth)

Hedges, A.A.C., 1973. *Yarmouth is an Ancient Town* (Yarmouth)

Priestly, U., 1987. *The Great Market* (*Norwich*) (Norwich)

Richards, P., 1990. *King's Lynn*, 46-53 (Chichester)

Wade Martins, S., 1988. *Norfolk a Changing Countryside* 1780-1914 (Chichester)

White, W., 1845. *Directory of Norfolk* (Sheffield)

61. Population Change 1801-1851

Sources

'Registrar General's Annual Report', from 1837/8 (HMSO). Census reports, every ten years from 1801 to 1851, prepared by the Registrar General (HMSO). All contain information for parishes, listed by county.

62. Population Change 1851-1951

Sources

Census reports, every ten years from 1851 to 1951 except 1941, prepared by the Registrar General (HMSO). All contain information for parishes, listed by county.

'Registrar General's Statistical Review of England and Wales', annual (HMSO).

63. Armada and 17th-century Defences

Cozens-Hardy, B., 1938. 'Norfolk Coastal Defences in 1588', *Norfolk Archaeology* 26, 300-314

Kent, P., 1988. *Fortifications of East Anglia* (Lavenham)

O'Neil, B.H. St J., 1941. 'The Fortification of Weybourne Hope in 1588', *Norfolk Archaeology* 27, 250-262

O'Neil, B.H. St J., 1945. 'A Plan of the Fortifications of Yarmouth in 1588', *Norfolk Archaeology* 28, 1-6

64. Napoleonic Fortifications

Kent, P., 1988. *Fortications of East Anglia* (Lavenham)

Rye, G. and Tooke, C., 1984. 'Great Yarmouth - The Fortifications - 1750', *Yarmouth Archaeology* 2, 9-12

Rye, G. and Tooke, C., 1985. 'Great Yarmouth - The Fortifications - 1781-c.1850', *Yarmouth Archaeology* 2, 26-32

65. Roman Catholic Recusancy

Anstruther, G., 1966. *The Seminary Priests 1558-1800* (4 vols) (Ware, Durham and Great Wakering)

Bellenger, D.A., 1984. *English and Welsh Priests, 1558-1800* (Bath)

Blackwood, B.G., 1986. 'Plebeian Catholics in the 1640s and 1650s', *Recusant History* (Catholic Record Society) 18, 42-53 (Southampton and London)

Bowler, H., 1958. 'Some notes on the Recusant Rolls of the Exchequer', *Recusant History* (Catholic Record Society) 7, 182-198 (Southampton and London)

Catholic Record Society, 1905-86. Vols 1-71 (Southampton and London)

Foley, H., 1877. *Records of the English Province of the Society of Jesus* (7 vols) (London)

Holt, T.G., 1980. 'Catholic Chapels of Norwich before 1900', *Norfolk Archaeology* 37, 153-168

Jessop, A., 1913. *One Generation of a Norfolk House* 2nd ed. (revised) (London)

McGrath, P.V. and Rowe, J., 1984. 'The Marian Priests under Elizabeth I', *Recusant History* (Catholic Record Society) 7 (2), 103-120 (Southampton and London)

Trappes-Lomax, T.B., 1962. 'Roman Catholicism in Norfolk 1559-1780', *Norfolk Archaeology* 32, 27-46

Whiteman, A., 1990. 'The Compton Census of 1676', *Records of Social and Economic History*, New Series 10

66. Protestant Nonconformity

Browne, J., 1877. *History of Congregationalism: and Memorials of the Churches of Norfolk and Suffolk* (London)

Cozens-Hardy, B., 1922. 'The first 70 years of Guestwick Independent Church', *Norfolk Archaeology* 21, 155-74

Dymond, D. and Martin, E. (eds.), 1988. *An Historical Atlas of Suffolk* (Ipswich)

Gay, J.D., 1971. *The Geography of Religion in England* (London)

A Member of the Houses of Shirley and Hastings, 1839. *The Life and Times of Selina, Countess of Huntingdon* (2 vols) (London)

Taylor, P.A.M., 1965. *Expectations Westward* (for an account of the Mormons and their emigration to America) (London)

Sources
1851 Religious Census for Norfolk. P.R.O. HO 129/193 and HO 129/228 - 249
Calendar of State Papers Domestic Charles II 1671-1673 ed. Blackburne, F.H., 1901 (p.xxxix for 1672 licences)
Compton Census of 1676 ed. Anne Whiteman, Records of Social and Economic History, New Series X, 1986
British Sessional Papers House of Commons 1852/53 Vol.89 - for summary of 1851 census figures
A list of the meeting places of The Society of Friends, The Librarian, Friends House, London, 1955. Norfolk and Norwich Library Service, Local istory Dept. C289.6

67. Workhouses Before 1834

Crowley, J. and Reid, A., 1983. *The Poor Law in Norfolk 1700-1850* (Cambridge)
Digby, A., 1978. *Pauper Palaces* (London)
Slack, P., 1990. *The English Poor Law, 1531-1782* (London)
Snell, K.D.M., 1985. *Annals of the Labouring Poor: Social Change and Agrarian England, 1660-1900* (Cambridge)
Wales, T., 1984. 'Poverty, poor relief and the life-cycle: some evidence rom 17th-century Norfolk' in Smith, R.M. (ed.), *Land, Kinship and Life-cycle* (Cambridge)

Sources
Abstracts of Returns made by Overseers of the Poor in 1776, Sessional Papers 31 (1777)
Brit.Parliam.Pap., 1803-4, XIII (Parochial Returns)
Brit.Parliam.Pap. 1818, XIX (Parochial Returns)
Brit.Parliam.Pap., 1844, XL (Return of Gilbert Unions)
Brit.Parliam.Pap., 1834, XXXI (Appendix to 1st Report from the Commissioners on the Poor Laws)
Norfolk Record Office, List of Poor Law Union Records (typescript)
White, W., 1845 (modern reprint) Directory of Norfolk

COMBINATIONS OF PARISHES AFTER 1764

INCORPORATED HUNDREDS

Date of Act	Name	House of Industry at	Maximum no. of parishes
1764	Loddon and Clavering	Heckingham	41
1775	East and West Flegg	Rollesby	20
1775	Launditch and Mitford (East Dereham separated 1801)	Gressenhall	50
1776	Forehoe Wicklewood (excluding Honingham)		23
1785	Tunstead and Happing (excluding North Walsham)	Smallburgh	42

Incorporation by Special Act

1806	Buxton	Buxton	9

GILBERT UNIONS

Date of Agreement	Name	House of Industry at	Maximum no. of parishes
1783	Brinton and Melton Constable	Melton Constable	3
1785	Bawdeswell	Bawdeswell	7
1786	Booton	Brandiston	2
1792	Acle	Acle?	18
1792	Oulton	Oulton	5
1805	Aldborough	Sheringham (Upper)	9
1805	Gimingham	Gimingham	9
1805	St Faiths or Taverham (excluding Beeston St Andrew)	Horsham St Faiths	18
1808	Hackford	Hackford	3-4

68. Poor Law Unions and Workhouses, 1834-1930

Boyer, G.R., 1990. An Economic History of the English Poor Law, 1750-1850 (Cambridge)
Charlesworth, A., 1983. An Atlas of Rural Protest in Britain, 1548-1900 (London)
Crowther, M.A., 1981. The Workhouse System, 1834-1929 (London)

Dickens, A., 1976. 'The Architect and the Workhouse', *Architectural Review*, 160
Digby, A., 1976. 'The Rural Poor Law' in Fraser, D. (ed.), *The New Poor Law in the Nineteenth Century* (London)
Digby, A., 1978. *Pauper Palaces* (London)
Hollis, P., 1987. *Ladies Elect. Women in Local Government, 1865-1914* (Oxford)
Jones, D., 1976. 'Thomas Campbell Foster and the Rural Labourer: Incendiarism in East Anglia in the 1840s', *Social History*, 1
Snell, K.D.M., 1985. Annals of the Labouring Poor: *Social Change and Agrarian England* (Cambridge)

69. Turnpikes and Roads

Albert, W., 1972. *The Turnpike Road System in England, 1663-1840* (Cambridge)
Hanson, H., 1983. *The Coaching Life* (Manchester)
Jefferies, R., 1949. *The King's Highway* (London)
Pawson, E., 1975. *The Turnpike Trusts of the 18th Century* (Oxford)
Reeder, W.J., 1969. *Hard Roads and Highways* (London)
Reeder, W.J., 1980. *Macadam* (London)
Robinson, B., 1982. *Norfolk Tracks and Roads* (Cromer)

70. Waterways

Boyes, J. and Russell, R., 1977. *The Canals of Eastern England* (Newton Abbot)
Darby, H.C., 1940. *The Draining of the Fens* (Cambridge)
Malster, R., 1973. *Wherries and Waterways* (Lavenham)
Summers, D., 1973. *The Great Ouse* (Newton Abbot)
Syson, L., 1965. *British Watermills* (London)

71. Railways

Allen, C.J., 1967. *The Great Eastern Railway* 4th edition (Shepperton)
Clarke, R., 1967. *Short History of the M&GNJR* (Norwich)
Gordon, D., 1977. *Regional History of the Railways of Great Britain*, Volume 5, *East Anglia* (Newton Abbot)
Joby, R.S., 1985. *Forgotten Railways: East Anglia* 2nd edition (Newton Abbot)
Joby, R.S., 1983. *Railway Builders* (Newton Abbot)
Joby, R.S., 1987. *Regional Railway Handbook* 2 (Newton Abbot)

Larkin, E. and J., 1989. *The Railway Workshops of Britain* (London)

Reed, M.C., 1969. *Railways in the Victorian Economy* (Newton Abbot)

Wrottesley, A.J., 1981. *The Midland and Great Northern Joint Railway* (Newton Abbot)

72. Worsted and Linen Weavers

Evans, N., 1985. *The East Anglian Linen Industry: Rural Industry and the Local Economy, 1500-1850* (Aldershot)

Sutton, A.F., 1989. 'The Early Linen and Worsted Industry of Norfolk and the Evolution of the London Mercers' Company', *Norfolk Archaeology* 40, 201-225

Priestly, U., 1990. *The Fabric of Stuffs: the Norwich textile industry from 1565* (Norwich)

Other Sources

Probate records of the Norwich Consistory Court, of the two Archdeaconry Courts and of the Peculiars of the Dean and Chapter, Great Cressingham and Castle Rising; National Apprenticeship Registers (PRO IR 1); *The Bury and Norwich Post*; census returns, parish registers and Poor Law records for certain parishes.

73. Tanners and Tanning

Crosby, A., 1986. *A History of Thetford* (Chichester)

Hudson, W., 1889. *St. Peter Permountergate Norwich* (Norwich)

Norfolk Archdeaconry Wills 1453-1560, *Norfolk Genealogy* 3 and 5

Norwich Consistory Court (N.C.C.) Wills 1350-1857 indexed in *Norfolk Record Society* 16; 21; 27; 34; 38; 47

Norwich Dean and Chapter Wills 1600-1857 (Norfolk Record Office MSS)

Owen, D., 1984. *The Making of Kings Lynn* (Oxford)

Pound, J., 1988. *Tudor and Stuart Norwich*, Chapter 5 (Chichester)

Waterer, J., 1956. *A History of Technology* 2, Chapter 5 (Oxford)

74. Brickmaking

Durst, D.W., 1977. 'Blickling bricks', *Journal of the Norfolk Industrial Archaeology Society* 2, (2) 4-8, pl.A1-5

Lucas, R., 1984. 'Excerpts from the memoirs of a Norfolk brickmaker (George Edwards)', *Journal of the Norfolk Industrial Archaeology Society* 3 (4), 141-4

Gunton, H.E., 1968-9. 'Costessey brickworks', *Transactions of the Newcomen Society* 41, 165-8

Hillier, R., 1981. *Clay that burns*, London Brick Company

Ives, R., 1980. 'The Peterstone brickyard', *Journal of the Norfolk Industrial Archaeology Society* 2 (5), 12-16

Lucas, R., 1995 (forthcoming). 'The brick-kilns of Norfolk', *Journal of the Norfolk Industrial Archaeology Society*

Mackie, I., 1971-5. 'Rougham brickworks site', *Journal of the Norfolk Industrial Archaeology Society* 1 (4), 4,16-18

Wiggins, J., 1840. 'On the mode of making and using tiles for under-draining, practised on the Stow Hall Estate in Norfolk, &c.', *Journal of the Royal Agricultural Society* First Series 1, 350-56, pl.I-IV

Sources

The printed maps of Norfolk by William Faden, A. Bryant and the Ordnance Survey which were used to create the map here showed, respectively, 49 brickyards, 122 and 92. A substantial number of sites appeared on two maps, a lesser number on all three maps. Such maps never, of course, included all brickmaking sites and the difficulty of distinguishing between operational and defunct brickyards was not resolved. Earlier indications of brickyard sites have been found in manuscript maps, namely, manorial and estate maps, enclosure maps and, most informative of all, the maps which accompanied the tithe apportionment introduced by the Tithe Commutation Act of 1836. The schedules accompanying tithe apportionment maps record field names and field use reaching back, not uncommonly, into the 17th century. Much of the necessary documentation for the study of brickmaking in the county is deposited in the Norfolk Record Office. It includes parish and estate disbursements for bricks and tiles, manorial licences to burn bricks and leases involving brickyards. The original returns from enumerators for the decennial census beginning in 1841 generate statistics for the workforce. Notices published in 18th- and 19th-century county newspapers have yielded valuable information on brickyard leases, the variety of stock, prices and transport. Over the same period, but starting later, trade directories named the owners and lessees of some of the brickyards and recorded also the other enterprises with which they may have been associated. Amongst the most important published sources have been the returns of 1836-45 for the brick-tax which was levied between 1784 and 1850; occupational abstracts of the decennial census, 1831-1951; the *Mineral statistics* for 1858; the separate *Memoirs of the Geological Survey*, treating of the districts of Norfolk and published between 1877 and 1899; and the periodically up-dated *List of quarries* submitted to Parliament under the provisions of the Quarries Act of 1894.

75. Malting and Brewing

Brigden, R., 1975. 'Norfolk Maltings', *Journal of the Norfolk Industrial Archaeology Society* 1 (8), 6-13

(Other issues of JNIAS also contain relevant articles)

Brown, J., 1983. *Steeped in Tradition: the Malting Industry in England Since the Railway Age* (Reading)

Corran, H., 1975. *A History of Brewing* (Newton Abbot)

Davison, A., 1991. *Justly Celebrated Ales: A Directory of Norfolk Brewers, From 1850* (Dartford)

Day, M., 1977. 'Brewing in Norwich' (*Norfolk Museums Service Information Sheet*) (Norwich)

Flood, R., 1986. 'E. Lacon & Co., Ltd.', *Journal of the Brewery History Society* 48, 29-31

(Other issues of JBHS also contain relevant articles)

Gourvish, T., 1987. *Norfolk Beers From English Barley - A History of Steward and Patteson, 1793-1963* (Norwich)

Mathias, P., 1959. *The Brewing Industry in England, 1700-1830* (Cambridge)

76. Paper Mills

Glendinning, S.E., 1928. 'Paper Making in Norfolk', *Eastern Daily Press*, 17th January

Hooper, J., 1898. 'Paper Making at Taverham', *Eastern Daily Press*, 1st December

Norgate, T.B., 1972. 'Taverham Paper Mill', *Norfolk Fair* 4 (12), 36-39

Shorter, A., 1958. *Paper Mills and Paper Makers in England 1495-1800* (Hilversum)

Stoker, D., 1976. 'The Early History of Paper Making in Norfolk', *Norfolk Archaeology* 36, 241-252

77. Watermills

Baldwin, J., 1982. *Fakenham Town on the Wensum* (Cromer)

Dence, C.S., 1980. *Portrait of a Village: Castle Rising* (Castle Rising)

Fitz Water Wheel Co., 1923. 'Water Power on the Farm Bulletin No.60', reprinted by *International Molinological Society*, 1979

Larkman, F., 1957. 'Watermills on the River Bure', *East Anglian Magazine*

Larkman, F., 1959. 'Watermills on the River Wensum', *East Anglian Magazine*

Luckhurst, D., c.1964. 'Monastic Watermills', *Society for the Protection of Ancient Buildings*

Miller, P.R., 1972 (2nd edition). *In Search of Watermills* (Norwich)

Messent, C.J.W., 1939. *The Old Watermills of Norfolk* (Norwich)

Norgate, T.B., 1969. *An Illustrated History of Taverham, Norfolk* (Taverham)

Vince, J., 1987. *Discovering Watermills* (Aylesbury)

Wilson, P.N., 1956, revised 1973 and 1985. 'Watermills an Introduction', *Society for the Protection of Ancient Buildings*

No author, 1991. 'Windmills and Watermills Open to View', Wind and Watermill Section, *Society for the Protection of Ancient Buildings*

78. Iron Founders and Agricultural Engineers

Alderton, D. and Booker, J., 1980. *The Batsford Guide to the Industrial Archaeology of East Anglia* (London)

Clark, R.H., revised 1988. *The Steam Engine Builders of Norfolk* (Yeovil)

Fewster, M.I., 1981. 'Thomas Smithdale and Sons. A Study of a Victorian Ironfounder', *Journal of Norfolk Industrial Archaeology Society* 3 (1), 23-33

Fisher, C., 1981. 'Soame of Marsham', *Journal of Norfolk Industrial Archaeology Society* 3 (1), 8-17

Osborne, D., 1990. 'Burrells of Thetford: further research on the beginnings', *Journal of Norfolk Industrial Archaeology Society* 4 (5), 175-186

Starling, P., 1972. 'Iron Foundries of Norfolk', *Journal of Norfolk Industrial Archaeology Society* 1 (1), 9-13

Wincote, K.W., 1975. 'Plowright and Sons, Engineers and Ironfounders', *Journal of Norfolk Industrial Archaeology Society* 1 (9), 10-16

79. Lime Burning and Extractive Industries

Jones, J. and J., 1977. 'Lime Burning in Norfolk', *Journal of the Norfolk Industrial Archaeology Society* 2 (2)

Manning, M., (ed.). *Journal of the Norfolk Industrial Archaeology Society* (Norwich), Volumes 2 to 4, articles by various authors.

80. Corn Windmills

Apling, H., 1984. 'Norfolk Corn Windmills', *The Norfolk Windmills Trust*

Beedell, S., 1975. *Windmills* (Newton Abbot)

De Little, R.J., 1972. *The Windmill Yesterday and Today* (London)

Freese, S., 1971. *Windmills and Millwrighting* (Newton Abbot)

Reynolds, J., 1970. *Windmills and Watermills* (London)

Scott, M., 1977. *The Restoration of Windmills and Windpumps in Norfolk* (Norwich)

Smith, A.C., 1982. *Corn Windmills of Norfolk* (Stevenage)

Vince, J., 1987. *Discovering Windmills* (Aylesbury)

Wailes, R., 1947-1948. 'Norfolk Windmills Part 1, Corn Mills', *Transactions of the Newcomen Society* 26

Wailes, R., 1971. *The English Windmill* (London)

Wailes, R., 1976. *Windmills in England* (London)

Wailes, R., 1979. *A Source Book of Windmills and Watermills* (London)

81. Windpumps

Wailes, R., 1955-7. 'Norfolk Windmills: Part 2. Drainage and Pumping Mills, including those in Suffolk', *Transactions of the Newcomen Society* 30, 157

82. Fishing and Maritime Industries, post 1600

Buckland, F., 1875. *The Fisheries of Norfolk* (London)

Davis, R., 1962. *The Rise of the English Shipping Industry* (London)

Dyson, J., 1976. *Business in Great Waters* (London)

Morey, G., 1968. *The North Sea* (London)

Wren, W.J., 1976. *Ports of the Eastern Counties* (Lavenham)

83. Seaside Resorts

Brooks, P., 1980. *Sheringham - the Story of a Town* (North Walsham)

Goodwyn, E.A., c.1979. *Mundesley Past* (Mundesley)

Hedges, A.A.C., 1973. *Yarmouth is an Ancient Town* (Great Yarmouth)

Reid, A. (ed.), 1986. *Cromer and Sheringham: the Growth of the Holiday Trade* (Norwich)

Rouse, J., 1982. *Coastal Resorts of East Anglia* (Lavenham)

Stibbons, P. and Cleveland, D., 1990. *Poppyland - Strands of Norfolk History* (North Walsham)

Warren, M.R., 1990. *Cromer - the Chronicle of a Watering Place* (North Walsham)

84. Population Change 1951-1981

Sources

Census reports, every ten years from 1951 to 1981, prepared by the Registrar General (HMSO). County reports contain information for parishes.

OPCS Monitors, various series, including PP.1 (population estimates for counties and districts.

'Population Trends', quarterly, from OPCS (HMSO). Contains information on national trends.

Norfolk County Council (Department of Planning and Property) prepare annual estimates of parish populations.

85. Rural Primary School Closures 1947-1990

Audit Commission, 1990. *Rationalising Primary School Provision* (London)

Norfolk County Council, 1947. *Development Plan for Primary and Secondary Education* (Norwich)

University of Aston, 1981. *The Social Effects of Rural Primary Re-organisation: a study on behalf of DOE and DES* (Aston)

86. The Pattern of Roads in the 20th Century

Note

This map is based on information supplied by the

Highways Department and interpreted by the author. There are some references in *Centenary: A Hundreds Years of County Government* in Norfolk published by Norfolk County Council in 1989.

87. First and Second World War Coastal Defences

Kent, P., 1988. *Fortifications of East Anglia* (Lavenham)

Kent, P., 1988. 'The Fixed Defences' in Glidden, G. (ed.), *Norfolk and Suffolk in the Great War* (Norwich)

Wills, H., 1985. *Pillboxes: A Study of U.K. Defences 1940* (London)

88. Agriculture in the 20th Century

Hall, A.D., *1914. A Pilgrimage of British Farming, 1910-12* (London)

Howkins, A., 1985. *Poor Labouring Men, Rural Radicalism in Norfolk, 1870-1923*

Hutchinson, Sir J. and Owers, A.C., 1980. *Change and Innovation in Norfolk Farming* (Chichester)

Keith, J., 1954. *Fifty Years of Farming* (London)

Kemp, R.W., 1961. 'Horticulture', *Norwich and its Region* (Norwich)

Mosby, J.E.G., 1938. 'Norfolk: Part 70' in Stamp, L.D. (ed.), *The Land of Britain* (London)

Rayns, F., 1935. 'The Agriculture of Norfolk' in Mottram, R.H. (ed.), *A Scientific Study of Norwich and District* (London)

Shotton, F.E., 1961. 'Agriculture', *Norwich and its Region* (Norwich)

Other Sources

P.R.O., MAF 68/2645; MAF 68/5286/7

89. Landscape and Nature Conservation

Blake, P.W. *et al.*, 1975. *The Norfolk We Live In* (Norwich)

Briers, F. (ed.), 1961. *Norwich and its Region*, Norwich)

Dymond, D., 1990. *The Norfolk Landscape* (Bury St. Edmunds)

Huxley, J.S., 1947. *Conservation of Nature in England and Wales*: (Report of the wildlife conservation special committee, Cmd 7122, London)

Petch, C.P. and Swann, E.L., 1968. *Flora of Norfolk* (Norwich)

Ratcliffe, D.A. (ed.), 1977. *A Nature Conservation Review* (Cambridge)

Washbourne, R. (ed.), 1976. *Nature in Norfolk: A Heritage in Trust* (Norwich)

Sources

National Parks and Access to the Countryside Act (1949)

Wildlife and Countryside Act (1981)

90. Conservation Areas

Cambridgeshire County Council, 1988. *The Cambridgeshire Guide to Historic Buildings Law*

H.M.S.O., 1990. *Planning (Listed Buildings and Conservation Areas) Act*

Suddards, R.W., 1988. *Listed Buildings* (London)

91. Listed Buildings

Norfolk County Council, 1987. *Historic Buildings in Norfolk: Problems and Opportunities*

Norfolk County Council, 1990. *Historic Buildings at Risk in Norfolk* 4th edition

Department of the Environment. 'Green Back' *Lists of Buildings of Special Architectural or Historic Interest*

92. Scheduled Ancient Monuments

Department of the Environment, 1979. *Ancient Monuments and Archaeological Areas Act*

Department of the Environment, 1990. *Planning Policy Guidance: Archaeology and Planning*, PPG 16

93. Local Government Since 1974

Halsbury's Statutes, 4th edition, 1986

Norfolk County Council Annual Report and Financial Statement 1987-88

Index of place-names appearing in the text